Penguin Books

Life in the English Country House

Mark Girouard is one of Britain's leading architectural historians, well known in the UK for his work on radio and television. He was born in October 1931, and educated at Ampleforth, Christ Church, Oxford, and the Courtauld Institute of Art. He worked for *Country Life* between 1958 and 1966, and from there went on to study architecture at Bartlett School, University College, London. From 1971 to 1975 he was on the staff of the *Architectural Review*. He was a founder member of the Victorian Society and he is also a member of the Royal Fine Art Commission, the Royal Commission on Historical Monuments (England) and Chairman of the Spitalfields Historic Buildings Trust.

His previous books, recently described in the *New Statesman* as 'each one a masterpiece', include *Robert Smythson and the Architecture of the Elizabethan Era*, *The Victorian Country House*, *Victorian Pubs*, *Spirit of the Age* (based on a BBC TV series) and *Sweetness and Light: the 'Queen Anne' Movement 1860-1900*. He has also contributed articles to *Country Life*, *Architectural Review* and the *Listener*. He was Slade Professor of Art at Oxford University (1975-6) when much of this book was written. *Life in the English Country House* was awarded the Duff Cooper Memorial Prize for 1978 and the W. H. Smith & Son Annual Literary Award for 1979.

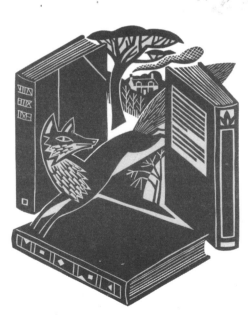

EX LIBRIS

Randy Manning

To Mom

from Randy

Nov. 21, 1980.

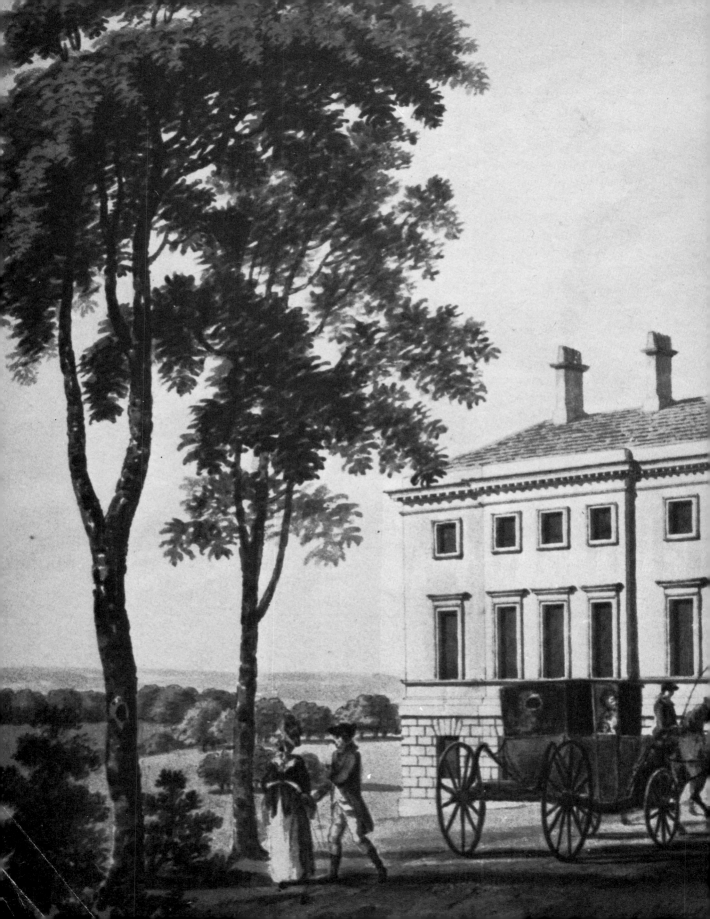

MARK GIROUARD

LIFE IN THE ENGLISH COUNTRY HOUSE

A Social and Architectural History

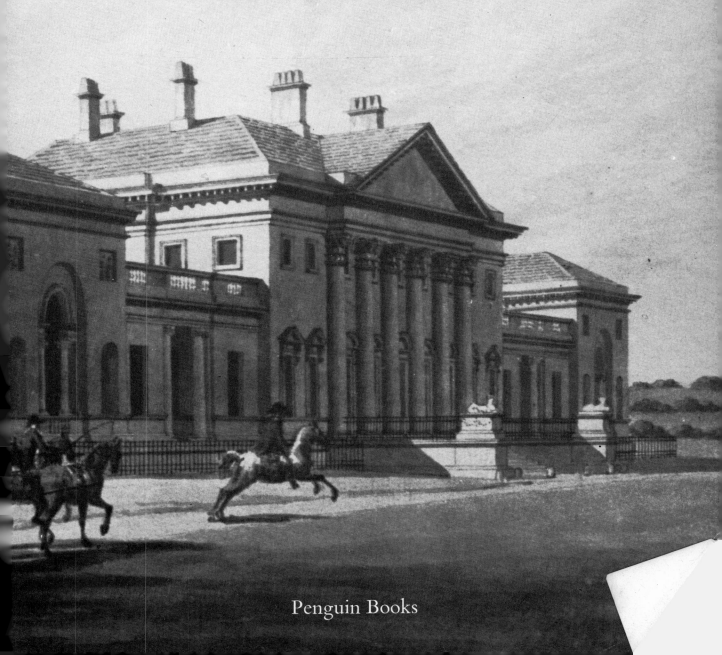

Penguin Books

Penguin Books Ltd, Harmondsworth, Middlesex, England
Penguin Books, 625 Madison Avenue, New York, New York 10022, U.S.A.
Penguin Books Australia Ltd, Ringwood, Victoria, Australia
Penguin Books Canada Ltd, 2801 John Street, Markham, Ontario, Canada L3R 1B4
Penguin Books (N.Z.) Ltd, 182–190 Wairau Road, Auckland 10, New Zealand

———

First published by Yale University Press 1978
Published in Penguin Books 1980
Copyright © Yale University, 1978

———

Designed by Dorothy Girouard

———

Filmset in Monophoto Bembo and printed in Great Britain
by Hazell Watson & Viney Ltd, Aylesbury, Bucks

———

PREFACE

ALTHOUGH English country houses are more visited and written about than they ever have been before, most people know comparatively little about how they operated or what was expected of them when they were first built. Even the most knowledgeable country-house enthusiasts tend to think in terms of architects, craftsmen or family history, but to know surprisingly little about how families used the houses which architects and craftsmen built for them. In recent years my own interests have begun to shift to this aspect of country houses, partly because of the enjoyment and fascination of investigating unexplored territory, partly because the results so greatly increased my understanding of country houses as a whole. This book is based on the Slade Lectures given at Oxford in 1975–6, but the original text has been substantially rewritten and nearly doubled in length.

The range of sources for an approach of this kind is almost infinite, and I cannot pretend to have done more than sample it. Moreover, instructive and enjoyable although it is for an architectural historian to adventure outside his own discipline, he is bound to make gaffes in doing so. I can only ask for indulgence for what is essentially a pioneering work.

I owe thanks to all those interested in the use and arrangement of houses who have helped me, especially John Cornforth, Marcus Binney and Gervase Jackson-Stops at *Country Life* and Peter Thornton, Maurice Tomlin, John Hardy, Simon Jarvis and Clive Wainwright at the Victoria and Albert Museum. Christina Colvin supplied me with late-eighteenth and early-nineteenth-century quotations, and Howard Colvin read and commented on my mediaeval chapters. John Harris let me have the run of his invaluable library; the Dowager-Marchioness of Cholmondeley took me round the eighteenth-century water supply at Houghton; Mary, Duchess of Buccleuch, and my father (who also helped with the index) gave me the benefit of their memories of country-house life between the wars. I have had nothing but help from the owners and custodians of the records I have consulted, both public and private, especially T. S. Wragg and Peter Day at Chatsworth, and Bob Wark, Mary Robertson, Winifred Freese and Virginia Renner at the Huntington Library. My visit to the Huntington was made possible by a welcome grant from the Paul Mellon Centre for Studies in British Art. Among others who have given help or information I would like to name Sir John Summerson, Colin Amery, Terence Davis, David Green, Anne Hawker, Patricia Morton, Valerie Pakenham, Faith Hart, Harriet Waugh, Susan Conder, Gavin Stamp, Robert Heber-Percy, R. H. Harcourt Williams, Sheelagh Lloyd, David Durant, George Clarke and the Marquess of Hamilton.

My final thanks must go to my wife for her elegant design and to my editor, John Nicoll, for constant help and encouragement with this and other books.

TO BILLA

IN MEMORY OF ROY

CONTENTS

1. (right) Houghton Hall, Norfolk (1722–32). The west front.

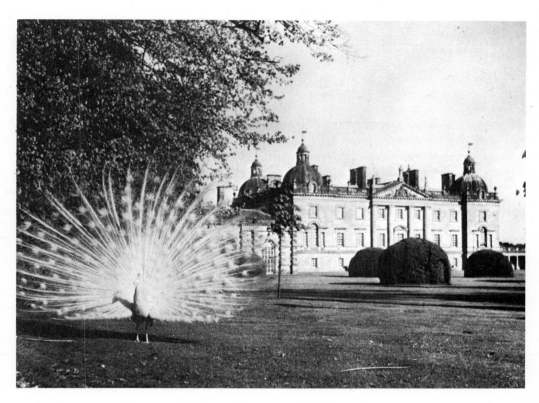

1 The Power Houses

WHAT were country houses for? They were not originally, whatever they may be now, just large houses in the country in which rich people lived. Essentially they were power houses—the houses of a ruling class. As such they could work at the local level of a manor house, the house of a squire who was like a little king in his village and ran the county in partnership with his fellow J.P.s at quarter sessions. They could work at a local and national level as the seat of a landowner who was also a member of parliament, or of a great magnate who was king in his own county but also had his gang of tame M.P.s and spent more than half the year in London, running the country in association with his fellow magnates. But basically people did not live in country houses unless they either possessed power, or, by setting up in a country house, were making a bid to possess it.

This power was based on the ownership of land. But land was not important to country-house owners because they were farmers. There were many exceptions over the centuries, but on the whole they did not farm for profit and often did not farm at all. The point of land was the tenants and rent that came with it. A landowner could call on his tenants to fight for him, in the early days of the country house, and to vote for him—or his candidate—in its later ones. He could use the money which they paid in as rent to persuade even more people to fight or vote for him, either by hiring them to do so, or by keeping up so handsome and impressive an establishment that they felt it was to their interest to come in on his side. Anyone who had sufficient resources and followers, and displayed them with enough prominence, was likely to be offered jobs and perquisites by the central government in return for his support. Acceptance produced money, which could be turned into more land, more power and more supporters. The more a landowner prospered, the more anxious his fellow landowners were to be connected with him. Through good connections and marriages with heiresses he or his descendants acquired the leverage for still more jobs and perquisites. Such, at any rate, was the ideal route to power; and although there were many pitfalls on the way, it was a route that led often enough to broad estates, a peerage, and the establishment of a dynasty.

For many centuries the ownership of land was not just the main but the only sure basis of power. Both power and money could be acquired by other means: by trade, by commerce, by fighting, by useful services to the government or by personal services to the king and queen. But money unsupported by power was likely to be plundered, power based only on personal abilities was at the mercy of time and fortune, and the power to be won through trade or commerce was limited. Until the nineteenth century the wealth and population of England lay in the country rather than the towns; landowners rather than merchants were the dominating class, and ran the country so that their own interests were the last to suffer. Even when the economic balance began to change, they were so thoroughly in control of patronage and legislation, so strong through their inherited patronage and expertise, that their political and social supremacy continued. As a result, from the Middle Ages until the nineteenth century anyone who had made money by any means, and was ambitious for himself and his family, automatically invested in a country estate.

Land, however, was little use without one or more country houses on it. Land provided the fuel, a country house was the engine which made it effective. It achieved this in a number of ways. It was the headquarters from which land was administered and power organised. It was a show-case, in which to exhibit and entertain supporters and good connections. In early days it contained a potential fighting force. It was an image-maker, which projected an aura of glamour, mystery or success around its owner. It was visible evidence of his wealth. It showed his credentials—even if the credentials were sometimes faked. Trophies in the hall, coats of arms over the chimney-pieces, books in the library and temples in the park could suggest that he was discriminating, intelligent, bred to rule and brave.

The qualities at a premium varied over the centuries, and so did the people who needed to be entertained, and the kind of entertainment which they expected. A country house was an expensive piece of plant which needed constant alteration as well as constant maintenance if it were to continue to fulfil its functions. Both new and old families financed this from a wide range of sources. Many houses were built or altered from the proceeds of rents alone, but perhaps even more were subsidized or entirely paid for by other means. Well before the Industrial Revolution had created a multitude of new fortunes, the wool trade, the law, service in India or sugar from Jamaica, lending money or supplying the army, had produced the means with which to buy estates and build houses on them. Other families both new and old made money out of the court or the government. The concept of a great nobleman serving the public for duty rather than for gain is a nineteenth-century one. Both Elizabethan statesmen and Whig magnates expected to do well out of their country. A farm of the customs or a monopoly of soap or starch could double a man's income. In the sixteenth century those with the right connections lined their pockets out of the monasteries, in the eighteenth century out of sinecures. Most court or government posts brought in handsome salaries and even more in the way of perquisites. Lord Burghley made enough out of being Lord Treasurer and Master of the Court of Wards to buy huge estates and build Burghley and Theobalds in the country and Exeter House in London— all houses on the scale of palaces. At Houghton Sir Robert Walpole built the most sumptuous house of its day out of the proceeds of public service (Pl. 1). In the 1750s even the relatively junior court job of Cofferer to the Household brought in enough to enable George Lyttelton to turn his ancestral house at Hagley into a handsome Palladian mansion.[1]

The size and pretensions of such houses were an accurate index of the ambitions—or lack of them—of their owners. When a new man bought an estate and built on it, the kind of house which he built showed exactly what level of power he was aiming at. If the head of an established family was ambitious to raise its status—or simply to keep up with new arrivals—one of the most obvious means towards doing so was to rebuild or improve his house. New houses could be a cause of much local stress and excitement—as was the case with Sir Robert Walpole's Houghton in Norfolk, and Lord Verney's Claydon in Buckingham- shire.

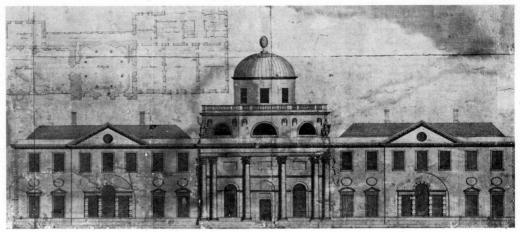

2. Claydon House, Buckinghamshire, as enlarged to the design of Sir Thomas Robinson in 1768–72.

The Walpoles had been minor Norfolk gentry until Robert Walpole, by a combination of good connections and his own great abilities, raised himself to a dominant position in the country. He consolidated his success in the time-honoured fashion, by buying land and building. His splendid new house at Houghton was started in 1721 and he moved into it a few years later. Built by the best architects of the time, fitted out by the best craftsmen, and housing the finest picture collection in England, it was incontrovertible evidence of his power, his wealth, and his discrimination. It became a source of bitter envy to his brother-in-law and neighbour, Lord Townshend, who had been a much greater man than Walpole, and had put him on the way to success. As Lord Hervey put it 'Lord Townshend looked upon his own seat at Raynham as the metropolis of Norfolk, was proud of the superiority, and considered every stone that augmented the splendour of Houghton as a diminution of the grandeur of Raynham.' He and Walpole had both a political and a private quarrel; he felt so bitter about Houghton that whenever Walpole was entertaining there he moved out of the neighbourhood. His bitterness and anger were justified; Houghton was not just a great house, it was a hostile move in the power game.[2]

In the long run, Walpole's efforts to raise the status of his family ended in failure. He bought insufficient land to support the house in its new glory; and although he married his son to an heiress the marriage was not only a disastrous failure but produced only one child, who was more than a little mad. This grandson wasted his fortune, sold the pictures and had no legitimate children; Houghton passed through the female line to a family whose main interest lay in another part of England.

But at least the house survived; the Verney ambitions ended in even greater disaster. In the 1760s, when Lord Verney decided to challenge the Grenvilles of Stowe for the political leadership of Buckinghamshire, an inevitable part of his campaign was the rebuilding of Claydon on a palatial scale (Pl. 2). But he outreached and overspent himself; the only result of his ambition was bankruptcy, followed by the demolition of most of his new building. The Verneys sank back to the level of Buckinghamshire gentry from which they had emerged a few decades previously.[3]

The history of English country houses is filled with similar stories of ambition, some successful and others not. Cautious families kept clear of such ventures. Few country house owners played the power game all the time and few, even of those that did, were entirely motivated by self interest. In every century parents admonished their sons, and moralists admonished both of them, that power brought responsibility. The amount that could be made out of office was regulated by standards which varied from generation to generation but were taken seriously, however lax they may seem today. Landowners were expected to foster their inheritance, look after their dependants, play their part in local government and be loyal to the interests of their own order.

Many of them took their responsibilities very seriously; but in their less serious moments they did the things they enjoyed doing, and saw their friends. Country houses were designed for pleasure as well as power. One of their main functions was to fill the leisure hours of their owners as agreeably as possible; and the less ambitious families had a great many leisure hours to be filled. Certain types of country house, such as hunting lodges in the sixteenth century or Thames-valley villas in the eighteenth, were designed almost entirely for pleasure. But although both duty and pleasure played a large part in the lives of their owners, the keeping up of their position lurked at the back of everything. Abusing power was one of the ways to lose it. There were friends and amusements which were suitable for a gentleman, and others which were unsuitable; they harmed his image, and so lessened his power and status, and the status of his class as a whole.

Pursuit both of pleasure and power was not confined to country houses and the property which surrounded them. Many landowners spent long periods away, fighting, hunting, staying with their friends, serving in the entourage of a great man, or attending parliament or the court. Although in the early Middle Ages court and parliament travelled round the country with the king, parliament seldom left London after the fifteenth century. By the end of the sixteenth century the court spent almost all the time either in London or close to it, mostly at Greenwich, Richmond or Hampton Court. Since monarch, court and government were all interconnected, the court had to be within easy reach of parliament, government offices and government officials in London.

Most people think of the English upper classes as having always been country-based—unlike corrupt French aristocrats, perpetually hanging around Paris or Versailles. But although poets like Jonson, Marvell or Pope and moralists like Addison constantly urged landowners to live on their estates, and praised and glamorized the lives of those who did,[4] from the sixteenth century onwards the upper classes were spending more and more time in London—or the area round London in which the court rotated. They were drawn there partly by the increasing power of the court and central government, and the profits to be won by standing well with them, partly by the pleasures of city life. The richer families acquired permanent houses in London, the less rich took lodgings. Even when landowners were in the country they were often longing to get out of it. In about 1590 Sir Henry Unton complained from the country that 'my clownish life doth deprive me of all intelligence and comfort'. Lord Pembroke, down at Wilton in

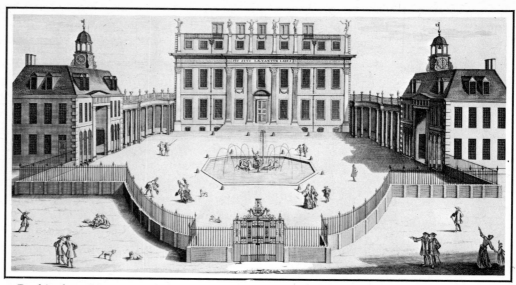

3. Buckingham House, London (William Winde, 1705).

1601, wrote 'I have not yet been a day in the country, and I am as weary of it as if I had been a prisoner there seven year.' Edmund Verney at Claydon a little later was 'weary of this deep dirty country life'. Lord Clifford, at Skipton Castle, had 'banished myself from all my friends and recreations'. Sir James Poulett at Hinton St George in Somerset felt 'tied to this dull dirty place'.[5]

William Cavendish, third Earl of Devonshire, is described in the histories of his family as a man who disliked London. Nevertheless his account books show that over a twelve year period in the 1660s and '70s he and his family were spending, on an average, a little under four months of the year in Derbyshire, where his main properties were, a little over a month at Latimers, the house in Buckinghamshire where he normally stopped on his way to and from London, and about seven months a year in London.[6] A hundred years or so later, in the time of the beautiful Georgiana, Duchess of Devonshire, the family were seldom more than three months a year in Derbyshire.[7] The rest of the year was spent mostly at Devonshire House in London, at Bath or at Chiswick. Chiswick was just outside London but conveniently in reach of it. It was part of the Thames-side zone which gradually filled up with the villas of rich people who wanted a rural retreat within a few miles of Westminster. The resulting landscape could reasonably be described as suburban, even if grander and more spacious than the suburbia of today.

Not all families were as London bound, even among the aristocracy. But a proportion of four months in London, a month at Bath or some other spa, a month travelling and six months at home was nothing out of the ordinary for a prosperous gentry family. The Georgian period was probably the age at which the upper classes as a whole were most addicted to living in towns—and best at creating them, as Bath, Clifton, Edinburgh, Dublin and Brighton still bear witness. Moreover, in this period it was more than the upper half of the upper classes that was involved. Towns like Nottingham, Newcastle, York, Norwich and Exeter filled up with the substantial town houses of county families, and

6

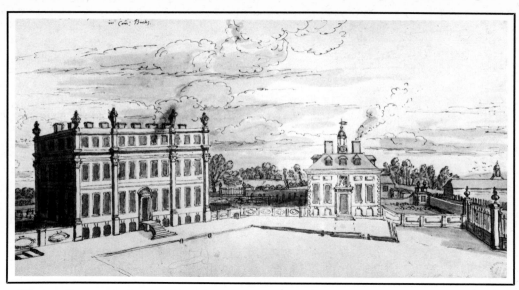

4. Wotton House, Buckinghamshire (1720).

acquired an assembly room, a theatre and a racecourse to provide recreation for those whose ambitions did not extend to London.

The absentee landlord, who dissipated his time and fortune in living it up in the city, became a stock figure in contemporary satire. But so did the boozy illiterate hunting squire, the Sir Tony Lumpkin or Sir Tunbelly Clumsy, who never left the country at all, or if he did only made himself ridiculous. For the ruling classes the sensible course was somewhere between the two. Their power was the result of a cross fertilisation between town and country. The roots of their power—their land, their tenantry and their neighbours—were in the country. They neglected it at their peril. But to neglect the town was equally perilous. The town provided jobs, contacts, and ideas. Those fully involved in court or government inevitably had to spend most of their time in London. Walpole, in spite of all the money, pride and affection that he lavished on Houghton, could only pass a month a year at it. Members of either house of Parliament, or those with a peripheral job at court, could get away more often. But the city was the place to meet friends from other parts of the country, make new contacts, arrange marriages, prosecute law suits, borrow money, hear the latest news, and catch up with the latest fashions.

The country benefited from all this flocking to the towns, to London and to the court. It is almost impossible to envisage how remote the country was until the arrival of railways—let alone the arrival of motor cars, radio and television. Country areas were almost completely isolated. The majority of the people living in them had never travelled more than a few miles to their local country town. But there was one great exception—the families at the big houses. Their annual migration to and from London involved not just the immediate family, but perhaps thirty or forty dependants as well. When they returned they brought strange and exotic figures in their train—servants from distant countries, poets, like Ben Jonson, brought by Lord Leicester to Penshurst, philosophers, like Thomas Hobbes, brought by the Earl of Devonshire to the wilds of Derbyshire or Jeremy Bentham, brought by Lord Shelburne to Bowood. They brought new

7

methods of transport, new forms of lighting, new furniture, new fashions, and new forms of building. All this contributed to their aura and therefore to their power; but it also made them agents of civilisation.

In the mid sixteenth century the building of Somerset House in the Strand brought the first strong taste of the Renaissance to the streets of London. It was quickly copied at Longleat in Wiltshire; and Longleat in its turn was copied at Sherborne Park in Gloucestershire. In the early seventeenth century Sir Charles Cavendish sent his surveyor up to London to make drawings of the latest buildings by Inigo Jones and others; and over the next ten years little nuggets of London detail were incorporated into his new house at Bolsover in Derbyshire.[8] In the late seventeenth and early eighteenth century two great London houses, Clarendon House in Piccadilly and Buckingham House on the edge of St James's Park, were so much admired by visiting country gentlemen that they were copied all over England (Pls 3 and 4).

These and countless other country copies of London fashions must have seemed strange enough when their balustraded parapets, classical detail or hipped roofs first appeared among the gables and battlements of older houses. But as local squires copied what the grander families were doing, and the yeomanry copied the squires, they were gradually absorbed into the local vernacular. The same kind of acclimitization affected parks and gardens. The straight avenues and canals with which the later Stuarts embellished their palaces in and around London were soon being installed all over England, until even modest manor houses and rectories had their miniature formal gardens. Then fashion changed, and fashion-conscious great people started to remodel the gardens that were only just beginning to mature.

In 1734 Sir Thomas Robinson reported that 'there is a new taste in gardening just arisen which has been practised with so great success at the Prince's gardens in Town, that a general alteration of some of the most considerable gardens in the kingdom is begun.'[9] The new type of garden had been pioneered by Alexander Pope at his Thames-side villa at Twickenham and made fashionable by William Kent, in the London garden which he designed for the Prince of Wales at Carlton House (Pl. 5). Its attraction lay in its complete contrast to the formal garden; it 'had the appearance of beautiful nature'. Trees were planted round the periphery, to shut out the neighbouring houses, and enclose an arcadian world of grassy glades and winding paths and water. These exquisitely artificial slices of nature in the midst of civilization were soon being copied on a larger scale all over the country. At first their encircling belts of trees, and the secret landscapes within, struck an exotic note in the surrounding context of commons, open fields or orchards. But their influence spread over the countryside and gradually changed it. A city garden on the site of the future Lower Regent Street had developed into what is now taken for granted as part of the English landscape.

In bringing town fashions into the country the upper classes had no sense of doing something controversial. Until the end of the eighteenth century there was little feeling that what was suitable for the town was unsuitable for the country. Even towards the end of the eighteenth century a rich landowner building in

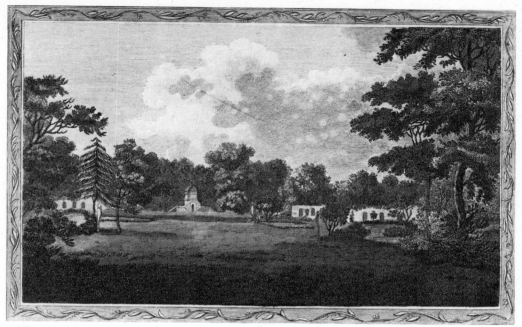

5. The garden at Carlton House, London, designed by William Kent in 1734.

Piccadilly would build a square brick box with a pediment, while another rich landowner, building in Suffolk, would build another square brick box, with another pediment. If someone saw furniture or hangings in a London house which took his fancy, he had no qualms about ordering the same thing for himself, and sending it down to the country. Rich people dressed with considerable formality in London, but with almost equal formality in the country. The Duke of Newcastle wore his garter-star in Piccadilly, and he also wore it when he was out shooting at Clumber, as his portrait by Francis Wheatley shows.

The portrait was painted in 1788. It is perhaps significant that when it was engraved in 1803 the garter-star was omitted.[10] Around 1800 a feeling began to grow among the upper classes that country life required a different set of fittings to town life. By the middle of the nineteenth century the feeling had become something more like a rule. In the 1840s one finds, for instance, the Earl of Ellesmere building a symmetrical Italian palazzo in Mayfair and an irregular Tudor-style mansion on his property in Lancashire—and, a few years later, Robert Stayner Holford doing the same kind of thing at Dorchester House in Park Lane and Westonbirt in Gloucestershire.

One of the reasons for this change was a change in the power structure. During the nineteenth century the upper classes lost their monopoly of power. They were increasingly ruling in partnership with the middle classes from the towns. They saw themselves, and were seen by others, as representing agriculture and the country, as opposed to industry and the towns. They were country landowners, living in country houses, built in a country style. This role has continued to the present day. When the first Duke of Devonshire, in retirement from London for political reasons, turned Chatsworth into a sumptuous palace in the midst of what Defoe described as a 'howling wilderness' he was introducing country folk to the

9

latest fashions from the city and the court. Today Chatsworth teaches city folk the ways of the country; little Brownies from Midland cities come there to watch demonstrations of milking, and gaze with amazement at milk spurting from a live cow instead of a bottle.

Country-house owners have survived owing to their ability to adapt to different situations over the centuries. The way in which they adapted, and the effect which this had on their way of life and therefore on their houses, makes a fascinating subject for study. Attraction to the central government in London, reaction back to the country as a result of the growth of the towns, and the resulting unity and then contrast between town and country architecture, is only one of many developments. Perhaps the most obvious and important change in country houses between 1400 and 1900 was that in 1400 they were designed for one community and in 1900 for two. In the Middle Ages (and indeed up till the early eighteenth century) when someone talked about his family he meant everyone living under his roof, including his servants; by the nineteenth century he meant his wife and children.[11] The early type can be epitomized by the great hall, in which the whole household ate together with its guests, and the later by the green baize door, dividing the servants' wing from the very different world of the gentry. By 1900 the gentry end of the house was made up of a complicated series of morning room, dining room, billiard room, smoking room and conservatory, designed for week-end parties drawn from all over the country. It accommodated a far more complex social life than had been found in the Middle Ages.

The decay of the single community and the elaboration of social life were in fact related. A great household of the Middle Ages contained members of all classes, spreading out in a hierarchy under the apex of baron or earl at their head. Its members cohered together for mutual protection in an age when force was more powerful than law. Households of this kind were formidable and largely closed groups. Their relations with other groups varied from caution, through suspicion, to hatred. Even in the late sixteenth century rural power groups such as the Talbots and Stanhopes in the Midlands could pursue a vendetta with a fury which must have made Shakespeare's portrayal of Capulets and Montagues entirely familiar to Elizabethan audiences.[12]

As a stronger central government produced a more law-abiding country, and as society grew more complex and full of opportunities, there was less and less reason for any but the lower social ranks to put themselves under the protection of the great by entering their service. Great households in the old style began to crumble; and as they crumbled society tended to reorganize on the basis of classes containing different groups rather than groups containing different classes. The mediaeval gentlemen who enrolled under the leadership—and often actually in the household—of a great lord had no feeling of solidarity with the gentlemen serving other leaders. Their loyalty was to their lord. But as they became more independent they began to live, work, visit and eat together as gentry, conscious of their identity with other gentry.

Once society began to reorganize on a class basis, the victory ultimately lay with the largest class. The centre of power began to move down the social scale. First the gentry, then the middle classes, and ultimately the working classes grew in power and independence. This posed the upper classes with a dilemma. Should they fight the movement or accept it? The most successful families were those who accepted it, and, on the basis of their inherited status and expertise, set out to lead the classes below them rather than to fight them. But leadership of this kind involved association; as a result, first the gentry and then the middle classes disappeared from great households as employees or subordinates, and reappeared as guests. Mediaeval dukes were unwilling to sit at table with anyone of lower rank than a baron; Victorian dukes were prepared to meet even journalists at dinner.

A Victorian duke would have found it inconceivable to be waited on by servants who served him on bended knee; but he would have been equally appalled by the idea of playing poker dice in the drawing room with his butler. This, transposed into contemporary terms, was the habitual practice of Henry, Lord Berkeley, who continued the mediaeval life-style deep into the sixteenth century. His biography mentions, in passing and as nothing out of the ordinary, that he used to play 'at the Irish game at tables' with his yeoman of the chamber in the great chamber at Berkeley Castle.[13] Mediaeval-style households combined ceremony with familiarity in a way which is difficult to grasp today, but was the result of the close weave of their social structure. Once the intermediate ranks in their hierarchy had disappeared, the gap between their upper and lower strata was bound to divide them into two sharply differentiated groups.

The division was accentuated by a growing feeling for privacy which became noticeable in the seventeenth century. Households in the old style had the disadvantages of all tightly-knit communities. Everyone knew what everyone else was doing, and quarrels and intrigues were endemic right across the hierarchy. As soon as families began to value their privacy they inevitably started to escape from their servants. But it would be a mistake to see country-house history in terms of greater and greater privacy. Separation between family and servants certainly grew steadily greater, but privacy on the family side of the baize door had to be reconciled with growing sociability. Privacy was perhaps at its greatest in the early eighteenth century, when servants had been moved out of the way, and individuals among both family and guests enjoyed the security of private apartments, each containing two or even three rooms. By the early nineteenth century apartments were shrinking and a German visitor, Prince Pückler-Muskau, complained of the social pressure which forced guests to leave their own rooms and spend the whole day in the communal life of the public rooms downstairs.[14]

Pückler-Muskau also commented on the independence of German servants, compared to the 'slavish reverence in the presence of their masters' to be found among English ones.[15] His comments underlined the fact that, in terms both of social life and of relations between employer and servants, Germany and the continent were (for better or worse) about a hundred years behind England. Differences in habits between one country and another are often more the result of differences in the chronology of their development than innate racial or national characteristics. The formal circle, for long the accepted vehicle for general conversation in country-house drawing rooms, started to disappear from England in the 1780s but still flourishes in old-fashioned *châteaux* in France. Poor relations still form (or formed until recently) an element in the upper strata of maharajahs' households, just as they did in great English households of the fifteenth and sixteenth centuries. The time lag can work down the social scale as well as across national boundaries. The extravagantly elaborate funerals which were common to all the European aristocracy in the seventeenth century began to be imitated by the Victorian middle classes in England just as they were going out of fashion in the top layer of society; and the best place to get some feel of this kind of funeral pomp today is in the slums of Naples.

The time lag can be observed at work even within country houses in the British Isles. The grander or remoter households tend to be more conservative. The royal household is full of survivals from many centuries. Well into the eighteenth century it was common enough in England for private orchestras to provide music during meals; Scottish lairds still circulate their pipers round the table at dinner and even at breakfast. At Blenheim in the early twentieth century the left-overs from ducal meals were still being fed to the poor in the local villages, exactly as in great households of the Middle Ages; the one change made by the Vanderbilt wife of the ninth Duke of Marlborough was to put the remains of meat, vegetables and sweets into separate tins, instead of cramming them all into the same containers.[16]

Even when the customs have gone the houses remain, enriched by the accumulated alterations, and often the accumulated contents of several centuries. Abandoned life-styles can be disinterred from them in much the same way as from the layers of an archaeological dig. Knowing how to disinter them correctly helps one to understand the architecture of houses as well as their arrangement. Although to some extent architecture follows its own rules it is also conditioned by the society for which it caters. The architects and builders of country houses were not producing pieces of abstract sculpture, but buildings designed to fit a particular way of life. This was not just a practical matter. The most successful country houses were those which managed not only to accommodate, but also to suggest and glamorize the life-styles of the people for whom they were built.

The researches of the past thirty years have thrown a flood of light on the history of the English country house. But they have mostly been devoted to working out when houses were built, who built them and how they developed stylistically. Only comparatively recently has much attention been paid to how they were used and what they were intended to do. This kind of approach no more provides a complete explanation of country houses than an art historical analysis. But it is sufficiently coherent to stand on its own; moreover, it has not been attempted before, at any rate in the form of a complete account from the Middle Ages to the twentieth century.

6. (right) A mediaeval cavalcade. Members of the French royal household processing on May Day, *c.* 1410.

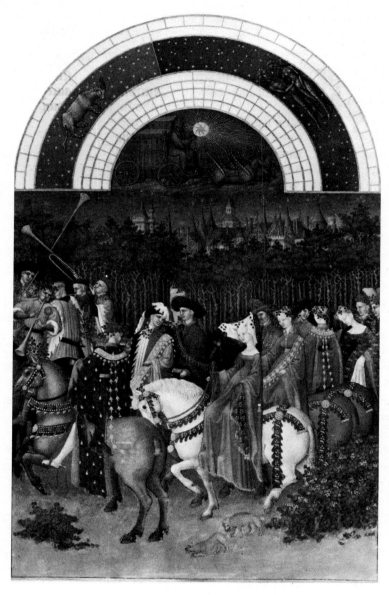

2 The Mediaeval Household

A GREAT household on the move was a familiar sight on mediaeval highways. It was also an impressive one. The number of people involved was unlikely to be less than a hundred, and could rise to well over five hundred in the case of a royal or semi-royal household. These numbers moved in three contingents of increasing size, probably spaced out several hours, and even days, apart.[1] First came a group of half-a-dozen or so people on horseback, hurrying ahead to announce that their lord was coming and to see that everything was in order at his destination. Then came a second and larger group, also mounted but far more decorative. It centred round the lord of the household and his wife, splendidly dressed and on splendidly caparisoned horses, with footmen running by their stirrups, a chaplain riding next to the lord, attendant gentlewomen riding alongside their lady, a crowd of perhaps thirty to a hundred gentlemen, yeomen and grooms riding before and behind, and a trumpeter at the head of the whole procession, blasting on his trumpet to advertise its approach. Gaily dressed in the family livery, with cloaks flying, swords clanking, and the family badge pinned to their sleeves, this mounted escort was an essential advertisement of the power and glory of a great man whenever he travelled.

The third group was even larger, not at all decorative, but equally impressive in its own way. It consisted of cooks, scullions, children, priests, household officials and other servants of all description, some on horseback but most on foot, swarming across the hedgeless countryside and accompanied by a long string of pack-horses or horses and carts, slipping and stumbling beneath their monstrous burdens. These, when unpacked at the other end, would disgorge plate, jewels, tapestries, table-cloths, clothing, hangings, coffers, musical instruments, carpenter's tools, mass-books, mass-vessels, vestments, linen, pots and pans, cooking-spits, and beds by the dozen.

A household on the move was like a tortoise without the shell. The shell, or rather shells, stood scattered ten, twenty, or several hundred miles apart, in the form of the castles, manors and lodges belonging to the lord of the household. For most of the year they were no more than shells, with a skeleton staff to look after them, and little except wooden forms, boards and trestles in the bare-walled rooms. It was only the arrival of the household which covered the walls with hangings and the boards with cushions and carpets, filled the rooms with people and household gear, and brought the buildings to life.

The houses had little meaning without the household in them, but the household could exist independently of the houses; every night wherever it lodged, whether in a house belonging to its lord, or an inn, or in the open under canvas, or even in someone else's house or castle, it organised itself in its traditional way, and did its best to create an acceptable setting and carry out the accepted rituals. Even the advance guard and the lord's own escort, which were known collectively as the riding household, were organised so that if needs be they could work in detachment from the rest of the household, and feed and look after their lord for a short stay or when he was on tour.

There is not much point in looking at the houses until one has looked at the

7. (right) A mid-fourteenth-century wagon.

households which the houses were designed to accommodate. Moreover, although what might be called gentle households varied greatly in size, the big household is the best one to start with. Big mediaeval households were not enlarged versions of small ones. Just as Victorian rectories and villas tended to be midget versions of country houses, in the Middle Ages it was the small households which did their best to copy the life-style and ritual of the big ones. They imitated them because they were familiar with them; the gentry were connected to the great families by numerous links of hospitality, service, or blood.

In 1420 the Earl and Countess of Warwick had a household of at least 125 people. In 1507–8 the Duke of Buckingham's household varied according to the season, from about 100 in Advent to 200 at the Epiphany. A few years later the Earl of Northumberland had 166 people on his check-roll. The Duke of Norfolk had a household of 144 at Framlingham Castle at Christmas, 1526.[2] Households could be even larger, especially those belonging to people of royal blood or with royal pretensions. In the middle of the fourteenth century, Thomas, Lord Berkeley is said to have had a household of 300; in the early sixteenth century Cardinal Wolsey's household amounted to around 500.[3] But in the later Middle Ages, at any rate, the normal household for a peer or great prelate varied between 100 and 200 people.

Even a household of this size seems exorbitantly large by our standards, but it was essentially functional; everything in it, including the element of conspicuous waste, had a practical purpose. Keeping the lord and his immediate family fed and comfortable was only part of what it had to do. It was also the main instrument with which he maintained his power and prestige and prepared the way for the jobs and marriage alliances which would increase them. It achieved this in four principal ways, which combined to make every great mediaeval house a mixture of office, barracks, court and hotel. It was the administrative and judicial headquarters of the great estates which produced the money, and, to a certain extent, the manpower on which the lord's power was ultimately based. It supplied the hard core of physical force through which he exercised his authority. It cocooned him in a mystique of continuous ritual, both secular and religious. It dispensed lavish hospitality to all ranks of society.

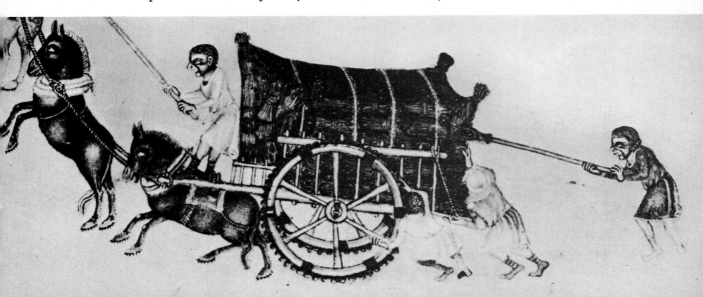

The organisation evolved to carry out these functions was complex and hierarchic.[4] A mediaeval household was a pyramid; its lord floated in splendour at its apex, but was supported on widening layers of gentlemen, yeomen, and grooms, approximating in function and status to officers, N.C.O.s and other ranks in the army today. The grander the household, the grander its upper members. The king surrounded himself with a circle of great noblemen and noble ladies (Pl. 8); a nobleman and his wife had their attendant circle of knights and people of gentle birth, a knight had his gentlemen and gentlewomen, and even a rich landowner without title had a household headed by members drawn from the squirearchy. The duties of these noble or gentle attendants were similar at all levels; from the royal household downward they acted as administrators, secretaries, bodyguards, companions and servants, sometimes a mixture of all five. The mixture can still be recognized in the royal household today.

Although socially diverse, the servants in a mediaeval household tended to come from the same catchment area. They were usually, though not invariably, recruited from families living in the areas where the lord had his main estates; the greater the lord, the bigger the catchment area. Yeomen servants and grooms were likely to come from his own tenantry. Gentleman servants could be the elder sons of local landowners, waiting for their fathers to die, or younger sons, who had entered the household as a career. They often belonged to cadet or illegitimate branches of their master's family, or were related to it through the female line. In a very grand household the senior officials were usually considerable local landowners and notables in their own right; they worked part-time only for their lord, and carried out much of their work through deputies.

Mediaeval households were not only pyramidal in organisation; they were power blocks as solid as pyramids in the front which they presented to the world and the weight which they gave to their members. The fact that an entire household, whether related to its lord or not, was described as his family accurately expressed its close-knit nature. It was a mutual benefit society, which worked not only for the power and glory of its lord but for the advantage and protection of everyone in it. The livery or badge of a powerful man was a sign of privilege not servitude. It showed that its wearer belonged to the exploiting rather than the exploited classes. Great households, the church or the law were the three main routes of advancement for people without fortune. Government service was scarcely differentiated from service in the royal household; and the royal household was only the grandest of a series of households all organised on the same lines and each equipped with its own administrative service, its own courts, and its own fighting force.

The heads of households, from the king downwards, extended and consolidated their power by attaching families of many social grades to them by ties of service, sentiment and self-interest; and they increased their prestige by having attendants of rank or gentle birth. For servants of all ranks household service meant increase in status, security and standard of living for themselves and their families, possibilities of advancement, and a widening of their horizons. For gentle

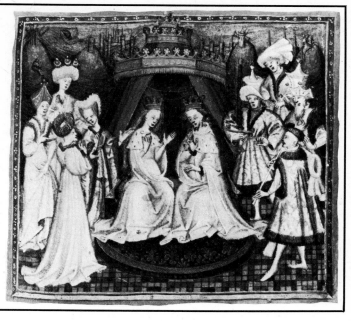

8. A king and queen with their courtiers.

servants, in particular, it was a way of acquiring social polish, administrative experience, and martial and sporting accomplishments. It provided a form of education at a time when schools scarcely existed, except those for the clergy. It was a way to travel and learn the ways of the world, especially when the lord and his household moved to estates in other parts of the country, or went to London or the court, or travelled abroad on an embassy or a campaign. It was sometimes a way to a wife, for in addition to gentlemen servants a great household contained a smaller number of gentlewomen acting as companions and ladies-in-waiting to the mistress of the house. For those without fortune it could be a route to independence and their own estates; many county families were founded by gentlemen (and even yeomen) servants on the winnings from their service to the great. Such originally penniless gentlemen made household service their career; elder sons stayed a few years, and when their parents died imitated what they had seen on whatever scale they could afford in their own houses.

Ben Jonson was later to look back on the system and celebrate great households as 'nurseries of nobility' providing

> the noblest way
> Of breeding up our youths in letters, arms,
> Fair mien, discourses, civil exercise,
> And all the blazon of a gentleman.[5]

The role of great households as noble nurseries stretched well back into the Middle Ages. Service could start literally at nursery age. The fifteenth-century *Babees Book* is the best known of a number of mediaeval verse-books of instruction for gently-born 'babies who dwell in households' who helped serve their master at table in the intervals of, and as part of, their education.[6] Ecclesiastical households were especially popular as means to literacy and social graces; mediaeval bishops and mitred abbots lived on the same scale as mediaeval lords, but tended to have better manners. In the twelfth century Thomas Becket, when Archbishop of Canterbury, had a selection of noble striplings in his household, including the king's eldest son.[7] So did his contemporary, William Longchamp, Bishop of Ely, of whom his secretary wrote

> All the sons of the nobles acted as his servants, with downcast looks, nor dared they to look upward toward the heavens unless it so happened that they were addressing him; if they attended to anything else they were pricked with a goad, which their lord held in his hand, fully mindful of his grandfather of pious memory, who, being of servile condition in the district of Beauvais, had, for his occupation, to guide the plough and whip up the oxen.[8]

In the early sixteenth century Cardinal Wolsey had nine or ten 'young lords' living in more genial conditions in his household, each with from two to five servants to look after them.[9] But not all of these household babies and boys came from such grand backgrounds, nor did ecclesiastical households have a monopoly. Geoffrey Chaucer, the son of a wine merchant, probably started his career in the 1350s as a child in the household of the Countess of Ulster; from there he moved on to royal households, fame, and a considerable fortune. In the 1480s Thomas More, the son of a lawyer, served as a child in the household of Cardinal Morton; in the 1520s Sir Anthony Wingfield brought Roger Ascham, the son of one of Lord Scrope of Bolton's upper servants, into his household, and he later paid for him to go to Cambridge and launched him on his career as scholar and humanist. In 1512 the household of the Earl of Northumberland included three 'henchmen' (the contemporary expression for pages) who were being educated there at his expense, and three more 'young gentlemen' who were being educated at the expense of their friends. Young gentlemen, henchmen, and Northumberland's own children were taught their letters by the 'Master of Grammar', a priest who was a permanent member of the household and had a clerk as 'usher of the school' to assist him.[10]

But the teaching role of a great household, although of some importance, was a side result of its four main functions of administration, power, state and hospitality. Of these, administration, vital though it was, involved the least people, for those in the household concerned with it were only the core of an organisation that included receivers, rangers, bailiffs and reeves, dispersed all over the lord's estates. In the central household a receiver-general collected and recorded all rents and other income from the estate; in very grand households a separate treasurer looked after the money once it had been collected. The steward, who was the chief household officer, spent much of his time on estate business; in particular he officiated, in person or by deputies, at all his lord's manorial courts. These deputies who gradually took over all the court business became known as 'stewards of the courts', and were usually lawyers; 'stewards of the household' and 'stewards of the courts' were the forerunners of the house and land stewards of later times. In the Middle Ages all these household officers were gentlemen, and were likely to have a clerk or two to assist them; a clerk, at least in the earlier

Middle Ages, had taken minor religious orders and was therefore literate, unlike most of the household. In addition, estate business produced a constant coming and going of people. Once or twice a year an auditor came to audit the accounts. In great households the lord's council, a consultant body composed mainly of lawyers, met to advise him on estate and other matters. Bailiffs or receivers came from the more distant estates to pay in the rents which they had collected. Tenants from the nearer manors came to pay in their rent in person; other tenants came with petitions or grievances. Most of these came with one or more servants. As the time of a business trip was conditioned by the speed of a horse, they all had to be given a meal, and many of them had to be put up for the night.

But although the ownership and smooth running of great estates was a prerequisite of power, the power was made actual by men not money. In the Middle Ages power was still largely based on physical force. A man's power depended on how many other men would fight for him. His physical backing gave him standing with the king when the country was stable, and enabled him to replace or put pressure on the king in times of trouble.

The most obvious way to wield physical power was to have a full-time army. There is, however, little evidence for the existence of these in the Middle Ages in England and then only on a comparatively small scale. In the mid fourteenth century, for instance, Maurice, Lord Berkeley had a following of twelve knights and twenty-four squires, with 120 attendants, all or mostly mounted, making a private army of 156 people which seems to have been independent of the rest of the household.[11] The drawback to private armies was their cost; to maintain, equip and pay fighting men all the year round was a heavy additional expense, when added to the already large expenses of running a normal household. In the intervals between fighting, which were likely to be long ones, money spent on a private army was wasted and its members could become bored and troublesome.

By the fourteenth century the feudal system by which land was held from the lord or king on condition that the tenant fought for him when called on had largely disappeared; the fighting obligation had gradually been compounded for a money payment. But there were two other systems by which fighting men could be obtained at an economic rate. These were the fighting household, and the use of retainers.

The origins of the former stretched far back into the Middle Ages. Part of the ordinary household normally acted as escort and bodyguard to their lord in addition to their other duties. The gentlemen and yeomen who attended on him and his guests at meals, or looked after him in his private quarters, also followed him when he went to fight, escorted and protected him in times of peace (and on occasions beat up or intimidated those who obstructed him), and in general rode about the country on his business. Normally they wore his badge and livery, and carried swords; but every house of any size had a reserve supply of horse and body armour, pikes and bows, hanging in the hall or kept in a separate armoury.

The fighting element in the household corresponded more or less exactly to the riding household. It rode out in its entirety on occasions such as that described at the beginning of this chapter, when the whole household was on the move. Its numbers could vary considerably. In 1420–1 the Earl of Warwick was travelling with a riding household of seventy-five and the Duke of Bedford with one of sixty-four. In 1458 the Duke of York rode into London with a riding household of 140. In 1512 there was a riding household of fifty-four on the books of the Earl of Northumberland. It made up about a third of his total household, which was perhaps the normal proportion.[12]

The riding household provided a core of well-trained and devoted fighting men. When more were needed, the retainers were called in. The popular image of mediaeval retainers bears little relation to the actuality. They were not a string of followers in constant attendance on their lord; their whole point was that they served on a part-time basis, and had no place in the regular routine of the household. On the strength of a written contract and, in most cases, payment of a comparatively small annual retainer in exactly the modern sense, they agreed to fight for, and attend on, whoever retained them whenever he called them out. When in attendance they, and the men who came with them, were maintained at his expense, and wore his badge and livery; not infrequently they also wore them when going about on their own business. The system was developed in the fourteenth century. Retainers could be both gentlemen and yeomen, although the Crown, which was always suspicious of retainers, tried to limit the system to gentlemen. They were substantial farmers, gentry and even knights, living in the geographical sphere of influence of their employer. Each retainer usually brought a band of followers with him, the size of which was often stipulated in the agreement.[13]

The system was a successful and long lasting one, because it worked in the interests of both parties. Basically it extended the already extended mediaeval family outside the limits of the household. The retainer had his fee, and the fact that he was known to be under the protection of a great man increased his status; the value of wearing a prestigious livery could be so great that some retainers were prepared to do so even without being paid a fee. The employer got a potential retinue or fighting force at a relatively small outlay. Even so, in the case of a very ambitious nobleman the combined total of retaining fees could amount to a formidable sum; by the early sixteenth century a quarter of the revenues of the Earl of Northumberland was being spent on retainers, and he was in financial difficulties as a result.[14]

Fourteenth-century retainers were usually called on for fighting services only. In the fifteenth century they were also brought in to supplement the regular household whenever their lord wished to make a show of state and power. The mounted and armed bands with which great noblemen rode into London, and astonished its citizens, were a case in point. The 400 horsemen who escorted the Earl of Salisbury in 1448, and the 200 with the Duke of Somerset in the same year, were composed of mixed riding household and retainers; when the Duke of York rode in in 1458 with only 140 horsemen, it was pointed out that he was travelling 'with his own household only'.[15]

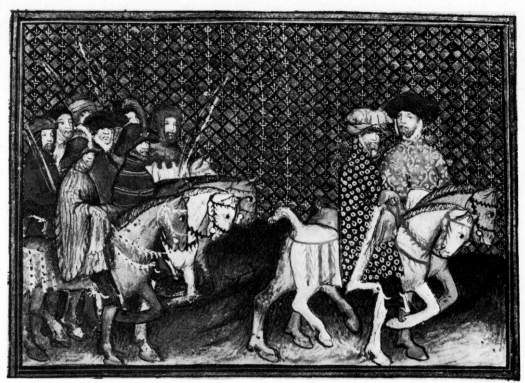

9. The Dukes of Exeter and Surrey leaving for Chester in 1399.

Retainers could also be called out when a great person, royal or otherwise, had to be entertained or impressed. In his life of Henry VII, Francis Bacon described an occasion when the Earl of Oxford entertained Henry VII at Hedingham Castle, probably in 1498. The king's departure took place through a long lane of attendants in the Oxford livery. The king asked 'These handsome gentlemen and yeomen, which I see on both sides of me, are some of your menial servants?' The earl's answer and the king's reaction to it underlined the advantages of the system and its dangers. The earl 'smiled, and said "It may please your Grace that were not for mine ease. They are most of them my retainers, that are come to do me service at such a time as this, and chiefly to see your Grace."' The king coldly pointed out that he was breaking the law; the consequence was that the earl had to pay a formidable fine.[16]

The Crown was naturally suspicious of a system which encouraged subjects to build up a great connection for comparatively little outlay. On the other hand, since there was no standing army in the Middle Ages, it was tempting for the Crown to allow its own supporters to keep retainers, in order to consolidate its own position. In 1468 Edward IV made retaining illegal; in 1504 the Crown took on the right to give exemption from the law to named individuals, for a stated number of retainers. This system of combined general illegality and licenced exemption survived through the sixteenth century, although it was often disregarded. At no time was any law passed limiting the size of private households, or their right to wear livery; a clear distinction was kept between retainers and household.

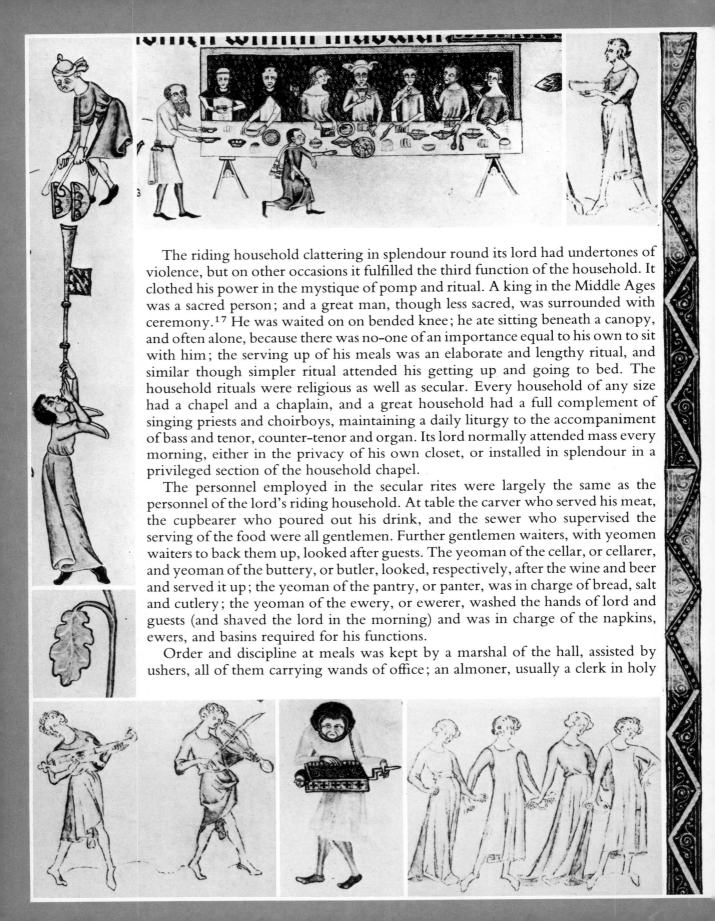

The riding household clattering in splendour round its lord had undertones of violence, but on other occasions it fulfilled the third function of the household. It clothed his power in the mystique of pomp and ritual. A king in the Middle Ages was a sacred person; and a great man, though less sacred, was surrounded with ceremony.[17] He was waited on on bended knee; he ate sitting beneath a canopy, and often alone, because there was no-one of an importance equal to his own to sit with him; the serving up of his meals was an elaborate and lengthy ritual, and similar though simpler ritual attended his getting up and going to bed. The household rituals were religious as well as secular. Every household of any size had a chapel and a chaplain, and a great household had a full complement of singing priests and choirboys, maintaining a daily liturgy to the accompaniment of bass and tenor, counter-tenor and organ. Its lord normally attended mass every morning, either in the privacy of his own closet, or installed in splendour in a privileged section of the household chapel.

The personnel employed in the secular rites were largely the same as the personnel of the lord's riding household. At table the carver who served his meat, the cupbearer who poured out his drink, and the sewer who supervised the serving of the food were all gentlemen. Further gentlemen waiters, with yeomen waiters to back them up, looked after guests. The yeoman of the cellar, or cellarer, and yeoman of the buttery, or butler, looked, respectively, after the wine and beer and served it up; the yeoman of the pantry, or panter, was in charge of bread, salt and cutlery; the yeoman of the ewery, or ewerer, washed the hands of lord and guests (and shaved the lord in the morning) and was in charge of the napkins, ewers, and basins required for his functions.

Order and discipline at meals was kept by a marshal of the hall, assisted by ushers, all of them carrying wands of office; an almoner, usually a clerk in holy

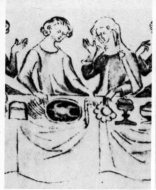
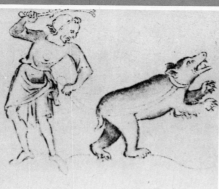
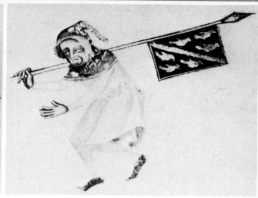

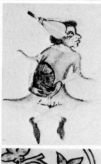

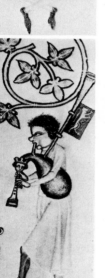

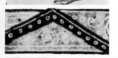

orders, said grace and collected and distributed the left-overs to the poor. In the lord's private chambers he was attended by a chamberlain (in the early Middle Ages or if he was very grand) and later by gentlemen and yeomen ushers of the chamber, with gentlemen, yeomen and grooms of the chamber to assist them. His beds, hangings and clothes were looked after by one or more yeomen of the wardrobe, assisted by grooms and arras-menders. The horses on which the lord and the riding household rode abroad were in the care of the yeomen and grooms of the stable, superintended by a master of the horse who was always a gentleman and was one of the main household officers. Grooms of the stable are the only ones of the numerous grooms employed in all departments of the household whose descendants have the same name and do the same work today. The personnel of the stables formed part of the riding household and joined the lord's escort when called on.

The ceremony of serving up meals centred round the lord, and could operate even when he was eating on his own. But most of the time there were visitors of all ranks to be entertained, coming sometimes for a meal, sometimes for a night or nights as well, and sometimes in very great numbers. The need to look after these guests added to the size of the household. Although many of them were on necessary business, to keep something approaching open house was an essential part of the image of a great man. To have crowds of people continuously coming to the house, to have drink flowing in abundance, to serve up far more food than could possibly be eaten, and to feed the poor waiting at the gate with the left-overs was all evidence of power, wealth and glory. It was a way of life which later generations looked back on nostalgically as 'the Ancient English Hospitality'.

On the whole, hospitality operated in the same sphere from which the owner drew his retainers and household. In addition to the coming and going of people

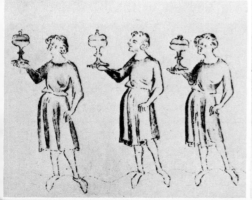
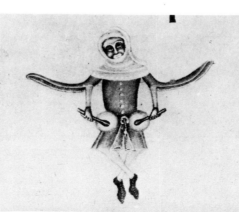
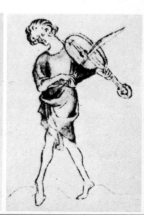

on estate and other business, the local gentry, many of whom were probably retainers, were regularly entertained, along with the attendants whom they brought with them as a necessary status symbol. But apart from this constant watering of the lord's own connection, there were always visitors from outside. At one end of the scale, passing pilgrims or respectable travellers of good standing were seldom refused hospitality when they asked for it. At the other were visitors of the same rank as, or higher than, that of the lord who entertained them. These arrived with a massive entourage—with, in fact, their own riding household—and expected to be put up in style; and, of course, the king, if he came, had to be entertained in the greatest style of all.

From the thirteenth century onwards, a number of household account-books survive which list these guests in greater or lesser detail. One of the most interesting is the account-book of Elizabeth Berkeley, Countess of Warwick.[18] It covers the years 1420 and 1421. During this period the Earl of Warwick was away fighting in France, but returned for a fortnight's visit along with an entourage of seventy-six people (only one of whom was a retainer). Other guests ranged from the Duke of Bedford (Henry IV's younger son) with an entourage of sixty-four, to bands of pilgrims, who were not considered respectable enough to be allowed into the house and were fed at the gate. There was constant coming and going of people from the family estates, ranging from receivers, auditors, and lawyers to bailiffs, clerks, messengers, falconers and huntsmen. People who came on business included a royal messenger bringing the earl a writ of summons to parliament, doctors, charcoal burners, two Irish fish merchants, embroiderers and goldsmiths. The household was entertained at Christmas by a travelling band of ten players, and the minstrel of the Duke of Clarence.

This kind of entertainment was only a portion of the junketings that enlivened the fourteen days from Christmas Eve to Epiphany every year in all households, from the largest castle to the smallest manor house. On New Year's Day everyone exchanged presents. Feasting went on during the whole period, and for at least one day something approaching complete open house was kept; as far as can be judged by the numbers involved, anyone who turned up from any level of society, except possibly the poorest, was entertained in the house, and even for the latter there must have been left-overs in abundance handed out at the gate.

In 1303 Thomas, Lord Berkeley 'kept open Christmas for all comers at Berkeley Castle: and John of Monmouth, then Bishop of Llandaff and many great guests kept with their lord the solemnity of that feast.' Two hundred years later little had changed. The Duke of Buckingham entertained 182 'strangers' to dinner at Thornbury Castle on Christmas Day, 1507, and 319 on the following Epiphany (all but forty of whom stayed on to supper). The twelfth-night guests included approximately twenty knights, gentry and clergy (among them the Abbot of Keynsham) with eighty-nine attendants, fifty estate officials, tenants and their servants, forty-two people 'from the town' and ninety 'from the country'. On 30 December, 1526, 235 'strangers' dined with the Duke of Norfolk at Framlingham Castle; thirty-five of these were knights, gentry, priests and their servants, the remaining 200 were 'persons of the country'.[19]

24

10. (previous pages) A high table, a bear leader, dancers, servants and musicians in the fourteenth century.

Entertainments provided during this period included plays, music and carols—the latter originally a combination of singing and dancing. Four 'waits from Bristol' came out to Thornbury, plays were put on by four visiting 'players of the Lord of Wrisell', and music and song was provided by two visiting minstrels and six trumpeters. The Earl of Northumberland's Christmas entertainments at Wressel Castle and Leconfield Manor in Yorkshire were largely home-made. His own choristers put on a nativity play in the chapel, his own trumpeters and minstrels played outside his chamber door on New Year's Day, his own bear-leader led on his performing bears for the amusement of the company. In the Northumberland household, as in others, an Abbot or Lord of Misrule was chosen from the household, and for three or more days presided over the high table, mimicked his lord, received homage, issued elaborately comic orders and indulged in what were called 'merry disports'. But at Wressel there were also entertainments from outside. The boy-bishops of York and Beverley—ecclesiastical equivalents of the Lord of Misrule—visited with their entourages; plays were put on by travelling players, some of them under the patronage of other great households.[20] Such travelling companies did not confine their attention to great houses; at Christmas, 1482, the household at Sir Thomas Stonor's manor of Stonor in Oxfordshire was entertained by both 'the players of Gloucester' and 'the players of Leighton'.[21]

The Christmas holiday was the culmination of the year's hospitality, but there was likely to be feasting on a lesser, but still considerable, scale on other feast-days—especially Easter and Whitsun—and at the auditing of the household and estate accounts. Other feasts were held to celebrate marriages and funerals; the funeral feast following on the death of a great nobleman could reach staggering proportions. The guests at all these entertainments were mostly drawn from a local catchment area; although very large numbers attended them, the numbers of great people and even independent gentry who came were comparatively small. Occasionally, however, feasts were held on a more than local basis. Excluding royal feasts, the most sensational of these of which there is a record was the Neville feast. It was held in September 1465, at Cawood Castle, near York. It almost certainly lasted several days. Although its ostensible purpose was to celebrate the enthronement of George Neville as Archbishop of York, it must also have been planned as a demonstration of the power, wealth and solidarity of the great Neville clan. Seven bishops, ten abbots, twenty-eight peers, an assortment of great ladies, fifty-nine knights and innumerable judges, lawyers, clergy, aldermen and esquires travelled from all over the country to attend it. Since they all came with an appropriate number of attendants the total number of people involved (including those serving and waiting) was somewhere in the neighbourhood of 2500 people; the food eaten included 113 oxen, 6 wild bulls, 1000 sheep, 2000 each of geese, pigs, and chickens, 12 porpoises and 4000 cold venison pasties.[22]

The feast given in 1504 to celebrate the enthronement of Archbishop Warham at Canterbury was less gargantuan, but still lavish enough. A feature of it was the serving up with each course of 'subtilties' or elaborate pieces of confectionery;

one of the simpler ones featured 'Saint Eustace kneelyng in a Parke under a great tree full of roses, and a white hart before him with a crucifix between his horns, and a man by him leading his horse'.[23] Another famous entertainment was the tournament and feast put on by Sir Rhys ap Thomas at Carew Castle on and around St George's Day, 1507. This was a piece of calculated showmanship by a jumped-up Welsh squire who had risen to great power and riches, and wanted to publicise the fact that he had been given the Garter. Thirteen jousters, all knights or men of substance drawn from all over Wales, were put up in the castle, presumably with their followers; another five or six hundred 'most of them of good rank and quality' were put in tents and pavilions in the park. Sir Rhys also assembled two hundred men in his own livery, 'tall men all in blue coats' who were probably a mixture of household and retainers. The grandest of the meals which punctuated the five days' feasting was given as though the king were present; food was served to an empty chair under a canopy, with fanfares of trumpets for each course. Only after this imaginary meal was assumed to be finished did the company sit down to their own food. Sir Rhys sat alone in grandeur in the middle of his table, with the Bishop of St David's at one end.[24]

Such festivities were exceptional, but even the everyday problem of feeding a household of one to two hundred people together with a varying number of 'strangers' was a considerable one. In the early Middle Ages great landowners had also been great farmers. From the fourteenth century onwards, for reasons which are still debated, there was a tendency for them to lease off more and more land. In the early sixteenth century almost all the food consumed by the household of the Earl of Northumberland was bought at local markets rather than grown on the earl's demesne land.[25] But in most houses, varying amounts of grain and meat, either produced on the lord's own demesne land or provided by tenants in lieu of rent, were sent in by the bailiffs of his local manors. The provision of food was the responsibility of the clerk of the kitchen. He was normally assisted by an acaterer or caterer (so called from *acate*—anything bought) who did the actual buying. Animals for eating were kept alive in meadows near the house until needed, then killed by the slaughterman; tallow from the oxen and suet from the sheep were handed over to the chandler to be turned into candles. All big households had their own baker and brewer, and a gardener to supply herbs but little else. All these servants were under the clerk of the kitchen, as were the yeomen of the buttery, pantry, ewery and cellar, the cooks, scullions, and boys to turn the spits— and the porter who kept the gate. The clerk's job was a responsible one, which could make him a small fortune, and hoist his descendants from the yeomanry into the ranks of the lesser gentry.

Once one considers the clerk of the kitchen and his troops, the hierarchies of the hall, chamber and wardrobes, the establishments of the chapel and stables, the receiver and the treasurer with their clerks, as well as miscellaneous servants such as armourers, minstrels, trumpeters, huntsmen, falconers, painters, joiners, the secretary who wrote the lord's letters and the fool who kept him amused—and once one realizes, in addition, that all gentlemen servants and probably also the senior yeomen officers had one or more personal servants to look after them—the great size of these mediaeval households ceases to be so surprising. At the head of the whole complicated organisation was the steward. He was always a gentleman, sometimes a knight, and traditionally a grave and respectable figure, with a gown, chain and white staff as insignia of his office. He was assisted as second-in-command by a comptroller, a necessary officer in view of the fact that the steward was often away, either on his lord's business, or, in the cases when he was a person of independent consequence and property, on his own. At mealtimes the steward presided over the head-officer's table, along with the comptroller, receiver, treasurer (if there was one), master of the horse, chaplain, possibly a few senior gentleman servants and any visiting gentlemen who were not considered important enough to make the lord's company.

All these servants were men. All cooking and cleaning as well as waiting was done by men. Women made up a minute proportion of the total household. The only women normally to be found in it were the lord's wife and daughters, the gentlewomen who acted as their companions, the female 'chamberers', not of gentle birth, who assisted the gentlewomen, the nurses of the lord's children, and one or more female launderers.

In the Northumberland household the proportion of women to men was 9 to 166, made up of the countess, her daughter, three gentlewomen, two chamberers, and two nurses; the laundry was sent out to the town. The Countess of Warwick, when running her own household during her husband's absence in 1420–1, had a female establishment of six gentlewomen (three of them married to the earl's gentlemen), three chamberers and one laundrywoman; but even in this woman-oriented household the proportion of women to men was only eleven to forty.[26] Most of the strangers entertained in mediaeval houses were men. Visiting nobility and gentry sometimes came with their wives, but much more often on their own; the people who came on business were almost entirely male and so, in all probability, were those (below gentry level) who flocked to the open house at Christmas. There were no women at Archbishop Warham's enthronement dinner or Sir Rhys ap Thomas's St George's entertainment; and although there was an unusual number of noblewomen and ladies with attendant gentlewomen at the Neville feast, they amounted to only sixty-seven out of the total of 2500 people involved.

The masculine nature of these households can perhaps be traced back to their origin as private war-bands. A wife and children (and accordingly women to look after them) were essential for the lord, if only for dynastic reasons; everyone else was organised like the personnel of a barracks, with no place for women except outside the walls. It is hard to believe that the majority of the household were totally celibate, but the whereabouts of its women, licit or illicit, remains mysterious. Many of the senior members of mediaeval households certainly owned or leased their own land, and had their own houses, with wives who looked after their affairs in their absence. It is possible that others were at least small-holders, and that their wives worked the land, as was common enough in the Middle Ages. Little is known about what leave of absence was allowed to members of the household; in some great establishments a system seems to have operated in which at least the senior members were 'in waiting' much as courtiers are today, and spent a quarter on the job followed by a quarter when they were free to go home.[27]

Inside the household, however, there was only a little cluster of women with its inner heart composed of the mistress of the house and her daughters and gentlewomen. The contrast between this island of womanhood and the masculine world that surrounded and served it must have been a violent one, and one likely to lead to tension, especially among the younger gentleman servants, and most of all among those who remained behind during the frequent periods when the master of the household was away. One of the advantages, and maybe one of the origins, of the code of chivalry was that it provided a viable relationship of passionate service and (in theory at any rate) sublimated sex between a young man and a married woman, or an unmarried girl and a young man who lacked the money or social status which would have made marriage a possibility.

Coming and going, of the neighbourhood and yet not of it, teeming, hierarchic, powerful, profuse, pregnant with hopes of wealth and wider horizons, subtly vibrating with sex, every great household must have had at least some of the magic experienced by Froissart in the household of Gaston de Foix: 'there was seen in his hall, chamber and court, knights and squires of honour going up and down, and talking of arms and of amours; all honour there was found, all manner of tidings of every realm and country there might be heard, for out of every country there was resort, for valiantness of this earl.'[28] The more the lord of the household could accentuate this image, the more people would seek to enter his service, or wear his livery, and the greater the hope of heiresses for his sons, alliances for his daughters, and honour or high position for himself. An essential part of the image consisted in the buildings in which power, ritual, wealth and hospitality were encased and expressed.

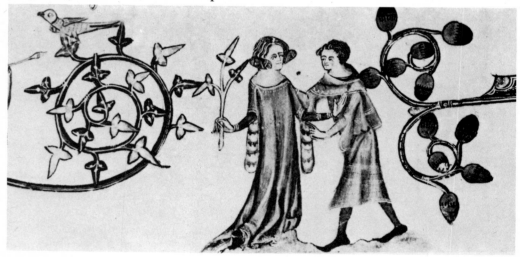

11. Courtly love.

12. (right) Haddon Hall, Derbyshire, from across the valley.

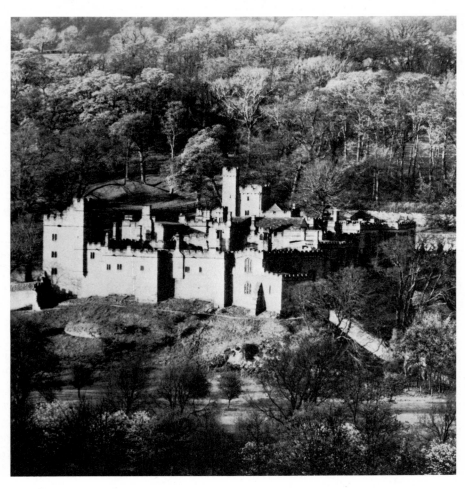

3 The Mediaeval House

ALL mediaeval houses of any size consisted of collections of smaller rooms grouped round a hall, kitchen and chapel. But during the Middle Ages the way in which these elements were arranged and the way in which they were used both changed considerably. Two forces were at work, one centripetal and the other centrifugal. The centripetal force affected the buildings, the centrifugal one the life lived in them. The buildings tended to start as a collection of separate structures, not so far removed from the individual huts in the encampment of a tribal chieftain; but, for reasons first of security and then of convenience and visual effect, they gradually merged into tighter and tighter groups round the hall. The life lived in the buildings was originally entirely dominated by the hall; a great household and many guests gorging together in a huge and magnificently decorated hall, to the accompaniment of fanfares of trumpets, was a supreme expression of power, ritual, wealth and hospitality. But the primacy of the hall was gradually eroded by the tendency of different elements of the household to eat in other parts of the house, for reasons of privacy, comfort, or state. Although this tendency had to work against the weight of tradition it gradually prevailed, and in doing so radically changed the nature of the country house.

Bishop Grosseteste, who drew up household regulations for the Countess of Lincoln in the late thirteenth century, twice drove home the importance of the whole household, including the Countess herself, eating together in the hall. 'Make your own household' he wrote 'to sit in the hall, as much as you may . . . and sit you ever in the middle of the high board, that your visage and cheer be showed to all men . . . So much as you may without peril of sickness and weariness eat you in the hall afore your many, for that shall be to your profit and worship.'[1] Three centuries later one half of his advice was still being carried out in most big households; it was not till the late sixteenth and early seventeenth century that the upper servants began to remove from the hall and eat separately from the rest of the servants in a parlour or steward's room. But by then the other half had long been disregarded; as early as the mid-fourteenth century, the lord and lady and their family had begun to eat and entertain in other rooms.

The move was lamented in a much-quoted passage of Langland's *Vision of Piers Plowman*, written in about 1362:

> Wretched is the hall . . . each day in the week
> There the lord and lady liketh not to sit.
> Now have the rich a rule to eat by themselves
> In a privy parlour . . . for poor men's sake,
> Or in a chamber with a chimney, and leave the chief hall
> That was made for meals, for men to eat in.[2]

The widely-held and constantly repeated belief that family and household continued to eat together in the great hall until Elizabethan and even Jacobean days is based on nineteenth-century romanticism. From the second half of the fourteenth century onwards a great man increasingly ate in other rooms, and only returned to the great hall on special occasions, which became rarer and rarer. The practice of the great gradually moved down the social scale until by the end of the sixteenth century even the lesser gentry had ceased to eat in their halls. The great hall was past its prime by 1400.

A vivid picture of what life was like when the hall still reigned supreme is given by the mid-fourteenth-century romance of *Sir Gawain and the Green Knight*. The romance starts in the great hall of Camelot during the Christmas festivities. New Year's gifts are being handed out and knights and ladies are running and laughing round the hall, fighting like children for them.

> All this merriment they made, till their meat was served
> Then they washed and mannerly went to their seats.[3]

Arthur and Guenevere, Arthur's nephews Gawain and Agravian, Bishop Baldwin and Iwain

> . . . dined on the dais and daintily fared
> And many a trusty man below at the long tables.
> Then forth came the first course with cracking of trumpets
> On which many bright banners bravely were hanging.
> Noise of drums then anew, and the noble pipes
> Warbling wild and keen, wakened their music
> So that men's hearts rose high hearing their playing.[4]

In the silence after the music the Green Knight, 'the largest man alive', glowing with green flesh and a mane and beard of green hair, glittering with the green diamonds scattered on his green clothes, and carrying a holly bush in one hand and a battle axe in the other, gallops unannounced into the hall on a huge green horse. He rides up to the dais and delivers the challenge on which the rest of the story depends.

Later on Sir Gawain, on his travels in search of the Knight, comes to a castle and asks for harbour.

> He called and soon there came
> A porter pure pleasant
> On the wall he learned his errand
> And hailed the knight errant
> 'Good sir' quoth Gawain 'Would you go mine errand
> To the lord of the house, harbour to crave.'[5]

Harbour is given. Knights and squires escort Gawain into the hall, and take his helmet, sword and shield from him. The lord of the castle comes down from his chamber to the hall to greet him. Dinner in the hall is over; Gawain is shown up to his chamber, given a change of clothes and fed with a sumptuous meal on a trestle table before the fire. After attending chapel with the rest of the household, he meets the wife of his host and her aged gentlewoman. He stays at the castle several days; much of his time is spent politely evading his hostess's attempts to seduce him, while her husband is out hunting. Life in the castle moves between hall, chapel and chambers. All meals take place in the hall. After supper the company in the hall amuse themselves with 'many noble songs, as canticles of Christmas and carols new'. It is in the hall that the lord displays to Gawain the animals he has killed out hunting, and in the hall that Gawain makes his formal farewell when he finally leaves. But on occasions, after both dinner and supper, the lord or his wife take Gawain into 'chamber'—not Gawain's guest chamber but the chamber (possibly two separate chambers) of his host and hostess. Here, in a more intimate atmosphere, they sit and talk by the chimney fire, and are refreshed with wine and spices.

> When they had played in the hall
> As long as their will them lasted
> To chamber he can him call
> And to the chimney they passed.[6]

The rooms, recreations and rituals described in *Sir Gawain* would have been familiar to the listeners who first heard the story in the halls or chambers of the West Midlands where it originated. Negotiation of the porter at the gate, daily services in the chapel, alternation between hall and chambers, provided the structure round which life in all big houses of the time was arranged; the only essential element left out is the kitchen, from which the feasts at Camelot and elsewhere would have originated. The fanfare of music which greeted each course at Camelot was, and remained, a familiar feature of all great dinners. Even at ordinary dinners the food was brought in by a formal procession headed by the marshal of the hall carrying a white staff; the grander the dinner became, the more elaborate was the procession and its accompaniments. The Green Knight's ride into the hall was only a more dramatic version of contemporary ceremony. At the banquets that followed the coronation of every sovereign, from that of Richard II in 1377 to that of George IV in 1821, a knight on horseback rode into Westminster Hall, and threw down his gauntlet as a challenge to all opposers of the king's title (Pl. 13). At other great banquets, in the fourteenth century and later (Pl. 14), the procession carrying in the first course was led through the hall by a household officer on horseback; at the enthronement feast of Archbishop Warham of Canterbury in 1504, for instance, the role was filled by the Duke of Buckingham, the mightiest subject in the land, who was acting as high steward of the feast.[7]

As in *Sir Gawain*, halls were used for receiving guests and saying good-bye to them, and for all kinds of entertainment. Christmas junketings all took place, or had their main centre, there. Royal halls, or halls where the king happened to be staying at the relevant time, were used for the meeting of parliament.[8] Courts of all kinds were sometimes held in halls; the shire court of the Palatinate of Cheshire sat for a time in the great hall of Chester Castle, and manorial courts sometimes (although by no means always) sat in the hall of the manor house.[9]

A hall could be cleared without too much difficulty for these functions because its tables were dismountable ones, made up of boards which were laid out on trestles when needed. But useful as it could be for other purposes, its main and far

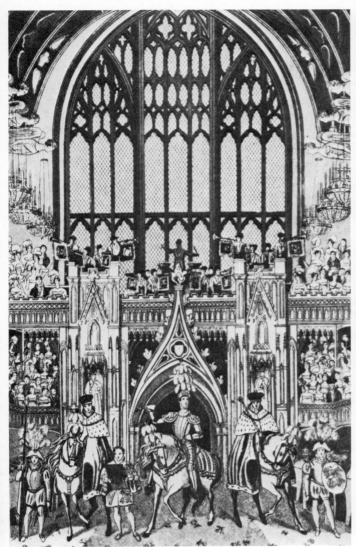

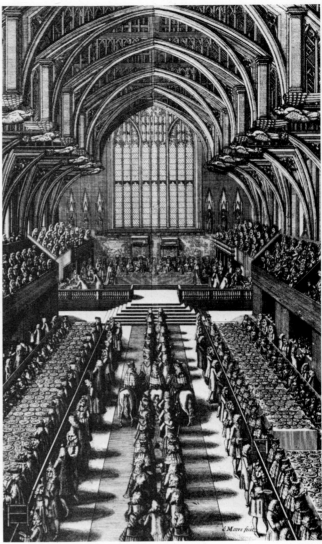

13. The King's Champion enters Westminster Hall at George IV's coronation dinner in 1821.

14. Arrival of the first course at James II's coronation dinner in 1685.

and away its most important function was that of an eating room. The fact that the halls of great men had to be large enough to seat households of around two hundred people at table, with room for even larger numbers at great feasts, explains their size. No other mediaeval hall came anywhere near the 239 ft 6 ins by 67 ft 6 ins of Westminster Hall; its immensity was the result of its unique function. In it (and overflowing out of it) took place the vast feasts involving several thousand guests which William the Conqueror gave every year, and later kings gave at least after their coronation. But in the thirteenth and fourteenth centuries plenty of halls exceeded 2500 square feet, including ones built both for royal, noble and ecclesiastical households. They range in size from those at Dartington and Penshurst (69 ft 9 ins by 37 ft 6 ins and 62 ft by 39 ft) to the huge and now roofless halls at Kenilworth Castle (90 ft by 45 ft) and the Bishop's Palace at Wells (115 ft by 59 ft 6 ins), or vanished halls such as that at the Archbishop's Palace at Canterbury, later the scene of the Warham feast, which measured 126 ft by 42 ft.[10] The earlier halls had to be divided by arcades, like a church, in order to roof them (Pl. 16), but improved joinery later enabled them to be covered by single-span timber roofs. The most famous example is the sensational roof which was constructed over Westminster Hall when its arcades were taken out in the late fourteenth century.

The architecture and fittings of a hall, as well as its dimensions, were geared to the supreme moment when the lord, his household and his guests feasted together, and demonstrated the strength and unity of the household and the wealth and generosity of its lord. The lord sat at the centre of a table across one end of the hall. From this position he 'showed his visage', in the manner recommended by Grosseteste, to his household sitting at tables placed along the hall before him. The household officers of gentle birth sat at a table presided over by the steward; other tables were supervised by the marshal of the hall, clerk of the kitchen, or other yeomen household officers. The lord's family and the more important guests sat to either side of him at his own table. Close by, one or more 'cupboards' (at that period seldom more than boards on trestles) were loaded with rows of gold and silver dishes, cups, bowls and other plate, to demonstrate his wealth. From the thirteenth century onward his table was often raised up on a dais, so as to become literally the high table. In later halls the importance of the dais was sometimes emphasized by the bay-window which lit one end, and by the coved canopy which ran along the top of the wall behind it; the latter was the architectural equivalent of a cloth of estate, which was suspended behind the seat, and canopy-wise over the head, of all great men. Wall-chimneys, which from the fourteenth century began to replace open hearths in the centre of the hall, were sometimes up on the dais, but more often in one of the side walls. They were often richly carved; so were the arcades of the hall, if it had them. Wall paintings or hangings on the walls, tracery in the windows, and a superb timber roof overhead all added to the impression of magnificence.

Something of the splendour of the hall often passed over into the kitchen, buttery, pantry and cellars which served it. A lord of the time of Sir Gawain, as he sat looking down the hall across the long lines of his household, normally saw three arches in the wall facing him (Pl. 15). The two side ones led to the pantry and buttery, from which the yeoman of the pantry dealt out bread, and the yeoman of the buttery beer and candles to whoever was entitled to them. Every effort was made to stop the two rooms from becoming private eating and drinking places, but by the end of the Middle Ages the upper servants sometimes had breakfast in the pantry, and visiting servants or other visitors of similar status were also entertained there.[11] The stairs from the beer cellar increasingly came up into the buttery, to give the butler control over his cellar. At mealtimes beer was served to everyone, wine only to the lord's and steward's tables. Wine for the top tables and plate for the cupboard and lord's table were both kept in a separate wine cellar, under the yeoman of the cellar; it was often behind or close

15. (upper right) Dartington Hall, Devon. Arches to buttery, kitchen passage and pantry (c. 1390).

16. (right) Oakham Castle, Rutland. The hall (c. 1180–90).

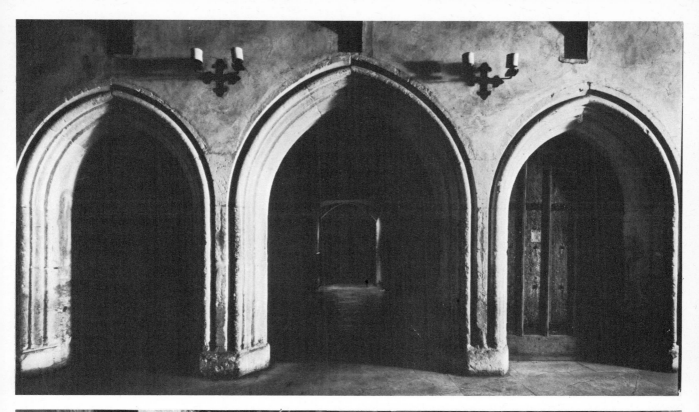

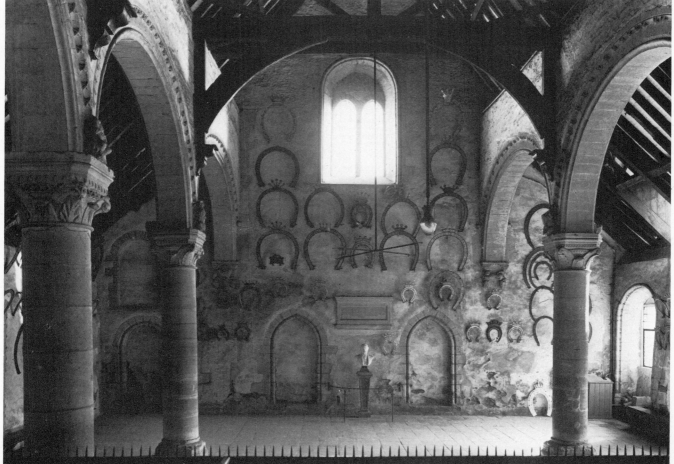

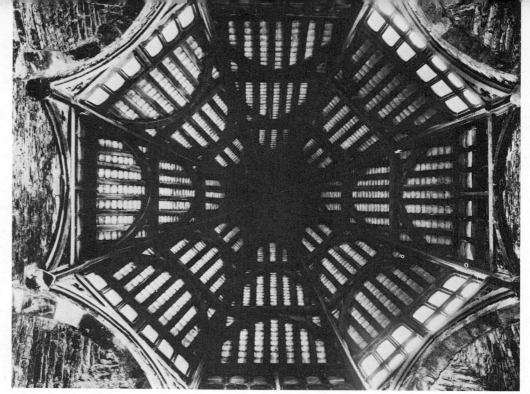

17. Stanton Harcourt, Oxfordshire. The kitchen roof (1485).

to the dais and vaulted with some elaboration, in tribute to the richness of its contents.

The middle one of the three arches was usually larger than the other two, and led by way of a broad corridor to the kitchen (Fig. 1). Baking was carried out, at least from the later Middle Ages, in brick-lined ovens, sometimes in a separate bakehouse, but all other cooking was done on open fires in the kitchen (Pl. 18), burning on open central hearths to begin with and then in huge open fireplaces. The amount of smoke, heat, smell and dirt produced by spit-roasting meat for several hundred people at open fires was very great. In the household of Henry VIII orders were given in 1526 that the scullions, who did the really dirty work (and cleaned the dishes in a separate scullery) should not 'go naked or in garments of such vileness as they now do'.[12] In an attempt to reduce heat and smell, big mediaeval kitchens were built very lofty, and ventilated through the roof. The effect of these kitchens, surrounded by great fireplaces and roofed by massive timbers or stone arches supporting a central louvre, can be cavernously impressive. Their architectural treatment is sometimes nearly as elaborate as that of the hall. Hall and kitchen were, after all, twin symbols of their lord's munificence. A number of fine examples survive, including great secular kitchens at Stanton Harcourt and Raby Castle (Pls 17 and 19), and the superb late-fourteenth-century kitchen which is now virtually all that remains of the abbot's house at Glastonbury.

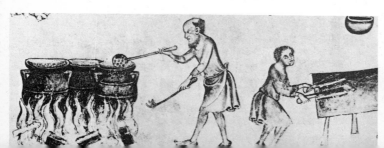

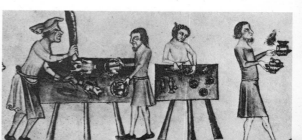

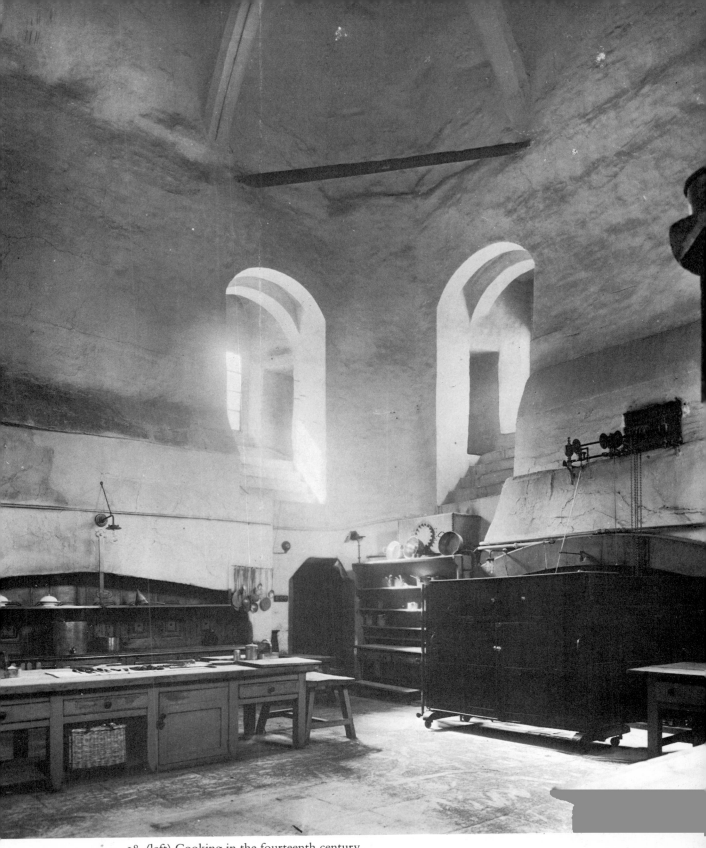

18. (left) Cooking in the fourteenth century.

19. (above) Raby Castle, Durham. The mid-fourteenth-century kitchen.

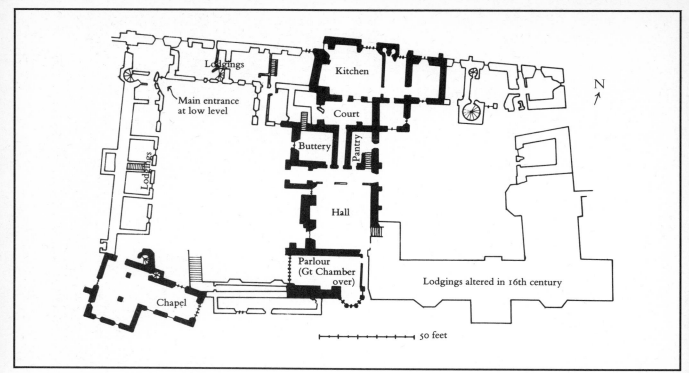

Fig. 1. Haddon Hall, Derbyshire.

The three arches at the kitchen end of the hall originally had a ceremonial as well as a practical function. They formed a triumphal arch or secular west portal. The procession carrying the lord's food collected it through a servery hatch from the kitchen, marched along the connecting corridor, and emerged through the middle of the three arches, with the ceremony appropriate to the occasion (Pl. 20). Later on in the Middle Ages, however (but seldom before the fifteenth century) the arches began to be concealed from the rest of the hall by wooden screens. Screens were originally designed to exclude the draught from the kitchen passage and from the entrance door, which usually opened straight onto the courtyard from the kitchen end of the hall. The earliest screens were movable; but they soon became fixed, and took over the function of the arches as a triumphal entry. Their ceremonial function was perfected when a musicians' gallery was built over them, as frequently became the case. The lord was then facing a fanciful portal crowned with trumpeters, who could burst into sound at the exact moment that the food and its escort emerged from underneath it.

No surviving room in England gives so vivid a feeling of the magnificence and functions of a great hall of the fourteenth century as the hall at Penshurst (Pl. 21). The traceried windows, the central hearth, the dais and the three arches in the kitchen wall all survive, although the arches are partly hidden by a later screen. But the elegant and spacious stone staircase which curves out of sight through an archway at the dais end of the hall is a later mediaeval addition (Pl. 22). It replaces a much more cramped newel staircase which was originally in the same position. At Penshurst and elsewhere such alterations became necessary once the owners had ceased to eat regularly in the hall. The procession carrying their food had to be

20. (upper right) A Garter dinner in St George's Hall, Windsor Castle, in the reign of Charles II.

21. (right) Penshurst Place, Kent. The hall (c. 1341).

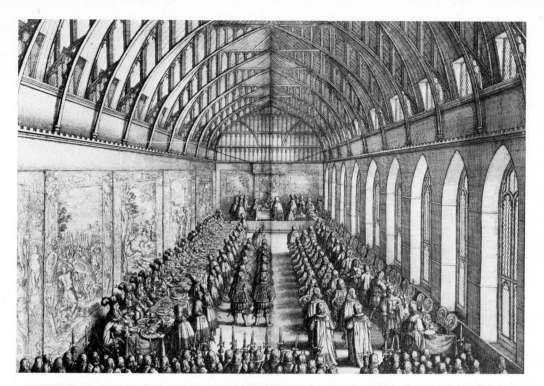

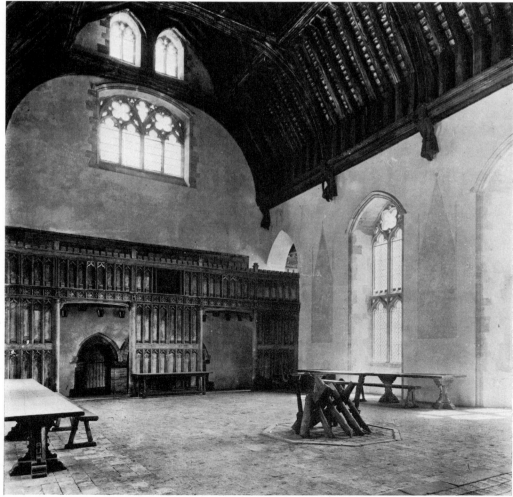

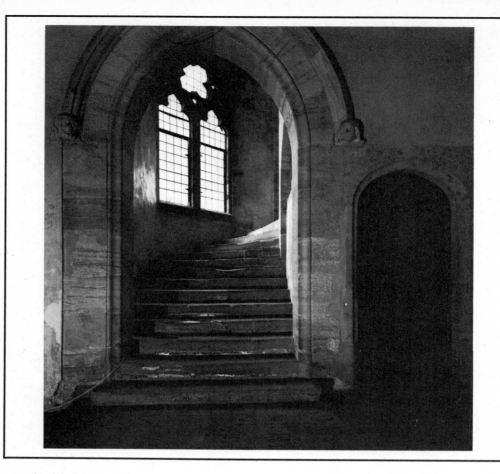

supplied with a sufficiently spacious route not only from the kitchen to the hall, but from the hall to the upstairs 'great chamber' or 'chamber with a chimney' where, as lamented by Langland, they now increasingly ate.[13]

The term 'great chamber' had begun to be used before it acquired its special meaning as the room of state for which the lord deserted the dais end of the hall. To begin with it just meant a large chamber, and was used as a distinguishing description in houses that had several chambers. In royal houses the great chamber invariably belonged to the king or queen, but in lesser houses it could be the chamber reserved for important visitors.[14] Chambers both great and small were used as bed-sitting rooms by guests or members of the family or household who occupied them. Even great people used the same chamber for sleeping, playing games, receiving visitors, and occasional meals. In the romance of *Guy of Warwick* the hero is invited into the chamber of the Emperor of Constantinople's daughter:

> Go we now to the chamber same
> In some manner to make us game
> to the chesses or to the tables,
> Or else to speak of fables,
> Before the bed of that fair maid[15]

40

22. The stairs from the dais end of the hall at Penshurst.

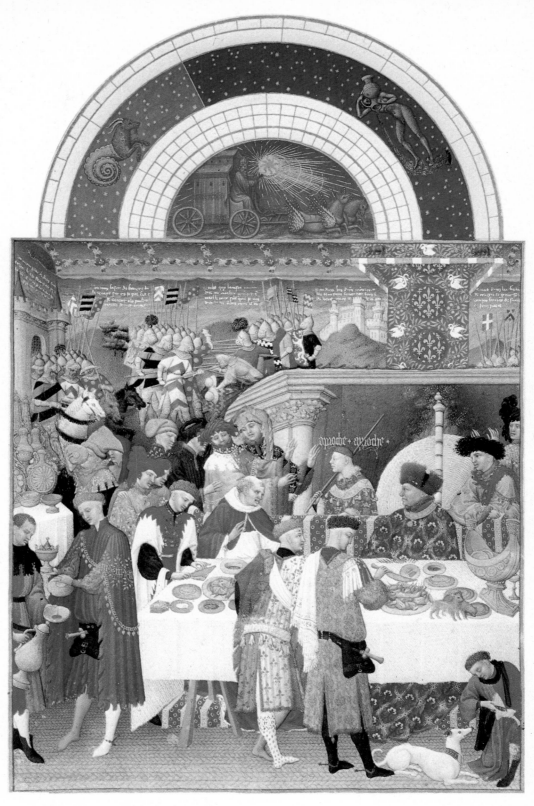

I. The Duc de Berry at dinner, as depicted in about 1410.

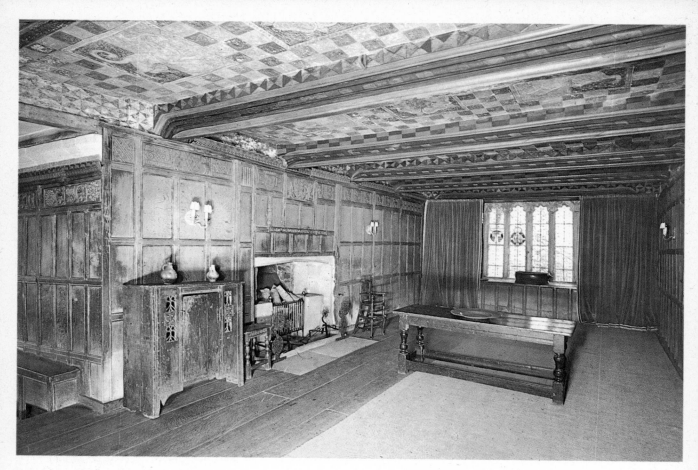

II. Haddon Hall, Derbyshire. The parlour (*c.* 1500).

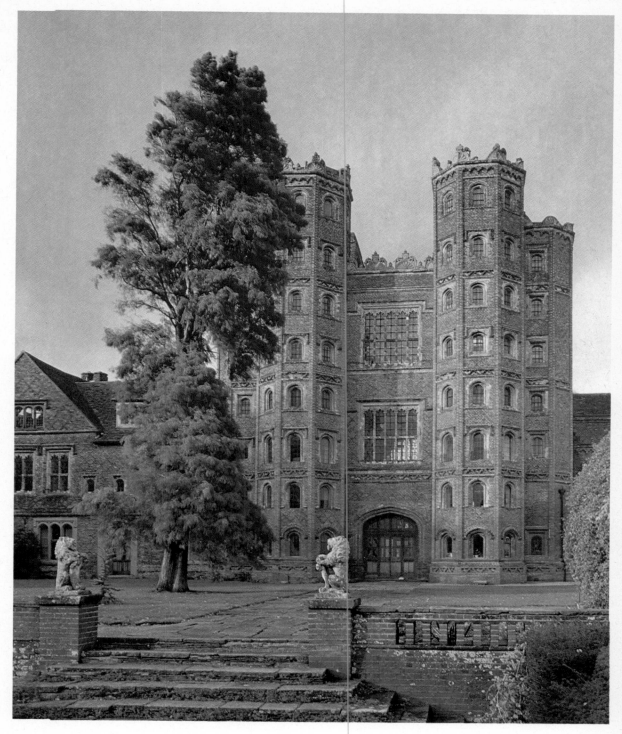

III. Layer Marney, Essex. The gatehouse (*c.* 1520–3).

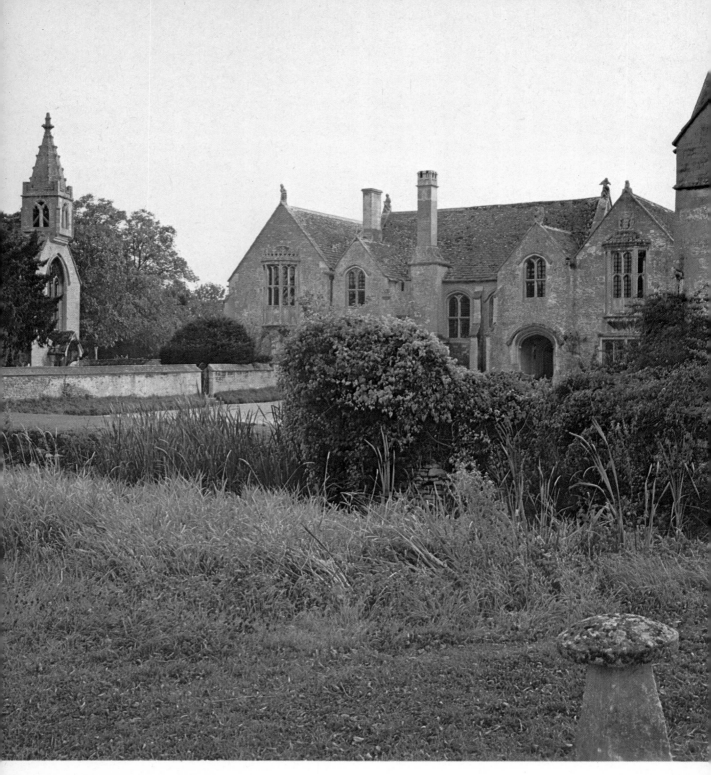

IV. Great Chalfield Manor, Wiltshire (*c.* 1470–80).

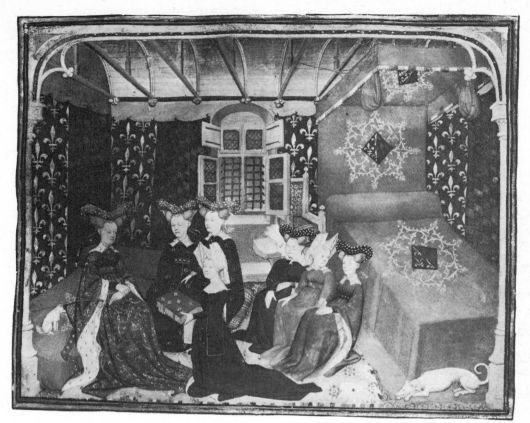

23. Christine de Pisan (*c.* 1364–*c.* 1430) presenting her works to Queen Isabel of France.

In the late fourteenth century Froissart presented a volume of love poems to Richard II in the king's chamber; the king 'put it on his bed, opened it, looked inside and read it at length'.[16] In a French miniature of the fifteenth century, showing Christine de Pisan presenting her *Livres des Trois Virtues* to Queen Isabel, the queen is sitting among her gentlewomen in her chamber which has a bed—indeed two beds—in it (Pl. 23).

Meals were also eaten in chambers, but to begin with this was the exception to the general practice of meals being eaten by the household sitting together in the hall. Sir Gawain was feasted in front of the fire in the castle guest chamber (which contained a bed hung 'with curtains of costly silk with clear golden hems') only because he had arrived too late for dinner in the hall.[17] Chambers were also places for intimate or amorous meals. Bishop Grosseteste's statutes suggest that the head of the household would eat in his chamber when suffering from 'sickness or weariness'.[18] On the occasions of great feasts ladies, if involved at all, often ate in a chamber, separate from the men in the hall—perhaps because it was taken for granted that the men would get drunk. The romance of *Guy of Warwick* describes how

> At Whitsuntide fell a day
> As I you tell may

The Earl made a great feast
Of lords of that land honest.
Knights, earls and barons
Came thither from many towns,
Ladies and maidens free
Came thither from many a country.
Knights sat in the hall
Ladies in the chamber all.[19]

At the Neville feast the women ate in the 'chief chamber'. Up to the eighteenth and nineteenth centuries ladies ate in a separate room at the Lord Mayor's banquet in the City of London, and were only allowed to watch from the balcony at the exclusively male coronation banquets served in Westminster Hall. Both these feasts had mediaeval origins.

The move of the high table from hall to great chamber was probably pioneered by the king. In royal palaces the chambers of both king and queen had been called great chambers from at least the thirteenth century. These early great chambers could be extremely large; the Painted Chamber in the palace of Westminster, which was built as Henry III's great chamber, was 80 ft 6 ins by 26 ft, and 31 ft high.[20] But there is no evidence that they were used for ceremonial meals until the fourteenth century. Some of the regulations drawn up in 1318 for the household of Edward II are worded in such a way as to suggest that the king was regularly eating in state in his great chamber.[21] By 1471, the date of the *Black Book* of regulations for the household of Edward IV, alternatives are given depending on whether the king 'kept estate' for meals in hall or great chamber.[22] By then the king and great commoners normally confined their presence in the hall to great feasts. The *Booke of Nurture*, a set of rhyming instructions for good behaviour compiled in about 1450, states unequivocally that

Pope, emperor, king, cardinal, prince with golden royal rod, duke, archbishop in his pall
All these for their dignity ought not to dine in the hall.[23]

According to the same source, other peers, bishops and mitred abbots can eat either in hall or chamber. But another verse manual of about the same period, the *Booke of Courtesy*, assumes that a 'lord' will eat in his chamber, and that the dais end of the hall will be occupied by the steward and other senior household officers — an arrangement which remained the standard one in big houses until the early seventeenth century.[24] Similarly, the Harleian regulations for the household of an earl, which date from the late fifteenth century,[25] take it for granted that the earl will eat in 'his great chamber'; the only occasions mentioned on which he frequents the hall are when he holds 'disguisings' or other pastimes there. By this is meant entertainment of the type especially associated with Christmas.

Retreat from the hall to the great chamber was far from being a retreat into informality. In the houses of great commoners as well as of the king, the ritual which had accompanied the serving of meals at the high table in the hall was

46

transferred to the lord's table in the great chamber; if anything it was elaborated. The procedure is described in detail in the Harleian regulations. In general these regulations give a vivid picture of the structure of life lived in a large late-fifteenth-century house. The Harleian earl and his household were drenched in ceremony from dawn until dusk. His getting up in the morning was a ritual performance, and so was the bringing up of what was called 'all night'—the loaves of bread, great silver jugs of beer and two great pots of wine which stood on his cupboard and sustained him and his wife through the night. His attendance at chapel involved a procession; even his hearing of mass privately in his own closet was a far from simple affair.

But the serving up of dinner and supper in his great chamber was the principal expression of his state.[26] The ceremony involved around twenty servants in its everyday form, and more on 'principal feasts'. Preparations for dinner started between ten and eleven 'after the levacion of high masse' (earlier, in some households), and for supper 'after Magnificat . . . towards five of the clock in the afternoon'. They were long and complex. First of all the grooms of the chamber set up boards on trestles, in order to make tables. The earl's board was set up on a carpet at the foot of a 'bed of estate' which still remained in the great chamber. The yeoman of the ewery prepared his own board, with cloth, napkins, basin and ewer. He, the yeoman usher of the chamber and another yeoman then laid the cloth on the earl's board, genuflecting to the board and kissing their hands before doing so. The yeoman of the cellar and others prepared the cupboard (at this period still a board on trestles) by covering it with a cloth and loading it with plate. Some of this was functional, in the form of cups for drinking, but much of it was purely for show. The grander the meal, the more plate was set out. Wine was brought up to the cupboard by the yeoman of the cellar, beer by the yeoman of the buttery; the yeoman of the pantry, escorted by the yeoman usher carrying his rod of office, brought up the great ceremonial salt along with bread, knives and spoons (forks were not yet invented). After making three bows to the earl's place, he set the salt slightly to the left of it and tucked the earl's knife and spoon under the 'state', a ceremonial fold in the tablecloth previously made by the yeoman usher and yeoman of the ewery when laying it.

Up to this stage only yeomen servants had been involved. Gentlemen now appeared, in the person of a sewer, carver, and cupbearer. The sewer and carver were ceremonially washed and fitted (or 'armed') with towels by the yeoman of the ewery. The sewer wore his towel rolled up and slung over his shoulder, like a sash; the carver also wore his rolled up but 'tippet-wise', that is hung round his neck, folded like a St Andrew's cross in front, and with the ends tucked under his girdle. He carried a napkin over his shoulder for the earl, and another over his arm for wiping his knife. His towel, second napkin and girdle were worn in exactly the same way as a priest wears a stole maniple and girdle for the mass. Once equipped, he took his knife and cut slices from all the loaves on the lord's table in order to take 'sayes' of them, that is, taste them; taking sayes was originally a precaution against poison, but by the end of the fifteenth century was assuming a purely ceremonial function. The 'state' fold in the table cloth was then unfolded.

Everything was now ready for bringing up the first course. The steward, comptroller, and gentleman usher took up position in the great chamber; the sewer, with an escort of gentlemen and yeomen (preceded on winter evenings by a yeoman carrying a torch), was sent down through the hall and screens to the servery in front of the kitchen dresser, in order to collect the food.

At the dresser there was a great deal more taking of says by the sewer before the attendant gentlemen and yeomen were loaded up with dishes. Since they were now carrying the earl's food, their return was much more of an event than their coming down. They were a procession carrying sacred meats. They were met at the entry of the hall by the marshal of the hall, carrying his rod of office, and the ushers of the hall; the marshal of the hall shouted 'by your leave, my masters' and everyone in the hall stood up, took their hats off, and stood in silence in honour of the food as it was carried through. On 'principal feasts' it was met as it left the hall by the steward, treasurer and comptroller. With or without them the procession then made its way up to the great chamber, where the sewer arranged the placing of the dishes on the table, and the carver took yet more says from the dishes.

It was only at this stage that a gentleman usher went to the earl 'giving him knowledge that his meat is on the board'. By now the meat must have been rapidly congealing, but this seems to have been of no concern in the Middle Ages. There was still more ceremony to be gone through. The earl and any one who was to eat with him assembled in the great chamber. The earl washed his hands in a basin, brought and taken away with suitable bowing and kissing by two gentlemen; one of them held the bowl on bended knee while the other manipulated a towel. The earl was helped into his great chair by the gentleman usher and two more gentlemen. The gentleman usher then placed the other guests at table. This was a tricky business, involving sound knowledge of precedence; great offence could be caused if it were done wrong. The most important guests ('seldom under a baron's son and higher, or a knight, and their wives' according to the Harleian regulations) were placed in order 'above the salt' on the right hand of the earl; this end of the table was known as the 'reward'. The other end of the table, below the salt, was known as 'the board's end' and, in the earl's case, was considered suitable for 'gentlemen of worship' such as 'esquires of ancient name'. Visiting gentlemen not considered important enough to eat at the lord's table ate at the steward's table in the hall.

Once everyone was settled, the almoner or clerk of the closet said grace, and eating at last began.

There were two tables in the great chamber—the lord's board and the knights' board. In some households (royal ones in particular) the knights' board was for knights and esquires without title who were not considered socially eligible even for the board's end of the main table.[27] The Harleian regulations, however, assign the knights' board to 'gentlewomen of presence', that is the countess's gentlewomen, and to the two gentlemen ushers, who sat down there once the first course had been served to the earl. A third table, outside the great chamber door,

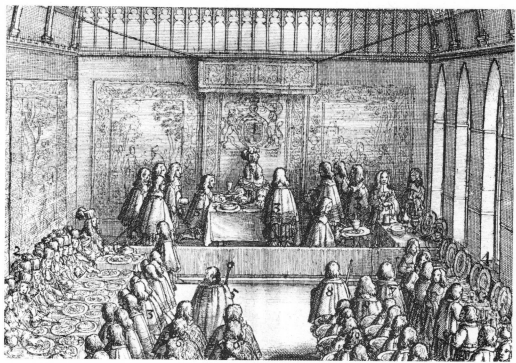

24. Dinner being served to Charles II (detail of Plate 20).

was for yeomen ushers and 'ladies' gentlewomen'; the latter were probably the gentlewomen's gentlewomen, gentle only by courtesy, like a gentleman's gentleman today. As soon as the earl was settled in, the steward and comptroller went down to the hall, and sat at its high table to preside at the household dinner or supper. This took place with almost as much ceremony as the meal in the great chamber, but was followed by a more easy-going second sitting for those who had waited or officiated at the main meal.

Who waited on whom at the various tables was ordered with as much sense of hierarchy as everything else. The earl's cupbearer looked after the earl alone, serving him on bended knee (Pl. 24) and holding a second, smaller cup under the earl's mouth to catch the drips. The earl's sewer and carver, assisted by gentlemen waiters, looked after the earl and the guests above the salt. The guests at the board's end were looked after by a separate sewer 'unarmed' that is without a ritual towel, and assisted by yeomen. The knights' board was waited on by yeomen only, the yeomen ushers' board by grooms, the gentlemen officers, gentlemen servants and yeomen officers by their own servants. The rest seem to have waited on themselves.

The amount of food dished out to each person varied according to his rank. The food was divided up by the sewers into fixed portions, known as messes. The normal division was four to a mess, eating from the same dish (hence messmates); bishops, earls and viscounts went two to a mess; a very great man had a mess to himself.[28] The great were, as a result, served up with far more than they could eat; it was part of their greatness. Their left-overs were passed on to one of the lower tables, and ultimately the broken meats of the whole household were distributed to the poor. The poor were also given at least a ritual portion of the best. The Harleian regulations describe how, while the earl is having his dinner, the almoner is to select a portion of the earl's meat for the alms dish 'the whole standard of beef on the flesh days, and on the fish days . . . the ling and cod, and part of other meat at his discretion.' This he later distributed at the gate to seven specified 'poor householders', a different seven each day of the week.

The Harleian earl's dinner and supper consisted of two courses, each made up of numerous dishes supplemented by 'potages'. The second course was introduced with even more ceremony than the first, since the earl was now seated in the great chamber. It was met at the great chamber door and escorted in by the two yeomen ushers carrying their rods. The enlarged procession was met inside the door by the two gentlemen ushers; the sewer made three curtseys: 'one at the entry of the great chamber, the second in the midst, and the third at his coming to the board', then knelt down and 'took sayes' from the dishes, each of which was offered to him by a kneeling gentleman.

The conclusion of the meal involved a lengthy and gradual stripping of the tables and emptying of their occupants. The knights' board was cleared; the people sitting at it had their hands washed; its cloth was removed and finally the board itself and its trestles were removed. The lord's board was cleared; its occupants (except the earl himself) and the occupants of the knights' board then rose from their stools or benches, curtseyed to the lord and moved to the end of the chamber by the door, where they stood in rows, with the more important in front. The earl's board and trestles, and all the stools and benches, were then removed. The earl rose from his chair and stood on his carpet. His hands were washed with the usual ceremony by two gentlemen. Grace was said. The hands of those who had been at his board were then washed by yeomen, as they stood at the other end of the chamber. All the gentlemen and yeomen who had officiated at dinner retired. Their places were taken by the steward and other officers and gentleman servants, who had been dining below in the hall. The earl was now standing alone on his carpet, at the foot of the state bed and before his great chair, looking across the empty floor at the respectful ranks of his guests and servants. He called for musicians and dancing began.

The ceremonies described in the Harleian regulations were the standard ones of their time. They relate closely both to the household ceremonies of Edward IV's *Black Book*, which dates from 1471, and to those in numerous surviving household regulations for other royal, noble and knightly households of the fifteenth, sixteenth and early seventeenth centuries.[29] On the other hand they are noticeably more complicated than anything in Bishop Grosseteste's thirteenth-century regulations, or other ceremonies described or alluded to in the thirteenth and fourteenth centuries.[30] The origin of English household ceremonies and their relationship both to contemporary religious ritual and household ceremonies in

50

Europe deserve more research. It is possible that in England household ceremonies became more elaborate in imitation of the court of Richard II, which through Richard's cosmopolitan wife was under strong influence from the continent and from France. Certainly, there is no better way of getting the feel of the type of meal described in the Harleian regulations than by looking at the illustration for January in *Les Très Riches Heures du Duc de Berry*, which date from 1409–16 (Col. Pl. I). This shows the duke dining. He is sitting under his canopy, with his salt in front of him, and his steward, complete with chain and staff, standing behind him. His sewer and carver, both armed with towels, are in attendance; his cupbearer is 'taking sayes' from the yeoman of the cellar in front of a cupboard loaded with gold plate.

Such meals were impressive rather than sociable, and indeed they were meant to be. Meals in the hall tended to become noisy, and the noise may have been one reason for the lord leaving it. One of the jobs of the usher of the hall was to walk up and down shouting 'speak softly my masters' whenever the row became too great. At meals in the great chamber Merry England was not much in evidence. Those attending them were arranged strictly according to rank, and usually sat along one side only of the lord's table. There was often a sizeable gap between the lord and the guests at the board's end and even (as shown in the *Très Riches Heures*) between the lord and his neighbour above the salt, if the latter was a degree below him in rank. Conversation would have been difficult anyway, and was further impeded by conventions as to who spoke when. At the table of Gaston de Foix in France in the fourteenth century the rule was straightforward: 'nul ne parloit a lui à sa table si il ne l'appeloit'.[31] In 1466 a German visitor was appalled at the formality of a dinner given for Edward IV's queen to celebrate her churching after the birth of her daughter. There were no other crowned heads present and the queen sat by herself according to the usual protocol, on a golden chair. Except for her mother and sisters-in-law, who were allowed to sit after the first course had been served, everyone remained kneeling while she ate; 'and she ate for three hours . . . And all were silent; not a word was spoken.'[32] This was an extreme example, involving a great occasion and a royal personage. But at the end of the sixteenth century William Harrison was to commend 'the great silence that is used at the tables of the honourable and wiser sort generally over all the realm (albeit that too much deserveth no commendation, for it belongeth to guests neither to be *muti* or *loquaces*)'.[33] There is no reason to suppose that behaviour was different a hundred years or more earlier.

Great chambers were usually on the first and more rarely on the second floor. Their commonest, but by no means invariable position was off the dais end of the hall. Early mediaeval halls were often up on the first floor too; at Westminster Palace, for instance, the White Hall, which was where the royal household ate, was on the first floor and opened straight into Henry III's great chamber. Later halls were almost always on the ground floor. What was to become the commonest relationship between hall and great chamber was carefully described in instructions for a new building at the royal castle of Bamburgh, issued in

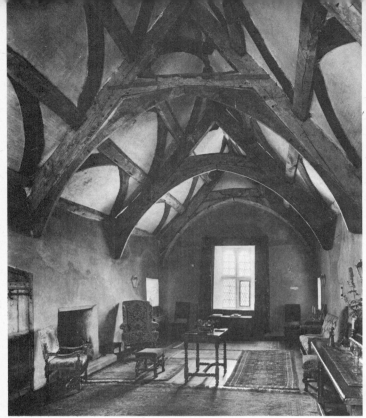

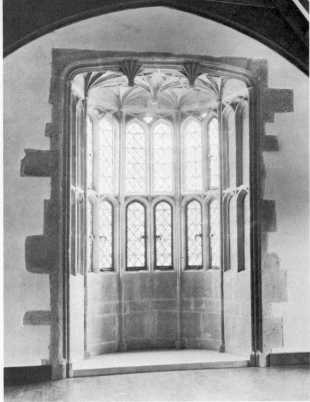

25. Cothay Manor, Somerset. The late-fifteenth-century great chamber.

26. Great Chalfield Manor, Wiltshire (c. 1470–80). The great chamber oriel.

1384.[34] A 'grande chambre', measuring forty six feet by twenty, was to be built on the first floor at the dais end of a ground-floor hall, measuring sixty-six feet by thirty-four. Below the great chamber were to be two vaulted rooms probably intended as wine cellars; in later houses this position was often occupied by a parlour.

The position of the great chamber on the first floor, or even higher, probably originated partly because first-floor rooms were drier, partly for reasons of security; a great chamber up a narrow newel staircase was easier to defend in an emergency, and the higher it was placed the larger the windows could be, without making the building it was in vulnerable to attack. But when defence became of less importance the position retained a ceremonial aptness. The retreat of the lord from the hall to great chamber may have led to a lessening of the sense of community in the household, but it accentuated its sense of hierarchy. Hierarchy was reflected not only in the gradation from the servants in the hall, by way of the officers up on the dais, to the lord higher still in the great chamber, but in the progress of the lord's food through the hall up to the great chamber, and of its remains down again, by way of the tables in the hall to the poor at the gate.

Changes in the ceremony and hierarchy of eating led to architectural changes. The processional route from the kitchen was often extended up a spacious and richly decorated staircase leading from the hall to the grand chamber, as at Penshurst. The hall tended to get smaller. This was only to be expected once the lord's removal had reduced both the numbers normally catered for in the hall and its ceremonial importance. But it was still the room by which great people entered the house, and its lord and his guests came back into it on great occasions, on feast days, or for plays. The lavish and ceremonial serving of meals in the hall and the generous entertainment of visitors there remained an essential part of the image of a great man, even when the upper level of both household and guests had been creamed off into the great chamber. Moreover, it had the weight of tradition behind it. So halls remained large and lavishly decorated rooms; but there were no more gigantic halls as in the earlier Middle Ages, except occasionally in a royal or collegiate context.

What the hall was losing, the great chamber was gaining. Great chambers inevitably began to grow bigger and grander. As they were usually up beneath the roof, they could have open timber roofs of any degree of elaboration (Pl. 25). Their chimney-pieces and windows were often richly decorated with panelled stonework, tracery and carving. A bay or oriel window was a frequent feature (Pl. 26). When the Countess of Salisbury entertained Edward III in her 'nobly apparelled' chamber at Wark Castle in 1341, Froissart describes how the love-struck king retired 'to a wyndow to rest hym, and so fell in a gret study'.[35] Such windows, besides being useful spaces to retire into for solitary thought or intimate conversation, could give a room extra dignity; and glass was still an expensive luxury, the lavish use of which underlined the wealth of the owner of the house.

But much of the splendour of mediaeval great chambers, as of mediaeval halls, was in their moveable furnishings. Tapestries 'nobly apparelled' them, damask and table-cloths concealed their boards and trestles, and plate loaded their cupboards. The use of great chambers for formal meals was ultimately to drive the beds out of them, but they survived for a considerable period even in the households of the great, and for a shorter time the lords of such households continued to sleep in them. In the *Booke of Courtesy* the lord entertains his guests on trestle tables set up at meal times in the same room in which he sleeps at night.[36] In the slightly later Harleian regulations, although the earl eats at the foot of a 'bed of estate', no-one appears to sleep in it: the earl sleeps in a separate chamber.

This arrangement may also have been derived from palaces. As early as 1307 Edward II ceased to sleep in Henry III's Painted Chamber; his own bed was in a new chamber added on next door, but he probably left the bed in the Painted Chamber.[37] The adjoining great chamber of Henry III's queen, Eleanor, still had a bed in it in 1501, although it was almost certainly no longer in use. In that year the room, which was by then known as the Parliament Chamber and used for sittings of the House of Lords, was the setting of the 'great and goodly Bankett' given to celebrate Katherine of Aragon's betrothal to Prince Arthur. The guests at the banquet sat at four tables: Henry VII presided at one, Prince Arthur at another and Queen Margaret at a third, described as 'standing at the Bed's feet, which was the table of most reputation of all the tables in the chamber'.[38]

By the years around 1500 the great chamber was in a state of considerable flux. In smaller houses (as, for instance Addington in Buckinghamshire in 1493) it was still being used as the principal lodging chamber, and the owner was eating in the hall or, more probably, the parlour.[39] In rather larger houses (as in Edmund Dudley's London house in 1509) the high table had been removed from the hall to the great chamber, but there was still a bed in the latter, for use either by the owner or an important guest.[40] At the grandest level the great chamber was being used for eating only. The Earl of Northumberland, in about 1512, seems to have been dining in his great chamber, sleeping in his wife's chamber, and using his own chamber as a dressing room; his household regulations refer to 'my lord's great chamber where he dineth', 'my lord's chamber where he maketh him ready', and 'my lady's chamber where she lieth'.[41] At this level houses were likely to have two great chambers, each with a suite of rooms attached to them. At Enfield in Middlesex Sir Thomas Lovell, who had been Henry VII's Treasurer of the Household and Chancellor of the Exchequer, had his own great chamber and rooms in one part of the house, and provided a separate great chamber for Henry VII in another, as part of a capacious royal suite of six rooms reserved for the king and queen.[42]

Suites of rooms such as those at Enfield were known as lodgings. But the term lodgings was in fact used for personal accommodation varying from a single chamber to a set of six or seven rooms assigned to a very great person. Both uses survive today; the head of an Oxford or Cambridge college lives in lodgings, and a landlady lets them. Mediaeval lodgings, whether consisting of a single chamber or a string of rooms, were the private territory of whoever occupied them. Access was allowed only to whomever their occupant invited in, and of course to his or her personal servants. In the case of an important man this meant his gentlemen, yeomen and grooms of the chambers. Anyone else who entered was asking for trouble. The idea that there was no privacy in a mediaeval house is based on a total misreading of the mediaeval plan. There was little privacy from personal servants, but a great deal of privacy from everyone else. What may appear to be passage rooms were in fact usually rooms of public access, such as halls or parlours, or rooms in a private sequence belonging to one person or couple, like the rooms in a hotel suite.

In the early Middle Ages, it is true, the supply of lodgings was rudimentary. Only the very great occupied more than one chamber, and even a single chamber was a luxury enjoyed by a limited number of people. Although in great households the steward and possibly one or two other household officers were likely to have a chamber of their own, the remaining gentlemen servants slept communally in a room known as the knights' chamber; it was a privilege to be promoted to sleep there, as happened to Guy of Warwick, the Earl of Warwick's cupbearer:

> The Earl loved that squire
> Before all others he loved him dear
> Of his cup he served him on a day
> In the knights' chamber he lay.[43]

Other dormitory chambers may have been provided for other members of the household; some of the grooms may have slept round the fire in the hall. Others

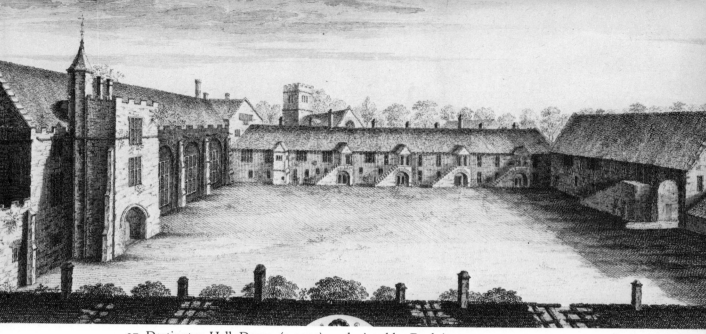

27. Dartington Hall, Devon (*c.* 1390), as depicted by Buck in 1734.

slept in, or outside the door of, their master's chamber on woven straw mats called pallets; the dimensions of nine feet by seven recommended for them in the *Booke of Courtesy* suggests that there were at least two grooms to a pallet.[44] As late as 1526, when efforts were made to stop them, the royal scullions were accustomed to 'lie in the nights and days in the kitchens on ground by the fireside'.[45]

Although this kind of sleeping around went on right through the Middle Ages among the lower strata of the household, the provision of lodgings for the upper and middle strata became much more generous. There is a noticeable change in the fourteenth century. One example is neatly documented at the royal manor of Easthampstead in Berkshire, in 1343. Two buildings to the left and right of the gate in the courtyard were converted to contain thirteen small chambers instead of six large ones. New stairs, windows, and 'oriels' (probably porches) were inserted to serve the new chambers, each of which had its own privy.[46]

The Easthampstead lodgings have long ago disappeared, but a number of other fourteenth-century lodgings of this new type survive, along with a great many fifteenth-century ones. Their usual arrangement is exactly the same as in an Oxford or Cambridge college: a row of external doorways each serving pairs of rooms on the ground floor, and a staircase leading to a similar pair on the floor above. At Dartington Hall in Devon there is a variant arrangement perhaps dating from the late fourteenth century: the first-floor lodgings also have external doorways, approached by long flights of external stairs framing the doors of the lodgings below (Pl. 27). Who went where in lodgings of this type is largely a matter of guesswork. It seems likely that some were for the household and some for guests, and that the less important servants and visitors were put two or more to a room (and probably two or more to a bed). In a big house an important household official like the steward probably had lodgings of at least two rooms.

As has already appeared, the lodgings of the master of the house and the lodgings reserved for an important guest were likely to be much more elaborate,

55

even to the extent of each being attached to a separate great chamber. If there was only one great chamber the lodgings of the family were not necessarily next to it; in some houses this position was reserved for guest lodgings and the family lodgings were placed elsewhere. But wherever sited, such lodgings could contain a closet, an inner chamber, an outer chamber, a wardrobe and at least one privy, in addition to the principal chamber.

The closet was to have a long and honourable history before descending to final ignominy as a large cupboard or a room for the housemaid's sink and mops. It was essentially a private room; since servants were likely to be in constant attendance even in a chamber, it was perhaps the only room in which its occupant could be entirely on his own. By the end of the Middle Ages it had acquired two of what were to remain its principal functions: it was a room for private devotions, and a room for private study and business. Early closets were sometimes also called oratories; these were probably for devotion only, but the same closet could be put to both uses. The two functions are epitomized by the 'Image of our Lady of silver and all well gilt . . . being in my closet' which the Earl of Oxford bequeathed to the cathedral church of Amiens in 1513, and by the 'divers evidence and other writings' which, along with a bag and purse of gold were in the closet of Edmund Dudley, Henry VII's unpopular minister, at the time of his arrest and attainder in 1509.[47] The Harleian earl heard mass in his closet before breakfast, when he was not attending it with his household in the chapel.[48] Such a chapel was an almost inevitable feature of any mediaeval house of any pretensions, and could be as large as a sizeable parish church. But from the late thirteenth century onwards closet and chapel began to be combined. The closet was placed like a gallery at one end of, and looking down into, a two-storey chapel (Pl. 28). The family and important guests attended services up in the closet, and everyone else down in the main body of the chapel.[49]

Much remains to be established about the names and uses of the other subsidiary rooms in large mediaeval lodgings. Personal servants could sleep in both outer and inner chambers, which then tended to be referred to as 'pallet chambers'. In some houses the inner chamber off the lord's chamber belonged to his wife; in the household of the Earl of Oxford in 1513 the 'inner chamber of my ladies' was off 'my lordes great chamber' where the earl slept.[50] The wife's chamber often had a chamber for her gentlewomen off or close to it. A wardrobe (and in very large households even several wardrobes) formed an important part of the lodgings of a great person. It usually contained a fireplace in front of which the yeoman of the wardrobe and his assistants could repair clothes and hangings.

A large set of lodgings invariably had at least one and sometimes several privies attached to it.[51] By the later Middle Ages a privy usually consisted of a small cell in which a pierced seat was placed over a shaft. The shaft connected to a pit, a drain, or just the moat or slope outside the building. Then, as now, the room produced numerous euphemisms. Privy, privy house or privy chamber were the commonest terms in the Middle Ages, but garderobe, withdraught, jakes, latrine, necessary and gong were also current. The terms can cause a good deal of

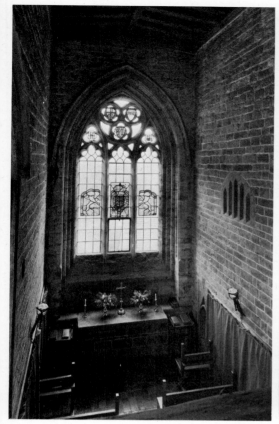

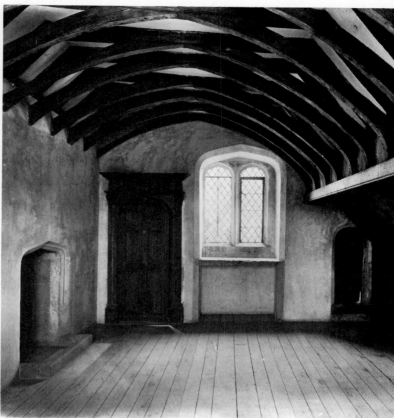

28. Looking down into the fourteenth-century chapel at Broughton Castle, Oxfordshire.

29. A Tudor closet at Compton Wynyates, Warwickshire.

confusion. Garderobe was the Norman French term for wardrobe, and was attached to privies because they were often built off wardrobes; the usage was similar to that of cloakroom today. The name 'with draughte' seems to have been applied to any small room attached to a large one, and need not necessarily imply a privy. In 1453 John Paston's 'drawte chamber' contained his writing board and coffers as well as a bed.[52] Similarly, 'privy chamber' seems to have been used both for the room through which a privy was reached and for the privy itself.

In royal houses the privy chamber seems to have started as a room between the great chamber, where the king was still sleeping, and his privy. It was probably the room in which he prepared himself for the privy. Privy and privy chamber were in charge of a minor official known as the groom of the stool or stole; the great chamber was under a much more important officer called the chamberlain. When the royal bed was moved out of the great chamber into the next room, the room was still called the privy chamber and was still in charge of the groom of the stole. In the later sixteenth and seventeenth centuries, as part of the constant series of retreats that make up the history of palace planning, the bed was removed from the privy chamber as well. It became a private dining and reception room, with a suite of private chambers beyond it, all collectively known as the privy lodgings. The groom of the stole remained in charge of the whole sequence; an official

57

whose original job had been to clean out the royal latrines had become one of the most powerful and confidential of royal servants.[53]

The lodgings built at Eltham for Henry IV and his wife in the years around 1400 had chambers and other rooms for the king and queen on the first floor, and parlours on the floor below.[54] Parlours have been referred to occasionally in the course of this chapter. A 'privy parlour' was one of the rooms in which, according to Langland, the lord and his wife ate in preference to the hall. But there is no mention of them in the Harleian or any other mediaeval household regulations. Even in Elizabethan and Jacobean ones they are only mentioned briefly, and in passing. This was not because of any lack of parlours but because they existed outside the ceremonial system. They were the small seeds from which was to grow the informal country-house life which later generations of foreigners were to admire and emulate.

Much remains to be established about the first appearance and use of parlours in English country houses. In the early Middle Ages parlours were only found in a monastic context. They were rooms in monasteries or convents in which visitors could talk (hence their name) to members of the community. The first secular parlours may have had a similar use, and been rooms in which members of the family or household could see visitors whom they did not wish (or were not allowed) to bring into their chambers. But by the second half of the fourteenth century, when domestic parlours first appear in contemporary literature, they have become more than this; they are informal sitting and eating rooms. Apart from Langland's 'privy parlour' there is a description of parlour life in Chaucer's *Troilus and Cressida*, written in about 1385. Chaucer describes how Pandarus goes to visit Cressida and finds her and two other ladies sitting

> Within a paved parlour; and they three
> Hearden a maiden reading them the geste
> Of all the siege of Thebes . . .

After a little conversation Pandarus suggests that, since it is Mayday, 'rise up and let us dance', but the ladies cannot be persuaded and more conversation follows:

> So after this with many wordes glad
> And friendly tales, and with merry cheer
> Of this and that they pley'd, and gonnen wade
> In many an uncouth glad and deep mattere
> As friends do, when they be met, I-fere[55]

The first inventories detailing the contents of parlours date from the fifteenth century.[56] Parlours of this period often have beds in them, suggesting that they were also used as guest bedchambers. In smaller houses they were sometimes the bed-sitting rooms of the owner of the house. As late as 1588 Thomas Phelips referred to 'the parlour where I do customably rest and lie' in the house at Montacute that preceded the very much grander house erected there by his son.[57] But early in the sixteenth century beds disappeared from parlours in houses of any

58

consequence, and they became eating and reception rooms only. The most common position for them was on the ground floor, immediately behind the dais end of the hall, and under the great chamber, where there had tended to be a vaulted cellar earlier in the Middle Ages. Parlours (or what can reasonably be assumed to have been parlours) are also sometimes found on the ground floor off the screens end of the hall. There is no evidence that they were ever on the first floor. The chambers on the first floor, especially the more important, usually opened into the roof, and in general were taller than those on the ground floor. The spatial contrast between low-ceilinged parlour and higher-ceilinged great chamber can still be savoured at Haddon Hall where the fifteenth-century parlour and great chamber are off the dais end of the hall, one above the other. The parlour has a flat ceiling, with painted panels between massive timbers, and its walls are lined with panelling (Col. Pl. II). It is an intimate room, even with very little furniture in it, and in winter must have been considerably warmer than the great chamber. It gives a good idea of why parlours became popular.

Some late-mediaeval houses have what seems to be a half-way stop in the retreat from the hall to parlour; the bay-window recess in the hall is enlarged until it becomes almost a separate little room, sometimes with its own fireplace. But whether this space was used to accommodate the lord's table or the steward's table remains uncertain; procedure probably varied from house to house and generation to generation.[58]

By the end of the Middle Ages most houses of any size probably contained a parlour. All of them invariably had the essential elements of hall, kitchen, great chamber, chapel and lodgings. These were the inevitable responses to the needs and rituals of the household. But on occasions one finds a doubling and even trebling up of this basic accommodation, resulting in buildings not only with two great chambers but with two or three halls, and two or three kitchens. Two different sets of circumstances led to this: either that of a building catering with extra lavishness for a single household or that of a building catering for more than one household.

Single-household units sometimes acquired two halls because a later and more ambitious generation built a new and larger hall, but did not demolish the old one (as happened, for instance, at Carew Castle in Wales).[59] But sometimes two halls seem always to have been intended to have two functions. Obvious examples, on the grandest scale, were the two halls at Westminster, the great hall and the long-demolished smaller hall, sometimes known as the White Hall. Although smaller the latter was far from small (120 ft by 37 ft); it was quite large enough to seat the members of the royal household. The great hall seems only to have been used for great feasts and for the supplementary functions that it later picked up as a law-court. In some non-royal houses with two halls one of them may also have been used for feasts and the other for the household; an example is the Bishop's Palace at Wells (Pl. 32) where the comparatively small hall built by Bishop Joceline in about 1202–42 was supplemented by the enormous hall built by Bishop Burnell in about 1275–92.[60]

The inventory of Sir John Fastolfe's Caister Castle, drawn up after his death in 1459, reveals another and completely different use to which a small and a large hall could be put. Its upper and lower halls are referred to in the inventory as the winter and summer halls. The winter hall was presumably designed for winter warmth; it was smaller than the summer hall and had a lower ceiling.[61] The existence of two halls in a house does not therefore necessarily mean that both were in use at the same time, or that the household was in some way split between them. There is no evidence for such a split; even the Harleian regulations, which are dealing with the very large household of an earl, give instructions for seating all its members at different tables in one hall, except for the few involved in the earl's meals in the great chamber.

But some mediaeval dwellings catered for an element outside and below the main household and its ordered hierarchy of gentlemen, yeomen, and grooms. When a large amount of land was attached to a house and was worked directly by the lord's own farm labourers, they would not necessarily eat in the hall. These labourers were called at the time *famuli*, and, for instance, at the preceptory of the Knights Templar at South Witham in Lincolnshire there is documentary evidence of a separate hall for them.[62] Such rooms were the precursors of the 'hinds' halls' (a hind was a farm labourer) which are found in some big Elizabethan houses. One of the Harleian regulations, laying down that 'at any meal time no man with a sleeveless coat to sit in the hall', suggest a reason for the segregation. Farm labourers were rough, dirty, ill-dressed, possibly serfs rather than freemen, and accordingly ineligible for the life of the household in the main hall, and the ceremony and degree of privilege that went with it.[63]

Some mediaeval halls, especially the earlier ones, were built above a much lower vaulted room (Pl. 30). Some of these rooms were certainly intended as cellars or store-rooms; occasionally they have fireplaces and may have served as either winter halls or hinds' halls. A great feast produced an exceptional situation and all rooms were pressed into service—not just two or more halls, if there were this number, but numerous chambers. Westminster Hall might seem big enough to have catered for the feasting ambitions of any monarch, but it was not big enough for the coronation banquet of Edward II, which filled not only Westminster Hall and the White Hall but a series of wooden halls built for the occasion. (The feast lasted several days, and in a court outside, a specially constructed fountain ran with wine during the whole period.[64]) The Archbishop of York's Cawood Castle had a 'main hall' and a 'low hall'; when the Neville feast was held there in 1465 the Archbishop presided over several hundred noble or gentle people sitting at seven tables in the main hall; the Duke of Gloucester (who was only a child) presided over three tables of noblewomen and ladies in the 'chief chamber'; a further selection of great people and gentlefolk were at five more tables in the great chamber and 'second chamber'; the low hall was filled with two sittings of 'gentlemen, franklins and head yeomen'. The household, and servants of guests were squeezed out of the halls altogether, and fed in the 'gallery'—an early precursor of the sixteenth-century long gallery.[65]

60

V. (right) Warkworth Castle, Northumberland. The Keep (late fourteenth century).

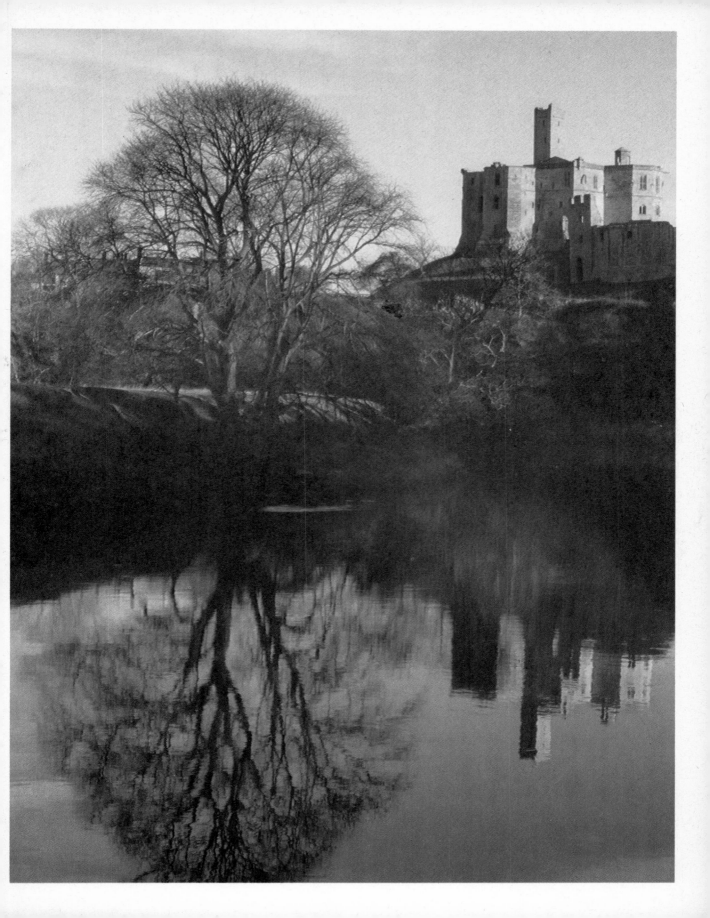

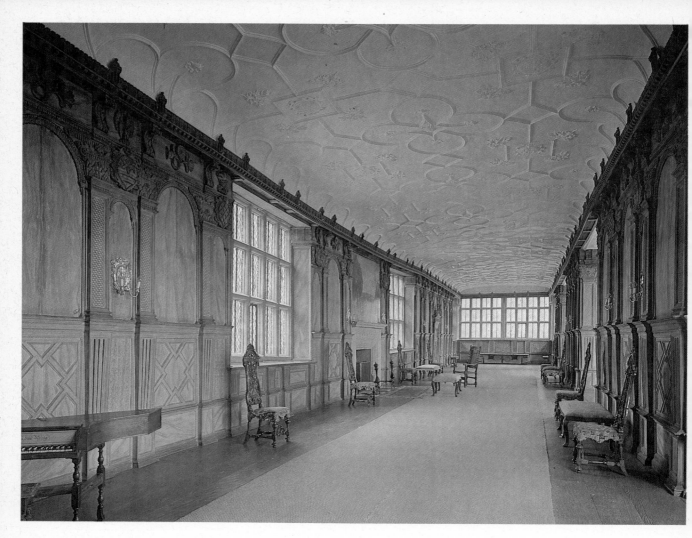

VI. Haddon Hall, Derbyshire. The gallery (*c.* 1600).

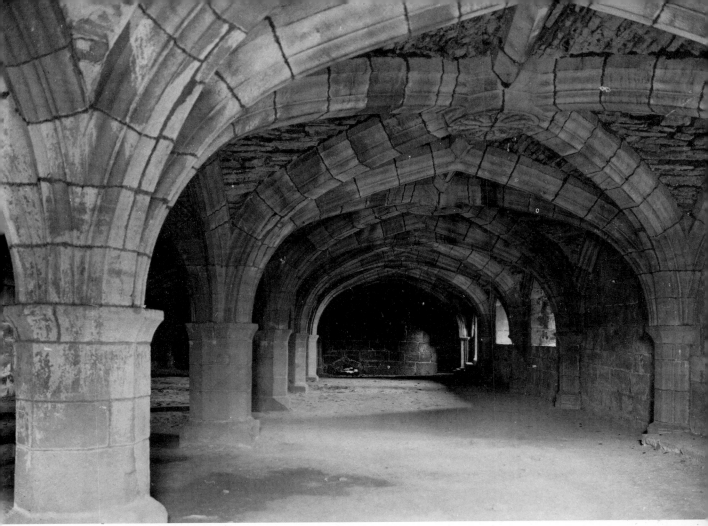

30. South Wingfield Manor, Derbyshire. The undercroft (*c.* 1450).

Castles are the most obvious and important examples of the quite different situation, where a multiplicity of halls was due to one complex sheltering several households. Any great castle with a strategic role to play attracted a hierarchy of households belonging to the different people involved with it. Its owner, whether king, prince or great magnate, might seldom or even never visit it, but quarters had to be available for him and his household when and if they came. The man responsible for actually running the castle was normally called the constable or keeper. He was appointed by the owner, but was not a member of his household in the same way as the steward or other senior officers, although he might be linked to it on a part-time basis; in the Earl of Northumberland's household, for instance, the constables of his castles of Prudhoe, Langley, Alnwick, and Warkworth each came into his household for one quarter each year to serve respectively as his carver, sewer of the board's end, cupbearer and gentleman usher.[66] The constable of a large castle, especially a royal one, could be a great person in his own right, and no more permanently resident at it than its owner. In such a situation the castle might have a resident deputy or lieutenant to look after whatever there was in the way of a permanent garrison. So a castle might have to provide separate accommodation for its owner, constable and lieutenant, each with his own kitchen, although there may have been cases where the kitchen was shared between two households.

The system survives in much-modified form at Windsor Castle (Pl. 31). Its arrangement is recognizably based on what existed in the Middle Ages. The queen has her own self-contained and very grand royal lodgings. The constables and other officials, acting or retired, have lodgings in various towers and outer courts; each lodging is a self-contained household, with a polished brass plate by its own front door. As a whole the castle is more like a little town than a single house; but its architecture provides it with a sense of unity, and St George's Chapel with a common place of worship.

Another occasion on which a great house or castle might have to accommodate what amounted to an extra household was the visit of a royal or very great person. Normal visits could easily be absorbed into the household routine, even though any visitor of standing came with a dozen or so servants. The visitor, if sufficiently important, sat at the lord's table in hall or great chamber; his following sat at the steward's or inferior tables, according to their status. The visit of a great man was a different matter. He probably came with a riding household of at least fifty people, which in itself produced problems of accommodation; and these were further complicated by problems of etiquette.

The etiquette of arrival is described in the Harleian regulations.[67] If the visitor was a baron or above, the great gates, normally kept closed, were opened at his coming, and he was allowed to ride into the inner courtyard on horseback. The head officers and attendant gentlemen waited at the gate to receive him, carrying their wands of office; if he was of higher rank than the earl they were instructed 'to deliver their staves to the head officers of the honourable personage, and like manner the porter and all other officers to give place to his officers during his abode there, and to be ministers under them.'

The situation resembled that of the Arab host who assures a guest that 'everything in the house belongs to you'. Ceremonially speaking, when a mediaeval host welcomed a guest of superior rank, the house belonged to the guest not the owner. The guest sat in the centre of the high table and presided over the meal, which was supervised by his ushers, sewer, butler and ewerer, not those of the owner. If the difference in rank between guest and host was sufficiently large the host was pushed out to a table of lower rank, and even out of the room altogether; a visiting king or queen normally ate at a table, and often in a room, on their own. Visiting royalty, and possibly other very great visitors, expected their food to be cooked in a separate kitchen by their own cook, who travelled with them. Even in the hall, the guest's servants and officers took precedence over those of the host all along the line.

All this caused a considerable disturbance in the host household. There were various ways of dealing with it. At one extreme the host could give up his own

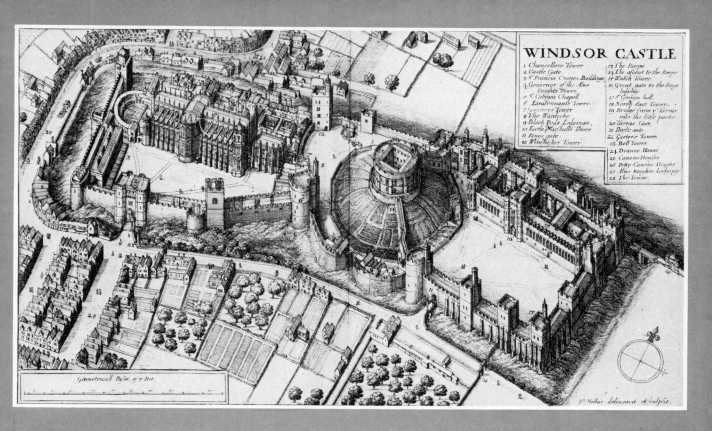

lodgings and efface himself before the greatness of his visitor. At the other he could provide a completely self-contained set of lodgings for the guest, with its own kitchen, hall and great chamber, so that the two households could exist independently side by side. The two great halls (each with its own kitchen) in the Prior's house at Ely are probably examples of this arrangement; Ely, like other religious establishments attached to a famous shrine, was particularly subject to great people coming on pilgrimage.[68] It was an arrangement that kept both guest and host contented but was, of course, extremely expensive; and there were many alternative variants.

The elements of which houses of all these varieties were made up developed according to a similar pattern from the early Middle Ages to the seventeenth century. They started detached, and tended to coagulate. The ground plan of the royal house at Clarendon in Wiltshire, as built in the twelfth and first half of the thirteenth century and revealed by excavation, looks like a collection of unrelated counters tossed at random onto a board.[69] By the end of the thirteenth century a number of houses were in a state of semi-coagulation. One can still get the feeling of this type of house at the Bishop's Palace at Wells today, but it comes across especially strongly in Buck's bird's-eye view of the palace as it was in the early eighteenth century (Pl. 32). Great hall, bishop's lodging, chapel and other accommodation are loosely tacked onto each other and sprawl in a great zig-zag across a huge irregular enclosure, the walls surrounding which are punctuated by a gatehouse and a tower of lodgings. Hall, chapel and bishop's lodgings were built

65

31. Windsor Castle in the mid seventeenth century.

in the thirteenth century; and although the enclosing wall and other buildings date from the fourteenth and fifteenth centuries the total impression is probably close enough to what existed in the thirteenth century, for there must always have been some kind of enclosure, and a thirteenth-century wooden kitchen and possibly other wooden buildings had disappeared by the eighteenth century.[70]

There was a good deal of wooden building in the houses and castles of the early Middle Ages; its subsequent disappearance tends to make them seem less diffuse than they originally were. Early kitchens were often of plastered wood, built round an open hearth. The danger of fire made it essential for them to be free-standing, although sometimes connected to the hall by a passage or covered way leading to it through the buttery and pantry; this was almost certainly the arrangement at Wells. When stone kitchens began to become the norm in the fourteenth century, the fire risk disappeared, and they could safely elide with the hall block.

Once the kitchen and its appurtenances had merged into one end of the hall, and the principal chamber and its appurtenances into the other, one of the most typical of all mediaeval plans had been created: the central hall with great chamber over cellar or parlour at the dais end, and kitchen, buttery and pantry (with one or more chambers on the first floor) at the screens end. This type of plan could be elaborated to produce a building of some splendour, but it was best suited to medium-sized manor houses. Examples began to appear in the fourteenth century, and proliferated in the fifteenth (Fig. 1).

At Great Chalfield in Wiltshire the type survives to perfection (Col. Pl. IV). Its architecture underlines both the plan and the hierarchy of the rooms and makes them immediately readable from outside. The hall is expressed by its porch, windows and generous roof, the great chamber (Pl. 26) by a richly decorated oriel, the screens-end chamber by an oriel which is slightly less elaborate but still very handsome. The latter is surmounted by the coat of arms of the family, a fact which suggests that the family lodgings were at the screens end and that the great-chamber end was for guests. The whole arrangement is exactly suited to the standing of its builder, an officer from a great household who had set up as a landed gentleman. It is both dignified and sensible; it exudes prosperous hospitality.[71]

Apart from houses like Great Chalfield, the plans of which can for convenience be classified as manorial, there were two other common mediaeval types, the tower house and the courtyard house. It is tempting to see both of them as developing from military origins, and to trace the tower house back to the twelfth-century keep, and the courtyard house to the curtain-wall castles of the late thirteenth and early fourteenth century.[72] Both types had defensive advantages; both could be developed to standards of magnificence of which the manorial type was not capable, and so add overtones of lordship and power to those of wealth and hospitality. In addition, the courtyard plan could conveniently house all the members of a large household at the level of increased comfort which began to be expected in the fourteenth century.

66

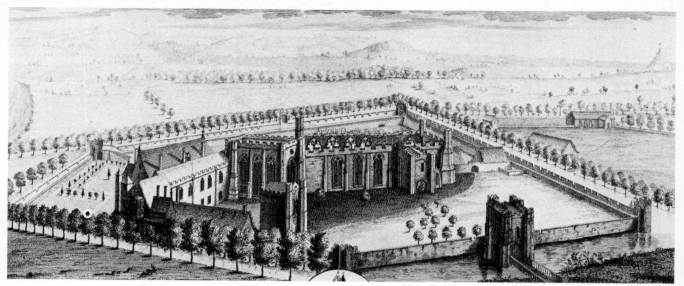

32. The Bishop's Palace, Wells, Somerset, in 1733.

The keep was a remarkable example of the way in which military considerations could force the normally scattered elements of an early mediaeval house into a single container. The grander twelfth-century keeps contained hall, chambers, privies, wardrobe, chapel, kitchen and cellars; they were, in fact, self-contained houses as well as military strongholds and formidable symbols of power. By the thirteenth century their military drawbacks had become clear, their accommodation was being found too cramped, and they went out of fashion as the central features of great castles. Suitably adapted, they continued to provide a useful formula for smaller establishments where there was a demand for a degree of security and a demonstration of power; as such they served, for instance, as the principal houses of border gentry (Pl. 33), or the lesser houses of great men, like the compact fortified house at Acton Burnell in Shropshire, built by Bishop Burnell of Wells at the end of the thirteenth century.

Keeps were pushed out of fashion by military technology's new model, the curtain-wall castle. Its sophisticated combination of perimeter walling punctuated and protected by projecting towers was worked out for military reasons; but the living accommodation necessary for a castle fitted very comfortably into the towers, or along the inside of the walls, and acquired a new shape in the process. Ranges of continuous, or nearly continuous, buildings surrounded one or more courtyards, entered by a gatehouse. Halls were usually too large for the towers and were built along the walls: kitchens and chapels fitted easily into towers; lodgings could be built either horizontally in ranges along the walls, or vertically in the towers.

Lodgings arranged horizontally around courts were neat and convenient, but it was more impressive to arrange them vertically in towers. The higher the tower the grander the effect, and, in times when such matters were of importance, the easier it was to give the upper rooms adequate windows without danger to security. Towers had always, for obvious reasons, had associations of power and

67

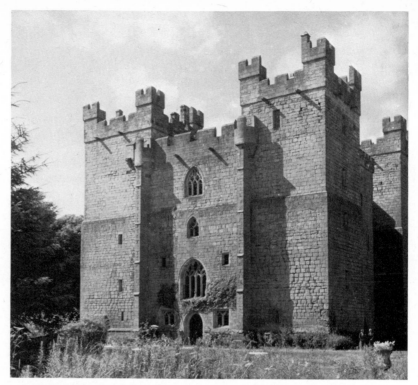

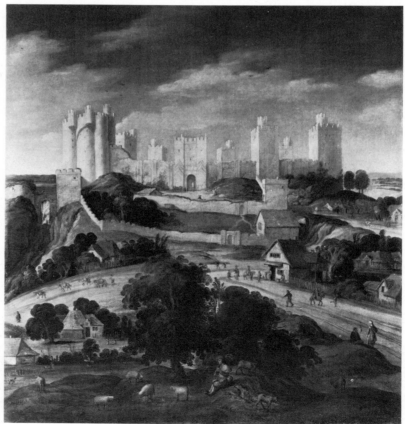

33. (top) Langley Castle, Northumberland (*c.* 1350).
34. Pontefract Castle, Yorkshire, as painted in the seventeenth century.
35. (right) A reconstruction of the intended entrance front at Thornbury
Castle, Gloucestershire (*c.* 1511–21).

lordship; it came naturally to a twelfth-century poet, when describing how the envoys of the 'young king' offered the border counties to the King of Scotland in the rebellion of 1173–4, to make them say 'You shall have the lordship, in castle and in tower'.[73] But towers also acquired associations of luxury; one can still envisage how liberating it must have been in mediaeval castles and fortified houses, where windows were either very small or looked inwards onto enclosed courtyards, to climb up above the courtyard roofs and look out through a spacious window to the surrounding countryside. This aura of power and luxury led to towers still being built when they had ceased to have a military function, and when objections to windows at ground level had long disappeared; it gave them a mystique which lasted on beyond the Middle Ages.

At the great house begun by the Duke of Buckingham at Thornbury in Gloucestershire in the early sixteenth century, the crenellated skyline and superb array of no less than six towers intended for the entrance front (Pl. 35) is made nonsense of, in military terms, as soon as one walks round the corner and sees the glittering lanterns of glass that break the outer walls and light the great chamber and accompanying rooms on both ground and first floor of the south front (Pl. 36). But the towers are not there for military reasons. The house combines two symbolisms to speak of power, wealth and luxury in terms so lavish that one is not surprised to discover that the duke was beheaded as an over mighty subject in 1521, leaving his great house unfinished.

Towers in mediaeval houses can appear singly or in squadrons, and be arranged symmetrically or asymmetrically. Both arrangements are traceable back to military origins: to irregular circuits of curtain walls following the contours of a naturally strong position, or great regular layouts on artificial moated sites, such as Edward I's royal castles of Beaumaris and Harlech, designed to dominate the Welsh by a combination of the latest technology and overawing symmetry.

The dazzling if disorganized effect of a great irregular circuit of lofty towers is brilliantly put across by the seventeenth-century painting which shows the long-demolished Pontefract Castle floating on its hill top like a vision of chivalry (Pl. 34). Something of the same effect still survives today at Raby Castle in Durham. Here, in spite of later alterations, all but one of the original haphazard circuit of ten towers survive (Pl. 39). One contained the chapel above a gate house, one the kitchen, one was the original keep, the others contained lodgings (Fig. 2).

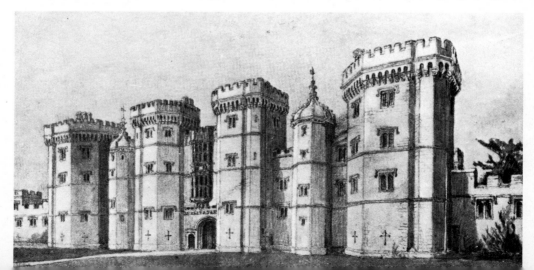

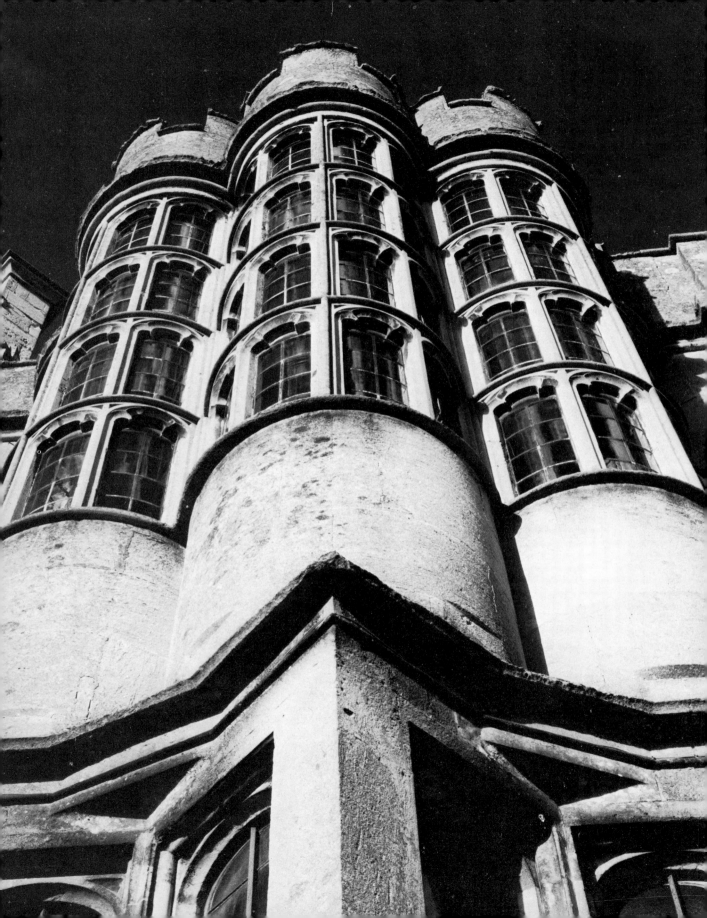

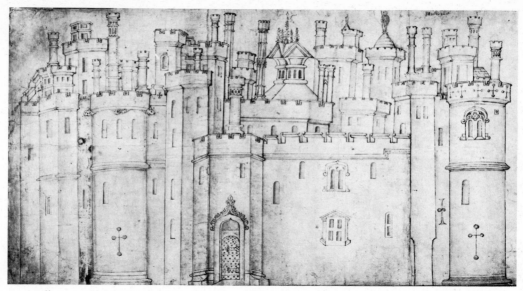

37. Melbourne Castle, Derbyshire. From an early-Elizabethan survey.

All this was largely a creation of the late fourteenth century. Grand though it is, it makes a curious contrast with its surviving contemporaries at Bodiam Castle in Sussex, Bolton Castle in Yorkshire, and Lumley Castle only a few miles from Raby. These have a circuit of towers almost as impressive as that at Raby, but arranged with meticulous symmetry around rectangular internal courts. The towers and fortifications of both types were, in the military sense, functional as well as impressive; but between them they were the immediate ancestors of innumerable fifteenth and sixteenth-century mansions built with more or less symmetry around square courts, embellished with gatehouse towers and corner towers, but, from a military point of view, not meant for serious business (Pls 1 and 40).

The type survives today not only in many country houses but also in Oxford and Cambridge colleges, and in their derivatives in schools and colleges all over the world. The resemblance between houses and colleges is not surprising, for the colleges were founded by the owners of the houses, who modelled both their organisation and their architecture on what they were familiar with. Just as Windsor Castle is a recognizable survival of one type of mediaeval community, so are the colleges of another. In them one can still see a family, in the extended mediaeval sense, in operation in buildings which, even when they are not mediaeval, are based on mediaeval models. The college life is centred round hall, chapel and lodgings. The lodgings are arranged off independent staircases and doorways around courtyards. Everyone eats in the hall except the head of the college; he only makes occasional appearances there and otherwise eats in his lodgings, which are much the grandest in the college. The dais in the hall is occupied by the dons, the senior members of the extended family, who retire from it to the senior common room, their equivalent of a parlour. Beer is dispensed in or from the buttery, and the porters at the gate control who comes in and out.

71

36. (left) One of the bay-windows on the south front of Thornbury.

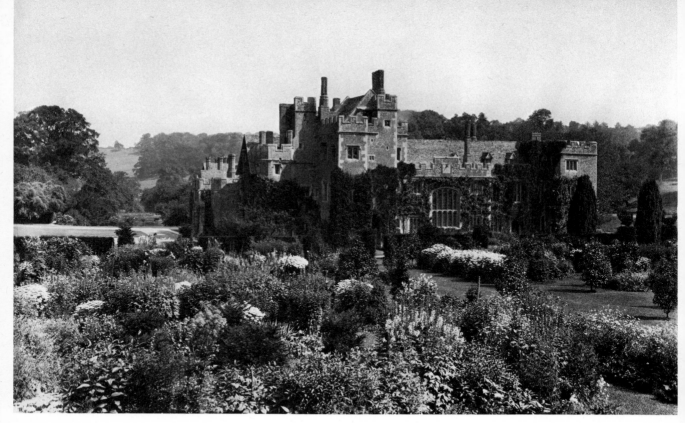

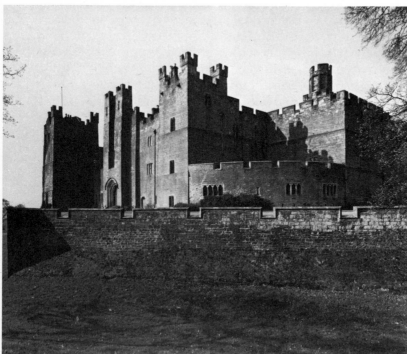

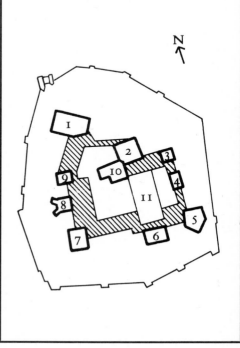

38. (top) Compton Wynyates, Warwickshire (early sixteenth century), from the south.

39. (above left) Raby Castle, Durham, from the north-east.

Fig. 2 (above right) Sketch plan of Raby Castle, Durham. 1, Clifford's tower. 2, Kitchen tower. 3, Mount Raskelf tower. 4, Chapel tower and gate. 5, Bulmer's tower. 6, South tower. 7, Joan's tower. 8, Neville gateway. 9, Watch tower. 10, Keep tower. 11, Hall. (Later additions not shown.)

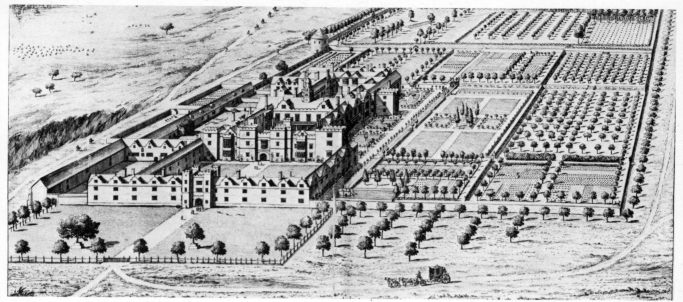

40. A bird's-eye view of Knole, Kent, a late-mediaeval house embellished in the early seventeenth century.

Colleges usually confined themselves to one tower, over the entrance. A few were more ambitious; Cardinal Wolsey's college at Oxford, later to become Christ Church, was designed to have an entrance front as impressively embattled as the Duke of Buckingham's contemporary *tour-de-force* at Thornbury. The use of towers varied very much from building to building. In some complexes one tower was made much bigger and more elaborate than the others, and some houses, like the colleges, had only one tower. It was a way of giving an extra fillip to a house of manorial type, for reasons of security or status (Pl. 38). Caister Castle in Norfolk was an example of a many-towered building with all the emphasis on one tower. The castle was built in four ranges round a courtyard, with a round tower at each external angle, but the north-east corner was a storey higher than the other ranges, and its slender brick tower still soars high above this, with five storeys of rooms rising above an undercroft to a total height of ninety feet (Pl. 41). At Tattershall in Lincolnshire an especially superb brick tower of five floors with octagonal corner turrets is the main survivor of the castle built in the mid fifteenth century by Lord Cromwell, Henry VI's Lord Treasurer; its lavish crenellation had little serious purpose, for there are large windows on every floor including the ground floor (Pl. 42). A slightly smaller brick tower, probably inspired by Tattershall, was added in the 1470s by Bishop Rotherham of Lincoln to his house at Buckden in Huntingdonshire.

The fashion for these super-towers started in the late fourteenth century, reached its height in the fifteenth century, and lasted well on into the sixteenth century.[74] Sometimes they are at or near the dais end of the hall. Sometimes they take the form of immensely grand gatehouses; the great early-sixteenth-century tower at Layer Marney in Essex is the culmination of these gatehouse towers, and, apart from being used as an entrance, is recognizably related to the towers at Tattershall and Buckden (Col. Pl. III). Sometimes the tower is detached from the

73

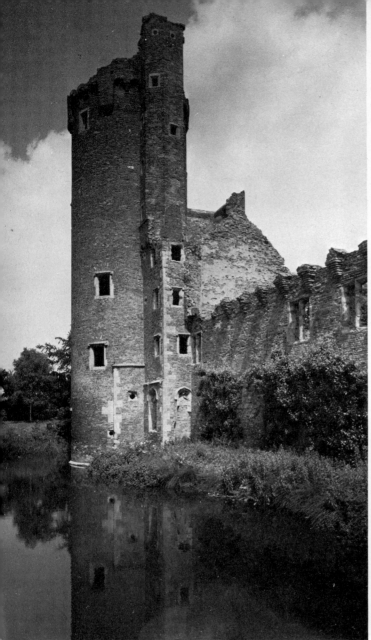

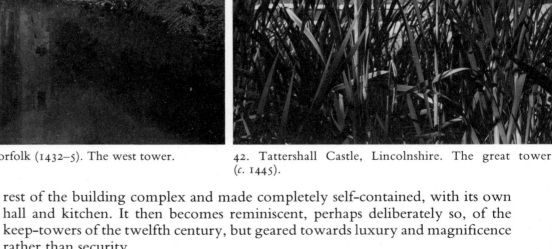

41. Caister Castle, Norfolk (1432–5). The west tower.

42. Tattershall Castle, Lincolnshire. The great tower (c. 1445).

rest of the building complex and made completely self-contained, with its own hall and kitchen. It then becomes reminiscent, perhaps deliberately so, of the keep-towers of the twelfth century, but geared towards luxury and magnificence rather than security.

In the late fourteenth century the earls of Northumberland built an early example of this variety of tower at Warkworth Castle (Col. Pl. V). The tower, normally and rather misleadingly referred to today as the keep, is built in the shape of a cross and is exquisitely planned and detailed to make it a self-contained

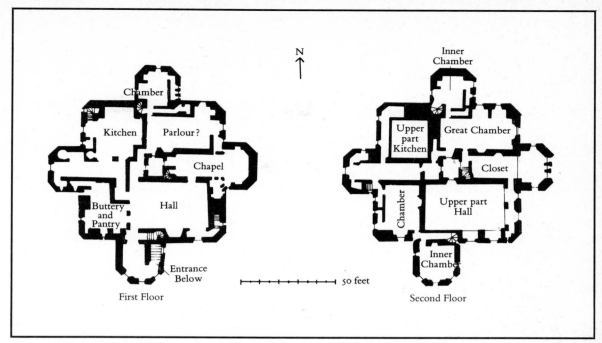

N

Chamber

Kitchen   Parlour?

Chapel

Buttery
and   Hall
Pantry

Entrance
Below

First Floor

Inner
Chamber

Upper
part   Great Chamber
Kitchen

Closet

Chamber   Upper part
Hall

Inner
Chamber

Second Floor

⊢————————⊣ 50 feet

Fig. 3. Warkworth Castle, Northumberland.

residence of the most luxurious nature. It stands in the main castle court, as does
the equally luxurious tower built by Lord Hastings at Ashby-de-la-Zouch in
about 1474. At Warwick Castle there are the remains of an even grander self-
contained tower of the 1470s, built astride the curtain wall; and at Raglan Castle
the so-called 'Yellow Tower of Gwent' was built in about 1460 by William
Herbert, Earl of Pembroke, on an island site in the moat, outside, but connected
to, the main castle complex. At all these places there was a separate great hall, with
attached lodgings and kitchen, in another part of the castle.

It has been suggested that these towers were built as self-contained units by
families who wanted to protect themselves from their own retainers.[75] The
suggestion is based on a misunderstanding of the nature of retainers, and of their
position, or rather lack of position, in the household. Some towers were almost
certainly built to contain the family's own lodgings, but it would be rash,
however, to assume that this was always their function, especially in the case of
self-contained towers with their own kitchens, which were too large for
constable's lodgings, but too small to take the main household. At Warkworth
and Ashby-de-la-Zouch there is evidence that the lord's lodgings were normally
in the main part of the castle. In the 1530s the Earl of Northumberland, when at
Warkworth, had lodgings beyond the dais end of the great hall, rather than in the
so-called keep; in 1574 they were specifically described as the 'lord's lodgings'.[76]
In 1596 the tower at Ashby-de-la-Zouch was almost unfurnished, and the lodgings
of the Earl of Huntingdon were in the main complex attached to the great hall.[77]
Although both these arrangements date from more than a century after the
towers had been built, great households tended to be conservative, and there is a
probability that they had been the same in the fifteenth century.

75

At the Bishop of Lincoln's house at Buckden, the tower was specifically described in a survey of 1647 as the 'king's lodgings' not the 'bishop's lodgings'.[78] This suggests one obvious possible use for towers, as royal lodgings, or lodgings for visiting great people. As such they would have been evidence less of their owner's power than of their special relationship with the Crown; the greatness of both Lord Cromwell and Lord Hastings did in fact rest on the favours of Henry VI and Edward IV rather than inherited estates and connections.

But perhaps it is a mistake to be too specific in looking for uses for these towers. Self-contained units within larger ones might have come in useful for different purposes within a comparatively short period. A tower which on occasions accommodated a visiting great person might also accommodate its own lord, when his main household was in another of his houses, and he came for a short visit, on business or for hunting. For visits of this kind it was not worth going through the formidable business of uprooting the main household; he would be accompanied only by his riding household, which would fit comfortably into a smaller unit. The same tower might also provide self-contained lodgings for a widow or married elder son.[79] Alternatively, it might be used when the lord was keeping his annual 'secret house'.

'Secret house' is an intriguing but somewhat mysterious custom, referred to in the early-sixteenth-century Northumberland household book. A similar custom existed in the household of the Earl of Derby in the 1580s.[80] Other big households probably kept some form of secret house from at least the late Middle Ages. The Northumberland regulations are for 'such times when his lordship keepeth his secret house at the New Lodge or otherwhere, when his Lordship breaketh up his house and takes the accounts of all the offices in his lordship's household.' It took place, in fact, at the yearly audit. During secret house the majority of the household seem to have gone on holiday while the relevant officers worked out the accounts; the main house was probably given a thorough cleaning at the same time. Meanwhile the earl moved to a smaller unit accompanied by a household of only thirty-five people, in which his own sons waited on him as his carver and sewer. He was attended in this retirement by a deputation of auditors and household officers, who came to make the declaration of the audit. One can see that, had the audit been declared at Warkworth, the tower there would have been a convenient place to retire to. At Leconfield the earl normally kept secret house at the New Lodge, a mile or so from the manor, which was his main residence. In 1589 the Earl of Derby's secret house was at another lodge, also called New Lodge, only a quarter of a mile from his castle at Lathom. But although such lodges may have come in useful for this particular event, they were almost certainly built for hunting.

Hunting lodges were always situated either in an impaled deer-park, or in or at the edge of a forest (Pl. 43). Some were lived in by the ranger who looked after the park, and were often very humble buildings, but others were built for the owner of the park or forest when he went hunting, and had more pretensions. A few were compact tower-like buildings, and they started a tradition for building

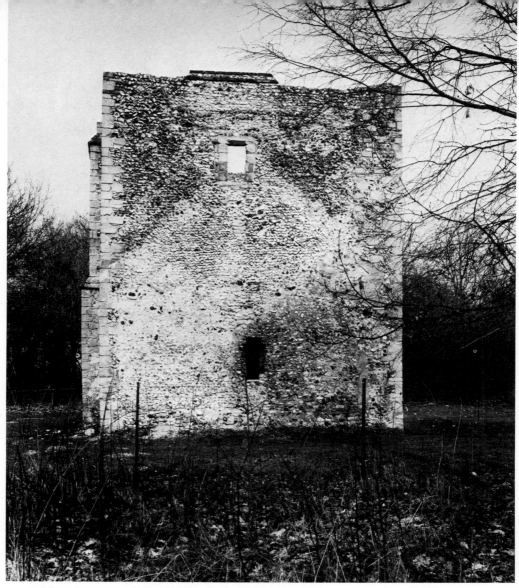

43. A fifteenth-century lodge in Thetford Warren, Norfolk.

lodges in this form which lasted well into the seventeenth century. The New Lodge built by Thomas, Lord Berkeley a few miles from Berkeley Castle as early as 1328–31 was described as a 'square pile of stonework'. Leland called the New Lodge at Leconfield 'a fair tower of brick'.[81] A tower format was a sensible one for houses which were normally used for short periods and by a reduced household, so that there was no need for large numbers of lodgings, and the roof or upper room could be useful for watching the movement of game. Such tower lodges were really only more detached versions of the tower lodgings that formed part of great houses or castles. 'Lodge' is just a variant of 'lodgings', and the term expressed the reality, that lodges were usually much simpler units than houses which had to fulfil complex functions of administration, power and state.

Although some hunting lodges were also manor houses, with a church and village attached, most were on their own, isolated from other people and isolated too from all the daily routine and the constant coming and going of visitors, officials and petitioners at the other houses, and from some degree of their ceremony. They were holiday houses. Some were in exceedingly remote country. Wharncliffe Lodge, for instance, was built early in the sixteenth century by Sir Thomas Wortley on the top of a crag in the then savage wilderness of Wharncliffe Chase; it is wild enough today, even though Sheffield is on its doorstep. An inscription carved on a nearby rock asked the reader to pray for the soul of Sir Thomas Wortley 'which Thomas caused a lodge to be made on this crag in the midst of Wharncliffe for his pleasure to hear the hart's bell [the stag's rutting cry], in the year of our Lord, 1510.'[82]

Pleasure, of one kind or another, tends to be an element in towers and tower buildings other than hunting lodges. At Hampton Court, if a seventeenth-century account is to be relied on, the garden contained 'some snug places of retirement in certain towers, formerly intended as places of accommodation for the king's mistresses.'[83] The tower called Mirefleur, originally built in 1433 by Humphrey, Duke of Gloucester, on the hill above his manor of Greenwich, where the Royal Observatory now stands, was rebuilt by Henry VIII and put to a similar use; he himself is said to have written, while being rowed up the river to Greenwich:

> Within this tower
> There lieth a flower
> That hath my heart.[84]

The tower's hilltop position must have been chosen largely for the pleasure of the view. A similar use of the top rooms or battlement walks of other mediaeval houses is suggested by a stanza in the fifteenth-century *Life of Ipomydon*, describing the aftermath of the Whitsuntide feast of King Ermones of Poyle-land:

> After meat they went to play,
> All the people, as I you say,
> Some to chamber and some to bower
> And some to the high tower;
> And some in the hall stood
> And spoke what they thought good.[85]

The tower at Tattershall has a broad and elaborately-finished walk round the battlements, with access at the corners into turrets lit by elegant trefoil-headed windows; all this was designed more for after-dinner strollers than for soldiers. At Melbury in Dorset the most prominent feature of the house built by Sir Giles Strangways in about 1530 is a hexagonal belvedere tower (Pl. 44); it rises from the middle of the main range of the house, and its circuit of twelve-light windows commands the surrounding countryside.

Apart from the one gesture of its tower, Melbury was a courtyard house with no frills. It was one of many similar early-sixteenth-century houses which did

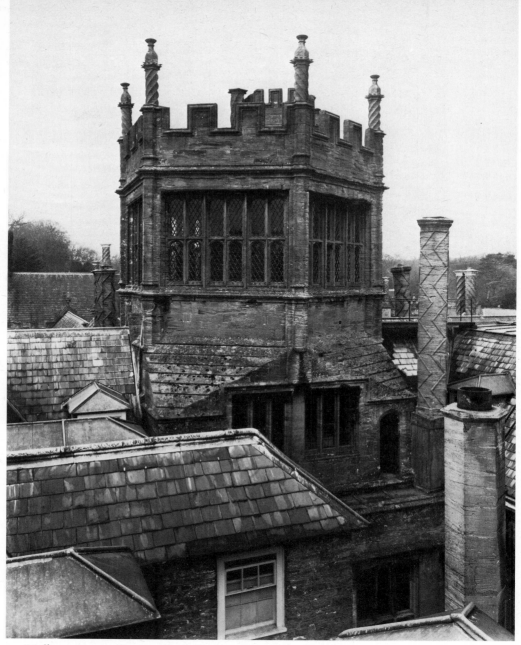

44. Melbury House, Dorset. The belvedere tower (*c.* 1530–40).

without the full pseudo-feudal rig and confined themselves to a single tower or a gatehouse. The courtyard type can be pursued down the scale to the point when it merges with the manorial type; this too can be followed down to its simplest form of a little hall sandwiched between little chambers (Pl. 45). A continuous thread links the smallest examples to the greatest, just as a link of service, as retainer or member of the household, was likely to join the owner of a small house to the owner of a great castle.

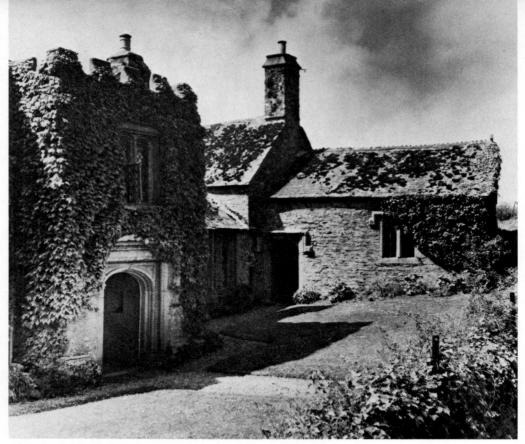

45. A miniature fifteenth-century manor house at Hareston, Devon.

The architectural progression from top to bottom can be traced easily enough in surviving buildings, or records of demolished ones. The progression in ceremony is harder to follow, because little documentation of daily life in small mediaeval manor houses has come to light. Of course such houses did not practise anything approaching the ceremony apposite for an earl. But it is likely that their ceremonies, like their households, were scaled-down versions of those of great people. Christmas feasts and plays certainly took place in very modest manor houses.[86] The lord of such a manor would not employ separate yeomen of ewery, cellar, buttery and pantry; the *Booke of Nurture* suggests that the four jobs could be combined in one person.[87] Similarly, he might imitate the practice of the Earl of Northumberland when keeping secret house, and employ his sons as carver and sewer, as Chaucer's squire was employed by his father the knight:

> Courteous he was, lowly and serviceable
> And carved before his father at the table.[88]

At all levels in the early decades of the sixteenth century one can see a growing realisation that the order and hierarchy which made each household a microcosm of the universe, as the Middle Ages saw it, could be echoed in architecture not only by hierarchy but by the order resulting from symmetry. In the course of the sixteenth century what had started as a refinement was to become a rule.

46. (right) Montacute House, Somerset (*c.* 1595–1601). Looking into the forecourt from the long gallery.

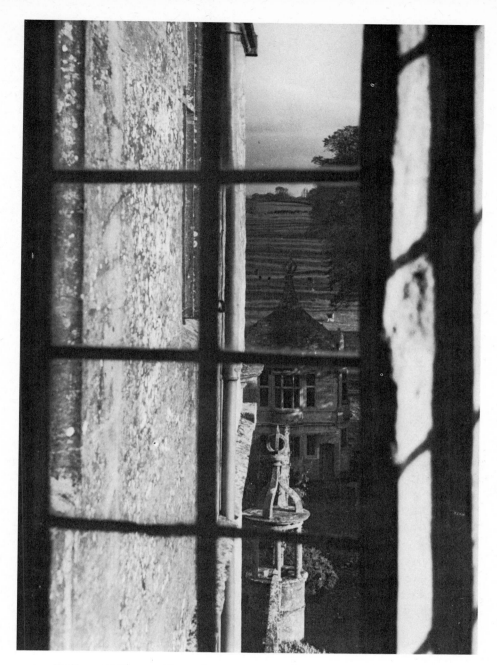

4 The Elizabethan and Jacobean House

In MOVING from a great household of the years around 1500 to its equivalent in the late sixteenth and even early seventeenth century, one's first impression is that the old machinery is still grinding away, almost without change. There were, in fact, changes, and some of them were important. But a remarkable amount remained the same, in spite of the Reformation and the Renaissance.

The household of the Earl of Derby, for instance, was still operating in the 1580s much as it must have done a hundred years previously.[1] Its size, exclusive of the family, varied from 115 to 140 people (and the women in it from three to six); its organisation was exactly the same as a household of the Middle Ages, from the earl's council down to the almoners and the trumpeters (but there was no fool). The hierarchy of gentlemen, yeomen and grooms was firmly based on the Stanley power-base of Lancashire and Cheshire. The earl's treasurer was Sir Richard Sherborne, who built his own great house at Stonyhurst and was one of the biggest landowners in Lancashire. The earl's steward, William Farington of Worden, was a member of a well-established Lancashire family, a substantial property owner, a magistrate and deputy-lieutenant of the county, and the son of a former upper servant of the earl's. His gentlemen waiters were all members of the local gentry. His clerk comptroller, William Fox, came from his own tenantry but was to found a family of minor gentry, as was his clerk of the kitchen, Michael Doughty, who was elected M.P. for Preston in 1589, on the earl's nomination.

The household moved ponderously from Knowsley to Lathom Castle, and from Lathom Castle to the New Lodge at Lathom. Once a year, when the earl attended court, the major part of it moved down to London. On two occasions a more mobile but still formidable household attended him on embassies to the continent. In Lancashire the earl's guests were almost all local people; of the 200 or so people named in the accounts, some of whom occur over and over again, all but a handful were from Lancashire, Cheshire or North Wales (and all but about a tenth were men). They came to celebrate Christmas, or the audit, or the christening of the earl's grandchild, to listen to plays put on in the hall by the Earl of Leicester's players and others, or to sermons delivered by local clergymen in the earl's chapel; they came to hunt; they came to sit on the earl's council, or attend the musters; they came in large numbers to pay their respects to the earl, whenever he returned to Lancashire from London or abroad.

As late as the 1630s the Earl of Worcester was being served dinner at Raglan Castle with similar ritual and at least as much state as would have attended his formidable ancestor the Earl of Pembroke in the 1460s.[2] Households with roots in the Middle Ages, such as those of the Earls of Derby and Worcester, tended to be especially conservative. But up to the early seventeenth century even new households of any pretension were likely to follow mediaeval models. Both Lord Treasurer Burghley and Lord Chancellor Ellesmere kept old-fashioned state, although they were self-made men.[3]

Lord Ellesmere's household arrangements are revealed by the full set of rules which he drew up in 1605 and which are closely based on the Harleian and similar late mediaeval regulations. A considerable number of other late-sixteenth and early-seventeenth-century regulations survive.[4] They range from a set of 1572 for the household of Sir Francis Willoughby of Wollaton, which show how ceremony was scaled down, but not discarded, for the household of a substantial commoner, to the immensely detailed regulations drawn up in 1596 for the great household of Viscount Montagu at Cowdray. Much the most personal of them are 'Some Rules and Orders for the Government of the House of an Earl', written in the early years of James I's reign by an anonymous R. B. 'at the instant request of his loving frende, M. L.'.[5] These take the form of advice to a friend, rather than a set of rules. They are full of the digressions and recollections of a shrewd and romantic old household officer, who looked back with nostalgia to the old order, which he saw with regret was beginning to crumble.

The households depicted by these regulations were still based on a hierarchy of gentlemen, yeomen and grooms; and there were still very few women in them. Household service was still a route to fortune. In the mid sixteenth century the profits of the Duke of Somerset's steward, Sir John Thynne, enabled him to build his great house at Longleat and launch his family on the way to a marquisate; and Bess of Hardwick used service in the households of the Zouches and the Greys as the first steps towards the succession of marriages which made her a countess and enabled her to found two dukedoms. In the later sixteenth and early seventeenth century Sir Walter Cope, who built what later became Holland House in Kensington, was launched on his career by service to the Cecils; and service to the Sackvilles and the Howards turned the Trevor family from penniless Welsh squireens into substantial landowners with at least two big houses and a brace of knighthoods to give them standing.[6]

To marry a member of one's household, even from its upper strata, was considered an appalling social misdemeanour. Even Bess of Hardwick never persuaded her employer to marry her, but such marriages did happen, and could provide a short cut to fortune, especially for a personable young man. Within a few years two young men on the make captured two widowed duchesses of Suffolk substantially older than they were. In 1553 Katherine Brandon, Duchess of Suffolk, married her gentleman usher, Richard Bertie, the son of a successful master-mason; their descendants ultimately became dukes of Ancaster. A few years later her step-daughter, Frances Grey, Duchess of Suffolk, married her master of the horse, Adrian Stokes. The latter marriage was considered especially ignominious since she was of royal descent, but at least there were no children.[7]

Such marriages may have been rare, but sexual intrigue between employers and their servants was probably not uncommon. The autobiography of Thomas Whythorne, who served as music tutor or gentleman waiter, sometimes both at the same time, in various big households in the 1560s and '70s, is full of virtuous accounts of his employers' unsuccessful attempts to seduce him.[8] One way in which the lower servants dealt with the frustrations of a predominantly masculine household is suggested by the call of one serving man to another in *Romeo and Juliet*: 'Good thou, save me a piece of marchpane; and as thou lovest me, let the porter let in Susan Grindstone and Nell.'[9]

Great people were still taking children into their households to educate them, giving gargantuan feasts, and keeping retainers. In the 1590s Bess of Hardwick's nephew George Kniveton was serving as a page in her household, and Sir Horatio Palavicino sent his eldest son to be brought up in the household of her stepson, the Earl of Shrewsbury.[10] As late as 1620 the Earl of Arundel dispatched his younger son, aged five or six, into the household of the Bishop of Norwich, equipped with a sheaf of good advice and the information that 'my grandfather of Norfolk, and his brother my good uncle of Northampton, were both bred as pages with bishops.'[11] At the funeral of the fifth Earl of Shrewsbury, held at Sheffield in 1560, dinner was provided for 'all manner of people who seemed honest'. About 1200 were served, and the remains, along with bread, drink, and twopence apiece were distributed to vast numbers of the poor. The funeral of the sixth earl, thirty years later, was said to have been attended by even greater profusion and magnificence.[12]

The throng of people who made up the funeral train of the Dowager-Countess of Huntingdon in 1576 included (besides her entire household, the Garter King of Arms, a countess with train as chief mourner, a knight carrying a great banner, poor men and singing men by the dozen, and all the usual crepe-encased paraphernalia of an important funeral) twenty gentlemen retainers and forty yeomen retainers belonging to her son.[13] The system of retaining survived under licence until at least the end of the sixteenth century.[14] The Protector Northumberland was lavish with licences, and so was Mary. Elizabeth was more cautious. She kept down the number of licences and never issued one for more than a hundred retainers; she and Lord Burghley did their best, not always successfully, to stop J.P.s and sheriffs from wearing the liveries of great men, a practice not calculated to inspire confidence in justice. But lords were still riding into London with a mounted entourage of gentlemen and retainers. In the 1560s Lord Berkeley never travelled with less than 150 gentlemen, many related to him and 'of remarkable families and descent'; they wore tawny cloth coats in summer, with the Berkeley badge of a white lion rampant embroidered on the left sleeve; in winter they wore coats of white frieze lined with crimson taffeta. In the 1570s the Earl of Southampton was attended by 100 gentlemen with gold chains round their necks. In the 1590s the Earl of Shrewsbury turned up at the Garter feast at Windsor attended by Sir George Booth and Sir Vincent Corbet, two landed knights of ancient lineage who were happy to wear his livery.[15]

Lord Berkeley was only able to support his 150 gentlemen, and the way of life that went with them, by reckless overspending. He had financial crises in 1560 and 1574, and was left with diminished estates and a household reduced to about seventy.[16] By the end of the sixteenth century the Earls of Southampton and Shrewsbury were both in serious financial difficulties.[17] By then gradual but cumulative changes in society were making the old mediaeval model seem out of date, for the good reason that it was ceasing to bring in results.

The changes were due to the gradual working of Tudor policy. By balancing one faction against another, by placing Crown-appointed Lord Lieutenants in charge of a local militia instead of relying on great people's retainers, by strengthening existing state courts and starting efficient new ones such as the Star Chamber, by successfully putting down a series of revolts and destroying or pruning over-powerful families, by boosting the glamour and prestige of the monarch and embroiling the upper classes in the hopes and excitements of court life, by judicial distribution of favours and perquisites, the Tudors, and Elizabeth in particular, had begun to replace the rule of force by the rule of law. Service to the Crown and influence or friends at court became a better route to power and fortune than individual factions based on local power structures. At the lowest level bribery had become more effective than bullying.

These changes should not be exaggerated. In a society with no standing army, no police force and by modern standards a minute civil service, the independent power of great landowners was still formidable. But the alternative structure was becoming harder for them to ignore. To work it to their own advantage involved loyal service to the Crown in their home county and long visits to London, to prosecute law business and attend at court.

Both of the latter were expensive occupations. In the late sixteenth and early seventeenth century grand families were likely to spend more money on the law than on anything else; in eight months in 1591–2 Bess of Hardwick spent £1200 on legal business; this was about fifteen per cent of her income and substantially more than the £340 a year she was spending on building Hardwick.[18] Court life for the ambitious involved prodigal expense on clothes, jewels, plate, carriages, presents and tips, quite apart from gambling losses resulting from high play in the long hours of hanging around the presence chamber. The compensations were the excitement and convenience of being where the action was, the hope of jobs, grants or perquisites which could double income and power overnight, and gossip, intrigue, spectacle, company and all the resources and excitements of London.

Few, if any, households could afford to combine the expenses of fashionable court and London life with the expenses of a mediaeval-type household and the way of life that went with it. And in London, at any rate, a great following was a liability rather than an asset. Once the great began to have doubts about the need for servants to fight and bully for them, and find that a crowd of gentlemen and yeomen brought little status in the town and was too expensive in the country, the size of their households was bound to shrink. They needed fewer people to attend on them at home and accompany them when they rode abroad; correspondingly, their visitors arrived with smaller entourages to be entertained. The shrinkage was gradual but continual from the mid sixteenth to the mid eighteenth century; after 1600 households of more than a hundred were increasingly rare.

Mildly streamlined households resulted in mildly streamlined houses. In such houses the combination of old and new power structures tended to produce a double way of life. The weight of tradition and the need to keep up local prestige maintained the old ceremonies, even if in reduced form; but court and city life had given the great a taste for a more private and intimate luxury, and for the conversational liveliness of meals uninhibited by ceremony. By the early seventeenth century ceremony was diminishing; 'R. B.' complained bitterly that 'noble men in these days (for the most part) like better to be served with pages and groomes, than in that estate which belongeth to their degree.'[19]

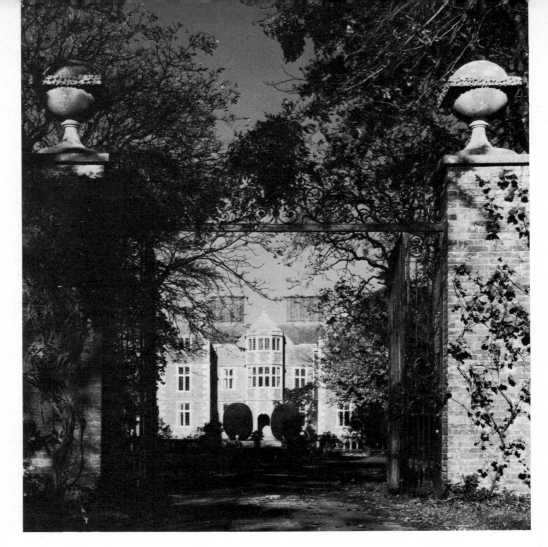

Changing tastes and ambitions produced a change in image, which affected houses as well as everything else. The qualities of the courtier and the lawyer became more fashionable than the qualities of the soldier; fighting was left more and more to professionals. A certain knowledge of the classics was considered desirable among the upper classes, and was echoed by classical detail and iconography in their houses. But it was more important to be witty than learned. Wit was demonstrated by quickness of repartee and by an ingenuity of mind of which the chief visual expression was the 'dévice'. The device at its purest was a hieroglyph, of an at first sight mysterious nature (though sometimes with an explanatory motto or verse attached): a cupid firing arrows at a unicorn, for instance, signified chastity under attack by sexual desire. All courtiers adopted their own devices as statements of their reaction to life in general or to a particular situation; they carried them enamelled on jewels, had them painted in the background of their portraits, and presented them to their mistresses. Devices could spill over into furniture, plate, buildings, or food; and the attitude of mind behind them led to a delight in anything ingenious or unusual even if it had no

86

47. Anderson Manor, Dorset (*c*. 1620–2).

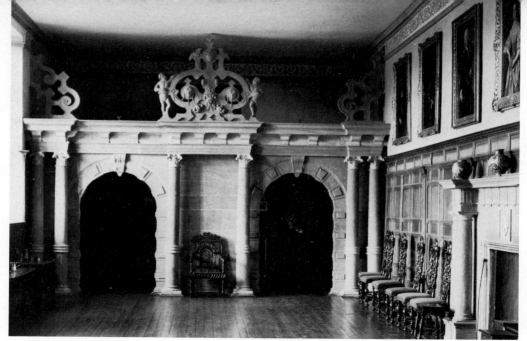

48. Montacute House, Somerset. The hall.

secret meaning. All such ingenuities tended to be loosely called 'devices'.[20]

The urge to express everything in terms of something else was based on more than a fondness for allegory. Such relationships were considered to be, in some mystical sense, real rather than allegorical; the structure and harmony of the universe was based on them. Of especial importance was the relationship between macrocosm and microcosm. The universe, with God at its head and centre, formed the macrocosm. Man was a microcosm of the universe, and his brain and will ruled over his animal parts, just as God ruled over the creation. Societies, including the little society of each household, were also microcosms. The household hierarchy, with its lord at its head, was based on the natural order, in exactly the same way as the hierarchy of the state. Hierarchies were not just convenient for those at the top of them. They were the only right and God-given way of organising men into societies.[21]

Such beliefs went back to the Middle Ages and beyond; but the Elizabethans pushed them further by projecting them into the objects with which they surrounded themselves, and especially into their buildings. The feeling that order and proportion in the household should be echoed by order and proportion in the architecture of the house had begun to appear in the later Middle Ages, but it became much stronger during the sixteenth century. In 1569 the Earl of Westmorland underlined the ineffectiveness of the old system of power politics by his part in the abortive Northern Rising, and died in exile in consequence. In 1570 the commissioners for dealing with his attainted estates visited his castle at Raby and were both impressed and appalled by its formidably disorganised circuit of towers (Pl. 39). They described it as 'a marvellous huge house of building wherein are three wards, and builded all of stone and covered with lead; and yet is there no order or proportion in the building thereof.'[22]

87

The main fronts of a new house of any size were now almost invariably symmetrical (Pls 47, 56, 62 and 63); but behind the facades the arrangements of rooms differed comparatively little from that of the later Middle Ages. The great chamber continued to head the hierarchy. Most large houses still had a chapel and chaplain; but smaller houses did without, and their master conducted daily or twice-daily prayers for the household in the hall or great chamber.[23] The hall was still used as the servants' dining and common room and as the room of entrance; the gentry still moved into it on occasions to watch plays or attend great feasts. Although halls were increasingly built one rather than two storeys in height (Pl. 48), those in the grander Elizabethan and Jacobean houses could still be rooms of some magnificence. But the great chamber was the ceremonial pivot of the house. The late sixteenth and early seventeenth century was the time of its greatest glory and magnificence. As one set of regulations put it in 1604:

> in that place there must be no delay, because it is the place of state, where the lord keepeth his presence, and the eyes of all the best sort of strangers be there lookers on . . . wherefore the gentleman usher is to take a special care herein, for their credit sake and honour of that place.[24]

Its chief function remained that of an eating place, in particular the place where, at least on occasions, dinner and supper were served by sewer, carver and cupbearer, with all attendant ceremonies and assistants, to the lord 'keeping his state' under a canopy (Pl. 65).[25] The arrangement of the first table remained the same, and strict social distinction was still kept between those above and below the salt, and those not considered eligible to eat with the host at all. Such distinctions could lead to frustration and annoyance among the neighbouring gentry; in about 1580, for instance, Mr Marlivate of Chevington in Suffolk complained indignantly to Sir Thomas Kytson of Hengrave that, instead of being placed at 'the Lord's board in the great chamber', he had been made to dine at the 'square board in the hall' with the steward.[26]

The dining function of the great chamber was so important that in the sixteenth and early seventeenth century it was often called the dining chamber, or sometimes the great dining chamber. But although this was its main function, it was far from being its only one. Great chambers were used for music, dancing and the putting on of plays and masques; for the lying-in-state of corpses before funerals; for playing cards, dice and backgammon in between meals; and for family prayers, especially in houses that had no chapel.

In 1607 the Dowager-Countess of Derby visited her daughter, Lady Huntingdon, at Ashby-de-la-Zouch castle. The visit was celebrated by a masque, put on in the great chamber. Goddesses spoke their pieces; clouds whizzed through the air on invisible machinery. At the culmination of the masque the masquers 'presented their shields and took forth their ladies to dance'. They danced measures, galliards, corantos and lavaltos until, 'the night being much spent', a shepherd sang 'a passionate ditty at my Lady's Departure', and the party ended.[27]

A few years earlier a masque in progress had been depicted in a curious painting showing the life of Sir Henry Unton (d. 1596) in strip-cartoon form. One of the episodes shows Sir Henry's wedding dinner. He and his party are sitting at table while a masque is performed before them by a circle of alternate black and white cherubs and pairs of women in exotic dresses and with red painted faces (Col. Pl. VII). An orchestra of six players provides music in the centre of the circle. The painting is too conventionalized to make clear whether all this is going on in the hall or the great chamber, but by this period the great chamber was certainly being used as an alternative venue to the hall for both masques and plays. Masques were usually put on by members of the household, with a cast composed of family, friends, and a selection of household gentlemen and gentlewomen;[28] it was usual for the masquers to break out of the masque and dance with the company, as at Ashby. To act in a play, on the other hand, was considered socially demeaning. Plays were normally acted by travelling companies, whose visits are often recorded in household accounts. In Shakespeare's *Midsummer Night's Dream* the play of *Pyramus and Thisbe* is mounted by a company of Athenian craftsmen in the great chamber of the Duke of Athens.

A masque always culminated in general dancing, but dancing frequently took place without a masque. At the end of the seventeenth century Roger North believed that great chambers had been primarily dancing chambers: 'After ye Scotch union . . . ye humour being then much after jollity and dancing, the Gentry affected to have one great room.'[29] Although this is bad history, it is true enough that the mediaeval taste for dancing continued and grew stronger under the Elizabethans and Jacobeans. Any big dinner usually ended with dancing in the great chamber, after the food had been cleared away. Good musicians, 'skilful in that commendable sweet science', as the mysterious R. B. put it, were much in demand, not only to supply music for masques and dancing, or to play the courses in at feasts, but to play at almost any time of the day. R. B. lays down that

> at great feasts, when the Earl's service is going to the table, they are to play upon Shagbutte, Cornets, Shalms and such other instruments giving with wind. In meal times to play upon Viols, Violins, or other broken music. They are to teach the Earl's children to sing and play upon the Base Viol, the Virginals, Lute, Bandera or Cittern. In some houses they are allowed a mess of meat in their chambers, in other houses they eat with the waiters.[30]

The musical functions of great chambers were sometimes commemorated in their decoration. The frieze in the great chamber at Gilling Castle in Yorkshire is mainly filled with the arboreal family trees of the Yorkshire gentry who were entertained there; but at one corner the trees give way to six musicians, three men and three women, seated at a long table with their music by their side (Pl. 49). Orpheus, patron of both song and dance, is portrayed surrounded by the nine muses in overmantel carvings from two vanished or rebuilt houses, Elizabethan Chatsworth and Toddington in Bedfordshire.[31] There is some evidence that the Chatsworth carving was originally in the great chamber there, but in the nineteenth century it was removed to its present position in the withdrawing chamber at Hardwick (Pl. 50). In the adjoining High Great Chamber is a lavishly inlaid table made in the 1560s, probably also for the great chamber at Chatsworth, although it has been at Hardwick since the house was first finished at the end of the sixteenth century. It is profusely inlaid with musical instruments and sheets of music (one has the motet 'Oh Lord in thee is all my trust' set to four parts) but also with playing cards and boards for chess and backgammon.

The chess and backgammon boards refer to yet another of the functions of the great chamber. According to the Cowdray regulations the yeoman usher of the great chamber was responsible for supplying 'cards and tables [i.e. games boards] for such strangers as shall be willing to play and pass the time thereat.'[32] Both gentlemen and yeomen servants joined in the games when either strangers or family wanted them to. In 1601 Lady Berkeley ordered the gentlemen servants at Berkeley castle to wear livery coats or cloaks, and not just jerkins or doublets when they came into the great dining chamber to 'sit at play with my Lord and me'.[33] Lord Berkeley's fondness for gambling for small stakes with his yeomen of the great chamber was described in Chapter 1.

Another use of the chamber was as the setting for the lying-in-state of a corpse. Directions of 1587 for the funeral of an earl require 'the corpse to be prepared, coffined and leaded, and to be placed within the chapel of his house or great chamber, till the day of the burial.'[34] The lying-in-state of a great man was arranged on the same scale of lavish gloom as his funeral. In the case of a duke, marquess or earl, the courtyard and entrance facade of the house were draped with hangings of black baize, as was the staircase and the first room leading up to the coffin. A second room was hung with black cloth; the room beyond it, where the coffin stood, was completely shrouded in black velvet. The coffin, covered with a black velvet pall, was placed on a raised dais in front of the empty state chair and canopy of the dead person, also caparisoned in black. Lesser corpses were not eligible for black velvet, but otherwise enjoyed the same sequence.[35] Mourners who came to pay respects to the corpse were given refreshments. John Smyth recalls how, at the funeral of Lord Berkeley in 1618, the tenants were 'called up into the great chamber to refresh themselves with wine and the like' and how 'I saw 100 pair of eyes at least pouring out (before that coffin) such passionate and sorrowful tears, as if their spirits should have followed those tears.'[36] After the funeral was over there was always at least a state dinner in the great chamber, presided over by the chief mourner.

As 'the place of state, where the lord keepeth his presence', the great chamber had to be fitted up with suitable magnificence. It was usually the most richly decorated room in the house, and was often as large as the hall. Its fittings tended to be more permanent than in mediaeval great chambers. Tables and cupboards replaced boards and trestles. Chairs and stools were covered with rich embroidery. Tapestries were supplemented, and sometimes replaced by pictures or carved and inlaid panelling. A plasterwork or painted frieze could be surmounted by an elaborate plasterwork ceiling. The windows were often filled

49. (upper right) Household musicians in the great chamber frieze at Gilling Castle, Yorkshire (1585).

50. (right) Hardwick Hall, Derbyshire. Detail of an overmantel (c. 1570) showing Orpheus and the Muses, originally at Chatsworth.

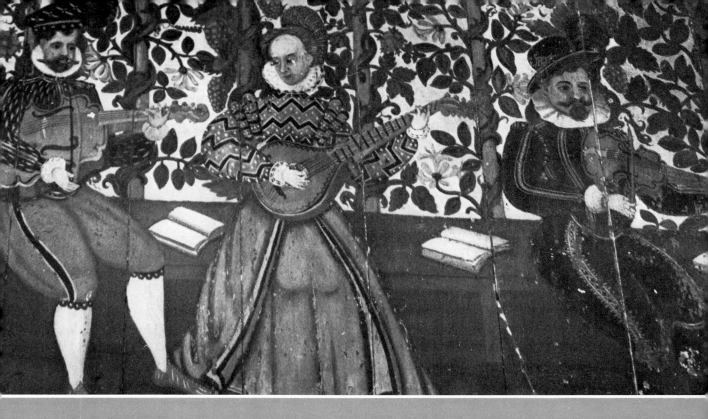

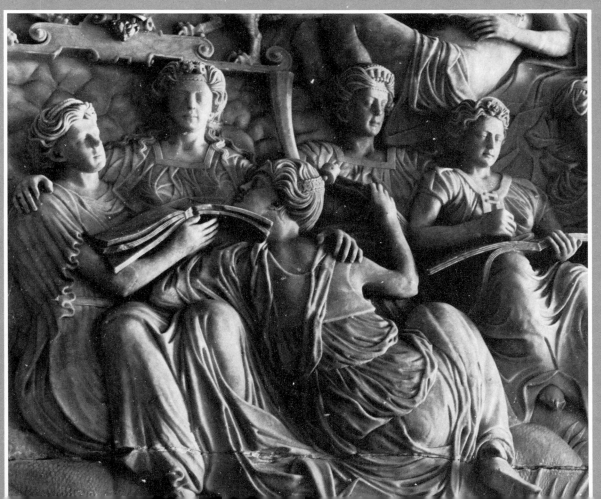

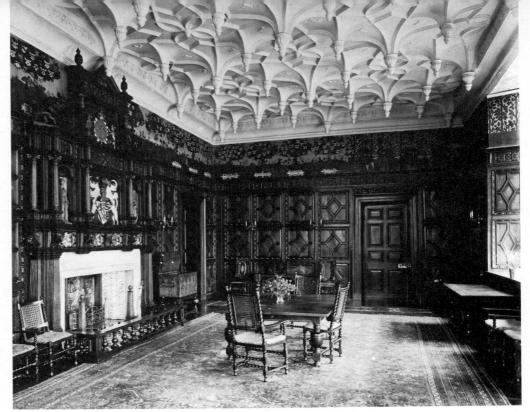

51. Gilling Castle, Yorkshire. The great chamber (*c.* 1585).
52. Knole, Kent. The main staircase (*c.* 1605–8).

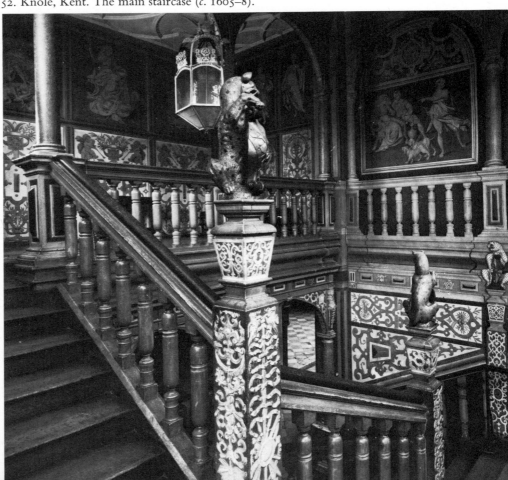

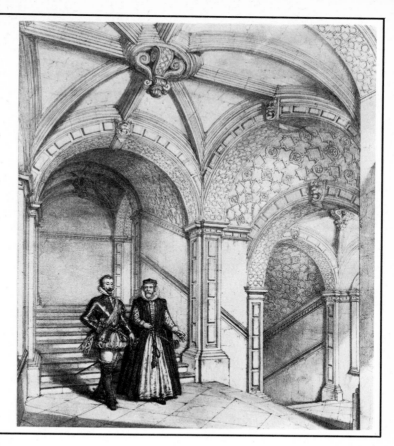

53. Burghley House,
Northamptonshire.
The stone staircase
(*c.* 1560).

with heraldic glass. The most sumptuous scheme of decoration to survive in an
Elizabethan great chamber is at Gilling Castle in Yorkshire, where every square
inch of walls and ceiling is glowingly encrusted with colour and ornament
(Pl. 51).

The ceremonial route to the great chamber remained as important as ever.
After Lord Burghley had visited Holdenby in 1579 he told Sir Christopher
Hatton, its owner, that 'I found no one thing of greater grace than your stately
ascent from your hall to your great chamber.'[37] Up till the end of the century,
main staircases were usually of stone, and turned in broad flights round a square
stone newel. At Montacute the newel is decorated with shell-headed alcoves; at
Burghley the staircase has a stone vault, magnificently coffered in the French
manner (Pl. 53). In the early seventeenth century improved techniques of joinery
produced the open-well wooden staircase, and such staircases, often resplendently
carved and painted (Pl. 52), became so fashionable that stone ones were
sometimes taken out to make way for them.[38]

The great chambers at the head of these staircases have often been redecorated,
and sometimes cut up into smaller rooms. Even those that have survived
relatively unaltered are either not used at all or used differently from how they
would have been in the sixteenth century. To get a feeling of their original
atmosphere one has to go to contemporary sources. There is an especially
evocative description in George Whetstone's *An Heptameron of Civil Discourses*
(1582), an account of a week of feasting and discussion spent by Queen Aurelia

and 'a chosen company' in her 'stately palace'. The company supposedly included Whetstone himself. Each day ends with supper in the great chamber, followed by dancing and masquing. Whetstone tells how on one evening, after the masque was finished, 'the Gentlemen and Gentlewomen began to shrink out of the great chamber, as the stars seem to shoot the sky, towards the breake of day.' In the next morning,

> coming out of my lodging somewhat timely, I entered the great chamber with as strange a regard, as he that cometh out of a house full of torch and taper lights, into a dark and obscure corner: knowing that at midnight (about which time I forsook my company) I left the place, attired like a second paradise: the earthly Goddesses, in brightness, resembled heavenly creatures, whose beauties dazzled men's eyes more than the beams of the sun; the sweet music recorded the harmony of angels, the strange and curious devices in masquers seemed as figures of divine mysteries. And to be short, the place was the very sympathy of an imagined Paradise. And in the space of one slumbering sleep, to be left like a desert wilderness, without any creature, save sundry savage beasts, portrayed in the tapestry hangings, impressed such a heavy passion in my mind, as for the time I fared as one, whose senses had forgot how to do their bounded offices. In the end, to recomfort my throbbing heart, I took my Cittern, and to a solemn note sung this following sonnet.

Whetstone then breaks into a song of passionate melancholy, starting 'Farewell bright gold, thou glory of the world'. His thoughts swoon with the 'charm of my passionate music', and meanwhile the sun 'decked in his most glorious rays' bursts through the windows and gives 'a *Bon Giorno* to the whole troop'.[39]

Elizabethan and Jacobean great chambers usually had an adjoining withdrawing chamber, with either the owner's bedchamber or the best bedchamber beyond it. A gallery was another room often found adjacent or close to the great chamber, although sometimes it was on the floor above. The origins of both galleries and withdrawing chambers date back to the fifteenth century, but consideration of them has been left to this chapter, because it was only in the sixteenth century that they became important.

'Withdraughte' or 'draughte' first appeared as a term apparently attached to almost any smaller room letting off a chamber. By 1496 Charlecote in Warwickshire had a 'withdrawing chamber' between the great chamber and the owner's own chamber; it contained little more than an 'old bed', a mattress and two blankets, suggesting that it was used as an antechamber and was occupied and slept in by the servant or servants of whoever was in the adjoining chamber.[40] During the sixteenth century withdrawing chambers gradually began to take over some of the functions that had previously belonged to chambers. They became the private sitting, eating and reception rooms of the occupant of the chamber to which they were attached. They continued to be slept in by his servants until at least the end of the sixteenth century (and in royal palaces until the late seventeenth century). In 1596 Viscount Montagu's yeomen of the chamber pulled out pallets at night in the viscount's withdrawing chamber at Cowdray and

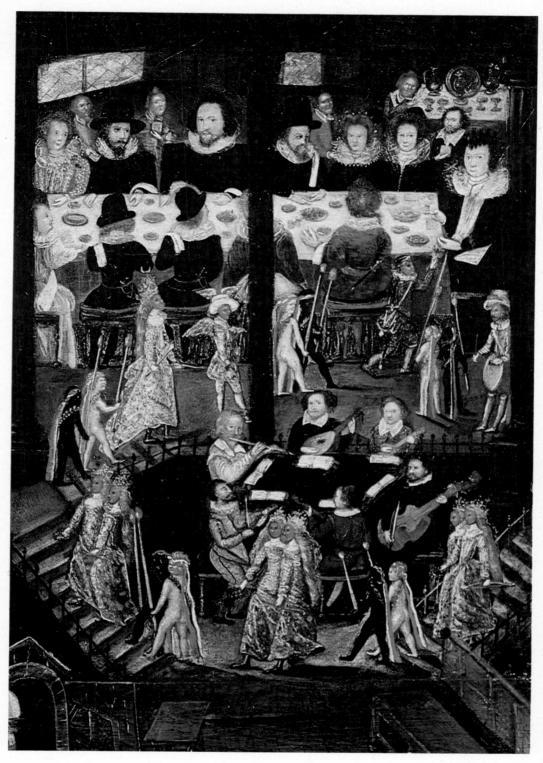

VII. Sir Henry Unton feasting. From the memorial picture painted after his death.

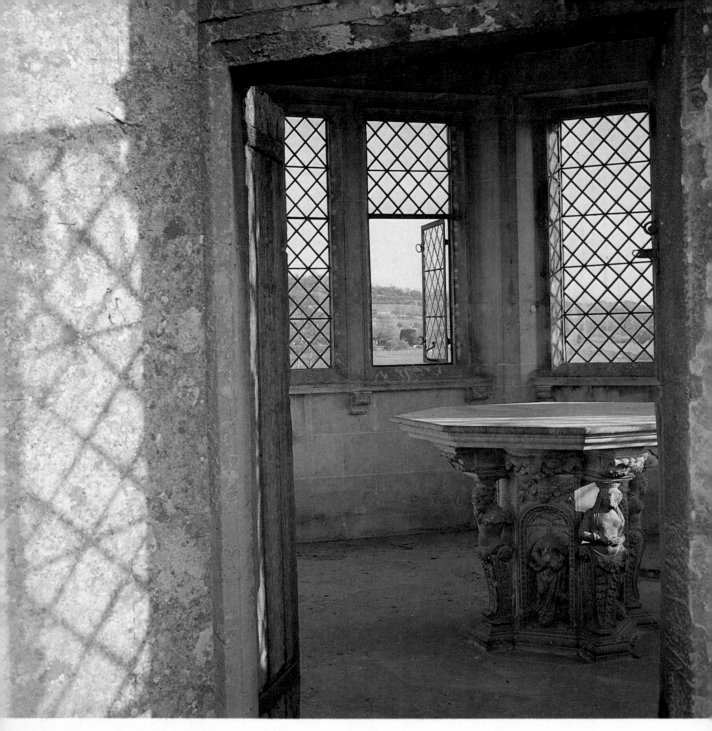

VIII. Lacock Abbey, Wiltshire. The banqueting room in the tower (*c.* 1550).
IX. (right) The Triangular Lodge, Rushton, Northamptonshire (1595).

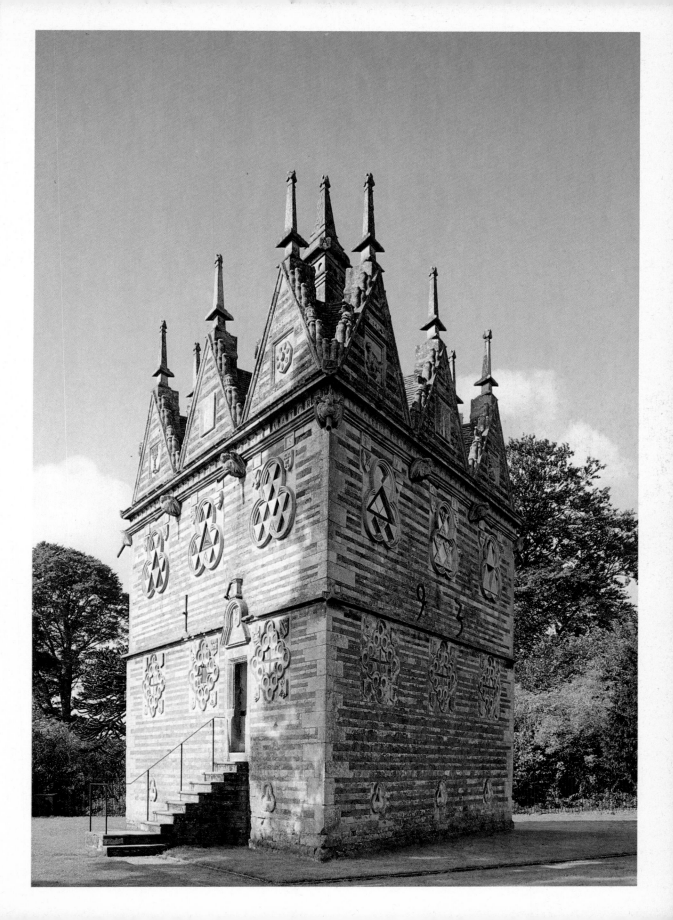

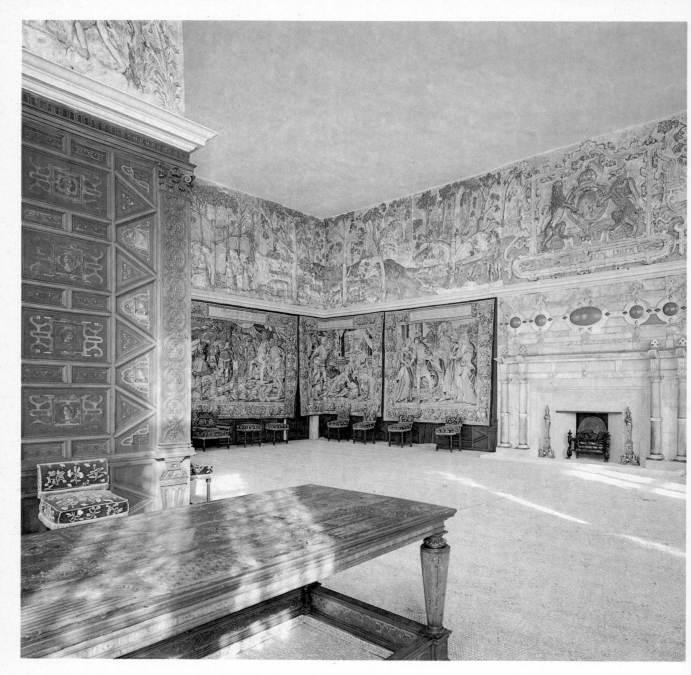

X. Hardwick Hall, Derbyshire (1590–7). The High Great Chamber.

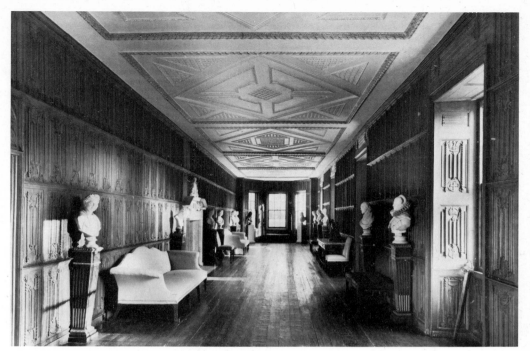

54. The Vyne, Hampshire. The gallery (*c.* 1520).

slept on call for their master in his adjoining bedchamber.[41] 'Bedchamber', incidentally, is a term which first became common in the mid sixteenth century; its appearance underlined the fact that such rooms were no longer bed-sitting rooms, as chambers had been in the Middle Ages, but were mainly used for sleeping in.

Viscount Montagu's yeomen of the chamber were also directed 'to attend me in my withdrawing chamber, if straight after mine own meal I come thither'. The use of a withdrawing or drawing chamber both as a room to retire into after meals and a room for private meals is described in many contemporary sources. In Whetstone's *Heptameron of Civil Discourses*, for instance, after dinner in the great chamber was ended, 'Queen Aurelia with a chosen company retired herself into a pleasant drawing chamber.'[42] Most of the discussions in the book take place in this drawing chamber. The company who retired into it included men and women. They were 'chosen', because by no means all those who attended dinner in the great chamber would expect to go into the drawing chamber; they would wait for an invitation from its owner.

On 4 April 1617 the Countess of Dorset, then in residence at Knole, wrote in her diary: 'This day we began to leave the little room and dine and sup in the great chamber.' The move was probably because the weather was getting warmer, and the 'little room' the earl and countess's withdrawing chamber. The countess continued to dine in the latter when she wished to be private; on the thirteenth the earl 'dined abroad in the great chamber, and supped privately with me in the drawing chamber.' Two days later 'I was so sick and my face so swelled that my Lord and Tom Glemham were fain to keep the table in the drawing chamber and I sat within', presumably in her bedchamber.[43]

The retiring function of the room naturally led people to think of it as the room to which they 'withdrew' from the great chamber or other eating place; its origins as a room hived off from a private chamber began to be forgotten. In the early seventeenth century withdrawing chambers unattached to bedchambers began to appear.[44] But this was not the normal arrangement; well into the eighteenth century anyone in a withdrawing or drawing chamber would expect to find a bedchamber beyond it.

Galleries originated as covered walks, sometimes roofed but open on one side, sometimes completely enclosed.[45] There is a reference to a gallery at Cawood Castle as early as 1465. It was used during the Neville feast as an eating place for visiting servants, presumably because, owing to the vast crush of people, there was nowhere else to put them.[46] By 1509 the house of Edmund Dudley in London had two galleries, one above the other looking into the garden; the upper one was closed, the lower was open and led to another 'great' gallery, also open. The house had a further closed gallery next to the great chamber.[47] A similar arrangement of galleries one above the other was incorporated in about 1520 into the west wing of the Vyne in Hampshire. The lower gallery is now enclosed, but was probably originally open. The upper one survives comparatively unaltered, and is the oldest long gallery in England (Pl. 54). It is about sixteen feet wide and seventy-four feet long and is lined with linenfold panelling, delicately enriched with grotesques, crests, arms and initials.

A different arrangement was to be found at Thornbury Castle (c. 1520), at the London house of the Marquess of Exeter (1530), and possibly at Richmond Palace.[48] At all these places the gallery resembled a cloister walk. It was carried round three sides of an enclosed garden and attached to the main body of the house on the fourth. At Thornbury there was an upper and a lower gallery, the lower one possibly open. At Lord Exeter's house the circuit had only one floor; it was built of timber, varied in width from twelve to eight feet, and was lit by twelve bay-windows, probably all looking inward onto the garden. It was hung with hangings and had a fireplace in its south walk.

The earliest galleries were probably intended to be no more than protected ways leading from one place to another, but they soon acquired another important function, as a place in which to take exercise under cover. The galleries at Lord Exeter's house and at the Vyne led nowhere, and can only have been for exercise; the Thornbury galleries connected the house to the church, and probably combined the two functions. Sixteenth-century doctors stressed the importance of daily walking to preserve health, and galleries made exercise possible when the weather would otherwise have prevented it. Closed galleries were especially useful in winter, open galleries in warm or wet summer weather. When conditions allowed it, galleries were deserted for raised walks in the garden, or walks along the leads of the house, where it was possible to catch the breeze and enjoy the view.[49]

Exercising galleries, communicating galleries and galleries that combined both uses were built in increasing numbers throughout the sixteenth century. The

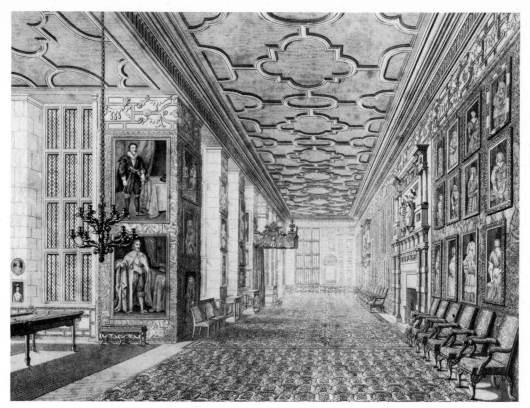

cloister-type went out of fashion as galleries were integrated into the main body of the house. Communicating galleries were normally no more than corridors. But exercising galleries, as rooms in constant use by the owner of the house and his family, gradually increased in pretensions and acquired other functions.

The first galleries contained little or no furniture, because they did not need it. But hangings and pictures soon began to appear on their walls to give the family something to look at as they walked. In 1547 there were no pictures (and almost no furniture) in the gallery at the Vyne, but nineteen pictures were hanging in Henry VIII's Long Gallery at Hampton Court.[50] In the course of the century pictures began to be found in houses other than royal. To begin with they consisted entirely, or almost entirely, of portraits. The fashion for collecting portraits was a sixteenth-century phenomenon, and the gallery became the main room in which they were hung. By the end of the century few galleries were without at least a handful of portraits, and the galleries of the great could contain from fifty to a hundred of them.

Portraits, which were not necessarily only of members of the family, were there to improve as well as to commemorate or entertain. An Elizabethan magnate, as he paced up and down his gallery, could look at the faces of his friends, his ancestors and relations, the great people of his day, the kings and queens of England, perhaps even the Roman emperors, contemplate their characters, and be inspired to imitate their virtues. That, at least, was the theory. Lord Howard of Bindon, for instance, asked Robert Cecil for the gift of his portrait 'to be placed in the gallery I lately made for the pictures of sundry of my

101

55. Hardwick Hall, Derbyshire (1590–6). The gallery, as depicted in 1835.

honourable friends, whose presentation thereby to behold will greatly delight me to walk often in that place where I may see so comfortable a sight.'[51]

The prominent display of Cecil's portrait—the equivalent of a signed photograph today—must also have demonstrated the importance of Lord Howard's connections to his visitors and neighbours. Although the Elizabethan upper classes were genuinely anxious to be morally and intellectually equipped for their responsibilities, they also had an eye for the main chance. Both portraits and galleries were used as pieces in the power game; galleries became status symbols as much as places of exercise. They grew longer, wider and higher (Pl. 55 and Col. Pl. VI). Although remaining almost unfurnished, they often approached the magnificence of a great chamber in their decoration. Sometimes they were next door to one; to have great chamber, withdrawing chamber, best bedchamber and gallery *en suite* on the first floor was the commonest Elizabethan and Jacobean recipe for magnificence. Sometimes they were on the second floor, usually above the great chamber, although occasionally this was built on the second floor as well.

A second-floor gallery had the advantage of the prospect. The gallery up under the roof at Montacute is terminated at either end by an oriel window from which those who walked in it could enjoy the view at the end of each 170 foot stretch (Pl. 46). The second-floor gallery at Worksop was a continuous lantern of glass raised fifty feet or so above the midland landscape. In fine weather promenaders could move higher still, and walk along the leads above it (Pl. 56). The Worksop gallery was 212 ft long and 36 ft wide. When it was built in the mid 1580s it was the largest gallery in England, but the competitive spirit of contemporaries was not going to let it remain so. In 1607 a correspondent described to the Earl of Shrewsbury, its owner, how he had recently visited the house that Lord Dunbar was building at Berwick, and 'heard (to use their own phrase) one of them creak, that Worksop gallery was but a garret in respect of the gallery that would there be.'[52]

Such splendid rooms naturally attracted extra functions. They tended to become supplements or alternatives to the great chamber, and be used for masques, games, and music. In 1601 Lord Petre's gallery at Ingatestone in Essex contained a shovelboard, fourteen feet long, in addition to six pictures, nine painted shields, and a few chairs and stools.[53] In 1607 one of Ben Jonson's masques was put on in the much grander gallery at Theobalds, to celebrate the handing over of the house to James I by the Earl of Salisbury.[54] The gallery at Apethorpe in Northamptonshire has an overmantel carved with King David playing the harp; underneath is the inscription:

> Rare and ever to be wished may sound here
> Instruments which faint spirits and muses cheer
> Composing for the body, soul and ear
> Which sickness sadness and foul spirits fear.

In contrast to the splendours of the great chamber, withdrawing chamber, and

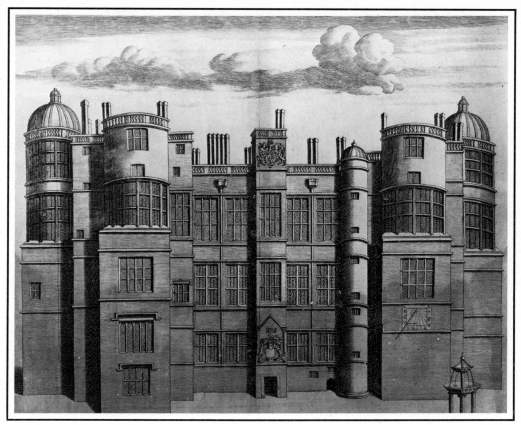

56. Worksop Manor, Derbyshire (*c.* 1580–5).

gallery up on the first or second floors were the parlour or parlours on the ground
floor. Parlours fulfilled much the same functions as in the Middle Ages, but more
houses had them, and they tended to be more handsomely decorated. Occasional
parlours still had beds in them (and were known as lodging parlours) but in
country houses their main use was as informal sitting and eating rooms. It is as
such that they appear in sixteenth-century literature. In the second book of the
Faerie Queene Spenser describes the parlour in the House of Temperance, and how

> in the midst thereof, upon the floor
> A lovely bevy of fair ladies sat,
> Courted of many a jolly paramour.[55]

In *The Taming of the Shrew* Bianca and the widow 'sit conferring by the parlour
fire', and in Sidney's *Arcadia* Kalander, when eating alone with Palladius, brings
him 'into the parlour where they used to sup'.[56] Parlours were used for dinner as
well as supper, and are sometimes called dining parlours on contemporary plans.
  Big houses often had several parlours. A small winter parlour, often near the
kitchen, was a common feature from at least the early seventeenth century. At
Longleat there was a string of three parlours letting off the dais end of the hall: the
great parlour, the little parlour, and the shovelboard parlour. The great parlour

was immediately under the great chamber, and of the same size; this was the commonest relationship between the two rooms, although in some houses the great chamber was over the hall. The name of the shovelboard parlour explains its use; it was the sixteenth-century equivalent of a billiards or games room.[57]

Notes made by Sir William Cecil in 1553, when he was living at Wimbledon, suggest that he and his family normally ate in the parlour, possibly with upper servants or at least with his wife's gentlewomen, but moved up to the great chamber on special occasions.[58] This was probably the commonest arrangement in houses with parlours through to the seventeenth century. But in some great houses the parlour was exclusively the room where the upper servants ate—an arrangement which may also have been found in the Middle Ages. At Knole in 1613–24 some twenty-one upper servants ate at one table in the parlour: they included the steward, the chaplain, the gentleman of the horse, the gentleman usher, the auditor, the secretary, two English and one French page and 'My Lord's Favourite'.[59] The earl and countess seem never to have eaten in the parlour although the earl may occasionally have sat there with his gentlemen. There was a similar arrangement at the Earl of Bridgwater's Ashridge in 1652; only upper servants ate in the parlour, and the earl laid down in his regulations that 'if any of my servants have been guilty of so much pride . . . as to exalt themselves (without direction therein received from me . . .) from the table in the hall to the table in the parlour, I expect they should withdraw from that place.'[60]

R. B.'s comment, made in the early years of the seventeenth century, that 'noble men in these days (for the most part) like better to be served with pages and groomes, than in that estate which belongeth to their degrees' has already been quoted.[61] This change in attitude led to an increasing reluctance to eat in state in the great chamber. In houses where the parlour was an upper servants' room the great chamber was sometimes replaced or supplemented by a much less grand dining chamber on the first floor. Such a change had taken place by 1634 at the Earl of Huntingdon's Donington Park in Leicestershire; the earl's dining chamber was simply fitted up, without tapestry or richly-upholstered furniture and his great chamber had been turned into a bedchamber.[62] But in most houses the shift was from great chamber to parlour. Parlours grew proportionately more important, until by the end of the sixteenth and beginning of the seventeenth century their ceilings and chimney-pieces were often not so very much less elaborate than those in the great chamber on the floor above (Pl. 57).

The tendency towards rather more privacy and rather less state, exemplified in the increasing use of parlours, can also be seen in the growing popularity of the banquet. The banquet was an institution which flourished greatly under Elizabeth, but its origins stretch back into the Middle Ages. It was often an intimate rather than a formal function, and bore no relation to a banquet in the modern sense of a sumptuous feast (although, confusingly, this other use of the word also existed in the sixteenth century).

The origins of banquets of this type go back to the mediaeval ceremony of the void.[63] This was originally a way of passing the time until the hall or great

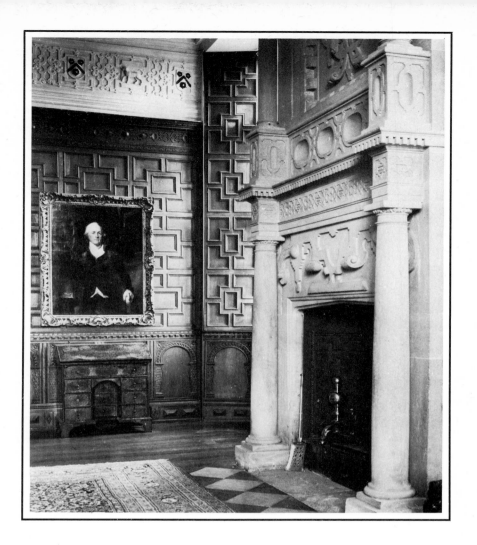

chamber had been prepared for after-dinner activities; a collation of sweet wine and spices was eaten standing while the table was being cleared or 'voided' after a meal. In the later seventeenth century when words of French origin became fashionable, 'void' was replaced by a French word of much the same meaning, 'dessert'. By then spiced delicacies were often replaced or supplemented by fruit. Once withdrawing chambers came into use the void or dessert was often served in them; college dons still retire from the dais in the hall at the end of dinner to eat dessert in the senior common room. But sometimes it was served in a special room, or in a turret on the roof or a building in the garden, and was known as a banquet.

Banquets in this sense were not confined to the after-meal period, although this was the commonest time to have them; they could be served at any time (like coffee and biscuits today), often to quite small parties of people. The list of exotic food suitable for banquets, given in Gervase Markham's *The English Housewife*, includes paste of quinces, quince cakes, quinces in syrup, ipocras, jelly, leech, gingerbread, marmalade, jumbals, biscuit-bread, cinnamon sticks, cinnamon

105

57. Montacute House, Somerset (William Arnold, *c.* 1595–1601). The parlour.

water, wormwood water, sugar-plate, spice cakes, Banbury cakes, marzipan, paste of Genoa, and suckets.[64] Something a little fanciful was always appreciated. Markham recommended that 'you shall first send forth a dish made for show only, as Beast, Bird, Fish, Fowl, according to invention'. Banquets were, in fact, a suitable vehicle for devices.

In the octagonal tower which Sir William Sharington added in about 1550 to his converted abbey buildings at Lacock in Wiltshire, there were two banqueting rooms. One was approached through the main rooms of the house, the other, on the floor above it, was only approachable by an external walk across the leads. Both contain octagonal stone tables, delicately carved with Renaissance beasts and ornament (Col. Pl. VIII); neither room could conceivably fit more than six people. The climb, the walk and the view must have made an agreeable after-dinner impression on Sharington's guests, including his friend Sir John Thynne of Longleat. In the 1560s Thynne scattered the roofscape at Longleat with little domed banqueting turrets, some square and some octagonal, and none of them much bigger than the rooms in the tower at Lacock (Pl. 58).

The after-dinner alternative to a climb up to the roof was a walk in the garden. All Elizabethan gardens of any consequence contained a banqueting house, which was sometimes used for meals as well as banquets. Banqueting houses tended to be of fanciful architecture, like the food served in them. Some were raised up on an arcade, for the benefit of the view. Some were in especially retired or unusual sites, and acquired other functions. The late-sixteenth-century banqueting house built on the edge of the great pool at Callowdon House in Warwickshire was 'the polite work of the Lady Elizabeth, wife of Sir Thomas Berkeley ... and the retired cell of her soul's soliloquies to God her creator.'[65] In about 1570 Richard Carew projected (but never built) a banqueting house on an island in the salt-water pond below his house at Anthony, in Cornwall. 'That perfectly accomplished gentleman, the late Sir Arthur Champernowne', devised it for him. The island was square, with round projections at each corner; the banqueting house had the same ground plan, but contained a round room within the square; above was a round turret containing a square room. There was a platform round the turret, and space off the two rooms for a little kitchen, a staircase, a store for fishing rods, and 'cupboards and boxes, for keeping other necessary utensils towards these fishing feasts'.[66]

Some banqueting houses were minute, others contained several rooms. The banqueting house built in about 1580–5 at Holdenby, only a hundred yards or so from the great house, was three storeys high and had six rooms to a floor; it was more a lodge than a banqueting house.[67] The point at which one shaded into the other was not always clear. Most big Elizabethan and Jacobean houses were within a hundred yards to a mile of a lodge, often with a deer-park attached to it. Such lodges were in the tradition of the lodges and self-contained towers of the Middle Ages, and suggest the practice of keeping 'secret house'. They could be used either as a destination for outings from the main house or as a place of residence, when the family wished to live in retirement or the main household

106

58. (right) Turrets and banqueting houses of 1568–9 on the roof at Longleat, Wiltshire.

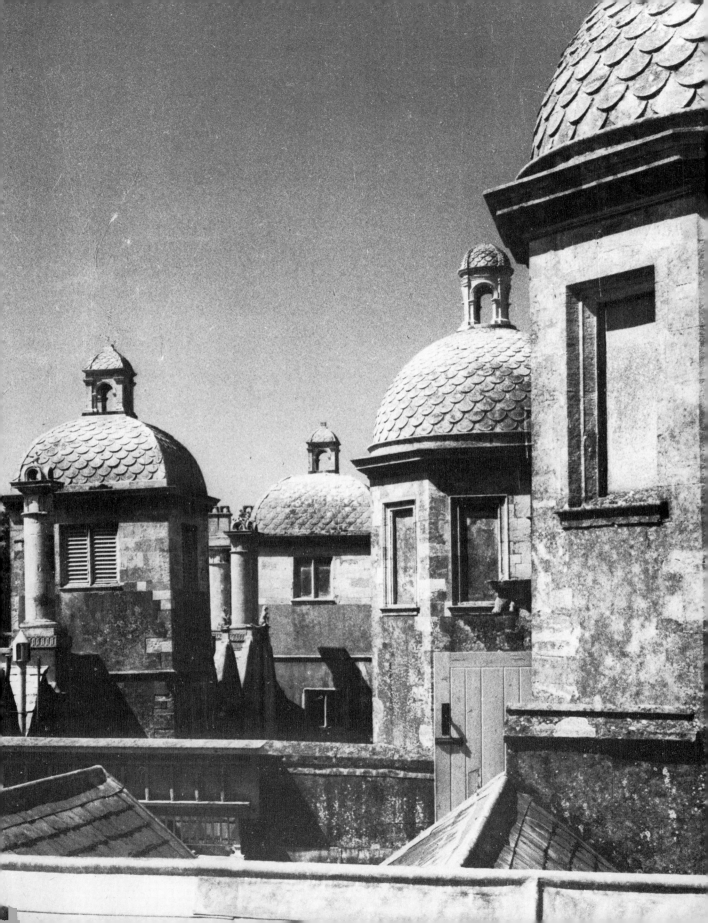

was elsewhere. Like banqueting houses (and like the hunting lodges which families often built in complete isolation from their main houses) their architecture was often fanciful, in sympathy with their holiday function. They were 'devices'. The lodge which Sir Walter Raleigh built half a mile away from his castle at Sherborne in Dorset had four pentagonal towers; the lodge at Wothorpe, which Lord Exeter built in the early seventeenth century a mile or so away from Burleigh 'to retire to out of the dust while his great house was a sweeping'[68] was built on a plan of a Greek cross, with four slender towers in its four internal angles (Pl. 59). The lodge which Sir Thomas Tresham began to build, but never finished, a few hundred yards from his house at Lyveden in Northamptonshire is also cross-shaped, and is delicately carved with emblems of the Passion. The little Triangular Lodge at his other house at Rushton is covered with mystic signs and numbers, all in multiples of three, in honour of the Trinity (Col. Pl. IX). But the Triangular Lodge, in spite of its name, was built as an especially fanciful and beautiful banqueting house rather than as a lodge.[69]

There is another cross-shaped lodge at Worksop in Nottinghamshire probably built in the 1590s by the seventh Earl of Shrewsbury. It is a little less than a mile from Worksop Manor—itself a lodge by origin, but enormously enlarged by the earl's father in the 1580s. The relationship between the two buildings is reminiscent of that between the lodges of Basilius and his daughter Pamela in Sidney's *Arcadia*:

> the lodge . . . is built in the form of a star, having round about a garden framed into like points; and beyond the garden ridings cut out, each answering the angles of the lodge. At the end of one of them is the other smaller lodge, but of like fashion, where the gracious Pamela liveth; so that the lodge seemeth not unlike a fair comet, whose tail stretcheth itself to a star of less greatness.[70]

Basilius's lodge was 'truly a place for pleasantness, not unfit to flatter solitariness'. Lodges were often built in secluded or remote situations, and were, as a result, lonely and romantic places—or for those unattracted by loneliness, melancholy places, so that Shakespeare could use the phrase 'as melancholy as a lodge in a warren'.[71] Their seclusion and separation from the coming and going of the big houses made them useful places for private meetings; in August 1590, for instance, when the great Irish rebel or patriot, the Earl of Tyrone, spent a mysterious night alone with the Earl of Derby, the earl left his main household at Knowsley and went to his lodge in the New Park at Lathom to entertain him.[72]

By their nature, lodges were not designed to accommodate large numbers of people. But by the end of the sixteenth century even large houses tended to have slightly fewer lodgings than they would have done a hundred years previously. It was an inevitable result of rather smaller households, combined with visitors who arrived with a rather smaller number of attendants. But all houses of any size had to have one set of lodgings of considerable splendour for an important guest. The best lodgings normally consisted of a withdrawing chamber, a bedchamber and an inner chamber beyond the great chamber; although this position was sometimes occupied by the family's own lodgings, they were more often in

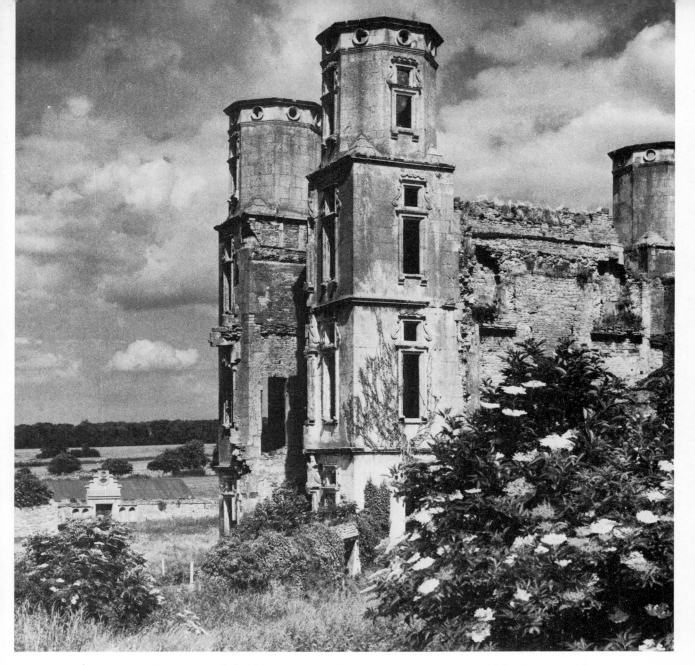

another part of the house. A really important guest would take over the great chamber as well as the best lodgings; some great houses still had two great chambers, one attached to the family lodgings and the other to the best lodgings, as in the later Middle Ages.

It was politic to make the best lodgings as handsome as possible. In addition to important friends and family connections, its occupants might include judges, privy councillors or officers of the government, sometimes coming on a specific mission from the monarch; it was important that they should go away feeling satisfied with their reception. And of course sometimes the visitor was the monarch in person.

59. Wothorpe, Northamptonshire (*c.* 1610).

Royal visitors were the one exception to the tendency of the great to travel with fewer people, and, moreover, in the sixteenth century the possibility of a royal visit became greater. Elizabeth, in particular, did little to maintain or bring up to date her numerous royal manors outside the metropolitan area. Instead, on her annual progresses, she preferred to park herself on her loyal subjects. It was a useful way of making her presence felt on the cheap, but for her subjects it was a doubtful honour. Against the possible advantages of royal favour was the appalling risk of an unsuccessful visit, and the inevitable and equally appalling expense. On occasions Elizabeth may have calculated her visits for political reasons; a long and ruinously expensive visit was a useful way of getting over-powerful subjects into such financial difficulties that the sting was taken out of them.

The size of royal lodgings in royal palaces had expanded considerably since the fifteenth century. Henry VII still used his great chamber in much the same way as his richer subjects, but under Henry VIII the process of withdrawal and subdivision entered a new phase.[73] The functions of the great chamber were taken over by a new room called the presence chamber; the great chamber became a guard chamber for the newly-founded yeomen of the guard. By then the privy chamber had ceased to be a bedchamber and became a private dining and reception chamber, with a withdrawing chamber between it and the royal bedchamber.

The process of withdrawal continued under Elizabeth. She ate more and more in the privy chamber, at the expense of the presence chamber. Her curious combination of actual withdrawal with ceremonial presence is described by Thomas Platter, a visiting German who was at the palace of Nonsuch in 1599.[74] He saw the royal table prepared for dinner in the presence chamber, to the accompaniment of all the usual ceremonies laid down in the Harleian and similar regulations. The first course was then brought in by forty yeomen of the guard. But the queen was not in the room and never appeared; she was at a separate table in her privy chamber. Sayes were taken, wine and beer were poured, three courses and a dessert were served, all with full ceremony to an imaginary queen at an empty table. At the end of each serving a portion of the food or drink was taken up and carried through to the actual queen next door. Finally 'the queen's musicians appeared in the presence chamber with their trumpets and shawms, and after they had performed their music, everyone withdrew.'

The royal coats of arms to be found incorporated in the decoration of many sixteenth-century great chambers underline their possible role as a chamber of state during a royal visit.[75] But it would have been absurd for most landowners, even when they rebuilt their houses, to supply anything approaching full accommodation for royalty on the off-chance of a visit. Most people hoped to get by with a handsome great chamber and accompanying lodgings for the queen; they gave over the remaining lodgings to her senior courtiers, and fitted in the rest of her entourage in surrounding houses or temporary accommodation. Some, like Sir Nicholas Bacon at Gorhambury, were given sufficient warning and hastily built on an extra wing. A few others responded in more sensational fashion, either because their loyalty was in doubt and had to be proved, or because they had a special connection with the Crown, or were in hopes of getting one.

In 1591 Elizabeth visited Edward Seymour, Earl of Hertford, at Elvetham in Hampshire. The earl was politically suspect; in early life he had spent nine years in the Tower as a result of having married Lady Jane Grey's sister, Catherine, whom some thought had a better claim to the crown than Elizabeth. The visit may have been intended as a chastening one, and the earl responded, of necessity, with lavish expressions of loyalty which very nearly bankrupted him. Apart from filling four days with festivities and peppering the surroundings to the house with a sham-castle on a lake and other recreational ornaments, he hurriedly ran up a shanty town of temporary buildings to supplement the inadequate accommodation of his mainly mediaeval house. These included a room of state and withdrawing chamber for the queen and her attendant nobles; a large hall for 'knights, ladies, and gentlemen of chief account'; various other large rooms or 'bowers' for his own servants and the queen's servants, footmen, and guards; and a buttery, spicery, larder, chandlery, ewery, pantry, wine cellar, boiling house, pantry 'with five ovens . . . some of them fourteen foot deep' and two great kitchens, one with 'a very long range for the waiters to serve all comers' in the best style of mediaeval hospitality.[76]

The situation of Lord Burghley was in a different class, and although even more expensive had its substantial rewards. Elizabeth visited him thirteen times at Theobalds, and Burghley obediently enlarged the house to make it, in effect, an alternative royal palace. Once the visits became regular, enlargement was imperative. A list of accommodation made by Burghley in 1583, when Theobalds was still a large but not unusually large Elizabethan house, shows the inconvenience to which a royal visit put him. The queen travelled with a substantial number of government officials as well as her personal attendants. Burghley had to find lodgings for twenty-four courtiers and members of the Privy Council (and, of course, their servants), including the Lord High Admiral, the Secretary of State and the Earl of Leicester; the last had special accommodation at the other end of a gallery off the queen's bedchamber. Other accommodation was required for the queen's gentlemen ushers, gentlewomen and grooms of the privy chamber, gentlewomen of the bedchamber, squires of the body, clerk of the kitchen, cooks, officers of the cellar and pantry, and groom porter. The total involved must have been somewhere in the region of 150 people, and much of the house had to be vacated by Lord Burghley and his household to make way for them. The queen took over his hall, parlour and great chamber as her own great chamber, presence chamber and privy chamber; Burghley removed his own table from the great chamber to a subsidiary gallery. His servants were pushed out of the hall and had to eat in the joiners' workshop; his steward removed from his lodgings to make way for the royal plate; other servants gave up their rooms and slept on pallets in a dormitory converted from a storehouse.[77]

At the time of this visit Burghley had already started to build a splendid new courtyard which was to solve these problems of accommodation by doubling the

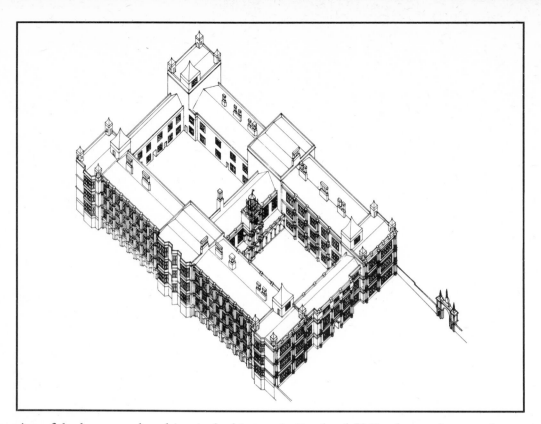

size of the house and making it the biggest in England.[78] But he made enough out of his various offices to more than pay for his building activities. Others were hopeful, but not so fortunate. In 1579 Burghley congratulated and condoled with Sir Christopher Hatton, the Lord Chancellor, on his equally enormous house at Holdenby (Pl. 60). 'God send us both long to enjoy her', he wrote, 'for whom we both meant to exceed our purses in these.'[79] More than loyalty lay behind the hope, for such houses could only be financed out of long years of office and profits. Hatton was a bachelor; he had no need for a house not so very much smaller than Hampton Court, and fell into appalling debt by building it. It stood, little used but full of waiting servants, for ten years, during which the queen never once visited it. Hatton died in 1591, aged only fifty-one. He left the house, estates, and debts to a nephew who could not afford to live there; the house was sold to James I in 1605 and was pulled down in the mid seventeenth century.

Burghley's son Robert Cecil, later Earl of Salisbury, was almost equally unlucky. When he built his great house at Hatfield in the early years of the seventeenth century, its plan was carefully devised in anticipation that he would frequently be entertaining James I and his queen. He died in 1612, aged forty-eight, when the house was only just finished. Not only did James I never visit it during Salisbury's lifetime, but the latter, in spite of making profits out of his offices that were considered excessive even by the standards of the early seventeenth century, had insufficient time to acquire estates on the scale he had planned for.[80] The Cecils entered on a slow decline until the 1820s, when marriage with an heiress relaunched the family on a new burst of power and prosperity.

60. A reconstruction of Holdenby House, Northamptonshire (c. 1575–80).

61. (right) Audley End, Essex (begun 1603). The porches.

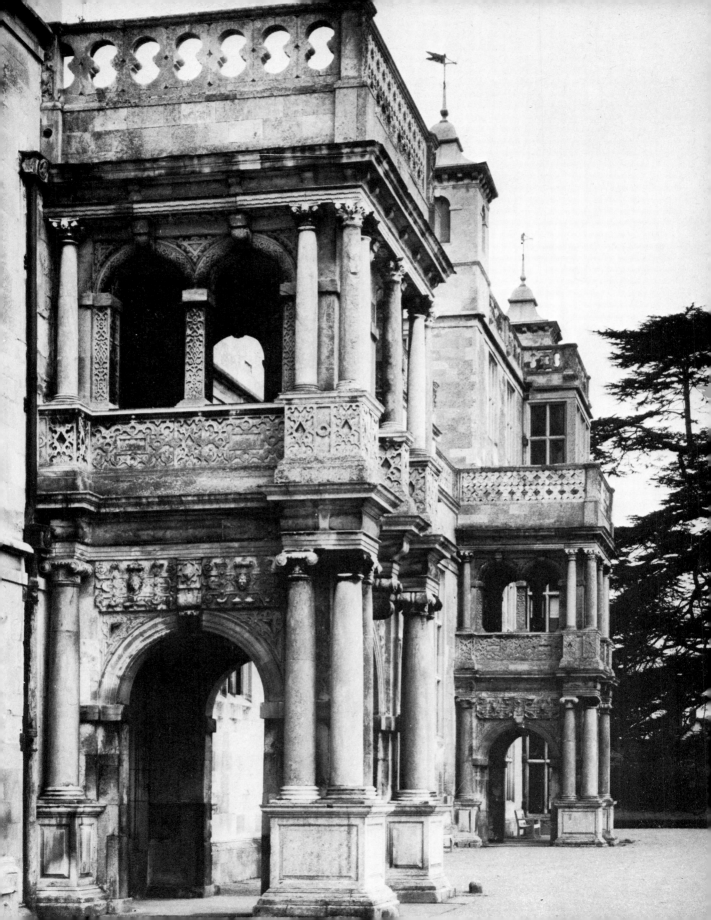

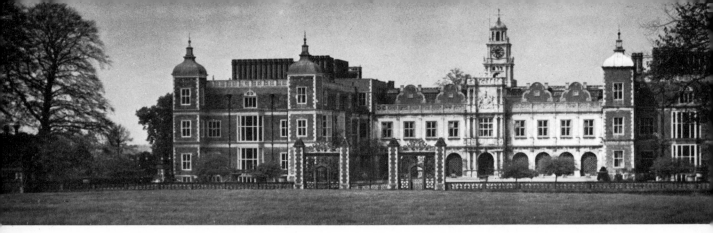

Hope of a special connection with James I also prompted the building of Audley End by Thomas Howard, Earl of Suffolk. At the beginning of his reign James relied heavily on the Howard family, and Suffolk probably saw Audley End as playing the role of Theobalds in a Jacobean context; the house was just as large and even more elaborately finished. At first all went well; and in 1614 Suffolk was appointed Lord Treasurer, as Burghley had been before him, and started milking his job for profit far more lavishly than Burghley had ever done. But James seems only to have visited Audley End once. In 1618 Suffolk, and the whole Howard clan with him, fell out of favour, was prosecuted for embezzlement and lost all his offices. Audley End became as much of a white elephant as Holdenby; after a brief spell as a royal residence half the house was pulled down in 1721, and the rest sold in 1751 in a semi-derelict condition.

These great houses with royal or would-be royal connections tended to follow the mediaeval arrangement, and be built round two or more courtyards, with a hall filling most of the middle range of the main courtyard. At Holdenby the queen's lodgings were to one side of the hall, beyond its dais end, and ran the whole length of the show front to the garden; Hatton's lodgings, with their own great chamber, were on the other side of the hall.[81] By the time Audley End was built the monarch was no longer single, and the main division in the house was between king and queen, rather than between monarch and subject. Suffolk probably had his own lodgings on the ground floor, and on the first floor the king and queen each had their own side, entered by its own magnificent porch (Pl. 61) and separated by a common hall and gallery.[82]

The courtyard plan remained in use into the seventeenth century, especially for larger houses. Courtyard houses usually incorporated a long gallery, sometimes with an open gallery beneath it; symmetry became the rule for all the main facades; and the house kept up with the times by a show of classical ornament or fashionable Flemish strapwork. Sometimes the lodgings round the court were built two rooms thick, rather than one as in the Middle Ages.[83] Sometimes they were linked by closed corridors or galleries, instead of having their own doors into the court; these gave no more privacy to the lodgings than they had had under the old arrangement, but made them considerably more convenient to get to.

Increasingly, however, there was a tendency for even large houses to do without courtyards and cohere into a single dominating symmetrical mass. Houses of this kind developed for a number of reasons. Security, which had made

114

62. Hatfield House, Hertfordshire (1607–12). The south front.

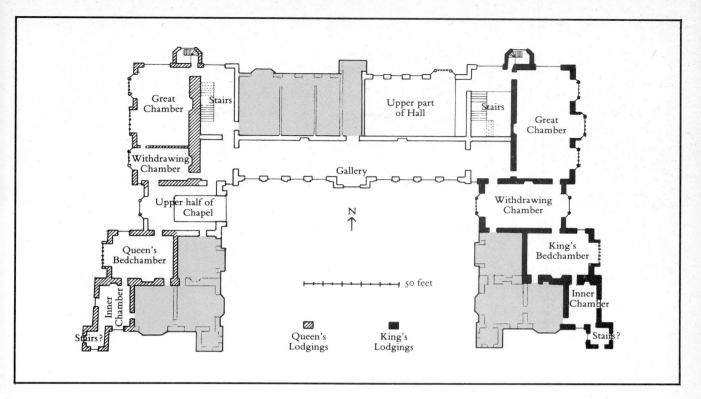

an internal courtyard, with rooms mostly looking into it, a sensible idea in the Middle Ages, was no longer important. The tendency for both households and the entourages of visitors to get smaller meant that fewer lodgings were needed. Earlier compact hunting lodges may have suggested the advantages of compression; some of the first examples (such as Worksop) were in fact designed as very grand hunting lodges, rather than to accommodate full-scale households (Pl. 56). But the main reason for the popularity of the type was probably aesthetic and symbolic. Houses which had been compressed into one soaring and stately whole were an irresistible advertisement of the dignity and glory of their owners.

By the early seventeenth century the compact house had become so prestigious that even Hatfield, with all its royal ambitions, was built as one (Pl. 62). The retention of the mediaeval bishop's palace a few yards from the new house made it possible to use the old buildings for subsidiary lodgings, in the event of a royal visit. The new house was built as, in effect, an immensely grand pavilion containing little but lodgings for the family and for the king and queen (Fig. 4). The royal lodgings, each with its own great chamber, were at either end of the house, up on the first floor and connected by a grand gallery; Lord Salisbury's lodgings were on the ground floor, beneath the king's and off the great parlour. The chimney-piece in the king's great chamber was suitably decorated with a statue of the king; in the same position in the queen's great chamber there was a mosaic portrait of Lord Salisbury, underlining the fact that Salisbury, rich though he was, baulked at providing three great chambers and used it as his own great chamber in the royal absence. The two royal lodgings each had, in fact, two sets of furnishings so that, when royalty left, the royal furniture could be carried out and the commoner's furniture brought in.[84]

115

Fig. 4. King's side and queen's side on the first floor of Hatfield House.

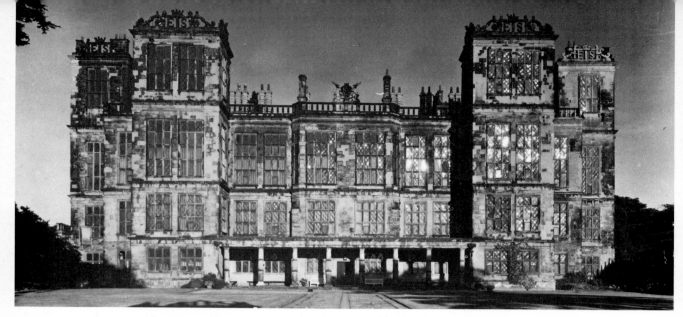

The second floor at Hatfield contained lower unpretentious rooms for servants and for Lord Salisbury's children. But at some great Elizabethan and Jacobean houses hierarchy of height matched hierarchy of state, and the grand rooms were pushed up onto the second floor. The finest surviving example of this arrangement is at Hardwick, a house which epitomizes so many aspects of Elizabethan life and architecture that its survival in relatively unaltered form can only be regarded as miraculous.[85]

The formidable Bess of Hardwick started to build it in 1590. By then she was the Dowager-Countess of Shrewsbury and the richest woman in England after the queen. As at Hatfield there was an existing house next door to the new site, which could be used to provide extra lodgings for servants and less important guests. The fact that Bess retained the old house, and that the great rooms in the new one were on a scale unequalled even at Theobalds and Holdenby suggest that she was in hopes of a special connection with royalty. No such connection existed, or was likely to develop, with the ageing Elizabeth. If Bess had expectations they must have been pinned on her grand-daughter Arabella Stuart, who still had a chance (which Bess may have exaggerated) of bypassing her cousin James and succeeding Elizabeth as Queen of England.

At the new Hardwick (Pl. 63), kitchens, hall, chapel, two great chambers, numerous lodgings, a gallery and two banqueting rooms were compressed onto a base plan so relatively compact that the house had to be a storey higher than usual to fit them in. As far as state and ceremony went, this was no disadvantage. The main great chamber, the gallery and the best lodgings were up on the second floor; the lesser great chamber, Bess's own lodgings and those of her son and of Arabella Stuart were on the first floor, where the rooms were considerably less grand; kitchens, servants' rooms and nursery occupied the ground floor, where the rooms were not grand at all (Pl. 64). The house is two rooms thick, and a two-storey hall pierces through its middle instead of running along its front. This variant on mediaeval practice, which ingeniously increased the symmetry of the plan, was probably inspired by the similar plan of the much smaller banqueting house or lodge at Holdenby.[86] And like so many lodges, Hardwick was a

63. Hardwick Hall, Derbyshire (Robert Smythson, 1590–6). The west front.
64. (upper right) Isometric drawing of Hardwick.
65. (right) Hardwick Hall. The High Great Chamber in 1835.

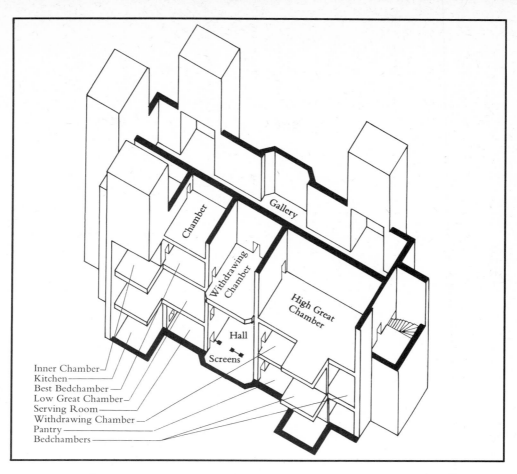

Chamber

Gallery

Withdrawing Chamber

High Great Chamber

Hall

Screens

Inner Chamber
Kitchen
Best Bedchamber
Low Great Chamber
Serving Room
Withdrawing Chamber
Pantry
Bedchambers

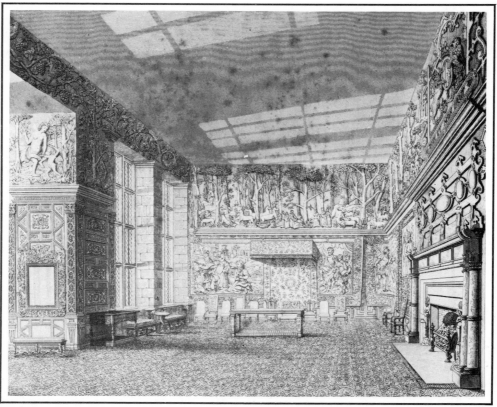

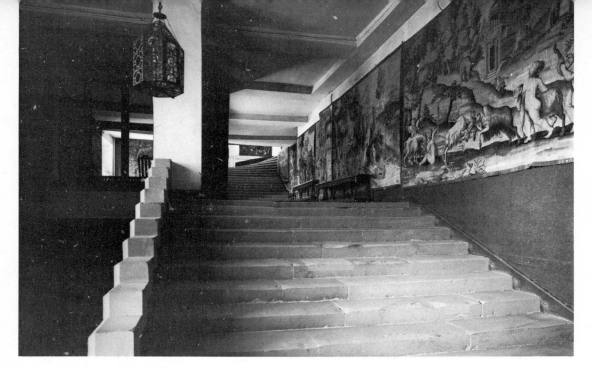

'device'; its plan resembling two linked Greek crosses, each with a tower at the end of three of its arms, was calculated to delight and surprise from both near and far.

One pay-off of the design was that it produced a grand processional route, from the kitchen, through the hall, up an extraordinarily dramatic and romantic stone staircase to the huge High Great Chamber at the top of the house (Pls 65, 66 and Col. Pl. X). Here the royal arms over the chimney-piece, and the court of Diana filling one side of the frieze which runs round the room, proclaimed Bess's loyalty and waited for the royal visit which never came in her lifetime. Meanwhile, Bess probably presided over the High Great Chamber herself on great occasions, and certainly paced with Arabella up and down the gallery.[87] As she did so, she could look at the alabaster figures of Justice and Mercy over the chimney-pieces and be encouraged to be just and merciful herself; or scan the portraits of her husbands and their increasingly powerful connections, and meditate on the mysterious movements of destiny which had raised her from the obscure daughter of an indigent squire to the position of what Horace Walpole called 'a costly countess'. Higher still, up on the leads of the roof, it was possible for her to contemplate the modest lands which her family had inherited, and the many lands which she had acquired by marriage or purchase, and pass on to a banquet in an elegantly decorated banqueting room in one of the six surrounding turrets.

From the outside the ascending hierarchy of a floor for the servants, a floor for the family and a floor for state is precisely expressed in the escalating height of the great windows on each floor. The surrounding ring of towers is reminiscent of the circuit of towers which enclosed houses like Raby Castle, and yet has in an abundant degree the 'order and proportion' which Raby had so noticeably lacked. For Hardwick was the ordered and compacted culmination of a way of life that went back deep into the Middle Ages. But glittering and splendid though it was, within fifty years of its completion it was to seem completely out of date.

66. Hardwick Hall. The staircase.

67. (right) Capheaton Hall, Northumberland (Robert Trollope, 1668). From a contemporary painting.

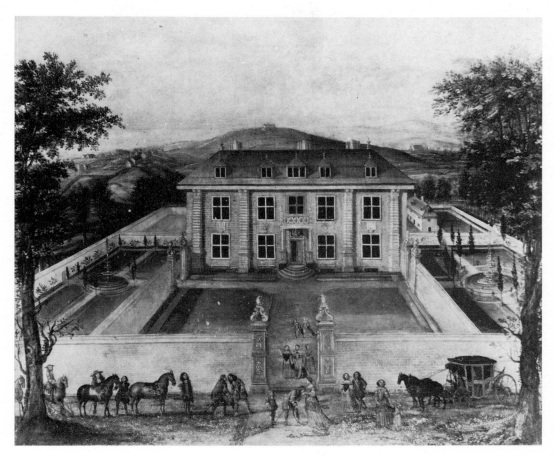

5   *The Formal House: 1630-1720*

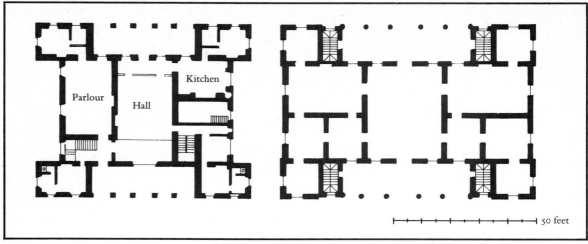

Fig. 5. A plan by John Thorpe based on (right) Palladio's Villa Valmarana.

IMPRESSIVE though Hardwick is, the symmetry of the exterior sits a little uneasily on the planning of the interior. Several of the great windows are false, and have chimney-pieces built across their inside face. Others have a mezzanine inserted behind them, so that they rise through two floors of low-ceilinged rooms instead of lighting a single lofty one. The High Great Chamber is the ceremonial centre of the house but it is not actually at the centre, but over to one side. This kind of discrepancy would have passed unnoticed in the Middle Ages; but once the idea that architectural order should reflect social order had begun to take root, symmetry was bound to be carried further.

In the course of the seventeenth century it *was* carried further. Its development was helped along by Palladio, whose influence first appeared in England in the decades around 1600. At first it affected the plans of country houses rather than their appearance. One of the main types of plan in his *Quattro Libri di Architettura* is one in which the centre of a house is filled by two large rooms, one above the other, with smaller rooms arranged symmetrically to either side of them. However Palladio intended this kind of plan to be used, to English eyes it immediately suggested a central great chamber above a central hall—an exquisitely appropriate arrangement, in which the owner of the house, dining in state in the great chamber, would not only be at the centre of the house, but also immediately above his household, dining with fitting but subordinate order in the hall below him.

The London surveyor, John Thorpe, produced a number of designs in which Palladian planning was adapted on these lines, but was combined with Jacobean or late Elizabethan detail (Fig. 5).[1] One house corresponding to the designs has survived, and a number of similar houses by unidentified designers are still in existence.[2] In them, and in Thorpe's plans, Palladian symmetry largely disappears once it comes to the arrangement of the rooms to either side of the two central areas. The usual English arrangement of especially grand lodgings for important visitors and rather less grand lodgings for the family did not adapt well to symmetrical pairing.

120

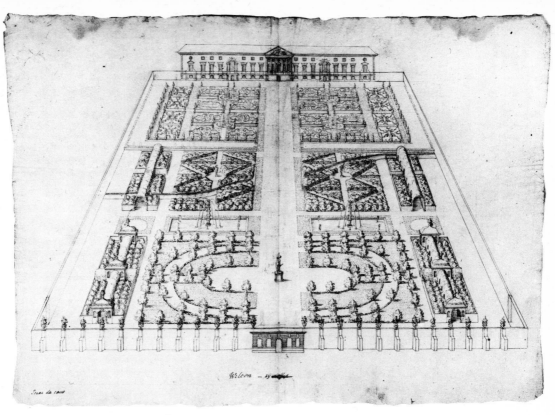

68. The original design (*c.* 1633) for the front of Wilton House, Wiltshire.

There was, however, one English context for which the arrangement was appropriate. This was the planning of palaces. A queen was normally the pledge and symbol of alliance with another nation. Unlike the wife of a commoner she had to be housed in independent state and on the same kind of scale as her husband. Once symmetrical planning began to be appreciated, the idea of balancing king's lodgings with queen's lodgings was bound to arise. As described in the last chapter, this kind of pairing can be found at Hatfield and Audley End, houses designed for the regular entertainment of royalty rather than palaces. But it was obtained by rather clumsily doubling the traditional English plan. The Palladian arrangement adapted better to pairing than the English one, and before long it replaced it.

One of the first recorded uses in England was, once again, in a private house planned for the entertainment of royalty. This was at Wilton, in the reign of Charles I. As John Aubrey put it 'King Charles I did love Wilton above all places and came thither every summer. It was he that did put Philip first Earl of Pembroke, upon making the magnificent garden and grotto, and to new build that side of the house that fronts the garden.' The new building was designed in about 1633, probably by Isaac de Caus, but heavily under the influence of Inigo Jones.[3] Its detail was Palladian as well as its planning. There is in fact no certain evidence for the plan, since only the elevation survives (Pl. 68). But this suggests that the new building was intended to contain a king's end and a queen's end to either side of a central room of state, where the two could meet. In fact, the design was never fully carried out. In 1640 the king fell out with Lord Pembroke and sacked him from his office of Lord Chamberlain. The royal family ceased to come to Wilton. Lord Pembroke scrapped the portico and the great room behind it, and built less than one half of the design, for himself.

The Stuarts were perpetually short of funds. In a royal context, although much was planned, the only example of this Palladian type to get built during the first half of the seventeenth century was a relatively modest building at Newmarket, designed in about 1620 for the Prince of Wales.[4] But the formula soon began to move down the social scale. There was something irresistibly attractive not only about the symmetry of its planning but about the way the function of the great chamber as a room of state could be expressed externally by facing it with a splendid and stately portico—or at least a pediment, with the arms of the owner prominently carved in its tympanum. As Roger North pointed out later in the century, in Roman days the pediment was a sign of rank; it was a status-symbol 'which few Romans were allowed, being a piece of state, and was called *fastigium domus*, than which nothing is more proper or agreeable.'[5]

There is a good example of a porticoed great chamber at Raynham Hall, in Norfolk. Raynham was built in the 1630s (and possibly started even earlier) by an up-to-date but not especially grand owner, Sir Roger Townshend. It is rather more Palladian than anything designed by Thorpe, but rather less Palladian than Wilton or the prince's lodgings at Newmarket. The position of the great chamber is prominently advertised by a first floor pediment surmounting a row of Ionic columns (Pl. 69). To either side of this were originally more or less matching lodgings, each consisting of withdrawing chamber, bedchamber and closets.[6] In other respects the plan did not follow Palladio. The great chamber was above the chapel, not the hall; the hall was on the other side of the house, with offices and other lodgings to either side of it.

Pediments and columns on the scale of Raynham were expensive, and may even have seemed presumptuous for a commoner. In about 1650 Roger Pratt designed a plainer version of the Palladian type for his cousin, Sir George Pratt, at Coleshill in Berkshire. Pratt was a gentleman amateur, fresh back from five years in France and Italy. He knew what was happening on the continent, but he also knew the needs of English country gentlemen. Coleshill was a brilliant attempt to supply these on the basis of a balanced plan derived from continental models (Fig. 6). The house (Pl. 70) was raised up on a basement. Above this, its centre was occupied by a two-storey hall leading to a great parlour on the ground floor and a great chamber above. This relationship of parlour to great chamber was a traditional one, but Pratt moved the two rooms from their traditional position on one side and placed them in the centre. 'Let the fairest room above', he wrote, 'be placed in the very midst of the house, as the bulk of a man is between his members.'[7]

The rest of the two main floors was divided into sets of rooms, each consisting of a larger room with two small inner rooms or closets off it. Pratt intended this

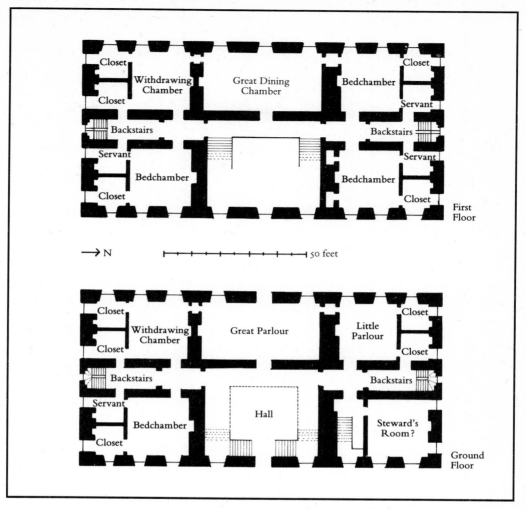

Closet | Withdrawing Chamber | Great Dining Chamber | Bedchamber | Closet
Closet | | | | Servant
Backstairs | | | Backstairs
Servant | | | Servant
Bedchamber | | Bedchamber
Closet | | Closet

First Floor

→ N   50 feet

Closet | Withdrawing Chamber | Great Parlour | Little Parlour | Closet
Closet | | | | Closet
Backstairs | | | Backstairs
Servant | | Hall | Steward's Room?
Bedchamber | | |
Closet |

Ground Floor

combination to be a flexible one, in which the larger room could be used either as parlour, withdrawing room, or bedroom. On the lower floor two of the sets were to be withdrawing chamber and a little parlour, with separate closets off for husband and wife. In case of need the withdrawing chamber could be turned into a bedchamber, complete with closets, and the little parlour be used as a withdrawing chamber. On all floors there was access to rooms and lodgings from long central corridors, running from end to end of the house. Although by this date corridors were familiar enough in England, the logical simplicity of their arrangement at Coleshill was something new.

The problem of how to fit the main staircase into a symmetrical plan was solved by putting it into the great hall. This made the hall an unsuitable room for meals. The servants were accordingly removed into a servants' hall, next to the kitchen, cellar and offices in the basement—a momentous break with tradition of which more will be said later. The hall became a superb room of entry, and a proud means of ascent or introduction to the parlour and great chamber (Pl. 71).

Externally, the 'fairest rooms' in the centre were expressed only by a wider spacing of their windows, and by pediments and flights of steps to emphasise the

Fig. 6. Coleshill House. Suggested original arrangement.

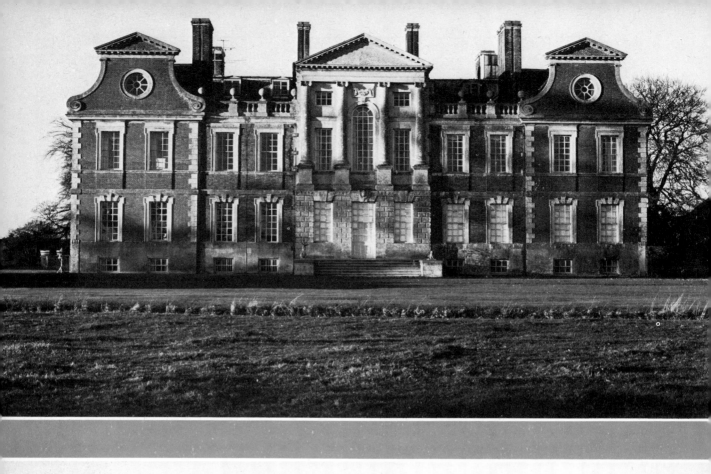

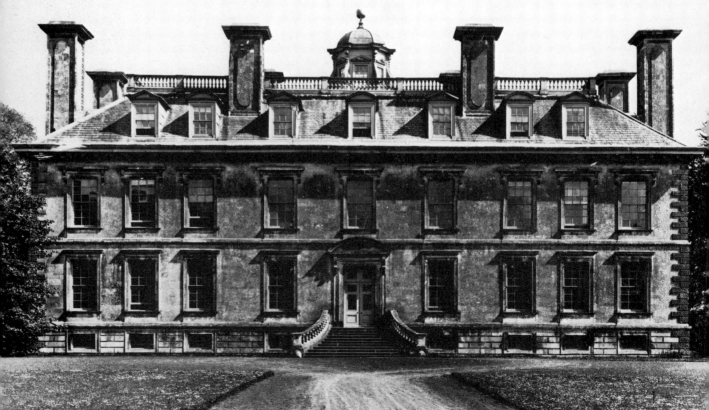

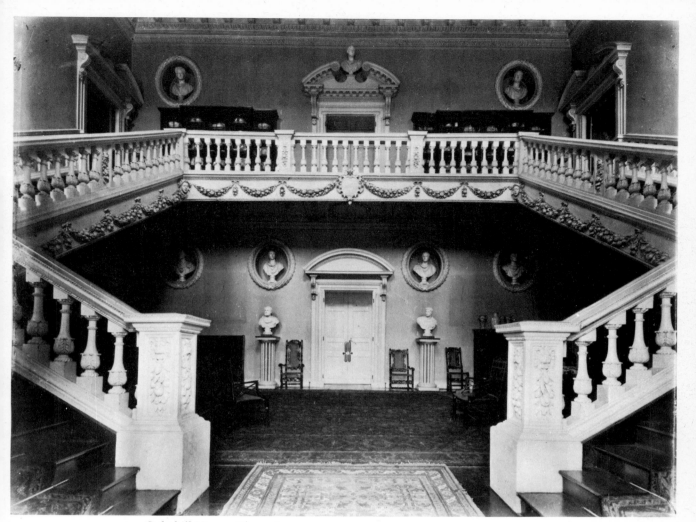

71. Coleshill House. The staircase.

doors into hall and great parlour. There was no large pediment or applied order; there was not even a break in the facade. The house was a single handsome block, capped by a noble hipped roof. The roof was filled with smaller lodgings, lit by dormer windows, punctuated by massive chimney-stacks, and surmounted by an octagonal cupola. This modestly handsome symbol of authority also served as a gazebo or banqueting room, with access to the railed-in promenade of the leads.

After the Restoration Pratt designed three more houses in quick succession.[8] They were all based on his Coleshill formula, but with variations. In all of them the central rooms were expressed more strongly than at Coleshill, by means of a pediment and a projection in the facade. The grandest of them, Clarendon House in London, had wings to either side, making it H-shaped (Pl. 72). Clarendon House was in Piccadilly, and was built for Charles II's first minister, the Earl of Clarendon. Its prominent position and powerful owner meant that, with or without the wings and central pediment, it was constantly imitated all over the country for the rest of the century.

69. (upper left) Raynham Hall, Norfolk. The east front (c. 1630).

70. (left) Coleshill House, Berkshire (Sir Roger Pratt, c. 1650–62).

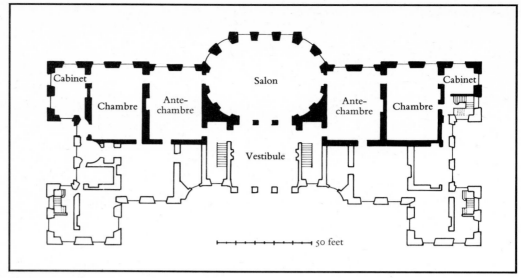

Fig. 7. Vaux-le-Vicomte. The ground floor.

Pratt's visit to, and return from, the continent was an early example of the upheaval among the upper classes caused by the Civil War. Many gentry and noblemen went to the continent, either to avoid unpleasantness at home or, like Clarendon, to follow Charles II into exile. At the Restoration those who were still abroad came flocking back. During their travels they had seen how the same type of planning, also derived from Italy, was developing on the continent. On their return they wanted something on the same lines.

The formal plan—as for convenience it can be called—was to be found on the continent on every kind of scale, and in France, Germany, Spain and the Low Countries as well as Italy. The Dutch examples were modest and charming, none more so than the Mauritshuis at The Hague, built for Prince Maurice of Nassau in 1633–5.[9] At the other end of the scale were houses like the château of Vaux-le-Vicomte, a few miles outside Paris (Pl. 73). It was built in the last years of Charles II's exile by Nicholas Fouquet, financial minister to Louis XIV. It had a formal plan of the utmost magnificence (Fig. 7). In the centre was a great oval room of state, rising through two storeys. To either side were lodgings for Fouquet and Louis XIV. The room of state was called a *grand salon*—a Frenchification of *grande salone*, and an acknowledgement of the plan's Italian origin. But the lodgings were made up of what had long been the traditional French sequence of *antechambre*, *chambre* and *cabinet*—the whole known as an *appartement*. The sequence approximated to the English one of withdrawing chamber, bedchamber and closet. But there were important differences, and as the French arrangement was to have a considerable influence in England, these need to be explored.[10]

Both France and England had started in the Middle Ages with the basic system of hall and chamber (in France *salle* and *chambre*), but the system had developed differently in the two countries. In England some of the functions of the hall had been hived off into the chamber, and the chamber had been subdivided into a

126

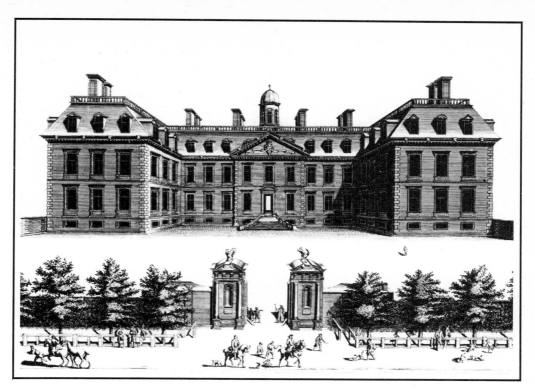

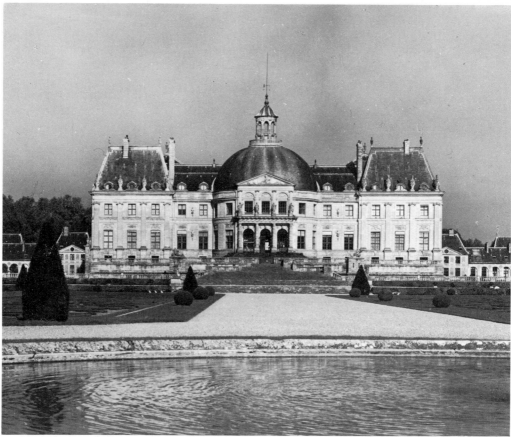

72. (top) Clarendon House, London (Sir Roger Pratt, 1664–7, as engraved before its demolition in 1683.

73. The Château of Vaux-le-Vicomte, France (1657–61).

great chamber for state, and a relatively private chamber for living and sleeping. No such development had taken place in France; nor had anything resembling the further subdivision of the chamber into withdrawing chamber and bedchamber. In the mid seventeenth century a *chambre* was still basically a bed-sitting room—even if, in a big house, a very grand bed-sitting room. It was used for the reception of visitors and for private meals as well as for sleeping. Its combination of functions was sometimes expressed by putting the bed in an alcove, like a room within a room. In a royal *chambre* the bed was separated from the rest of the room by a balustrade, like an altar rail in a church, and only courtiers above a certain rank were allowed behind it.

The rooms before and beyond the *chambre* accordingly had functions rather different from those of their English equivalents. The *antechambre* was, as its name implies, essentially a waiting room for visitors hoping to get access to the *chambre*. Sometimes a great person would come out into it, so that people not considered important enough to be admitted into his *chambre* could pay their respect or present petitions. The room had little of the private nature of a seventeenth-century withdrawing room.

The public, or relatively public, nature of *antechambre* and *chambre* was reflected in the status of the *cabinet*. An English bedchamber of any size almost invariably had a room leading out of it, sometimes an inner chamber with a bed in it for a child or a servant, sometimes a closet for private study or prayer. Such rooms were useful but not essential. French *cabinets* were essential, because they were *the* private rooms. To get into the *cabinet* of a monarch or great man one had to be in the inner ring of power. *Cabinets* could vary a good deal in size; usually they were small rooms but very richly decorated, and they often contained their owners' most precious pictures, coins, medals, bronzes and curiosities. They were like little shrines at the end of a series of initiatory vestibules.

At the other end of the sequence, the *grande salle* or *grand salon* was used for the same kind of functions as a great chamber but had a different lineage. It descended from the mediaeval *salle*, rather than the *chambre*. The *salle* had developed in exactly the opposite way to the English hall. Instead of the family and their guests moving out of it and the servants staying, the family had stayed and the servants been removed. Accordingly a French *salon* was either entered directly from outside, like an English hall, or was preceded by a vestibule (or, if it was on the first floor, by a staircase). Vestibules could be richly decorated but they were never large; they were rooms to pass through, not to linger in.

The *salon* was normally expressed on the exterior by some kind of frontispiece. At Vaux-le-Vicomte this rises up through two storeys into a dome. Dome and frontispiece form the dominant feature of the facade; to either side the two *antechambres*, as the rooms of least importance, are treated as a relatively plain interlude before the *chambre* and *cabinet* at the privileged end of each *appartement*. The position of these is shown on the outside by pilasters and separate roofs forming terminal pavilions. The combination of a state centre for the saloon and pavilions for the priviliged end of the apartments was to become one of the commonest ways of organising facades all over Europe.

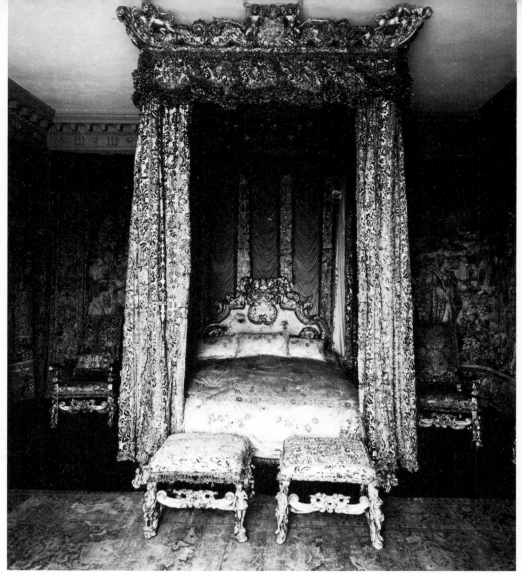

74. The late-seventeenth-century state bed in the Venetian Ambassador's room at Knole, Kent.

The formal plan, deployed with a Dutch or French rather than an Italian accent, grew in popularity after the Restoration, until by 1700 it had become more or less obligatory for anyone wanting to be in the fashion. To begin with the Dutch influence was the strongest but, among grander houses especially, France gradually overtook Holland, as a result of close contact between the English and French courts and the growing power and prestige of France under Louis XIV. The injection of French influence into the English version of the formal plan had two results. One was that the names changed. The central room gradually ceased to be called a great chamber, great dining room, or dining chamber—all names current in the mid seventeenth century—and was increasingly called a *salone*, *salon*, or saloon, as indeed were some great chambers or parlours not in a central position. Closets, especially if they were elaborately decorated or furnished, were sometimes called cabinets (in the same way as voids became desserts, and yeomen

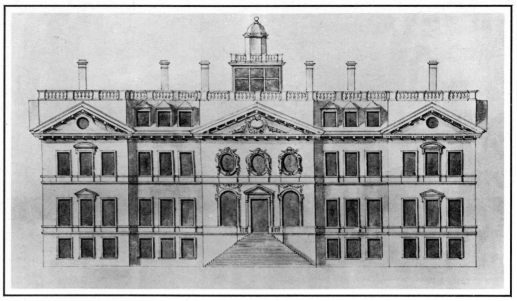

75. A design by Robert Hooke for Ragley Hall, Warwickshire (*c.* 1679).

of the chamber *valets de chambre*). Lodgings increasingly came to be called apartments.

The use and arrangement of rooms tended to be modified as well as their names. Closets or cabinets became more important and more richly furnished. The occasional antechamber began to appear, sometimes instead of a withdrawing chamber, sometimes in addition to it. More often, withdrawing chambers became more accessible, less like private sitting rooms and more like general reception rooms. Bedrooms became more public, though perhaps never quite as public as in France. They were decorated with the sumptuousness and furniture appropriate to important reception rooms. Their walls were lined with rows of richly upholstered chairs and stools; their occupant received visitors lying in bed framed by splendid curtains, under a tester decorated with plumes of ostrich feathers, and with his coat of arms carved or embroidered on the bed-head behind him (Pl. 74).

The style was set by Charles II. His withdrawing room, which in 1661 was a room of limited access, became steadily less select. By 1678 he was directing that any 'Person of Quality as well our servants as others who come to wait on us are permitted to attend and stay us in the withdrawing room.'[11] The periodic emergence of the king or queen to talk to such waiting 'Persons of Quality' was the precursor of the 'Drawing Rooms' which were the most regular feature of court life in the eighteenth and nineteenth centuries.

Charles II's bedchamber was less public, but still far from private. Princes of the blood were allowed into it of right and at any time. Principal officers of state and privy counsellors had access, but had to ask permission first. For someone of lower rank to be admitted was a notable compliment: in his diary, John Evelyn recorded with the greatest complacency the occasions when Charles II invited him in. Besides receiving privileged visitors, Charles ate there when he wished to dine or sup in private. His bedchambers in his various palaces were arranged in the

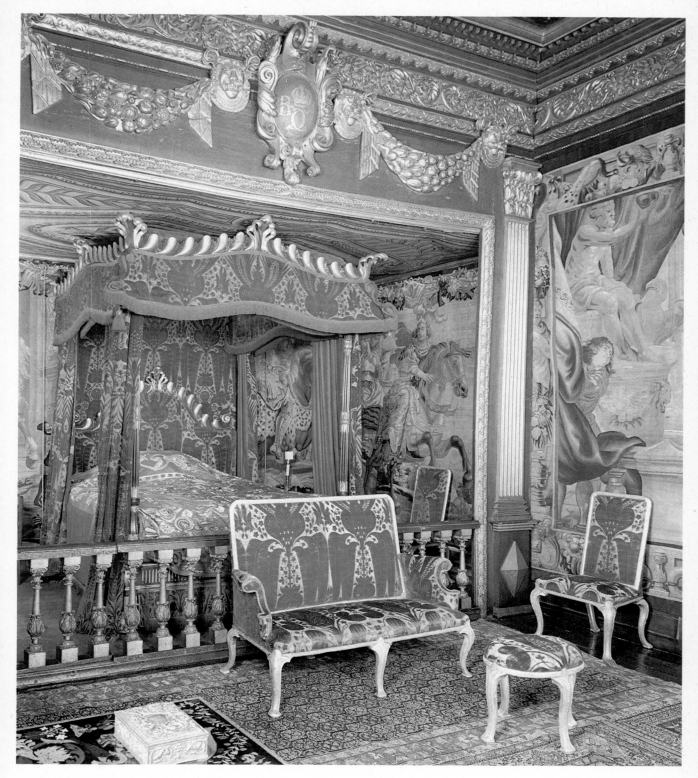

XI. Powis Castle, Powys. The state bedroom, as decorated for Charles II in about 1665.

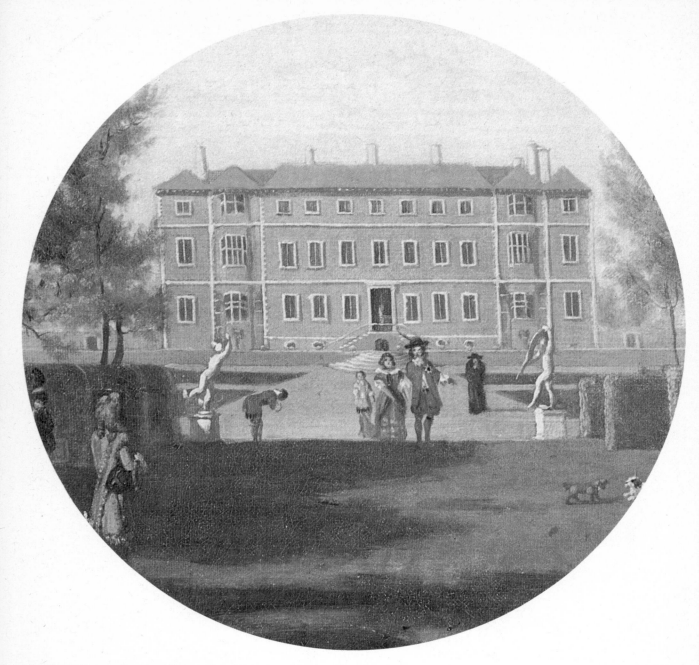

XII. Ham House, Surrey. The garden front, as painted in about 1680.

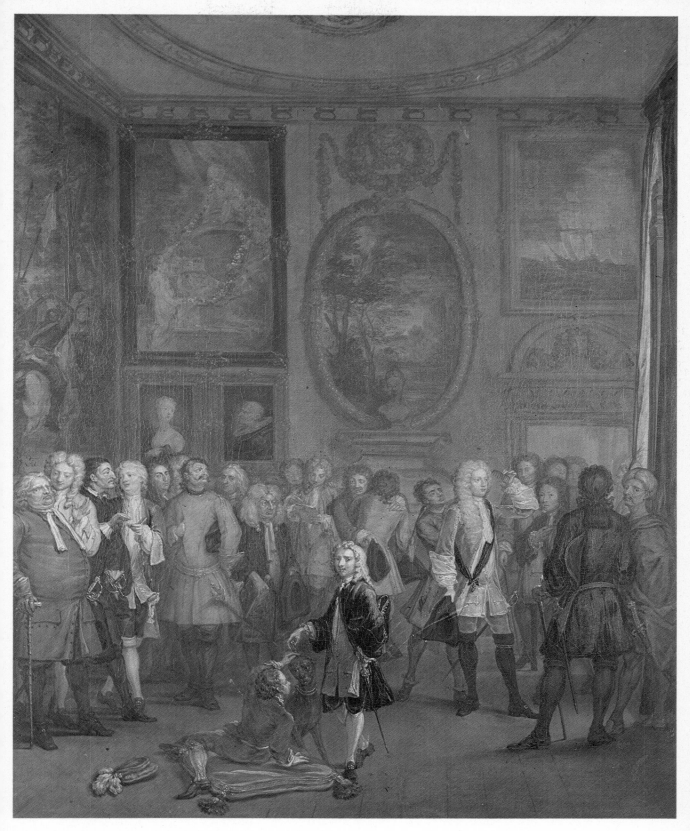

XIII. A Nobleman's Levée. By Marcellus Laroon, *c.* 1730.

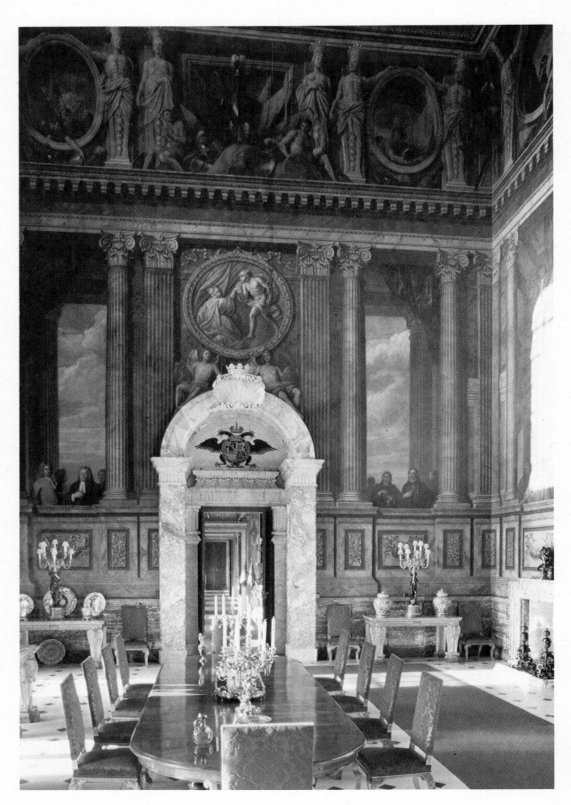

XIV. Blenheim Palace, Oxfordshire (1705–25). The saloon .

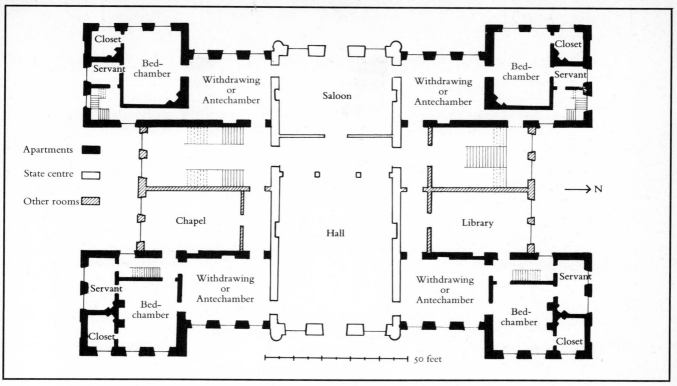

Fig. 8. Ragley Hall, Warwickshire. The ground floor.

French manner, with the bed in a railed-in recess; they have all disappeared, but a bedchamber prepared for him at Powis Castle in Wales still survives complete with its balustrade (Col. Pl. XI).[12]

The king's serious business was carried on in his closet, sometimes called his cabinet. It was there that he discussed policy with his inner circle of advisers; the king's cabinet council was the ancestor of the prime minister's cabinet of today.[13] His cabinets or closets were fitted up with French richness; in 1664 Pepys was shown his Whitehall closet, and reported 'such variety of pictures and other things of value and rarity that I was properly confounded and enjoyed no pleasure in the sight of them.'[14] But Charles II never managed to build a new palace—although he came nearer to it than his father and grandfather.[15] Moreover palaces were rapidly acquiring a complicated series of introductory rooms, which made them increasingly unlike private houses.

A typical grand house of the period, influenced by Pratt, France, and English court practice is Ragley Hall in Warwickshire (Pl. 75). It was designed in about 1678 by Robert Hooke for Lord Conway, Charles II's Secretary of State. Hooke was a distinguished scientist and a member of the Royal Society, as well as an architect. Ragley as he left it (it has been much altered) was an example of the scientific method applied to the rational arrangement of a country house (Fig. 8). There was a state centre, of two-storey hall leading into 'salon' or dining room. Round this were four symmetrical apartments, each with a drawing room or antechamber leading to a bedroom, and with two small rooms and a backstairs beyond the bedroom. Between the apartments were two front staircases and two extra rooms—a chapel and a library. The backstairs descended into a basement, which contained the kitchens, cellars and servants' hall. There was no great chamber on the first floor. Its function was filled by a 'salon' or dining room (it is called both on the plans) on the level of the hall. As at Vaux-le-Vicomte both the state centre and the bedroom ends of the apartments were given external expression.[16]

Two features of Ragley deserve closer examination—the arrangement and use of the big rooms in the centre, and of the small rooms and backstairs at the extremities. The English, for whom the saloon took the place of the great chamber rather than the hall, had to decide what to do with the hall. Should it be reduced to a vestibule, on the continental model, or kept to something resembling its traditional English size? In the long run the vestibule-hall was to be the winner, but well into the eighteenth century the weight of tradition retained old-style halls in many country houses. In addition to being rooms of entry and waiting, these big halls were used for dining on special occasions. As late as 1756 Isaac Ware suggested that, while halls in town houses need only be vestibules, in the country they should be 'large and noble'. A country-house hall, he pointed out, was more than a waiting room for 'people of the second rank; it serves as a summer-room for dining . . . and it is a good apartment for the reception of large companies at public feasts.'[17]

During the long intervals between great occasions, halls tended to pick up other functions. By 1678 the Elizabethan hall at Longford Castle in Wiltshire, besides being used as a 'great Banquetting Roome' for 'Christmas or such a time of extraordinary festival' contained a shovelboard and a newly-installed music gallery. The latter was probably used for music at all times of the year, and not just to provide musical accompaniment to banquets. The walls and screen in the hall were decorated with 'very great heads of foreigne or English deere'.[18] Sets of antlers on the walls, and occasional use for games or music, were to be features of halls for many years to come. Some halls were still hung with arms and armour, at first for use and later for decoration. In 1723 the Duke of Chandos's servants were hanging up their arms on circular boards in the hall of the duke's house at Cannons;[19] by the 1760s Robert Adam was decorating the hall at Osterley with low-relief plaster panels of military trophies, in memory of a custom that no longer had a practical function.

In 1678 the servants at Longford had their own 'little hall' to eat in. The upper servants had a separate parlour on the kitchen side of the screens. The banishment of servants from their traditional eating place in the hall produced a major change in country-house life. Pratt may have been a pioneer of the development. At Coleshill in or around 1650 (as already described) he put the servants into a servants' hall in the basement.[20] By the end of the seventeenth century a servants' hall combined, in grander houses, with a steward's room or parlour had become the standard arrangement. Such servants as remained in the main hall were only there in waiting, on call to perform services or carry messages.

Once the servants had ceased to eat in the hall, the special appropriateness of having the room of state elevated a floor above it ceased to exist. The dignity of

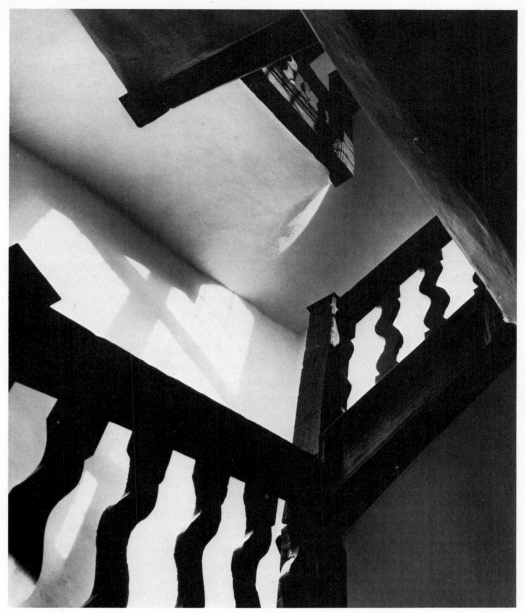

76. Nether Lypiatt Manor, Gloucestershire. The backstairs.

approaching it up a grand staircase began to be offset against the advantage of having it what Roger North called 'easy and grateful in ye access',[21] on the level of the hall. Something of the dignity of a staircase approach could be retained by elevating hall and great room above a basement; entrance could then be by means of a handsome flight of steps, or, as Pratt called it, 'a most graceful ascent out of the court'.[22] To have hall and saloon adjoining each other, as at Ragley, was both dignified and, on great occasions, useful. From the late seventeenth century onwards great chambers on the first floor gradually disappeared—although the power of tradition was still producing occasional first and even second-floor great rooms well into the eighteenth century.

137

Before the introduction of saloons, the only large rooms at hall level had been the main parlour. To begin with, rooms filling the functions of saloons were quite often called parlours—usually great parlours or great dining parlours, to underline their new dignity—but the term saloon gradually ousted the traditional one. The upgrading of the parlour meant that another room was needed to fill its traditional informal function as a family sitting and eating room. The second parlour was normally called a common parlour—common being used in the sense of everyday. Common parlours were often on the ground floor, but were sometimes in the basement, if the house had one; the latter arrangement was recommended by Roger North, who wrote a treatise on house planning at the end of the seventeenth century.[23]

The ejection of servants from the hall revolutionized one aspect of the country house. Another was transformed by the equally revolutionary invention of backstairs (Pl. 76)—and of closets and servants' rooms attached to them. Roger North thought this the biggest improvement in planning that had taken place during his lifetime.[24] The gentry walking up the stairs no longer met their last night's faeces coming down them. Servants no longer bedded down in the drawing room, or outside their master's door or in a truckle bed at his feet. They became, if not invisible, very much less visible.

Some form of backstairs had existed in France since the sixteenth century. In England they appeared in embryo in the first half of the seventeenth century, but their systemization seems to have been the work of the great innovator Roger Pratt. He wrote down the principles in 1660, when he had already carried them out at Coleshill. Bedchambers must 'each of them have a closet, and a servant's lodging with chimney, both of which will easily be made by dividing the breadth of one end of the room into two such parts as shall be convenient'. The servant's room should have backstairs adjoining. In general, a house should be 'so contrived . . . that the ordinary servants may never publicly appear in passing to and from for their occasions there.'[25]

By the time Hooke designed Ragley, with its four backstairs, the system had reached the height of sophistication. A closet for prayer, study and private meetings, a little room for a servant, possibly a wardrobe, and a backstairs adjoining became the essentials of luxurious living. Sometimes one or more of these little rooms were put in a mezzanine; such mezzanines survive at Kinross in Scotland and Easton Neston in Northamptonshire, and give the latter its distinctive north facade (Pl. 77).[26] The servant often shared his room with a close-stool; it was not till the eighteenth century that luxury advanced to the stage of putting these two useful aids into separate rooms. The servant, the contents of the close-stool, and anything that was undesirable or private could move or be moved up and down the backstairs, preferably to offices in the basement.

The servants thus neatly tidied away were a somewhat different body from the servants in an equivalent household a hundred years earlier. There were fewer of them, their social status was lower, and there were more women (though fewer gentlewomen) among them. The Earl of Derby at Knowsley in 1585, and the Earl

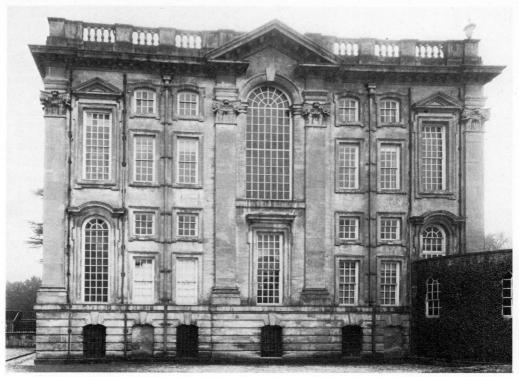

77. Easton Neston, Northamptonshire (Nicholas Hawksmoor, c. 1700–2, probably remodelling a house by Wren of c. 1690). The north front.

of Dorset at Knole in about 1620, had households of 115 and 111 people.[27] Both were living in great state. The Duke of Chandos, living in equivalent state at Cannons in 1722, had a household of ninety; this included a private orchestra of sixteen musicians, which was an unusual feature for that period, even for a duke.[28] Reduction in numbers was accompanied by reduction in ceremony. Some remnants survived. On Sundays at Cannons, and when the duke had guests, the usher of the hall 'with his gown on and staff in his hand' preceded each course into the dining room, with the clerk of the kitchen walking behind him. But all the panoply of bowing, kissing and kneeling, of sewers, carvers and cupbearers, had disappeared.[29]

The reduction in numbers at Cannons was due to several causes. There were fewer gentlemen servants. Receiver, treasurer and comptroller had gone for good, and so had sewer, carver and other gentlemen waiters, although the loss of the latter was to some extent compensated for by an increase in the number of pages. The duchess only had two gentlewomen, half what she would have had a hundred years previously. The surviving gentlemen were of lower rank than their predecessors, and therefore needed fewer personal servants to look after them. Lord Derby's steward had three servants, the Duke of Chandos's steward had none. Among the lower servants there were reductions in all departments except the stables. Lord Derby had twenty-four people to wait on him at meals, the Duke of Chandos had fifteen; Lord Derby had twelve in the kitchen, the duke had six.

The gentlemen servants no longer included elder, or even younger, sons of good county families. They were recruited from, at best, a respectable middle-class background—the sons of merchants, clergymen and army officers. The duchess's gentlewoman was the daughter of a Liverpool knight, not a country squire. In 1724 a Mr Drummond, related to the Earl of Perth and the banking Drummonds, put in for the job of steward, but was rejected as too good for the job.[30] The steward at Cannons was a shadow of the stewards in great households of earlier days. His office had lost its social prestige, and lacked the value deriving from professional qualifications; in all large establishments estate business was now conducted by a separate land steward who usually did not live in the house. At £50 a year the house steward at Cannons was paid less than the master of music and head gardener (£100) or the secretary, chaplains and librarian (£75). On this salary-scale he was clearly no longer the chief household officer. Accordingly a new office of master of the household had been created and given to an ex-army officer, Colonel Watkins.

All these gentlemen ate at their private table in the chaplains' room, except for the chaplain-in-waiting and Colonel Watkin, who ate with the duke.[31] There was a gap in prestige and possibly social background between the upper servants at the chaplains' table and the lesser gentlemen and gentlewomen, who ate in the gentleman-of-the-horse's room. These included the gentleman of the horse, who ran the stables, the gentleman usher, who looked after the main rooms, the duke's two gentlemen, descendants of the earlier gentlemen of the chamber, who were his personal attendants, the duchess's two gentlewomen, and the pages.

The decline or departure of gentlemen servants produced a corresponding increase in status of the former yeomen officers—now just known as the officers. They were promoted to the dignity of 'Mr', and ate in the gentleman-of-the-horse's room, although at a separate table. They included the clerk of the kitchen, the clerk of the check (roughly equivalent to the clerk-comptroller of earlier days), the head cook, the butler, and the groom of the chambers. The butler had absorbed the jobs of the yeomen of buttery, ewery and pantry, and was beginning the rise that was to lead to his nineteenth-century eminence. In 1726 the Cannons officers were amalgamated with the lesser gentlemen and sat at the same table with them. By then the latter were probably gentle only by courtesy, and the duke's gentlemen not so very different from the 'gentleman's gentleman' of later days.

All other servants ate in the kitchen or the servants' hall. Kitchen staff, other than the head cook and clerk of the kitchen, ate in the kitchen. Footmen, under-butler, porters, coachman, grooms, stable-boys, gardeners, odd men and maids other than kitchen-maids ate in the servants' hall.

Footmen had had a curious history. In the later Middle Ages and the sixteenth century a footman was an attendant who walked or ran on foot by the side of his master or mistress when they rode out on horseback or in a carriage.[32] He was mainly there for prestige, but could also be used to lead home a lame horse and to run messages, especially in London. A fast-running footman with plenty of

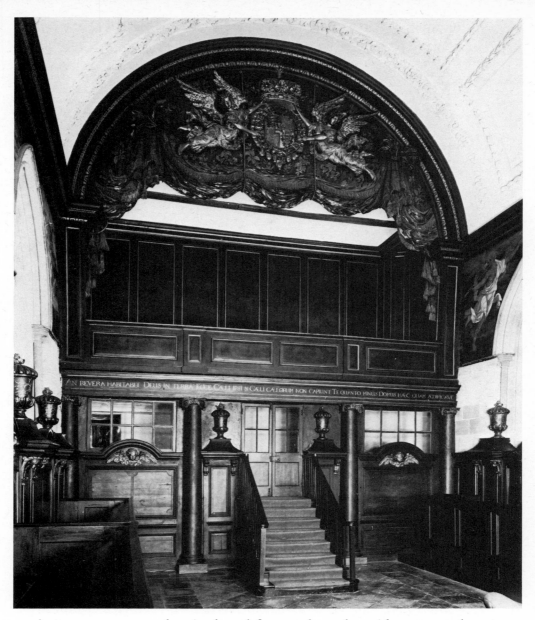

staying power was much prized, and from at least the mid seventeenth century owners were racing their footmen against each other, and betting heavily on the result.

During the seventeenth century footmen began to come into the house to help wait at the less important tables.[33] By the end of the century both gentlemen and yeomen waiters had entirely disappeared, and footmen (at times supplemented by pages as personal attendants to important people) were waiting at the first table, under the butler and under-butler. At Cannons the duke and duchess had seven footmen, one of whom was still employed as a running footman. Colonel Watkins had a footman of his own, and another waited at table in the chaplains' room.

141

78. Petworth House, Sussex. The Duke of Somerset's gallery in the chapel (1689–92).

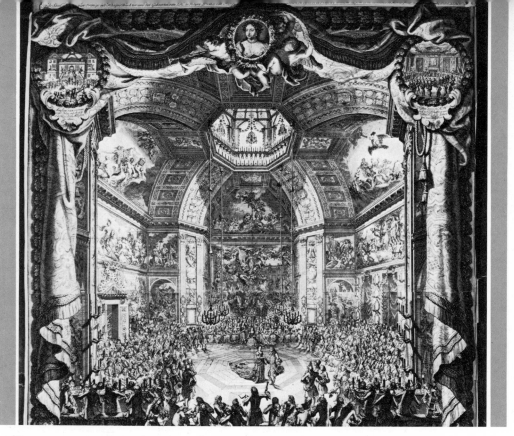

Footmen supplanted waiters because, originally at any rate, they came from a lower social class and were cheaper. During the seventeenth century the same reasons of economy began to bring women into the non-ceremonial sections of the household. Women were invariably paid less than men for doing the same job. They had always been nurses, laundry-maids and personal attendants on the ladies of the house, but they now began to clean and cook. At Cannons all the cleaning and some of the cooking was done by women. There were two laundry-maids, a dairymaid, three housemaids and two cookmaids, as well as 'chairwomen' working in the laundry and kitchen. The female staff was under a housekeeper who had an assistant housekeeper to help her.

In the sixteenth century a housekeeper had been a person who looked after the house of a widower or a bachelor. As female staff increased during the seventeenth century, she became a regular feature of large households of all sorts. At Cannons she supervised the linen and the housework, controlled the supplies of tea, coffee, sugar, preserves, soap and candles, and showed the house to visitors. She still ranked low in the household hierarchy; she sat at the officers table but, at £10 a year, was paid less than any of them.[34]

Cannons is an example from the later days of the formal house. In the intervening period different houses had changed in different ways and at different rates. The Duke of Beaufort at Badminton in the 1680s had a household and style of living not so very different from that kept by his grandfather at Raglan Castle in the 1640s.[35] But the general drift was inexorable. By the end of the seventeenth century the ancient ceremonies had almost entirely disappeared. Large

142

79. A ball in honour of the birthday of William of Orange, given at the Huis ten Bosch in Holland in 1686.

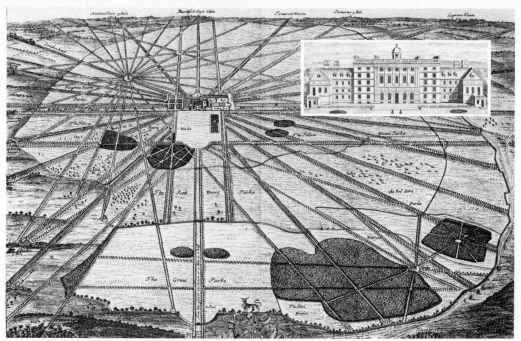

households were recruited from lower social grades. Servants were kept out of sight except when actually about their business, and even then kept as invisible as possible if their business was at all insalubrious. The departure of the servants from the front part of the house was accompanied by the departure of all the tenants, visitors on business and hangers-on who used to eat with them in the hall. Everyday hospitality at this level still went on, but it was kept out of sight of the grander visitors. It was a very different system from the communal and public hierarchy of great mediaeval or even great Elizabethan houses.

The changes were partly due to a growing feeling for privacy and a growing fastidiousness. But they also reflected the changing nature of society and the power structure. Great houses were no longer settings for the display of a united following of all social ranks, tied to their lord by service and hereditary loyalty, bound together by shared ceremony and ritual, and prepared if needs be to fight for him. The power of the central government and the institution of a standing army had destroyed the point and possibility of such followings. The protection offered by a great lord to his servants no longer attracted gentlemen of any standing, once the state maintained reasonable law and order, and numerous other routes of advancement were available to them. Grammar schools and universities offered a better education than could be picked up by the page of a great man. Younger sons went into commerce, the law, the armed forces or the government rather than household service. Moreover the Civil War, and the parliamentary battles which preceded it, had given many of the gentry a taste for independence. Some form of gentry service lingered on in a few houses. As late as 1700 Lord Paget, at Beaudesert in Staffordshire, still had the right to summon certain of the local gentry to wait on him 'on some solemn feast days' and occasionally exercised it. But, as Celia Fiennes commented, 'these things are better waived than sought'.[36] It had become demeaning for a gentleman to be a servant.

143

80, 81. Badminton House, Gloucestershire, as remodelled *c.* 1665–70. The north front, and bird's-eye view of the park.

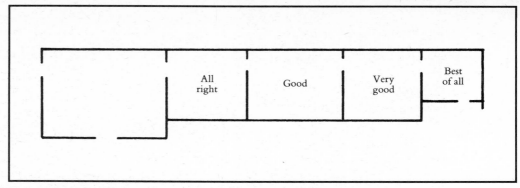

Fig. 9. The axis of honour in the formal house.

The growing independence of the gentry from the aristocracy presented both classes with a dilemma. Should the gentry act as loyal servants of the king or fight for greater political power at his expense? Should the aristocracy try to maintain their status by becoming powerful at court, or by leading the gentry in their aspirations for political independence through parliament? From the 1630s to the end of the century the dilemma split both gentry and aristocracy and divided family from family, brother from brother, and father from son. The division into what came to be called court and country parties ultimately ended in victory for the country party and for parliament. But as far as the architecture of country houses was concerned, the pace was set by the court party.

The court party maintained the sixteenth-century belief that a hierarchy under a single head was the only right order for society, because it was ordained by God and followed his model of the universe. But it placed much greater emphasis on the supreme power of the king, and on the central authority of the state, which derived from the king. This authority was absolute, because it came from God not man.[37] Outside their own households the members of the aristocracy had authority only because the king gave it to them. Because they were his chief servants and filled the top rank of the hierarchy below him they had to be treated with honour and respect. They still received visitors, or ate in state, under a canopy. They sat in their chapels framed in flamboyant pomp of curtains, coats of arms and coronets (Pl. 78). Their wives walked with a train and a page to carry it, even through their own gardens (Col. Pl. XII). But they were not what they had been.

The formal house flourished because it reflected absolute monarchy and the society that went with it. In the late seventeenth and early eighteenth century, when absolute monarchy was at its most powerful, saloons between matching apartments were springing up from Russia to America,[38] and from Sweden to Sicily. The immense prestige of Louis XIV and his court set the fashion, but it was imitated by the opponents of France as well as its allies—by Prince Eugene at the Belvedere and the Duke of Marlborough at Blenheim. In England it flourished especially among adherents of the court, but even the leaders of the country party were unable to ignore it.

In 1686, when William of Orange opened his birthday ball in the central saloon at the Huis ten Bosch in Holland, the two little figures gravely turning under the

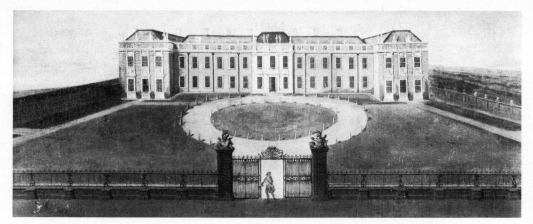

82. Petworth House, Sussex. The west front (1688–93), from a contemporary painting.

dome (Pl. 79) were like jewels of great value in a setting where everything was designed to lead up to them and to set them off—not just the circle of admiring courtiers round them, but the subordinate apartments round the saloon, and the subordinate buildings and long garden vistas round the palace. When the Duke of Beaufort dined in state in the saloon behind the central frontispiece at Badminton, he was at the hub of a web of converging avenues stretching far into the surrounding countryside, underlining the fact that all the local avenues of power and influence converged on him—not just as a great landowner and heir of an ancient family but as Lord Lieutenant and Lord President of Wales (Pls 80 and 81). A saloon with apartments to either side, long axial vistas leading up to the saloon or through the apartments to their inner sanctuaries, and the extension of such vistas through the surrounding gardens and countryside, became essential features of all great houses—and were imitated in miniature in smaller ones. They suggested with vivid appropriateness a hierarchy under a supreme ruler, and ordered and regulated movement within the hierarchy.

As far as country houses were concerned, the functions of the lower ranks within the hierarchy were now only those of respectful service to their superiors. They lived in the basement, or in subordinate wings to either side of the house. The main rooms were designed as the orderly setting for meetings between gentlemen, lords, and princes, who seldom forgot their rank. But behind the rigid etiquette which regulated their intercourse, continual jockeying for power, position and favours went on. The central government was a rich source of jobs and perquisites, which were distributed either by the king himself, or by his ministers and favourites. The main power of the court aristocracy now lay in its power of patronage; it was constantly being solicited for favours.

The formal house was beautifully calculated as an instrument both to express etiquette and to back up negotiation. Since each room in the sequence of an apartment was more exclusive than the last, compliments to or from a visitor could be nicely gauged not only by how far he penetrated along the sequence, but also by how far the occupant of the apartment came along it—and even beyond it—to welcome him (Fig. 9). The situation changed radically depending on whether the visitor was grander or less grand than the person he or she was

145

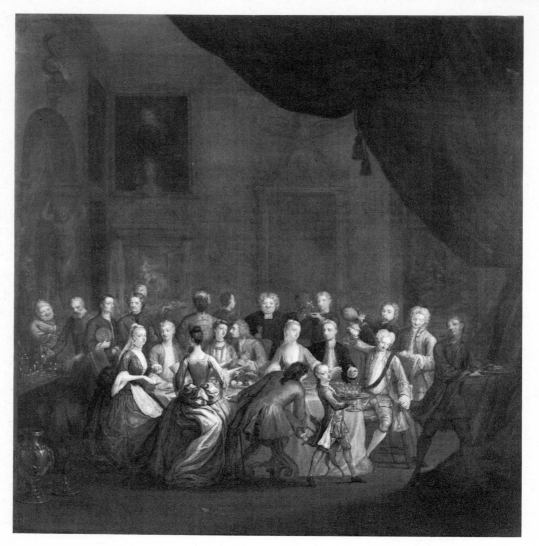

visiting. The less grand visitor hoped to penetrate as far as possible along the line, but did not always succeed. The grander visitor was pressed to penetrate to the inner sanctuary, but could not always be tempted.[39]

The system can be watched in action in a contemporary account of a visit paid by the King of Spain to Petworth in 1703.[40] The front half of Petworth had been built by the Duke of Somerset in the 1680s (Pl. 82). His new building was a very grand example of formal planning, possibly designed by a Frenchman. It consisted of four apartments, stretched out to either side of the centre in two sets of two, one above the other. The lower two were probably for the duke and duchess, the upper two for important guests. In the centre was an entrance hall, and above it, under statues and a dome, there must originally have been a two-storey saloon.

The reception party for the King of Spain consisted of the Duke of Somerset, and Queen Anne's husband, Prince George of Denmark. The first point of etiquette was that the prince, being the queen's husband, acted as though

146

83. Dessert being served at an early-eighteenth-century dinner. From the painting by Marcellus Laroon.

Petworth were his own house. It was he who welcomed the king, and he who showed him round the house; the principal function of the duke seems to have been to pay the bills.

As the king arrived he was welcomed at the door by the prince and escorted to the entrance of his apartment on the first floor. After a decent interval to allow the king to settle in, a series of state visits were paid between the various great people. First, the prince sent a message to the king to ask if he could call on him. Permission being given, the prince emerged from his apartment, and proceeded through the ante-room and withdrawing room of the king's apartment to the door of his bedchamber. The king, who was sitting in an armchair in his bedchamber, came to the door—but no further—to welcome him, and sat him in an armchair opposite him—an armchair being a rank above a chair without arms, and two ranks above a stool (if it had been the case of one reigning monarch entertaining another, or if the business had been one of policy rather than courtesy, they might have gone into the cabinet). After they had passed the time of day for a few minutes, the prince returned to his apartment. Shortly afterwards the king sent a message to ask if he could call on the prince. Permission being given, the king emerged from his apartment and was met by the prince who, being of an inferior grade of royalty, came out of his own apartment to the top of the stairs to greet him. He was then conveyed to the prince's bedchamber, where *he* passed the time of day for a few minutes. At some stage the duke had appeared, and the king now asked him if he could pay a call on the duchess. King, prince and duke then proceeded down to the duchess's apartment on the ground floor. The duchess 'came forward several rooms, even to the bottom of the stairs, to meet the King, and making a very low obeisance she received a kiss from him, as also the two young ladies her daughters, whom she presented to him.' The king, however, advanced no further into the duchess's apartment than a 'little drawing room', where he passed three or four minutes in polite conversation. He was then shown round the rest of the house—by the prince of course, not the duke. Everyone now having called on everyone else, and the honours having been done, king, prince, duke and duchess finally emerged from their various apartments to have supper together in the saloon.

The supper was described as 'served up with so much splendour and profusion, yet with so much decency and order that I must needs say I never saw the like.' But the description gives no details. However, a detailed account survives of a combined dinner, ball and supper, 'the finest that ever was seen', given by the Earl of Portland for Prince Eugene of Savoy in 1711.[41] The entertainment lasted from six in the evening till five in the morning. It was held at the earl's house in St James's Square, mostly in a new room which Lord Portland had built on. It was referred to variously as a hall, 'sale', or great room, and filled the function of a saloon.

The evening started with dinner at the late hour of six o'clock to fit in with a sitting of the House of Lords; the normal time was now one or two o'clock. It was attended by the prince, seventeen noblemen, and no ladies. The waiting was all

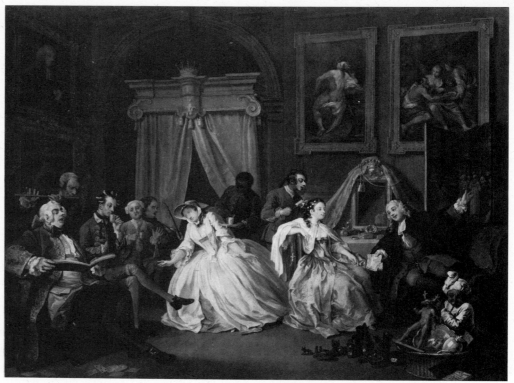

84. The Countess's Levée. From the *Marriage à la Mode* series, by William Hogarth.

done by volunteer gentlemen 'that offered themselves to have an occasion to see the feast'. There was a buffet loaded with gilt and silver plate, and during the whole meal 'trumpets and kettle drum play'd in a room adjoining'. After dinner the company removed to Lady Portland's apartment on the first floor. Here 'several persons of both sexes had been invited to cards' and to hear a symphony performed by twenty singers and musicians from the opera. While this was going on, the saloon was cleared of tables and buffet for a ball. The company returned there at ten, and the ball lasted till three. The company then moved downstairs to Lord Portland's apartment, where supper was served. There were two separate tables, for gentlemen and ladies; Prince Eugene insisted on serving the ladies in person before he ate himself, and the other men followed his example. Supper concluded with much drinking of toasts. Everyone left at about five in the morning.

The separation of men from women at the dinner was still in the mediaeval tradition. Another interesting feature of the evening is the relatively small number of people involved. Eighteen sat down to dinner, fifteen couples danced at the ball. The entertaining was 'the finest that ever was seen' because of the style and richness of the accompaniments, not because of its size. This was typical of the period. Feasts for several hundred people were still being given in the country, to prepare for an election or celebrate Christmas, births, weddings, and comings of age. They usually centred round dinner in the hall, and could involve all the neighbouring gentry and near-gentry, and even the tenants and local freeholders.

148

But the entertainments which enjoyed the most prestige were small but elaborate ones for relatively few people (Pl. 83)—just as the prestigious part of the house was devoted to a few large apartments for great people coming on what amounted to a state visit. A hard line was still drawn between the inner ring of the great and smaller fry.

The smaller fry were most likely to penetrate into a great house on the occasions of its owner's levy or levée. Although a big landowner often held a levée when he returned to the country, levées were, on the whole, London events. Great men (and the king) held them every morning. A man's levée was attended by men only.[42] It started while the giver of the levée was being powdered and curled in his bedroom—or, in some cases, in a separate dressing room or ante-room leading up to his bedchamber. The select few might be invited to talk to him in his bedroom or dressing room, but most waited patiently outside until he appeared in the ante-room, sometimes pursued by his barber putting the final touches to his toilet (Col. Pl. XIII). The giver of the levée could gauge his rating by the number of people attending it; Lord Hervey describes how Sir Robert Walpole's levée suddenly emptied on the death of George I, when everyone expected him to be turned out of office. In the same way, those attending the levée could gauge how they stood with the great man by his affability—or lack of it—towards them.

Levées were especially used to present petitions, or to ask for jobs or favours. Of course, nothing in the least bit private could be discussed in the crowd in the outer room. That was reserved for the bedroom or better still, the closet or cabinet. And here the backstairs revealed yet another asset. While the crowd was hopefully approaching the great man by the official path—through the saloon and along the axis of honour—the person or persons to whom he really wanted to talk could bypass them entirely, and be quietly introduced at the inner end of the sequence by being brought up the backstairs.

In the time of Charles II and his successors, the backstairs acquired a recognized function in the king's political and private life. William Chiffinch, Charles's senior page of the backstairs and keeper of his cabinet-closet, was an extremely useful person to know, and an invaluable servant to the king. Under his supervision, priests, whores, opposition politicians and anyone else whom the king wished to see in secret, came discreetly up the backstairs.[43] Well into the eighteenth century the backstairs played a similar useful role in all palaces and large houses; hence the phrase 'backstairs intrigue'.[44]

The levée of a woman was of a more intimate and less official nature than that of a man. It was held entirely in her bedroom or dressing room and was angled towards flirtation and amusement rather than politics. As Goldsmith put it:

> Fair to be seen, she kept a bevy
> Of powdered Coxcombs at her levy[45]

He was writing at the end of the reign of the levée. A hundred years or so earlier, in 1683, John Evelyn had been fascinated but also shocked when he was brought

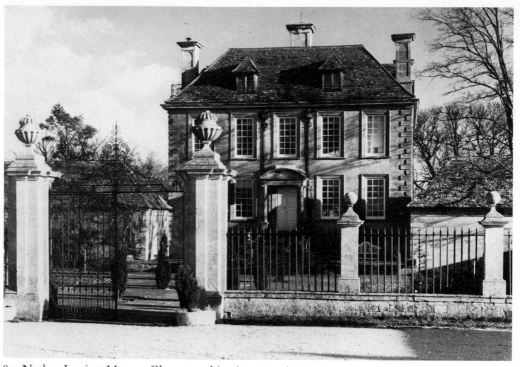

85. Nether Lypiatt Manor, Gloucestershire (*c.* 1700–5).

to the levée of the Duchess of Portsmouth, Charles II's mistress, and found her 'in her morning loose garment, her maids combing her, newly out of her bed, his majesty and the gallants standing about her'.[46]

The Duchess of Portsmouth's levée took place in her dressing room, within her bedroom. Dressing rooms seem to have been an English refinement. They were the result of English couples, even very grand ones, tending to share the same bedchamber, rather than visiting each other from separate bedchambers, as in France. As early as the beginning of the sixteenth century, 'My Lord's chamber where he maketh him ready' at Wressel Castle was clearly a dressing room in fact if not in name.[47] The term 'dressing room' seems first to have appeared in the second half of the seventeenth century. In grand houses of this period there could be two separate dressing rooms, for husband and wife, 'so that at rising each may retire apart and have several accommodation complete', as Roger North put it.[48] But at the end of the seventeenth century it became fashionable for women to dress in their bedchambers, probably as a result of French influence. Although the use of dressing rooms came back in strength in the eighteenth century, as late as 1743 Hogarth's *Marriage à la Mode* series shows a fashionable countess holding a levée in her bedchamber (Pl. 84). The bed is in a recess in the French manner, and among her visitors and little court is a barber, a beau, and an antique dealer. It was probably French influence, too, which made separate apartments for husband and wife more common in the late seventeenth and early eighteenth century, especially in grand houses. At a period when marriages were still almost invariably arranged it was, after all, a sensible arrangement.

Although the basic idea of the formal house was a simple one, it admitted of endless variations. Formal houses were not necessarily large. Hooke's Ragley

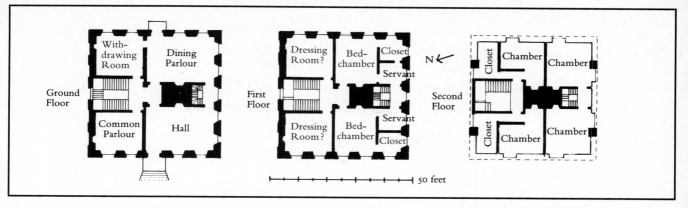

First Floor

Dressing Room? — Bedchamber — Closet

Servant

Dressing Room? — Bedchamber — Servant — Closet

N

Second Floor

Closet — Chamber — Chamber

Closet — Chamber — Chamber

50 feet

should be compared with the more modest, but exquisitely formal, house which he designed in about 1680 for Sir William Jones, the Attorney-General at Ramsbury in Wiltshire (Pl. 86). Even a house as small as Nether Lypiatt in Gloucestershire, where there was no room for a central hall and saloon, was arranged in the form of matching sets of apartments laid parallel to each other, with front and back stairs in between (Pl. 76 and Fig. 10). Externally it was completely formal, from the disposition of the chimney-stacks to the arrangement of the subordinate pavilions each echoing the shape of the central house (Pl. 85).

One of these pavilions may originally have contained the kitchen. The 1680s saw the beginning of the practise of moving the kitchen out of the main block and putting it in a separate pavilion.[49] The move had the practical advantage of taking kitchen smells out of the house, a convenience which seems at the time to have been thought to make up for the distance between kitchen and eating rooms. But it also suggested an aesthetic of house between pavilions which suited the contemporary feeling for hierarchy—as long as at least two pavilions or wings were provided. The problem then arose of what to put into the second pavilion. Should it be the stables—the most common solution? Or laundries and breweries? Or a chapel? Numerous different variations were adopted. The only one never found in England (as opposed to Ireland or America) was Palladio's arrangement of putting the farm in the wings. Although Palladio's villa plans had a strong influence on similar plans in England, a close connection between house and farm was entirely at variance with the English tradition.

Many decisions of this sort had to be made by the designers of formal houses. Should the saloon be put on the first floor, or on the level of the hall? Should there be two state apartments, or only one, balanced by a family apartment? Should there be one family apartment, or two, for husband and wife? What floor should they be on? How should the state centre be expressed externally? How could a grand staircase, chapel or gallery be fitted into a plan without disrupting its symmetry? How many concessions should be made to convenience or tradition, at the expense of symmetry? Endless variations can be found, from houses which are exquisitely and ingeniously symmetrical, to houses based on traditional sixteenth-century planning, but brought modestly up-to-date by the provision of backstairs, closets and a formal exterior.

Formal planning could be applied to the alteration or remodelling of old houses as well as the building of new ones. Roger North was especially delighted with

151

Fig. 10. Nether Lypiatt, Gloucestershire.

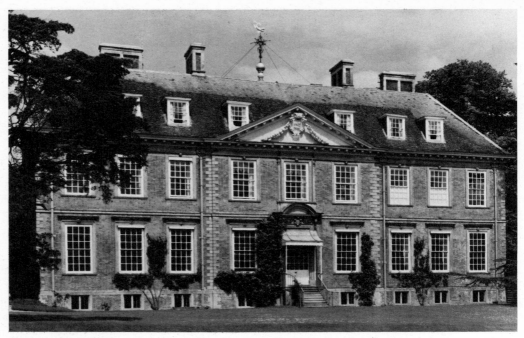

86. Ramsbury Manor, Wiltshire. The west front (Robert Hooke, 1680–3).

the remodelling of Ham House, as carried out by the Duke and Duchess of Lauderdale in the 1670s.[50] The main feature of this was the provision of a new range between the arms of the H-shaped Elizabethan house, in order to provide matching apartments for the duke and duchess (Col. Pl. XII). These were on the ground floor, to either side of a private dining room. As the scale of the rooms is small, but the decoration extremely luxurious, the result is both intimate and formal. Above these two apartments the new range was filled by a single state apartment known as the Queen's Apartment because Catherine of Braganza occupied it. The queen's bedchamber has been somewhat changed,[51] but her closet survives unaltered, and gives a vivid idea of the nature of these minute but important rooms (Pl. 87).

Formalizing an old house could lead to problems of design, as happened at Chatsworth. Its main block appears to be a new building of the late seventeenth century, but is in fact an Elizabethan house sumptuously remodelled. The layout of the rooms was conditioned by this. There was no space to fit a saloon and matching apartments of appropriately grand scale into the main front. Instead a great dining chamber—in effect a saloon—at one end of the front led into a single apartment containing antechamber, withdrawing chamber, bedchamber and cabinet, filling the rest of the front. The arrangement is very grand, but lopsided (Fig. 11). That it was felt to be so at the time is shown by the fact that at one end of the great dining chamber, where the missing apartment should have been, a mirror is set into the wall to reflect the enfilade of doors through the existing apartment (Pl. 89). As long as one stands in the right place, the complete arrangement appears to be in existence. The lopsidedness is reflected in the exterior: the great dining chamber at one end of the front and the state bedroom

152

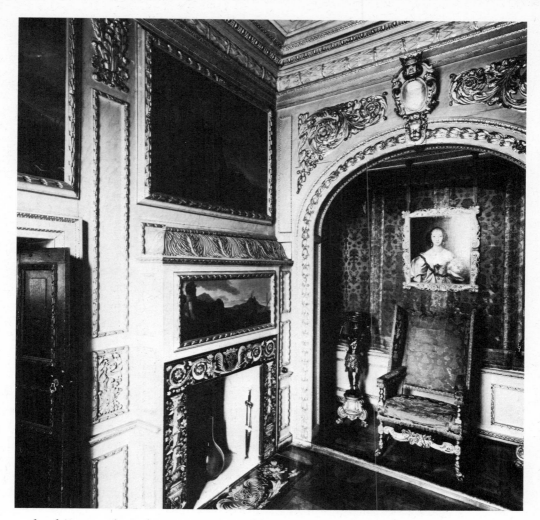

and cabinet at the other are expressed by pilasters, but in the centre, where one would expect a portico or some external feature, there is nothing—quite logically, for there is nothing to express (Pl. 88).

There was no such problem on the entrance front which was remodelled some years later (Pl. 90). Here the first and second floors were each given over to a central room between two family apartments. As these were considerably smaller than the state apartment on the south front, there was no problem about fitting the rooms behind the facade although the need to incorporate a staircase prevented perfect symmetry. A pediment and columns suitably expressed the ground level entrance into the courtyard and the dignity of the central rooms above. The upper one of these survives relatively unaltered. It is magnificently frescoed by Thornhill, but originally had no fireplace (Pl. 91). It was designed as what Roger North called an ante-room.[52] He considered such an arrangement 'the perfection which one would desire, and if understood easily obtained because it fits the humour of a front, whereof the middle windows may serve the ante-room, and on either side the chambers.' The central room 'need not have a chimney, because it is for passage, short attendance or diversion. Music is very

153

87. Ham House, Surrey. The queen's closet (c. 1675).

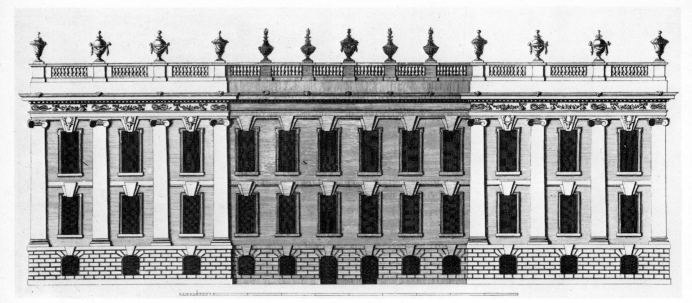

88. Chatsworth, Derbyshire. The south front (William Talman, 1687–8).

proper in it. And it is scarce known what a life is given to the upper part of a house, when it is conveniently layed out and adorned.'[53]

At the end of the seventeenth century an architect of genius took the formal plan and used it to produce results that were both closely adapted to the needs and values of his clients and expressive works of art. The architect was Vanbrugh. Vanbrugh started with the two main elements of formal planning, axial vistas and symmetrical hierarchies, and dramatized them. His axial vistas are exquisitely interlocked, interminably extended, and vibrant with incident. Every part of his houses, from the smallest out-building by way of kitchens and stables to the apartments and saloon, is made to play its part in an extended hierarchy that gradually builds up to the central crescendo.

Vanbrugh is often thought of as an impractical architect. Most people consider Blenheim the acme of waste and ostentation. But by the standards of its times (and apart from the extravagances of its skyline) Blenheim was functional. It was, of course, on an enormous scale, because it was a palace for a national hero. But every element in the plan had its purpose.

Blenheim is based on the standard formal plan (Fig. 12). A hall (Pl. 93) in the north front leads into a saloon between matching state apartments on the south front (Pl. 92). This provides the major theme. It is echoed on a smaller scale by the minor theme of twin apartments for the duke and duchess, placed to either side of a central vestibule (which soon became a private dining room) on the east front. An inner zone, behind the main ranges of the apartments, contained corridors, backstairs, dressing rooms, wardrobes and closets.[54]

On the west front the space corresponding to the private apartments is filled by an enormous gallery. This provided display space for Marlborough's great collection of pictures, and a state route to the chapel in the west wing. The chapel corresponds in position to the kitchen in the east wing; the balance between

154

89. (right) The enfilade at Chatsworth reflected in the great-dining-chamber mirror.

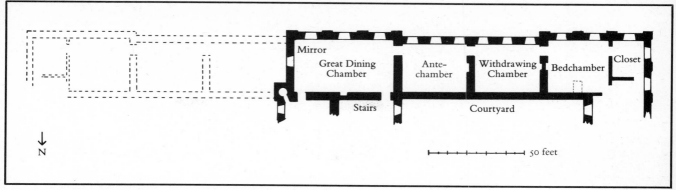

Fig. 11. Chatsworth. The state apartment on the second floor of the south front.

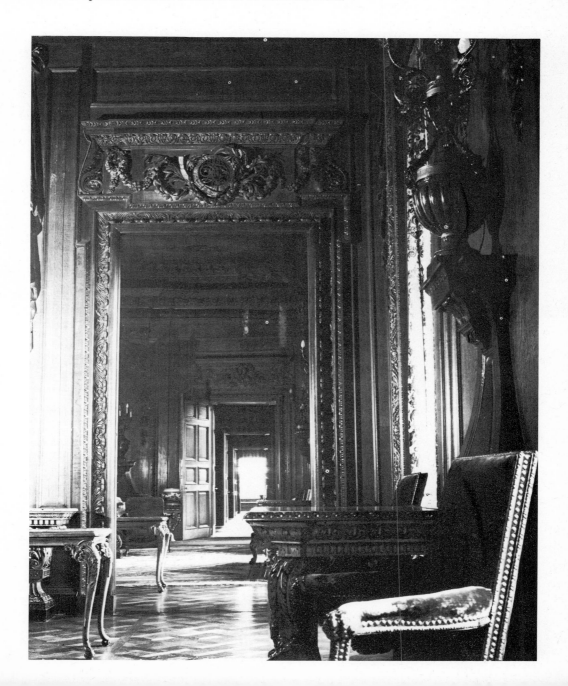

90. Chatsworth. The west front (1700–3).

spiritual and physical nourishment may have amused Vanbrugh. Beyond the kitchen is the kitchen court, and beyond the chapel the stable court; a cross axis across the main courtyard connects the two through a vista of archways, and is also the axis of the approach from Woodstock.

The main axis runs through saloon, hall and great court and continues across Vanbrugh's epic Roman bridge to a column on the hilltop a mile from the house. The duke, dining in state in the saloon, would (had he survived to see it all completed) have been enthroned on the line of a continuous celebration of his greatness. The column is surmounted by his statue, and a roll call of his victories is carved on its base. The ceilings of both hall and saloon are painted with his apotheosis. Externally they are crowned with trophies of victory, in the form of statues of prisoners and the bust of Louis XIV; the position now occupied by the bust was originally intended for a statue of Marlborough on horseback, trampling

156

91. (right) Chatsworth. The Sabine Room (1706).

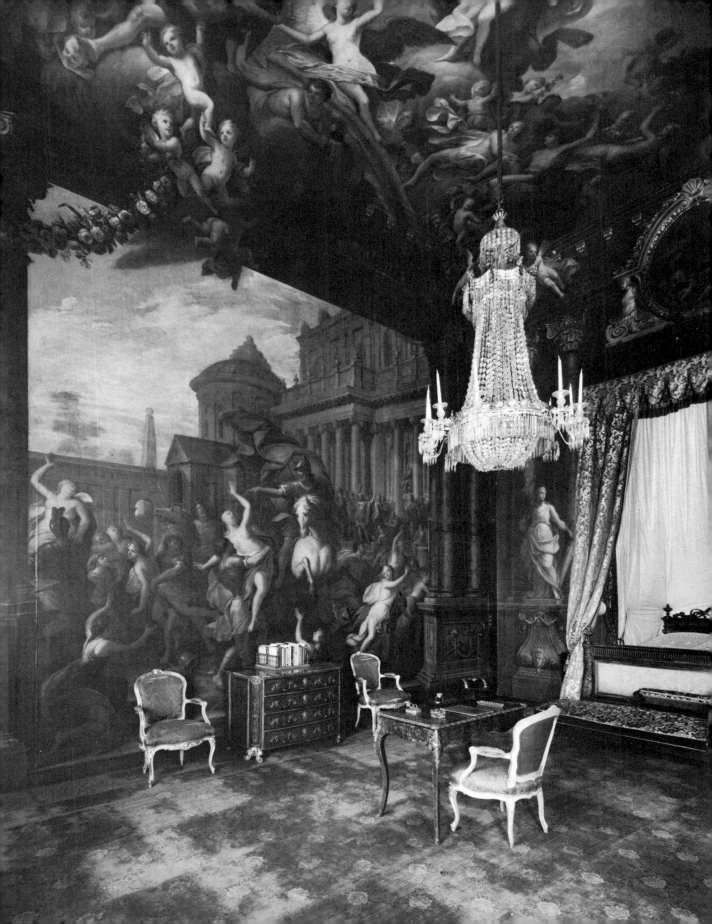

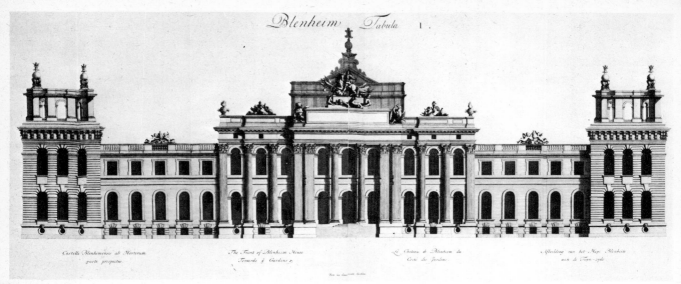

92. Blenheim Palace, Oxfordshire (Sir John Vanbrugh, 1705–20). The south front.

on his enemies (Pl. 92). A triumphal arch, surmounted by the royal arms and cherubs blowing trumpets, leads from the hall to the inner glories of the saloon (Pl. 93 and Col. Pl. XIV).

The hall was a room for great dinners, the saloon for grand ones. Both rise through two storeys. On a balcony under the arch between them musicians could transpose the fanfares of the cherubs into real life while dinner took place; the balcony originally opened onto both rooms.[55] It also gave access to lesser apartments, on the first floor above the family and state apartments. As these upper apartments were of minor importance the staircases leading up to them are relatively inconspicuous; there is no grand staircase. In the nineteenth century the bedrooms from the lower apartments were moved upstairs, and the ground floor rooms run together as an interminable and largely meaningless sequence of twelve state rooms. The point of the plan had been destroyed.

At the beginning of the eighteenth century Vanbrugh and the Baroque went out of fashion and Palladianism came in. To begin with Palladianism did not mean a change of plan in the country-house world, it only meant a change of uniform. The reign of the saloon between apartments went on—but now the ceremonial centre could be neatly expressed in terms of a temple, with a portico at one or both ends. As in earlier models, the result did not necessarily have to be grand, and there was scope for a variety of arrangements. The apartments could vary in size from two rooms to four. The hall and saloon in the centre could be large or small. In some scaled-down versions hall and saloon were elided into a single hall-saloon. The apartments could be arranged to produce houses with wings extended—that is to say with apartments strung out at length along one axis—or with wings folded, with apartments turned back along either side of the hall and saloon to produce a compact, approximately square plan. The type with wings extended was much used for houses at the centre of great estates, where show was considered essential. The results were the immensely extended facades of houses like Stowe, Wanstead or Wentworth Woodhouse (Pl. 94). The wings-

93. (right) Blenheim Palace. The hall.

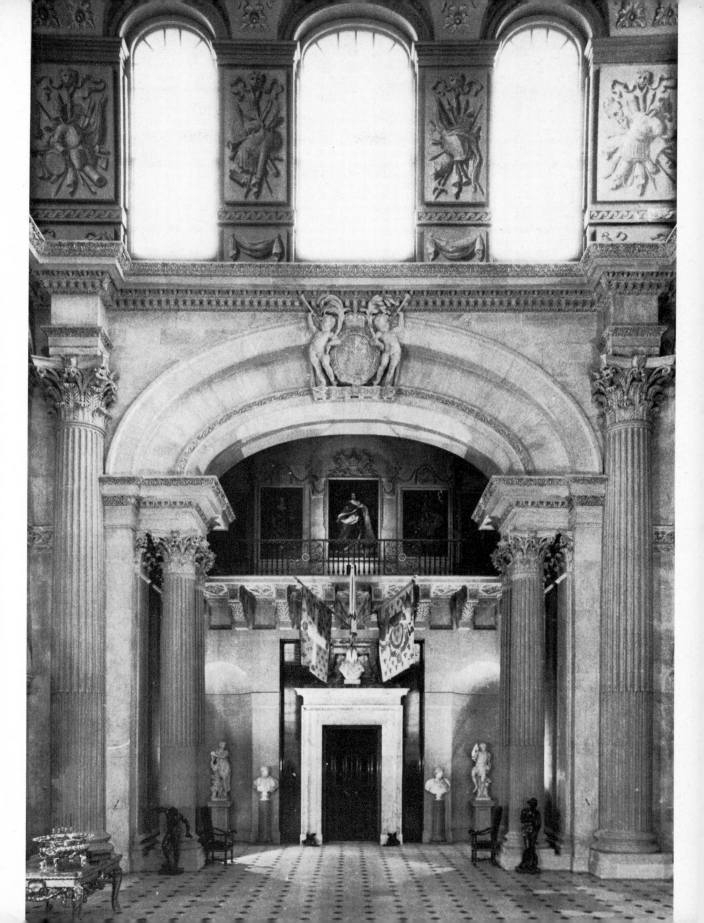

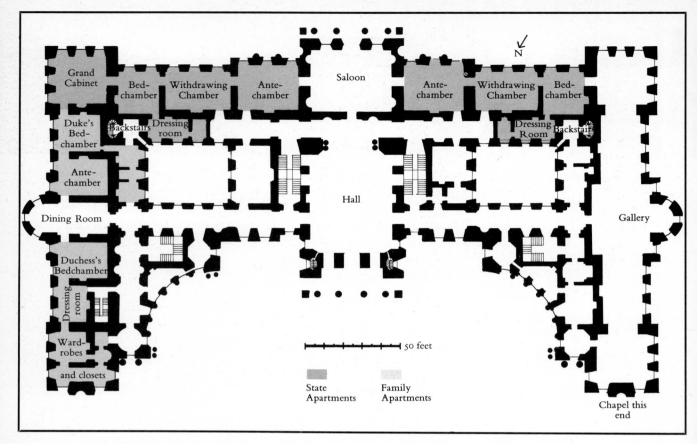

Fig. 12. Blenheim Palace, showing the state and private apartments.

folded arrangement worked very well for houses built for people of moderate fortunes but sophisticated tastes, or for the subsidiary and more private residences of the great (Pl. 95). Such houses were known in the eighteenth century as villas, and were built in especially large numbers in areas within comfortable reach of London.[56]

Externally, English Palladian houses almost invariably followed the same formula, even if with many variations. Their lower storey was rusticated, and acted as a basement podium for one or more smooth-faced upper storeys, the proportions of which were dictated by a central frontispiece or portico. The basement storey was known in the eighteenth century as 'the rustic'. The arrangement derived ultimately from Roman temples, by way of Palladio and Inigo Jones. The main entrance was sometimes into the rustic, but was usually into the hall behind the portico, by way of an external flight of steps built in front of the rustic; in the latter case there was normally a subsidiary entrance into the rustic, under the main one.

The arrangement adapted well enough to English practice. In some houses the rustic was entirely filled by kitchen, cellars and service rooms. More usually it was divided between service rooms and informal living rooms. There were many variations. At Wanstead, in 1722, there were three complete apartments in the rustic: one of five rooms, for the owner, Lord Castlemain, one of four rooms, for his wife, and one 'designed for the entertainment of their friends'. The floor above was 'for the rooms of state' and contained four more apartments, in addition to

160

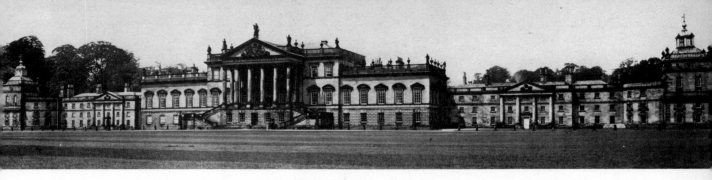

the hall and saloon.[57] At Wolterton (a considerably smaller house) there were only four gentry rooms in the rustic; these may originally have been designed as one complete apartment, but by 1750 were being used as a family dining parlour, drawing room, study and breakfast room.[58] Houghton seems never to have had bedrooms in its rustic. Instead it was liberally supplied with informal living rooms, in the form of a breakfast room, supping parlour, hunting hall and coffee room, all grouped round a central vaulted hall, known as 'the arcade', and used for 'walking and *quid-nuncing*'.[59]

   Twice yearly at Houghton Walpole gave what became famous as his Norfolk 'congresses'. A mixed party made up of his colleagues in the government and of local gentry assembled in large numbers to drink, hunt, eat and indulge in bawdy, gossip, sight-seeing and politics. The social life of the congresses went on entirely in the rustic. Here, as Lord Hervey, one of the guests, described it, they lived 'up to the chin in beef, venison, geese, turkeys etc. and generally over the chin in claret, strong beer and punch.'[60]

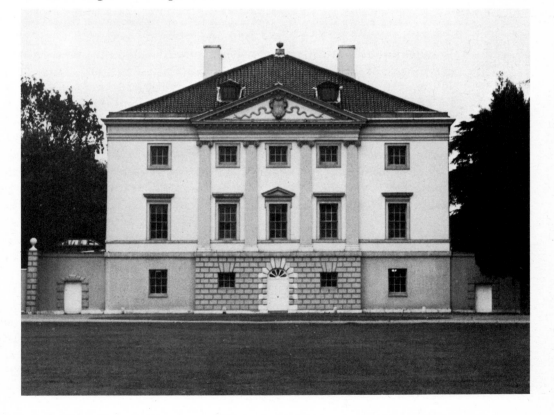

94. (top) Wentworth Woodhouse, Yorkshire. The east front (Henry Flitcroft, *c.* 1734–40).

95. Marble Hill, Twickenham, London (Roger Morris, 1728–9).

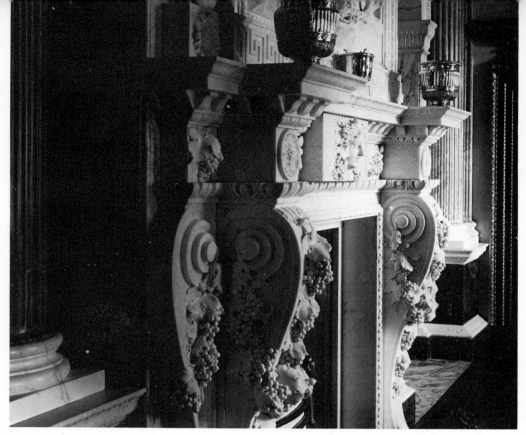

The floor above was described by Hervey as 'the floor of taste, expense, state and parade'. Its rooms were grouped in four matching apartments to either side of a hall and saloon, both two storeys high and decorated with extraordinary grandeur. The two eastern apartments were occupied by Walpole and his wife, but the rest of the floor only came to life on great occasions, such as the visit of the Duke of Lorraine, husband of the Empress Maria Theresa, in 1731. On this occasion 'the consumption both from the larder and the cellar was prodigious. They dined in the hall which was lighted by fifty wax candles, and the saloon with fifty.'[61]

On a first view the symmetrical arrangement of the main floor and the grandeur of the hall and saloon make Houghton the epitome of a formal house. But in fact it was one of the first great houses where the formal system began to crumble. It was not only that the bias of its social life was shifting to the informality of the rustic. In the year of the Duke of Lorraine's visit the main room in the north-west apartment was being fitted out as a dining room—not just an everyday dining room or a dining room for upper servants, but a state dining room richly furnished, lined with marble and designed to take over the dining function of the saloon (Pl. 96).

Once the saloon had ceased to be used for formal meals its position as the ceremonial pivot of the house had gone—and the reasons for putting it in the centre of the house with a great portico in front of it had gone also. The balance of the system had dissolved and the days of the formal plan were numbered.

96. Houghton Hall, Norfolk. A detail in the dining room (William Kent, c. 1731).

97. (right) English connoisseurs in Rome in about 1750.

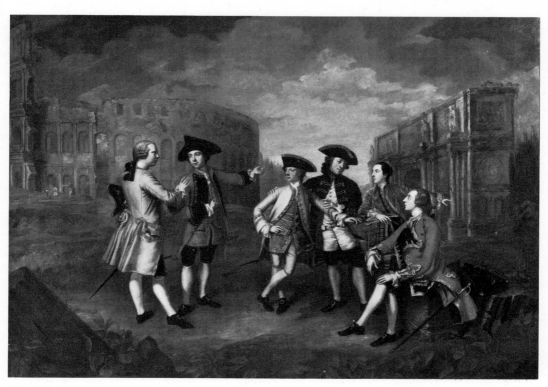

6 *First Interlude: Virtuosos and Dilettanti*

BY THE beginning of the eighteenth century books and pictures were needing special accommodation in more and more houses. They were to become such an essential part of country-house life that one tends to forget how deep into the seventeenth century many houses had almost no books and only a handful of pictures. In the Middle Ages learning, and even literacy, were not considered necessary acquirements for a great lord. The qualities expected of him were bravery, dash, a certain magnificence and easiness of style, perhaps the practical good sense of a man of the world, but not learning. Such men set the pace for lesser landowners, and their style tended to be imitated even by those who had pushed their way into the landowning classes by less swashbuckling routes, and made money as lawyers, merchants, or sheep farmers. The reactions of one particular gentleman, as reported in the early sixteenth century, were reasonably typical: 'I'd rather that my son should hang than study letters. For it becomes the sons of gentlemen to blow the horn nicely, to hunt skilfully and elegantly, to carry and train a hawk. But the study of letters should be left to the sons of rustics.'[1]

But any generalization about degrees of culture among the mediaeval upper classes needs to be qualified.[2] From the fourteenth century most great lords were literate and a few were even literary: the books of Duke Humphrey of Gloucester, younger son of Henry IV, form the nucleus of the Bodleian Library at Oxford. Richard II read and collected books and patronized poets. His tastes inevitably influenced his court. His steward of the household and close personal friend, for instance, was Thomas Percy, Earl of Worcester. Worcester was one of Froissart's patrons and may have been responsible for installing libraries in the two great houses which he owned or built in Yorkshire, Wressel Castle and Leconfield Manor. These libraries still existed in the early sixteenth century, when the house belonged to the fifth Earl of Northumberland, who also had literary tastes. The Northumberland household book refers to both 'my Lord's Library' and 'my Lady's Library' at Leconfield in about 1512.[3] In the 1540s Leland was delighted with the library at Wressel. It took the form of an octagonal closet in one of the towers, and was fitted with desks for the books. It was known as 'Paradise'.[4]

A much more important exception was provided by the spiritual lords—both bishops and mitred abbots. Though often coming from relatively obscure origins they rivalled the lay lords in wealth, power and style of life, and much exceeded most of them in education—for which reason they were employed by the Crown to fill the major administrative posts in the government. Books were inevitably to be found in their households, sometimes in such number that a separate room was needed for them. An inventory of 1423, for instance, specifically names a *liberaria* in the house of Henry Bowet, Archbishop of York.[5]

The Reformation, by altering the balance of power, contributed to the spread of education among the upper classes. The power, wealth and number of great clerics decreased. Instead the Tudors created their own new secular bureaucracy. It was mostly recruited from the lesser gentry, but it acquired wealth and possessions until it became a new hereditary governing class. These Tudor bureaucrats were strongly under the influence of Renaissance ideas. They took books and learning very seriously; and as a result of the spread of printing, there were increasing numbers of books for them to buy.

From the early sixteenth century onwards the governing classes—which to all intents and purposes meant the landowning classes—were being urged both to read and to acquire books. In his manual *The Booke Named the Governour*, published in 1531, Sir Thomas Elyot, himself an ex-civil servant and ambassador, discussed the education best calculated to produce suitable members of the ruling classes. He stressed the importance of encouraging a delight in books from the earliest years. He looked at reading from a moral point of view. Books, in particular the Greek and Latin classics, were to be read to acquire knowledge but even more to learn the principles of good conduct—especially by reading about the exploits of good and great men, in order to be encouraged to imitate them, and of bad men, in order to know what to avoid. After a certain age a young man was even to be allowed to read lascivious poets, in order to learn to 'condemn the folly and dotage' which they expressed—from Elyot's point of view one would have thought rather risky advice.[6]

Romances, books of poetry—lascivious or otherwise—song books and other books designed for entertainment rather than instruction did in fact form an element in sixteenth-century libraries. They were bound to do so, in an age when to write elegant love poems was considered a desirable accomplishment for a gentleman. It was an aspect of English upper-class life that reflects Castiglione's *Book of the Courtier* rather than Elyot's *Booke Named the Governour*. *The Courtier*, as translated into English by Sir Thomas Hoby in 1561, was widely read in England and suggested a new dimension of gracefully employed leisure and courtly love-making as a corrective to Elyot's soberer and more high-minded approach. But even so, books suited for a courtier remained only a small element in upper-class libraries; books bought for instruction or edification were to dominate them for many years to come.

In spite of this increase in literacy, the numbers of books in country houses remained, by our standards, very small. Many country houses still had no books at all. Outside immediate government circles the doctrines of Sir Thomas Elyot and his friends only penetrated slowly. Many gentlemen, especially in the remoter parts of the country, still preferred to hunt and hawk; in Northumberland, in the 1560s, ninety-two out of the 146 leading gentry were unable to sign their name.[7] In 1601 Bess of Hardwick, in spite of contacts with the Greys, Cecils, and other highly educated families, only had six books at Hardwick, kept in her bedchamber. Sir William Fairfax, who installed the magnificent great chamber at Gilling Castle, owned thirty-nine books. Only a dozen or so members of the upper classes (exclusive of clerics) are known to have owned more than a hundred books in the sixteenth century, and although this figure is based on fairly superficial research the real figure is unlikely to have exceeded a hundred. Only two great men—Lord Lumley and Lord Burghley—owned more than a thousand books.[8]

It is uncertain just how or where Burghley and Lumley kept their books. The average literate landowner's collection of around fifty to a hundred books did not need a separate room to accommodate it. Theological books were sometimes kept in, or next door to, the chapel,[9] but the normal place in which a gentleman kept his books was in his closet. This was usually off his bedchamber, less often off the great chamber or parlour. In addition to books it could contain a miscellaneous collection of personal items ranging from bows and arrows to chests full of leases, and from money bags to bridles for horses.

An inventory of 1556 lists the contents of the closet of Sir William More of Loseley in Surrey, an educated and conscientious landowner who was also an M.P. and a faithful servant of the Tudor dynasty.[10] His library was one of the bigger private ones of the sixteenth century. It contained 273 books and was kept in his closet, off his bedchamber. Besides books, the closet contained maps of the world, and of France, England and Scotland, a painting of Judith, a desk, two chairs, a coffer, a pair of scales, a pair of scissors, pens, seals, compass, a rule, a hammer, a perpetual calendar, a slate to write on, an ink stand and a counting board. The books were classical, religious, medical, legal and political. Light relief was provided by a volume of Boccaccio, a song book and 'an old book of fables'.

It is easy enough to imagine More and similarly conscientious landowners at work in their closets. To imagine is the best one can do, however, for no such sixteenth-century closets survive in England in anything approaching their original state. The nearest one can get is a design for a closet made about 1600 by Robert Smythson—for whom or where is not known (Pl. 98). It is a workmanlike design which would have accommodated the books and possessions in More's closet well enough. In addition to built-in writing desks, spaces for hanging maps, and receptacles for ink, writings and loose papers, the walls of the closet are lined from floor to ceiling with open compartments gradually decreasing in size as they rise to the ceiling.[11]

The compartments were probably designed as storage space for a mixture of manuscripts, papers and books. The proportions of the openings suggest that the books were as likely to be laid on their sides, one on top of the other, as vertically—probably in the same kind of random manner as is shown, for instance, in the *trompe l'oeil* paintings in the *studiolo* of Federigo Montefeltro at Urbino. Stacks of bookshelves with books compactly stored in them seem, today, such an obvious device that one forgets that books were originally housed in a much more haphazard or inconvenient manner. Small collections of books were usually kept in chests. In England compact book-storage seems first to have arrived with the organised institutional libraries of the early seventeenth century—especially the Bodleian at Oxford, where the great double tiers of shelves with ladders and galleries which Bodley introduced into Duke Humphrey's Library must have seemed a miracle of technological virtuosity when they were installed in 1610–12.

The Bodleian, and the college libraries which imitated it on a more modest scale, served as models and encouragement to the elder sons of landowners, who were now coming to the universities in increasing numbers. In the course of the

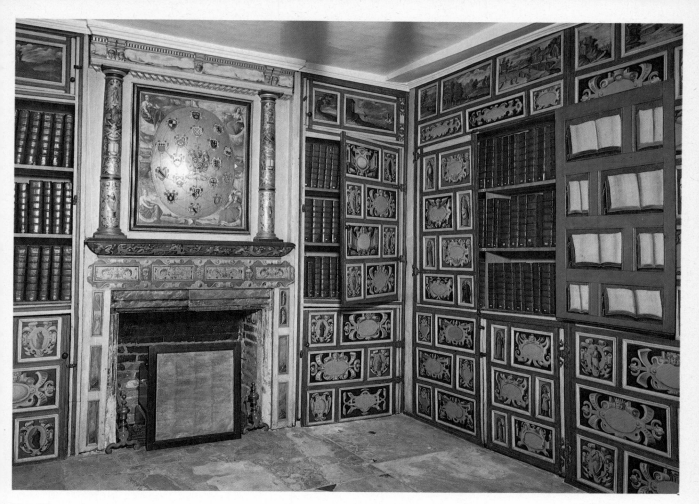

XV. The Kederminster Library, Langley Marish Church, Buckinghamshire (*c.* 1620).

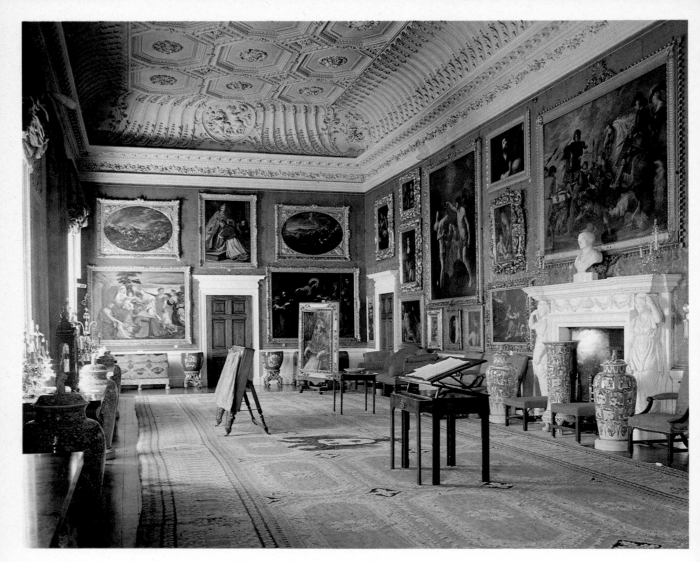

XVI. Corsham Court, Wiltshire. The gallery (*c.* 1762).

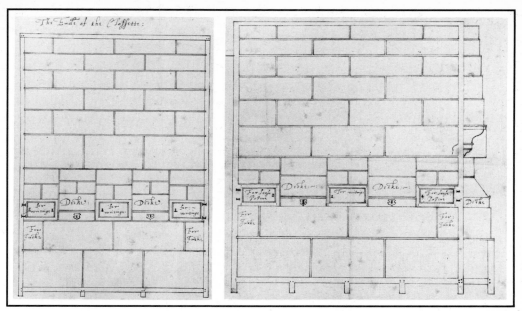

98. Design for a closet. By Robert Smythson, *c.* 1600.

seventeenth century country-house libraries left their pioneering period and began to become a standard piece of country-house equipment. They were still unlikely to contain more than a few hundred books, which were often still kept in a closet, rather than given a room of their own. Books began to feature, however, in the portraits of country-house owners, as well as in their closets. One of the self-portraits of Sir Nathaniel Bacon, a talented amateur artist of the early seventeenth century, shows him sitting in a rather idealized closet complete with a pile of books, an open atlas, his palette, a painting of Minerva, and his dog—the complete picture of the cultivated country gentleman.

In April 1617, Lady Anne Clifford, Countess of Dorset, recorded how she spent the evening at Knole 'in working and going down to my Lord's Closet, where I sat and read much in the Turkish History and Chaucer'.[12] But neither Lord Dorset's nor Sir Nathaniel Bacon's closet survives. Surviving rooms fitted out for books in country houses of the first half of the seventeenth century are extremely rare, if not non-existent. Much the best example of the closet of a cultivated Jacobean gentleman is, in fact, not in a country house at all, but in a church. In about 1620 Sir John Kederminster, a learned landowner, built a little library attached to the church at Langley Marish in Buckinghamshire, and left it a collection of his books at his death. There they and the library still are (Col. Pl. XV). The books are kept behind doors in shelved cupboards or presses, as they were called at the time. The doors and joinery are elaborately marbled and painted with grotesques, views of Windsor Castle and of Sir John's house, little landscapes, portraits of Sir John and his wife, and the Kederminster family tree, given pride of place over the chimney-piece.[13]

In the second half of the seventeenth century, rooms called libraries became more common in country houses. But they were still rare enough to call for notice. John Evelyn always remarked on libraries when he came across them in private houses. All the rooms which he describes or mentions have disappeared, as has his own library at Sayes Court, although its contents survived intact until 1977. An engraving made in about 1690 of Pepys's library in Buckingham Street in London gives a good idea of what a private library looked like in the late seventeenth century (Pl. 100); the room was dismantled in his lifetime but the books, and the presses which he had made for them, are now at Magdalene College, Cambridge. But the oldest surviving country-house library (in the sense of a room rather than a collection) is probably that installed in the 1670s by the Duke of Lauderdale at Ham House (Pl. 99).

The books at Ham are kept in two rooms, described as the library and the library closet in contemporary inventories. Neither of them is at all large. In one corner of the library is a built-in set of drawers and a flap that lets down to form a writing desk. The two rooms are on the first floor, off the gallery; they are distinct from the duke's own closet, which was off his bedroom on the floor below and had its own writing-table and small collection of books. The library and library closet may originally have been approachable from his closet by a backstairs, but they could also be reached through the great chamber and long gallery. They were half way between rooms private to the duke and rooms accessible to others. The duke did in fact let others have the use of his books. His friend, Roger North, brother of the Lord Keeper of the day, describes how Lauderdale, being learned and having a choice library, 'took great pleasure in Mr North's company and in hearing him talk of languages and criticism. And these brothers were not seldom entertained at the great house at Ham, and had the freedom of the gardens and library.'[14]

The gallery next to the library at Ham was (and still is) hung with family portraits, and was kept free of furniture to leave room for walking. The style of fittings and portraits had changed, but the room was still in the Elizabethan tradition. Elsewhere in the house, frescoed ceilings and paintings of landscapes, seascapes and mythologies, either set into the panelling or hanging on the walls, introduced a note that was new since Elizabethan, and indeed Jacobean days. Along with marble busts in alcoves on the entrance front, celestial and terrestial globes in the gallery, books in the library, pendulum and repeating clocks in the private apartments, and paintings in the duke's closet and the library closet showing chemists at work in their laboratories, they demonstrate the influence that the concept of the virtuoso was having on the country house.[15]

Although as early as 1547 there were nineteen pictures other than portraits hanging in the gallery at Hampton Court,[16] well into the seventeenth century portraits were the only pictures to be found in most country houses. Pictures other than portraits seem to have been bought at random, and largely for their subject matter. Informed buying was virtually non-existent until Charles I, the Earl of Arundel (Pl. 101) and other members of the court circle built up their collections in the 1620s and '30s.

Arundel set a pattern that was to be followed by increasing numbers of noblemen or rich gentry over the next two centuries. He travelled on the continent, toured the monuments of classical Italy, and had drawings made of

170

99. (upper right) Ham House, Surrey. The library (*c.* 1675).

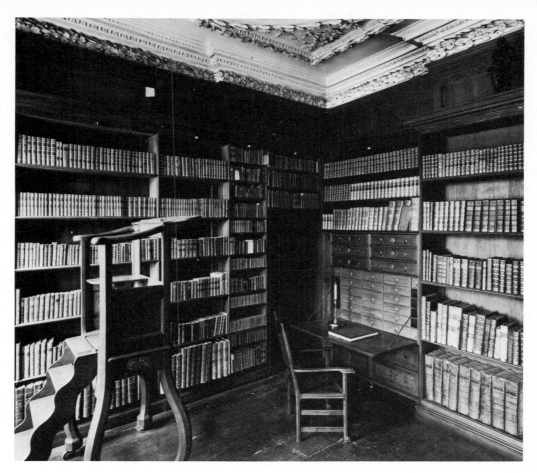

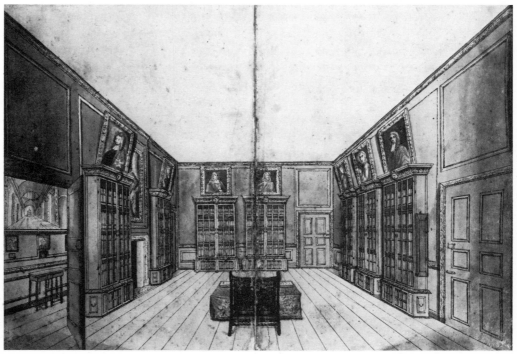

100. The library of Samuel Pepys's house, Buckingham Street, London, in about 1690.

them. He visited galleries or cabinets of pictures, statues, and rarities collected by kings and princes. He formed his own collection and brought it back to England. The range of his purchases was impressive. He collected paintings, drawings, statues, inscriptions, sarcophagi, altars, manuscripts, incunabula, gems, coins and medals.

The residue of the Arundel marbles, after adventures as picaresque and unlikely as those of any hero of romance, ended up in the Ashmolean Museum at Oxford. But the Ashmolean and the University Museums also house the bizarre and rather pathetic remains of the collection formed a generation later by Elias Ashmole, who gave the Ashmolean its name. His collection epitomized the shift of interest away from art towards science which characterized the second half of the seventeenth century. It comprised remarkably interesting and complete collections of minerals, insects, fishes, birds and animals (the remains of his dodo are still in the University Museum) but also such oddities as a woman's breeches from Abyssinia, a purse made of toad skin, 'figures and stories neatly carved upon plum stones', Edward the Confessor's gloves and Henry VIII's dog collar.

Ashmole was described by his contemporary, Anthony Wood, as 'the greatest virtuoso that ever was known or read of in England before his time.' Early in the eighteenth century the third Earl of Shaftesbury defined virtuosos as 'real fine gentlemen . . . lovers of art and ingenuity'. He continued to define them at some length, but the pith of the matter was in those two phrases. Virtuosos were essentially not only gentlemen, but real fine gentlemen—the fine flower of the upper classes with ample private means. But they were also fine gentlemen in pursuit of art, and therefore collectors of it—and of ingenuity, that is to say of science and the by-products of science.[17]

The motives behind the virtuosos were summarized as early as 1605 by Francis Bacon when he analyzed why 'men have entered into a desire of learning and knowledge'. He gave three reasons, and applied a metaphor to each: 'sometimes upon a natural curiosity and inquisitive appetite . . . as if there was sought in knowledge a couch, whereupon to rest a searching and restless spirit . . . sometimes to entertain their minds with variety and delight . . . [making of knowledge] a terrace, for a wandering and variable mind to walk up and down with a fair prospect . . . [and] sometimes for ornament and reputation . . . [using it as] a tower of state, for a proud mind to raise itself upon.'[18]

Bacon rather tartly contrasted all three aims with what he considered the only true aim of knowledge and learning—'benefit and use'. Some gentlemen did, it is true, put their knowledge to practical use, and because of the prestige newly attached to science and art such activities were considered acceptable for a gentleman. There were gentlemen artists like Sir Nathaniel Bacon, gentlemen architects like Sir Roger Pratt, gentlemen chemists like Roger Boyle, and gentlemen engineers like Sir Samuel Morland. But on the whole it was for curiosity, pleasure or prestige rather than use, and as collectors rather than practitioners that most gentlemen virtuosos of the seventeenth century involved themselves with both art and science. Members of the upper classes, whose status

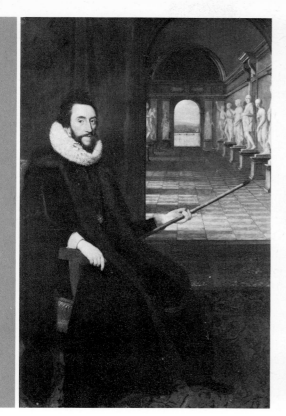 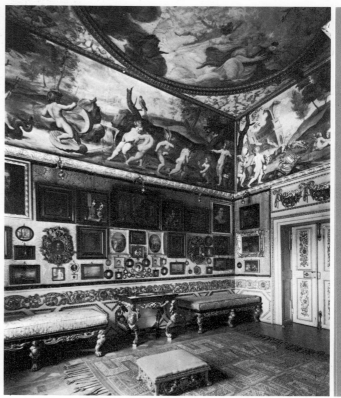

and wealth had been securely founded by their fathers and grandfathers, felt able to take life at an agreeable pace. The closer relationships between England and the continent in the seventeenth century made travel abroad easier than it had been under Elizabeth. To have travelled added to a gentleman's prestige and qualifications, and it was tempting to bring something back as evidence of these travels. Some collected for the love of it, some because it had become the fashion, some for reasons of prestige. To form a collection needed leisure, knowledge and money; the possession of one added to the owner's mystique and helped to separate him from lesser men. It did indeed, as Bacon said, raise him on a 'tower of state'; it added to the exclusiveness of the upper-class club and helped to keep out 'intruding upstarts, shot up from last night's mushrooms'—as George Peacham described them in his contemporary treatise *The Compleat Gentleman.*[19]

Motives varied from virtuoso to virtuoso. They were probably almost always mixed. Even the Earl of Arundel, whose love and delight in works of art is undoubted, may also have been influenced by a desire to reinstate the glories of his family—sadly diminished, for religious reasons, under Elizabeth—and to re-acquire the attainted dukedom of Norfolk. But whatever the motives, in the course of the seventeenth century to have the reputation of a virtuoso, and to enrich ones house with rare and splendid collections, became an accepted part of the image of a great man—and a desirable part of the image of a gentleman.

Collections, once formed, had to be put somewhere. Two types of rooms were obvious receptacles for them: the gallery for the larger objects and the cabinet, or closet, for the smaller ones. Galleries were already associated with pictures, and

101. (above left) Thomas Howard, Earl of Arundel, in his gallery. By Daniel Mytens, *c.* 1615.

102. (above right) Ham House, Surrey. The Green Closet (*c.* 1637–9).

continued to attract pictures even when they were not portraits. Closets or cabinets were already accepted as the rooms where the owner of a house kept the most precious or favourite of his personal possessions; pictures, medals, and rarities joined in naturally with his books and personal papers. It was a development which had already taken place on the continent. Cabinets of pictures or curiosities were a familiar feature of the palaces and great houses visited by Englishmen on tour—as indeed were galleries, so that Richard Burton, in his *Anatomy of Melancholy* could write

> who will not be affected . . . to see those well furnished Cloisters and Galleries of the Roman Cardinals, so richly stored with all modern pictures, old Statues, and Antiquities . . . Or in some Prince's Cabinets, like that of the great Duke's in Florence, of Felix Platerus in Basil, or Noblemen's houses, to see such variety of attires, faces, so many, so rare, and such exquisite pieces, of men, birds, beasts.[20]

As collections grew the owner's personal closet or cabinet was likely to prove inadequate to house them. Separate libraries became more common. Little extra cabinets appeared, devoted entirely to precious objects. The Green Closet at Ham, off the withdrawing room there, survived into the age of photography, along with many of the original contents listed in the inventories of the 1670s, to give a vivid feeling of the atmosphere of one of these exotic little rooms (Pl. 102). The pictures shown in the photograph may have been added to and rearranged, but the incrustation and total indifference to modern ideas of tastefully spacious arrangement was genuinely seventeenth-century; the closet is only twelve feet by sixteen, and in the 1670s there were already fifty-five pictures in it.[21]

In the course of the eighteenth century the pendulum of upper-class fashion, which had swung away from art towards science, swung back to art again. The numbers of the upper classes who travelled, the numbers who collected, and the size of their collections all increased. Books and works of art, instead of being objects of rarity or pieces of technical equipment to be kept in special rooms, began to be absorbed into the everyday life of the house.

Art overtook science partly because of inevitable changes of fashion and shifts of interest, partly because some of the scientific virtuosos of the later seventeenth century had managed to make themselves ridiculous, or at least to attract a good deal of ridicule. Once the mystique that surrounded the early days of science wore off, much of what had been collected began to look absurd to sharp-eyed literary gentlemen in London. In 1645 John Evelyn could describe in his diaries, with uncritical enthusiasm, the contents of the cabinets of the ingenious Signor Rugini in Venice. In addition to Greek and Latin medals, they abounded, as Evelyn put it, with 'things petrified, eggs in which the yolk rattled, a piece of beef with the bones in it, a whole hedgehog, a plaice on a wooden trencher turned into stone and very perfect, a morsel of cork yet retaining its levity' and, in another cabinet, 'a diamond which had a very fair ruby growing in it' and a crystal containing 'a drop of water not congealed, but moving up and down when shaken'.[22]

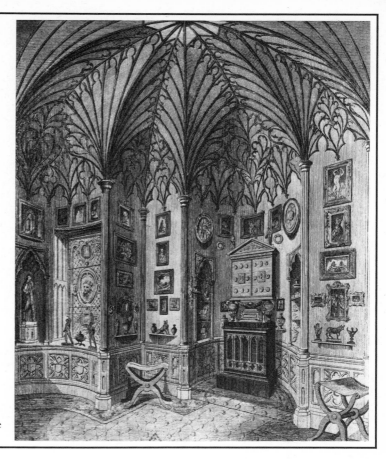

103. Strawberry Hill, Middlesex. The tribune or cabinet (c. 1765).

By 1676 Thomas Shadwell was already beginning to satirize collecting in his play *The Virtuoso*, which centres round the ridiculous exploits of the virtuoso himself, Sir Nicholas Gimcrack. From then on dramatists and journalists had a lot of fun. In 1710 Addison amused himself and his readers by making up Gimcrack's will, and publishing it in the *Tatler*. It was full of absurd legacies: one box of butterflies, a female skeleton and a dried cockatrice to his wife; 'my receipt for preserving dead caterpillars' and 'three crocodiles eggs' to his daughters; 'my rat's testicles' to his 'learned and worthy friend Dr. Johannes Elscirckius', and so on. His son was cut out of the will for 'having spoke disrespectfully of his little sister, whom I keep by me in spirits of wine'.[23]

As William Wotton put it in 1694 'nothing wounds so much as a jest; and when men do once become ridiculous, their labours will be slighted, and they will find few imitators.'[24] In the early eighteenth century virtuosity tended to shift back into its old channels, away from the pursuit of science and back to the collection of pictures, marbles, statues, gems, and medals. This form of collecting had certainly not died in the second half of the seventeenth century, but it had become less fashionable. Moreover, the attitude of late-seventeenth-century gentlemen to works of art had been conditioned by their scientific dabblings. They admired examples of extreme realism or ingenuity, such as Vandervaart's violin at Chatsworth painted to look as if it were a real violin hanging on a door, or the

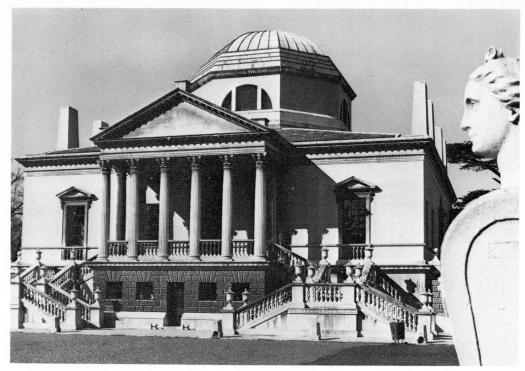

104. Chiswick House, London (The Earl of Burlington, c. 1725).

'cherry stone cut in the form of a basket, wherein were fifteen pair of dice distinct' which delighted Evelyn.[25]

In contrast, the virtuosos of the eighteenth century were Platonists. They were seeking for the re-creation of the ideal in classical statues or contemporary Italian pictures, just as, in their own gardens, they tried to re-create ideal landscapes. Both activities contributed to the pursuit of perfection which some of them, at any rate, entered into with extreme seriousness, to fit themselves as members of the ruling class. Such eighteenth-century gentlemen were as convinced as the sixteenth-century gentlemen walking in their long galleries that to contemplate and understand their possessions led to moral improvement. But the means were different: contemplation of the ideal of harmony, balance and proportion in the human figure or the ideal landscape, rather than the virtues and vices of actual people. As the Earl of Shaftesbury, the theorist of eighteenth-century virtuosos, put it, 'the science of virtuosos, and that of virtue itself, become, in a manner, one and the same.'[26]

Virtuosos in the eighteenth century tended to call themselves dilettanti. To be a dilettante had, in the beginning, none of the patronizing connotations of the word today. A dilettante was someone who delighted in the arts. One reason why the term spread may have been because virtuoso had become a devalued and derided expression. A new name was needed for very much the same thing. There was little difference of approach between the two, except that eighteenth-century dilettanti—like early-seventeenth-century virtuosos—were concerned almost entirely with the pursuit of the arts.[27]

176

105. (right) The Pantheon, Ince Blundell, Lancashire (1802–10), before the contents were dispersed.

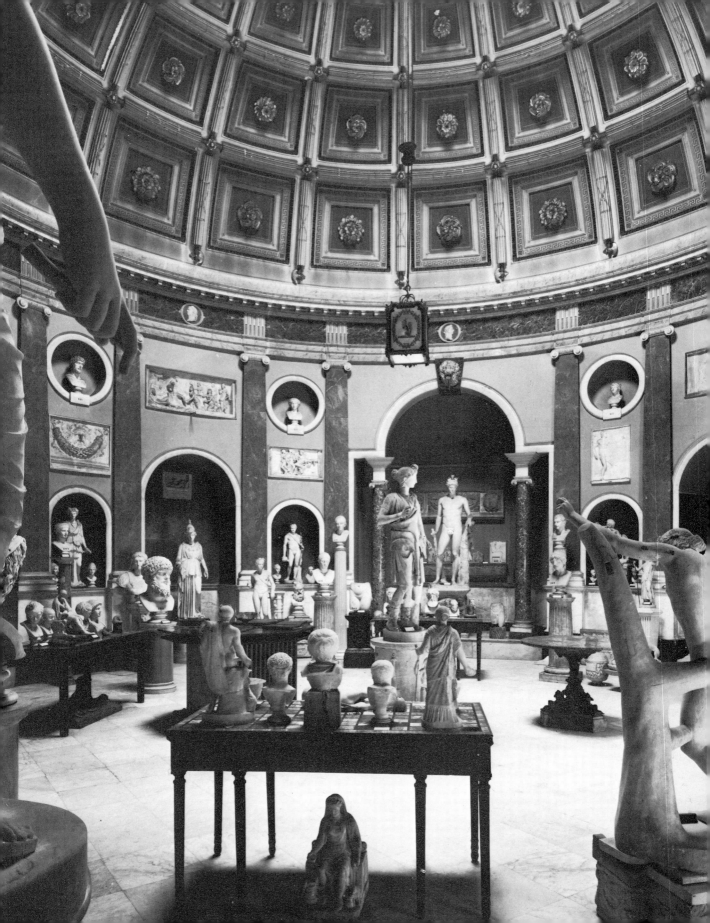

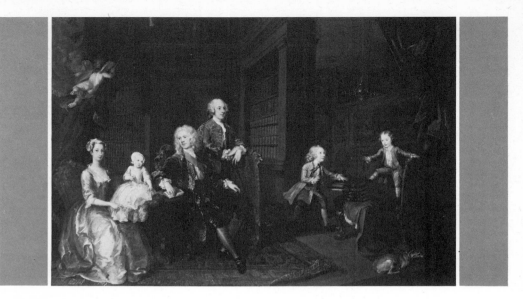

The emphasis on delight in the name 'dilettante' underlines their increasingly sociable nature. The Earl of Arundel and his friends who collected in the first half of the seventeenth century were a small group. In the second half of the eighteenth century it became a stock part of the education of every young man of wealth and birth to travel round the continent, to form a collection, and often to continue collecting on the London art market after he had returned. Travel was increasingly easy, the wealth and power of Britain were growing, and so were the numbers and wealth of the upper class. Every year, troops of well-born young men set out from England to make the grand tour. Some were filled with high-minded aspirations, some were only out to enjoy themselves. They flocked round picture galleries, they congregated in the ruins of Rome, they directed excavations, and they bought Greek and Roman statues—often faked—and old masters of doubtful authenticity from the dealers who crowded round them. They survive for us today in the amiable caricatures of Thomas Patch and others (Pl. 97), in Zoffany's splendid painting of the Tribuna at Florence, in the portraits that they commissioned from Pompeo Batoni and other artists in Rome, and in the objects that they brought home with them.

Space had to be found for the combined accumulation of objects collected by previous generations and by the new dilettanti. Libraries were enlarged and enriched by new books or portfolios of engravings concerned with travel, classical architecture, statues or pictures. Galleries and cabinets continued to flourish. The gallery and 'cabinet room' added in about 1762 to Corsham Court in Wiltshire, to contain the pictures collected on the continent by Sir Paul Methuen earlier in the century, survive complete with pictures (Col. Pl. XVI). At Strawberry Hill Horace Walpole's Gothic gallery and cabinet (or tribune, as he sometimes called it) have lost their original contents, but they are illustrated and listed in his own description of the house. The tribune (Pl. 103) was filled with a miscellany of objects as bizarre, in the aggregate, as anything recorded by Evelyn—from miniatures, bronzes, enamels and cameos to the great seal of King Theodore of Corsica, a bronze phallus, and a set of Turkish beads.[28]

106. The Cholmondeley family in their library in 1732. By William Hogarth.

107. (right) Holkham Hall, Norfolk. The library (William Kent, c. 1745).

In about 1725 the Earl of Burlington—the Arundel of his generation, and an architect as well as a collector—designed a villa at Chiswick for his own use (Pl. 104). It was originally built as an appendage to an existing Jacobean house, and was intended to contain his collections. Pictures and sculpture were kept on the main floor in a series of exquisitely finished little rooms of different shapes, grouped round a domed central rotunda. Books and manuscripts were in the rustic. The handsome Corinthian portico had nothing but a passage behind it. It expressed the contents of the building and the tastes of its builder, rather than its ceremonial centre.

A number of other houses were given extensions designed for similar purposes. In about 1770 Robert Adam added a series of chastely classical rooms to Newby Hall in Yorkshire, to contain William Weddell's collection of Greek and Roman sculpture. A sculpture gallery in the form of a reduced version of the Pantheon was added to Ince Blundell Hall in Lancashire in 1810 (Pl. 105). Both these additions were self-contained appendages, like the villa at Chiswick. More often, an attempt was made to integrate the collections into the normal life of the house. The gallery and cabinet room at Corsham also doubled up as a saloon and withdrawing room (Col. Pl. XVI). Lord Leicester's collection of sculpture at Holkham was displayed in the hall, the dining room, and a gallery which was used on occasion for dancing or great dinners.[29] In the breakfast scene in Hogarth's *Marriage à la Mode* series, the earl and countess are taking breakfast in a drawing room hung with their suitably fashionable collection of Italian pictures.

But the most obvious example of acclimatization was the library. Pepys's library (Pl. 100), as it was drawn in about 1690 was essentially a study. Although Pepys lavished a great deal of care and love on it, and had the portraits of his friends hanging round it, it had none of the attributes of a sitting room. In contrast is Hogarth's portrait of the Cholmondeley family, painted in 1738 (Pl. 106). The family are shown sitting in a room which has clearly been adjusted by Hogarth for artistic effect. But there is no doubt that it is a library, that both Lord and Lady Cholmondeley are sitting in it, and that their children are in it with them, having fun with the books.

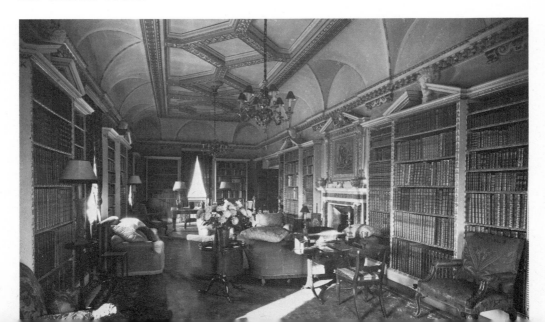

By the time the picture was painted, books had ceased to be the accoutrements of the expert and had become an everyday part of upper-class life. The library and its contents were no longer the personal equipment of the owner of the house; they had become the common property of the family and his guests. They included novels, plays, and journals for the idle hour as well as books for serious study.[30] The library began to be used as a living room, and people found what a very pleasant room it was, used in this way. In 1745, for instance, the library at Wrest in Bedfordshire was being used by the family as a sitting room in the evenings. Lady Grey, the mistress of the house, wrote enthusiastically to a friend: 'You can't imagine anything more cheerful than that room, nor more comfortable than reading there the rest of the evening.'[31] In 1755 the Countess of Kildare, staying with her aunt at Holland House on the edge of London, wrote 'I have got now into the library, which is a mighty pleasant room, and you will find it is a great improvement to Holland House to have a room in common so.'[32]

Book-lined studies, the personal sanctums of their owners, continued to exist as well as libraries of common resort; large houses could contain both. But communal libraries became increasingly popular. Up till the end of the eighteenth century they tended to be used mainly as family living rooms, like the library installed by Kent in the 1740s, between the Earl and Countess of Leicester's apartments in the separate family wing at Holkham (Pl. 107). But by the end of the eighteenth century libraries were also essential adjuncts to the entertainment of a house party. About these late-Georgian libraries, richly equipped with games, books, portfolios of engravings and scientific toys to amuse guests on wet afternoons, more will be said in Chapter 8.

In the course of the seventeenth and eighteenth centuries it became more and more important for a gentleman to be cultivated as well as literate. Culture became an essential part of the image of a worthy ruling class. Uneducated country gentlemen could still be found, but they were much criticized by their own class. One function of a country house was to demonstrate the culture, or lack of it, of its owner. Porticoes and pediments could be symbols of culture as well as of state. As Greek and Roman civilization continued to be considered the basis of modern civilization, the language of the classical orders remained the most common way of expressing culture in architecture. But by the middle of the eighteenth century it was beginning to be recognized how much England owed to the Middle Ages. The Gothic past offered an acceptable, if inferior, option for study by educated gentlemen; and Gothic began to be an acceptable alternative for country houses. Horace Walpole's antiquarian enthusiasm produced Strawberry Hill; a generation later Walter Scott built Abbotsford.

There tended, in fact, to be a relation between the contents of libraries or picture galleries and the architecture of the houses which contained them. But the absorption of books and works of art into country houses affected their plan as well as their detail. The arrival of the library as a communal living room, and the need for picture and sculpture galleries, helped to destroy the balance of the formal house and bring about its replacement by new types of planning.

180

108. (right) The view from the entrance portico of Stowe House, Buckinghamshire, in 1739.

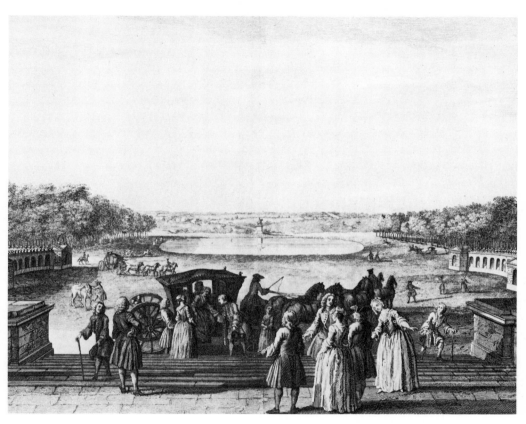

7 The Social House: 1720-70

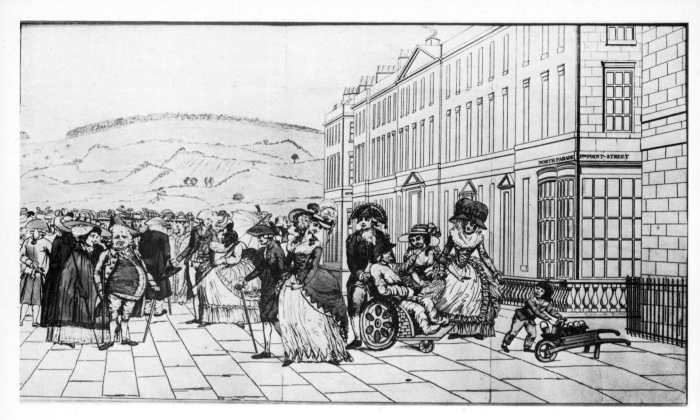

THE seventh Duke of Somerset, who has already featured in Chapter 5 as the man who rebuilt Petworth and entertained the King of Spain there, was one of the most celebrated characters of his day. He became known as the Proud Duke of Somerset. He is said to have insisted on his children always standing in his presence, and to have cut off the inheritance of one of his daughters when he fell asleep and woke to find her sitting down.[1] But the point about the Duke of Somerset was perhaps not so much that he was proud as that he was old. He lived until he was eighty-five, and died in 1750. In the 1740s, and even in the 1730s, the kind of protocol which had reigned in 1703, when the King of Spain came to Petworth, was beginning to seem a little absurd. Although dukes were still great people they could no longer expect the attention which they had taken for granted fifty years previously.

The point was underlined by Hogarth, when he painted his *Marriage à la Mode* series in 1743–5. The first picture in the series shows the marriage contract between the bridegroom and bride being signed by the bride's father, an ancient and haughty earl (Pl. 110). Not only is almost every available surface encrusted with earl's coronets, but the earl is sitting holding his family tree—if not exactly under, at any rate in front of, a canopy also surmounted by an earl's coronet—just as his predecessor would have done in the early seventeenth century.[2] Hogarth is clearly making fun of this kind of behaviour, which by the 1740s seemed as pompous and stuffy as the Proud Duke himself.

Perhaps the best place at which to watch the pride of the great beginning to be cut down to size is at Bath—that most typical of all the creations of the eighteenth

109. The North Parade, Bath, in about 1770.

110. (right) The Marriage Contract. From the *Marriage à la Mode* series, by William Hogarth.

century. At Bath one can start with a symbolic episode, once more in a ducal context. The Duchess of Queensberry turned up one evening at the Assembly Room at Bath wearing a white apron—that is to say not bothering to take off her day-time clothes. Beau Nash, the master of ceremonies—a man of very unpretentious middle-class origins—stripped the apron off her and threw it to her attendant ladies. The duchess swallowed the rebuke, and did not appear in an apron again.

The background to this incident is sketched out by Oliver Goldsmith, in his life of Nash.[3] 'General society among people of rank or fortune was by no means established. The nobility still preserved a tincture of gothic haughtiness, and refused to keep company with the gentry at any of the public entertainments of the place.' Beau Nash's achievement was to get rid of this 'gothic haughtiness' and establish 'general society among people of rank or fortune'. By that he meant a society in which the nobility and gentry mixed together, if not with complete equality, at any rate with much more social ease than they had before.

The social pattern of Bath was echoed by its architecture. There were no great axial vistas leading to a central feature, like the central avenues leading to the palace of the prince in towns that were being developed at the same time in France, Germany and Italy. Instead there were a series of focal points—the different baths, the assembly rooms, the pump room and the abbey—surrounded or linked by terraces and crescents. People strolled from one to the other, meeting friends on the way and talking to them (Pl. 109 and Col. Pl. XVIII).

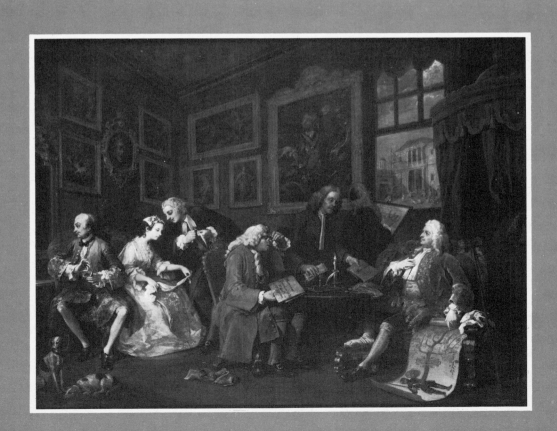

The Beau achieved what he did at Bath through the force of his personality. But a change would inevitably have come sooner or later because it reflected a change in society. Its middle strata, shading from the lesser gentry to the professional classes and richer merchants, were increasing in numbers, wealth and independence. They were comfortably off, well educated, and socially presentable. The great could no longer win the support of such people by taking them into their households as upper servants, or inviting them to dinner once a year and putting them at a separate table or even in a separate room to themselves. But their support was important. It meant votes, and control of enough votes meant one or more seats in the House of Commons. By the early eighteenth century Parliament had won its battle with the Crown. Influence in the House of Commons was now the basis of power. It had become more important than having the ear of ministers or the king; it was, in any case, the best means of getting their ear.

The core of a man's voting strength was his own tenantry; as voting was still open, tenants normally voted as their landlord directed them. But he extended this core by forming what was known as his 'interest'. An interest was built up by constant entertaining, by giving favours small and large and by getting jobs for individuals and their dependants. All landowners inherited a certain amount of patronage, in the form, for instance, of jobs on their own estates and presentations to livings. They used their interest to get government jobs which gave them additional patronage; and they used the additional patronage to extend their interest. A political operator like the Duke of Newcastle could have an interest which extended over the whole country and included a string of parliamentary seats; a country squire had his little local interest, which people like the duke would bid for by dispensing favours and by entertaining him in a dignified but affable way.[4]

At the beginning of the eighteenth century only about five per cent of the population had a vote. The lower strata of the voting body consisted of the smaller freeholders. Some of these were tenants, politically tied to their landlord, but by no means all of them were. In contested elections much wooing of the smaller freeholders went on, and lavish dinners were given for them by local landlords. But in the course of the eighteenth century the larger property owners, assisted by the professional classes who also normally had a stake in property, succeeded in eliminating most of the friction from the political system. There were fewer and fewer contests at elections, which were usually fixed beforehand, by mutual agreement among local interests. The small freeholder became less important. In 1762 Samuel Egerton, M.P. for Cheshire, refused to entertain his freeholders, and when asked why said that 'he did not value them'.[5]

The combined results of the growing independence, culture and prosperity of the lesser gentry and professional classes, the sewing up of the parliamentary system, and the resulting decline in importance of the smaller freeholder was a growing gap between the polite world of the gentry and the impolite world of servants, farmers and smallholders. In terms of the country house this meant an increasing split between gentry upstairs and non-gentry downstairs. Gentlemen

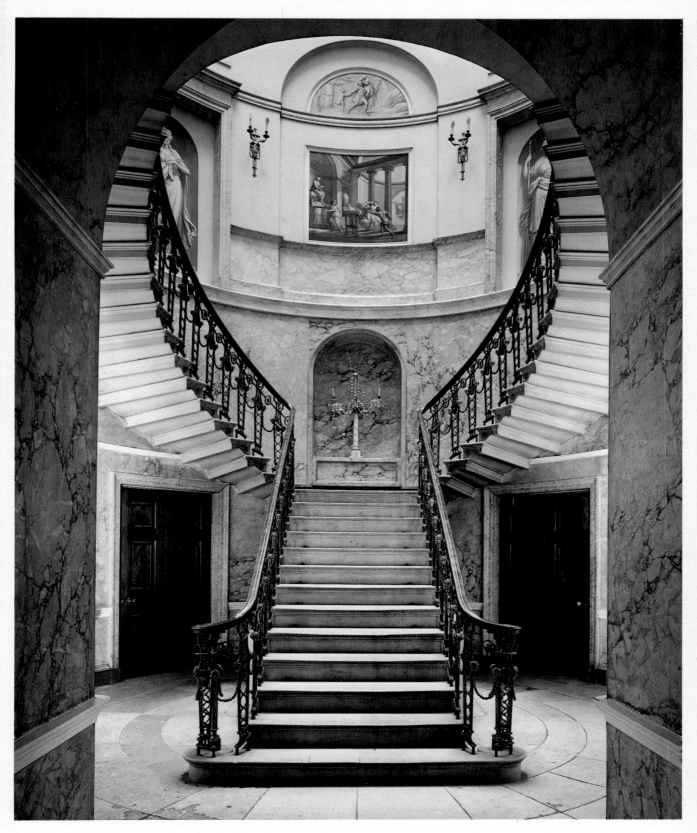

XVII. 20 Portman Square, London (1775–7). The staircase.

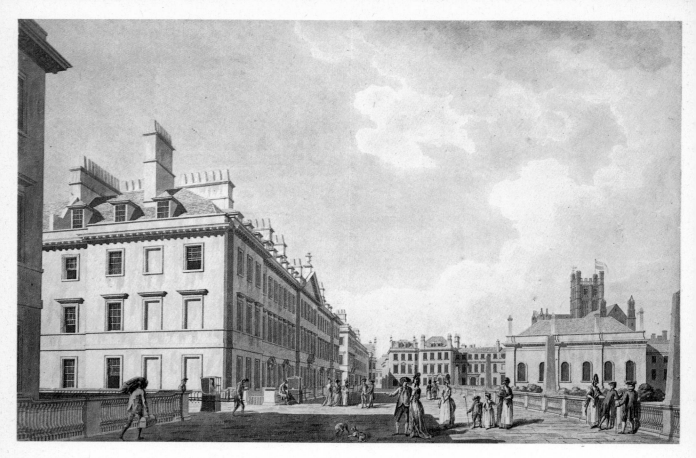

XVIII. View of the North Parade, Bath. By Thomas Malton, *c.* 1777.

XIX.   The Drake–Brockman family in the rotunda at Beachborough House, Kent. Attrib. to Joseph Highmore, *c.* 1745.

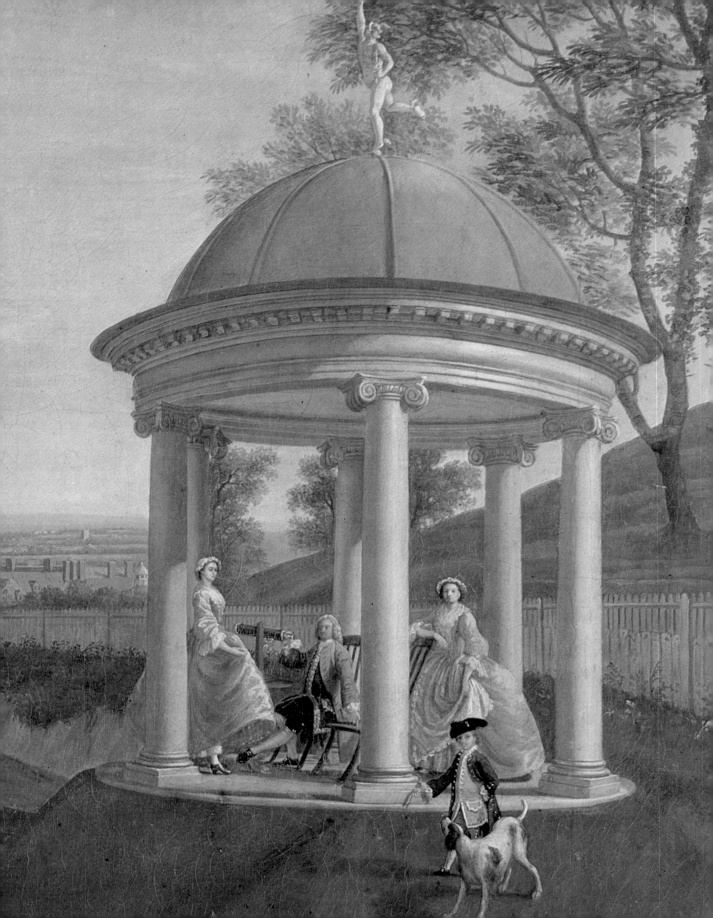

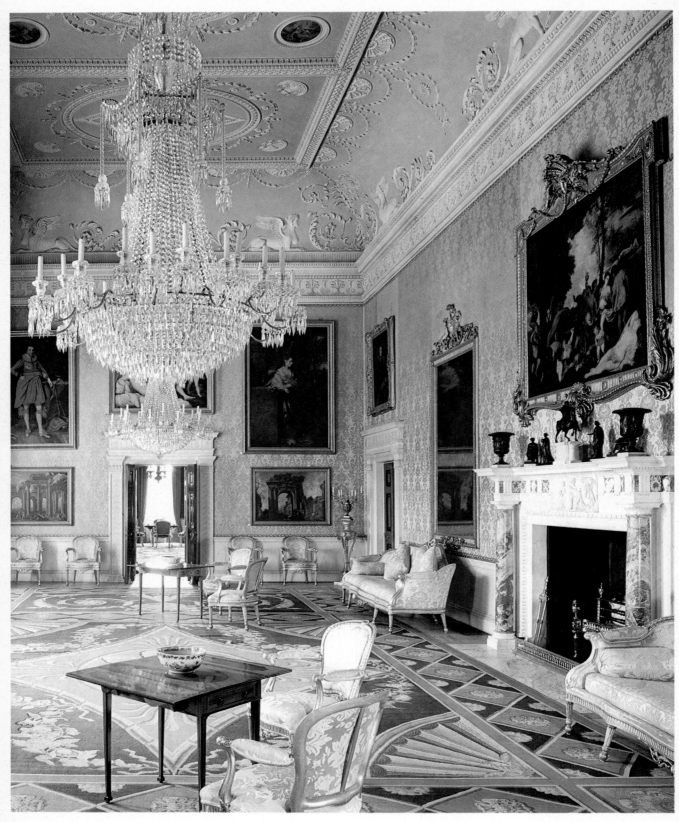

XX. Saltram, Devon. The saloon (1768).

could now only enter household service as librarians, tutors or chaplains; in which case they did not consider themselves servants and ate with the family or on their own. The tenants and freeholders, on the other hand, had sunk in status with the upper servants. Up till the early eighteenth century they were still being entertained on occasions in the hall and even in the parlour; in the course of the century they were exiled to the steward's room, or to a separate tenants' hall or audit hall in the servants' part of the house.

With this change of venue went a tendency to cut back on the kind of casual hospitality which had survived in some houses from the Middle Ages. In 1720 the Duke of Chandos had directed that all visitors to Cannons 'if honest substantial men and not idle loose fellows be asked to drink before they go away and more especially this be observed towards tenants.'[6] By 1735, at the Duke of Newcastle's two ancestral Sussex houses at Halland and Bishopstone, steps were being taken to put an end to the practice of 'giving small beer and doles of wheat to all the people of the country about them, without stint or limitation, and of entertaining all comers and goers with their servants and horses, another boundless expense.'[7]

Hospitality at this level did not disappear altogether. Tenants and others who came on business of any importance could still expect a meal or at least refreshment. The traditional celebratory dinners on special occasions still continued, even if they were now moved downstairs and possibly reduced in scale. They consisted of two kinds: regular dinners given at least once and sometimes twice a year, in the Christmas season and when rent was paid at the audit, and dinners given to celebrate a birth, a wedding, an election or a coming-of-age. Different houses had different traditions. There could be combined or separate dinners for household, tenants and local tradesmen, and either sit-down dinners or distribution of food and drink for the labourers and cottagers. Dinners were often followed by dancing, and the gentry sometimes put in an appearance at these events. But in the mid eighteenth century complaints were being made that they were tending to stay in London over Christmas and enjoy the pleasure of polite entertainment instead of taking part in the traditional festivities alongside their dependants.[8]

To outsiders, the polite world could seem both exclusive and corrupt. But like all ruling classes, it worked out an ethical justification for itself. Between 1650 and 1714 there had been two revolutions, a republic and a change of dynasty. Most of the landowning classes had been involved in at least one, and sometimes all, of these events. Only a small minority continued to support the concept of a monarch as the source of all power, with authority derived from God, presiding over a complex of lesser hierarchies, all miniatures of the divine model. Instead, property became the basis and justification of government.[9]

The polite world saw themselves as an elite, whose claim to run the country was based on having a stake in it as property owners, and was reinforced by the culture, education and *savoir-faire* of which its country houses were an advertisement. The monarch was the head of the government, but his powers were defined and restricted, and derived from consent not right. The nobility were given the respect due to major and long-established property owners, but not the reverence due to gods in miniature. The members of the property-owning elite moved among themselves with relative equality. They no longer found the rigid hierarchies of the formal house a sympathetic setting.

The growth of what Goldsmith called polite society, and the quality of life inside it, can be savoured in the diaries of Caroline Girle, later Mrs Lybbe Powys. She was the daughter of a prosperous surgeon of Lincoln's Inn Fields, who was also a small property owner in Berkshire. All through her life she was an indefatigable traveller. In 1757 she and her parents travelled up to Yorkshire and back. Among the many places they visited was Chesterfield, in Derbyshire, where they went to the races, and to a ball at the Assembly Room in the evening. In Caroline Girle's words, 'About ten we went to the Assembly Room, where the Duke of Devonshire always presided as Master of the Ceremonies, and after the ball gave an elegant cold supper where, by his known politeness and affability, it would be unnecessary for me to say how amiable he made himself to the company.' A couple of days later, after another day at the races, the duke came back to take tea with the Girles and their host. Two years later Miss Girle was at Bath, where she had already been twice before—'a city' she calls it 'more worth seeing than any I was ever at, the great metropolis excepted'.[10] The affability of the duke to the gentlemanly surgeon and his daughter, the presence of Londoners at balls in the Assembly Rooms at both Chesterfield in the north and Bath in the west, the actual existence of both Bath and assembly rooms, tells one a good deal about polite eighteenth-century society—its size, its mobility and its almost inexhaustible appetite for social life.

One of the factors which contributed to this mobility, and therefore helped both to spread the upper crust of polite people all over the country, and to make them more polite, was improved transport. The invention of carriages, more-or-less sprung, in the late sixteenth century had helped to encourage a rush of the upper classes to London—and a disinclination to leave it—which James I and others tried to discourage. But these early carriages, however convenient for the middle-aged, the unadventurous or the delicate who could not face the effort of a long journey on horseback were, even so, very crudely sprung and ponderous, slow and uncomfortable. After jolting a hundred miles or so along appalling roads to London the natural inclination was to stay there as long as possible. During the eighteenth century the design, and especially the springing, of carriages became increasingly sophisticated. By the mid-century better-sprung carriages were being supplemented by smaller and lighter chaises, chariots, curricles and phaetons. Both long-distance and local travel became easier, especially for women; the predominantly male make-up of earlier upper-class entertaining began to disappear. To begin with, better-sprung vehicles made travel over bad roads quicker and less uncomfortable, but from the middle of the eighteenth century the roads began to improve too. By the end of the century an energetic young man, driving himself in a racing phaeton, could make week-end visits within a hundred-mile radius of London. Phaetons were the sports cars of the eighteenth century. 'My will is yet unsigned, and I don't choose to venture in a phaeton with a young man while that is the case', Fanny Burney makes Mrs Selwyn say to Evelina in 1778.[11]

But well before then the whole of polite society was increasingly on the move. Some members of it were rotating in bigger circles than others, but all the circles were constantly intersecting. Once the London season was over, a large section of society went down to Bath for further social life. At Bath they met other polite people from all over the country and a contingent from Ireland. Meanwhile other chunks of society were travelling to enjoy the company and take the waters at other spas, such as Clifton, Buxton, Tunbridge Wells, or Scarborough. Others were going to race meetings and taking part in the attendant gaieties, in the form of balls and assemblies, held in the new assembly rooms at provincial centres such as York, Norwich, Nottingham, Exeter and Shrewsbury—or, as has appeared, Chesterfield, not a town one would connect today with eighteenth-century elegance.

In between these various centres they were constantly stopping to stay at the country houses of friends, or to visit the country houses of strangers. Within the club of polite society, both the grounds and the interiors of all country houses of any size were normally open to view, so that during the summer season the more famous and accessible houses, could appear like country versions of the Parades at Bath or Tunbridge Wells (Pl. 108).

One result of the nobility and gentry becoming more mobile and mixing more together was new kinds of parties. From the sixteenth to the early eighteenth century, whenever people decided to entertain, they did so in much the same way. They gave either a dinner on its own, or a dinner combined with dancing. The latter combination started with a meal, sometimes enlivened by music. After dinner the company retired to a withdrawing room, and passed an hour or so by taking tea or dessert, or playing cards, or listening to more music. They then returned to the room where they had dined, for dancing or as it tended to be called, a ball; in the early eighteenth century as few as seven couples dancing together could be described as a ball.[12] After dancing there was normally some kind of light refreshment, and then everybody went home. The refreshments at the end might, according to the century, be described as a banquet or a supper, the room for dinner and dancing a great chamber or a saloon; the dances danced, the music played and the food eaten changed, but the pattern remained much the same. The guests did one thing at a time, and they all did it together.

The eighteenth century introduced more variety. Balls developed and grew larger and more elaborate. The assembly, the masquerade, the rout, the drum, the *ridotto*, the *ridotto al fresco* and the musical party were all new forms of entertainment which only got under way in the eighteenth century, even if some of them had their origins in the seventeenth.

The most important of these was the assembly (Pl. 112). Assemblies varied in their details, but basically conformed to the definition made in 1751: 'a stated and general meeting of the polite persons of both sexes, for the sake of conversation, gallantry, news and play'.[13] They took place in the evening. The guests either

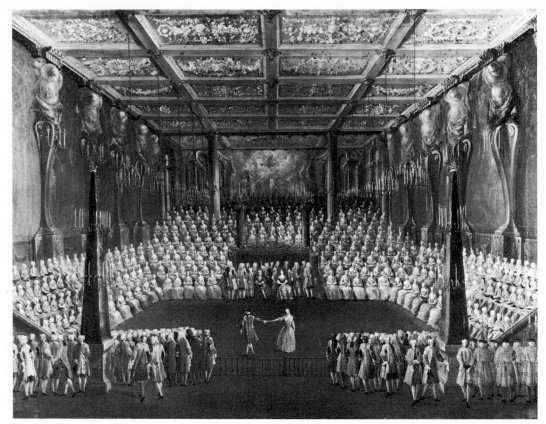

111. A ball at Dublin Castle in the 1730s.

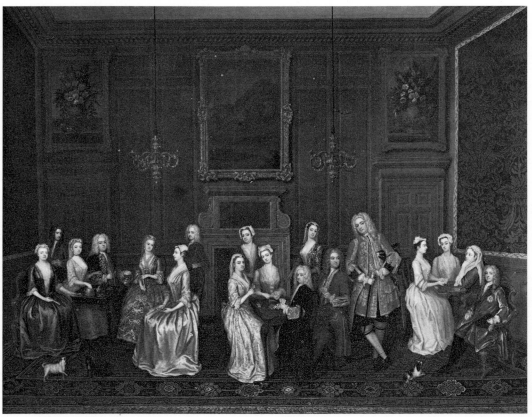

112. An assembly at Lord Harrington's. By Charles Phillips.

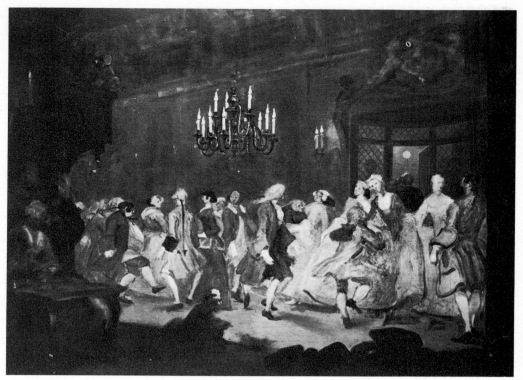

113. The Wedding Dance. By William Hogarth, c. 1745.

played cards, or drank tea, or just walked around talking and flirting. Some assemblies, but by no means all, ended with supper.

To modern eyes assemblies sound staid enough entertainments, but at the time they represented a breakthrough. They involved several activities going on at the same time, and this made them notably less formal than earlier types of entertainment. Moreover they could easily be extended to cope with the growth of society. Assemblies in the early eighteenth century involved comparatively few people, and could take place in a single room; in the course of the century they tended to expand in size until they could fill half a dozen rooms or more.

In 1731 Peter Wentworth wrote to his brother Lord Wentworth that 'Mr Howard opens his assembly with a ball'.[14] This would have been a ball in the old-fashioned sense, a series of dances which all the guests either took part in or watched, before they moved on to the card-playing and tea-drinking of the assembly (Pl. 111). But in the mid century assemblies and balls merged together. Dancing, tea-drinking and cards went on at the same time, usually in different rooms (Pl. 113). Such ball-assemblies (they were called both at the time) almost invariably included a supper. Normally, everyone stopped what they were doing and proceeded together into the supper room; but on occasions a running supper was provided, and the guests went in and out of the supper room as they felt like it.

Masquerades were balls or ball-assemblies at which the guests wore masks, at any rate for the first half of the evening. *Ridottos* combined dances with concerts,

193

and *ridottos al fresco* were *ridottos* held in the open at public gardens such as Vauxhall or Ranelagh. Routs and drums seem to have been little more than large assemblies. Musical parties, which were extremely popular in the eighteenth century, were basically assemblies with a concert included.

One of the great features of the eighteenth century was the popularity, and the increasing size, elaboration and sophistication of public meeting places, in the form of assembly rooms and pleasure gardens. They were a product of Goldsmith's 'increase in general society'. They could provide a little of everything that the eighteenth century enjoyed—musical entertainments, places to eat, places to dance, places to walk up and down, meet one's friends or pick up new ones, and indulge in gossip or flirtation. Naturally, they catered for larger numbers than private houses. But ambitious hostesses soon started to emulate them. To begin with, they hired public rooms and gave large parties for their friends in them. Before long, they started to add on to their own houses. As Isaac Ware commented in 1756, 'We see an addition of a great room now to almost every house of consequence.'[15] This was in London. In the country some houses already had their great halls, but they were in the wrong place. Halls were all very well for dinners given to unsophisticated tenants and local gentry of the old style, who came tumbling in from outdoors straight to the table. Polite society needed its big rooms to be several removes from the front door.

As a result, the formal house ceased to work. Instead of a hall and saloon, between apartments which were the private territories of the people occupying them, what was now needed was a series of communal rooms for entertaining, exclusive of the hall and all running into each other.

The first step in this direction was to open up the state apartment on occasions to general company. There had been occasions in the past when the best lodgings or state apartment had been the scene of general gatherings—at christenings or funerals, for instance, when the mother or the corpse, in suitably festive or funereal splendour, was on display in or adjoining the state bed. But this was when the bedchamber had an occupant with a functional part to play. The next stage was to throw the whole apartment open for assemblies, with card-tables in the withdrawing room and the guests parading through the unoccupied bedchamber and closet to admire their fittings and decorations.[16] The stage after that was to increase the number of rooms in the state apartment, so that it could accommodate a big assembly or assembly-ball. The final stage was to hive the state bedchamber off from the apartment, leaving just a sequence of reception rooms.

In the formal house the state apartment had normally been strung out along the straight line of the axis of honour. The eighteenth century discovered that, for its changed needs, the most attractive and convenient way to arrange it was in a circle, around a top-lit central staircase. Top-lit staircases had first appeared in England in the late seventeenth century; but it was not until well into the eighteenth century that their convenience began to be appreciated.

A circuit of reception rooms round a staircase made, if not its earliest, its first

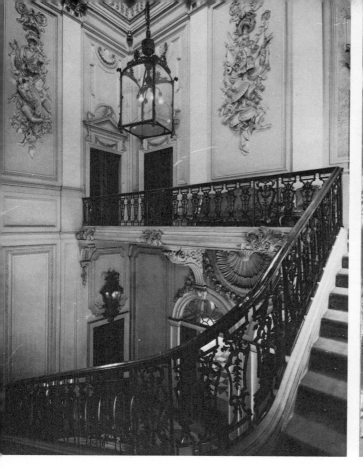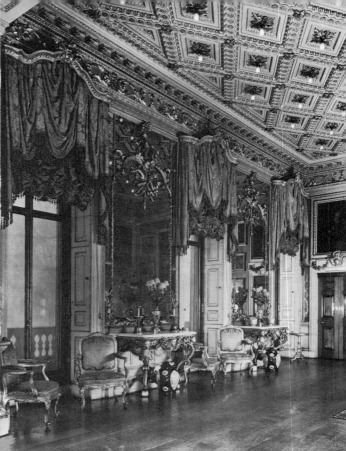

highly-publicized appearance at Norfolk House in St James's Square. It was designed in about 1750 by Matthew Brettingham for the Duke of Norfolk. Brettingham was also working at Holkham in Norfolk which was slowly taking shape in the 1740s and '50s.[17] He adapted a type of plan which had been used in the wings at Holkham and made it the mainspring of Norfolk House (Fig. 13). The centre of the house was filled by a top-lit staircase, and the reception rooms went all the way round it on the first floor (Pls 114 and 115). Each room had a different colour scheme, and most had a different style of decoration; guests at a big assembly could climb the splendid staircase, make their way round the circle, stop to enjoy the various distractions provided for them, enjoy a sequence of different visual experiences, and finally make their way down the stairs and out again.

The circuit included one room bigger and grander than the others, known as the great room or great drawing room. There were four rooms before it on the circuit, and a state bedroom, dressing room and closet after. The great room was no longer the ceremonial centre of the house; it was the richest in a series of rich episodes. The bedroom, dressing room and closet were thrown open to company for big receptions, and were probably seldom used by an individual. With the exception of the occasional eminent foreigner, people moving in London society expected to be lavishly entertained, but not invited to stay.

114. (above left) Norfolk House, London (Matthew Brettingham, 1747–56). The staircase.

115. (above right) One of the reception rooms in Norfolk House.

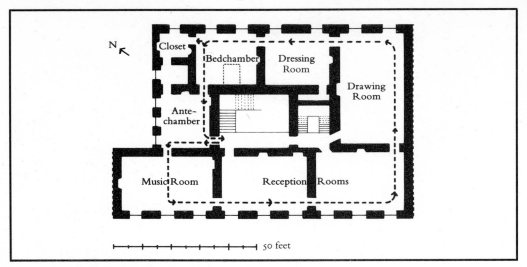

Fig. 13. Norfolk House. The first floor.

The opening assembly at Norfolk House was given in February 1756. It was the most talked about social event of the year. It produced an elegy on the distress of Lady Townshend, who for political reasons was not asked:

> Oh could I on my waking brain impose
> Or but forget at least my present woes
> Forget 'em—how? each rattling coach suggests
> The loath'd ideas of the crowding guests
> To visit—were to publish my disgrace
> To meet the spleen in every other place
> To join old maids and dowagers forlorn
> And be at once their comfort and their scorn . . .
> This night the happy and the unhappy keep
> Vigils alike—Norfolk hath murdered sleep![18]

Horace Walpole, who inevitably *was* invited, gave one of his sparkling impressionistic descriptions which leaves one with no very clear idea of what was where. William Farrington went round room by room, and described the whole circuit in detail.[19]

Farrington was an obscure captain in the Indian army; the fact that he was invited gives an idea of the growing range of London society. He was much impressed by the 'vast crowd and the great blaze of diamonds' and by the way in which 'every room was furnished with a different colour, which used to be reckoned absurd, but this I suppose is to be the standard.' He describes how the company was received by the duchess in the room after the antechamber, at the head of the staircase. This was the white and gold music room, now in the Victoria and Albert Museum. Then came two rooms, one hung with green and one with crimson damask. Then the great room, hung with tapestry and containing the duke, his niece, and the card-tables—Horace Walpole repeated a remark that 'all the company was afraid of the duchess, and the duke afraid of all the company.' Then came a dressing room and the bedchamber, hung with blue

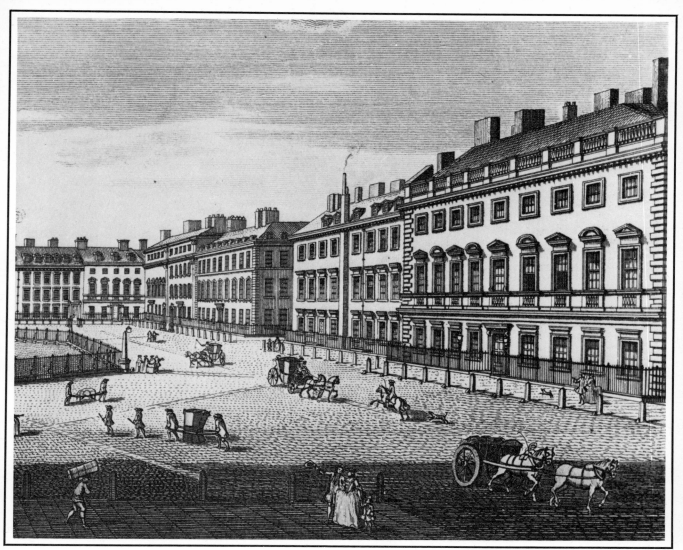

116. Norfolk House. The exterior, from St. James's Square.

velvet. In the latter was the state bed, surrounded by a brass rail to protect it from crowds. The last room was the closet, 'filled with an infinite number of curiosities'. From it guests went out on the stair again.

From the outside Norfolk House presented a bland but handsome facade. It had no columns, no central pediment, just rows of windows with pediments to mark the big rooms on the first floor. The design was criticised at the time as 'insipid',[20] but in fact the regular succession of pedimented windows, with no central feature, accurately suggested the regular succession of rooms, with no one ceremonial centre, behind them (Pl. 116). One advantage of the plan was that it was not necessary to use the full circle of rooms. For a smaller entertainment, for instance for a musical party, the first two or three rooms could be used on their own.

The Norfolk House type of plan became the standard one for London houses. Within the next couple of decades it was to be developed or varied with even

197

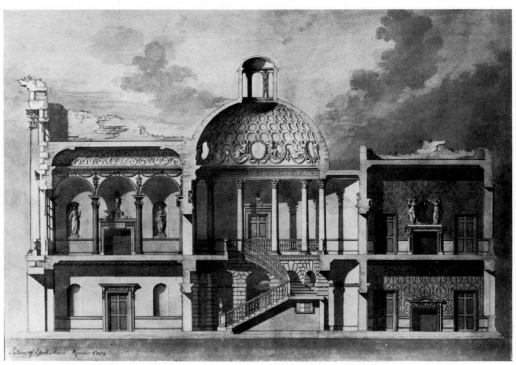

117. A section of the house designed by William Chambers for the Duke of York in 1759.

greater panache, and with more delicacy and sparkle, by architects such as Robert Adam and William Chambers. Adam varied the shapes of the rooms in the circuit, and worked out a style of ornament which expressed to perfection the sophistication, gaiety and elegance which polite society aimed at. He tended to be dealing with houses on more constricted sites than that of Norfolk House, and for them he developed a type of plan based on a half-circle, with the staircase to one side. But the principle remained the same; guests could come up the stairs, circulate through two or three rooms rather than six or seven, and find themselves back on the stairs again. Such smaller circuits had no bedroom in them; and at a ball, supper was usually served in a dining room on the ground floor. Adam's supremely elegant staircases thus became the setting both for the first approach of guests to their host and hostess, and for the descent and ascent of the whole party to and from supper (Col. Pl. XVII).

The section drawn by Chambers in 1759 for a proposed London house for the Duke of York is a brilliant exposition of the attractions of a house with a central staircase leading to a suite of rooms for entertainment (Pl. 117). It was never built; but James Paine adapted the design a few years later on an even grander scale, and with an almost identical staircase, for Wardour Castle in Wiltshire. In the second half of the eighteenth century houses with central staircases became popular in the country as well as in the town. They could be very grand, and they could be not

198

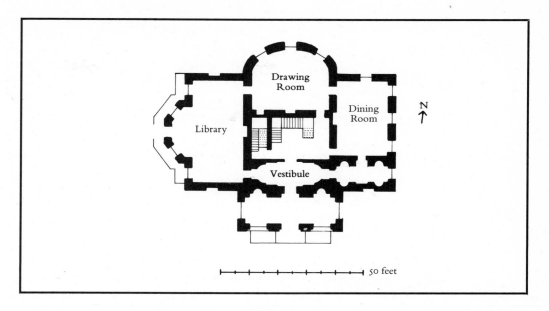

grand at all. The credit for developing the plan for more modest country houses lies with Sir Robert Taylor. He was not actually the first to do it, but he was the first to adapt it to new social usages and do it in independence of the saloon-with-apartments system.[21]

The first of Taylor's country houses was Harleyford Manor in Buckinghamshire, designed in about 1755. Its main rooms are all on the ground floor, above a basement. There are no apartments on this floor; all the bedrooms are upstairs. The hall is little more than a vestibule and the floor is mainly occupied by three more-or-less equal rooms, originally the dining room, drawing room and library (Fig. 14). In the centre is a staircase core, consisting of a main stairs with a back stairs to one side of it. Each room can be reached without going through one of the other rooms, there are no long corridors, the house is compact and was therefore cheap to build, and eminently usable for everyday life. But it was also perfectly adaptable for a social event. For a 'very elegant ball and supper' such as Mrs Lybbe Powys attended there in 1790,[22] it had the essential minimum of three rooms—one for dancing, one for cards and one for supper—neatly arranged with a convenient flow round and into the staircase. Moreover, Taylor anticipated Adam and made each room a different shape, so that going round from room to room was a series of contrasts. The way the house works is beautifully expressed by its exterior. There is no portico, and no dominant feature or facade. Each facade is different; a walk round the exterior produces a series of different groupings in the same kind of way as a walk round the interior (Pl. 118).

In formal houses of the early eighteenth century where hall, saloon and main apartments had all been on the same floor, staircases had tended to become relatively utilitarian. In town houses, or smaller country houses like Harleyford, where even the main bedrooms and dressing rooms were on the upper floors, and

199

Fig. 14. Harleyford, Buckinghamshire. The ground floor.

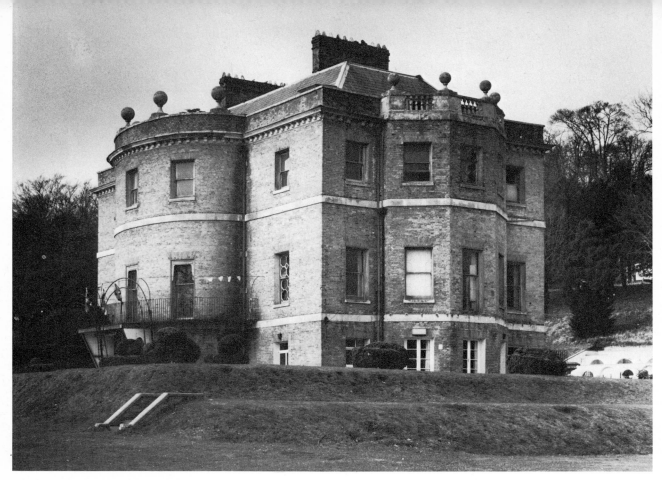

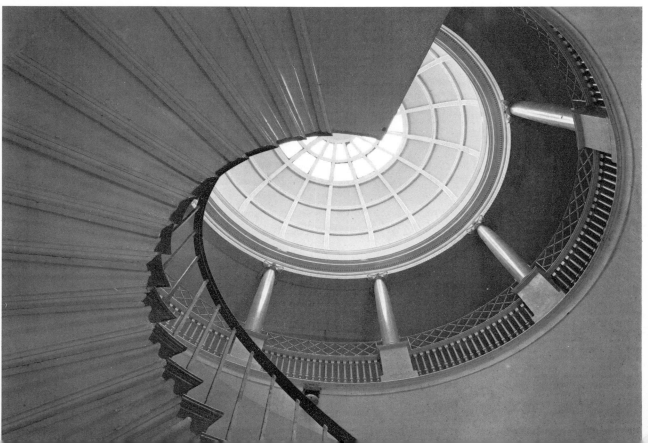

at ground-floor level the staircase hall was in constant use as a circulation space, they needed to make more of a show. But there was no reason, and usually no space, for them to be as grand as the staircases leading up to first-floor state rooms in sixteenth and seventeenth-century houses. Taylor and others evolved the solution; a top-lit circular or oval cantilevered staircase, often made of stone and fitted with a wrought-iron balustrade. Such staircases were spacious without being over large, and could be supremely elegant (Pl. 119).

More important houses than Harleyford occupied more ground space and often still had one or more apartments on the ground floor. In such houses, however, the rooms tended to be arranged in a different manner to that found in formal houses. Sometimes they were lavishly expanded versions of the central staircase plan, perhaps with pavilion wings, as at Wardour Castle. More often their plan was based on two overlapping circuits. Hagley Hall in Worcestershire is an early example of the latter type. It was designed in about 1752, by Sanderson Miller and others, for George Lyttelton—later Lord Lyttelton.[23] It was planned with a private section to the east, grouped round one staircase, and a public section to the west, grouped round another staircase (Fig. 15). The private section contains three apartments, all with dressing rooms, and the library. The public section was designed on the circuit system, but was nicely contrived to be usable partially or in whole. It consisted of hall, saloon, drawing room, gallery (Pl. 120) and dining room. When the family were there on their own they could cross the hall from the library to eat in the dining room; when they had company they could use the drawing room in conjunction with the dining room; and for big parties they could open up the whole circuit.

The link between the two circuits is provided by the hall and saloon in the centre. To this extent Hagley bears a superficial resemblance to formal houses. But although the plan is obviously influenced by them, it is adapted for different purposes. The two sides of the house have different functions and arrangements. The saloon is the first of a circuit of rooms and not noticeably grander than any of the others. The centre of the house is no longer a ceremonial centre in the early-eighteenth-century manner and so there is no portico (Pl. 121). Lyttelton thought about having one, because a portico in this position had become the conventional thing, but decided against it.

Central rooms on the axis of the hall, such as the saloon at Hagley, continued to be called saloons in some new houses as late as the early nineteenth century. But the tendency was for them to become less and less important, until they ended up as little more than vestibules. Alternatively, the name 'saloon' was shifted to a large room further round the circuit, in the same kind of position as that of the great room at Norfolk House or the gallery at Hagley. Indeed, according to their shape, such off-centre rooms could either be called galleries, as at Hagley and Harewood, or saloons, as at Saltram and Brocket. They served for the display of pictures and as ballrooms; their new position fitted more conveniently into the routine of the eighteenth-century ball, because the rooms preceding them in the circuit could be used for the reception of guests on their first arrival. Saloons in

118. (upper left) Harleyford, Buckinghamshire (Sir Robert Taylor, 1755).

119. (left) Chute House, Wiltshire. The staircase (Sir Robert Taylor, c. 1768).

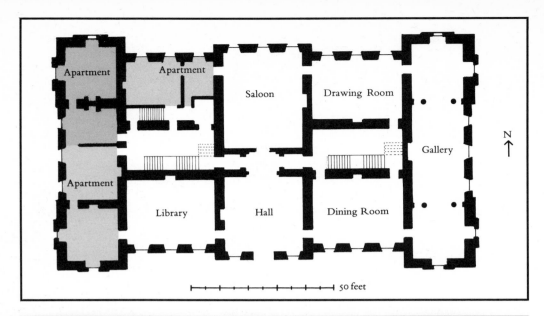

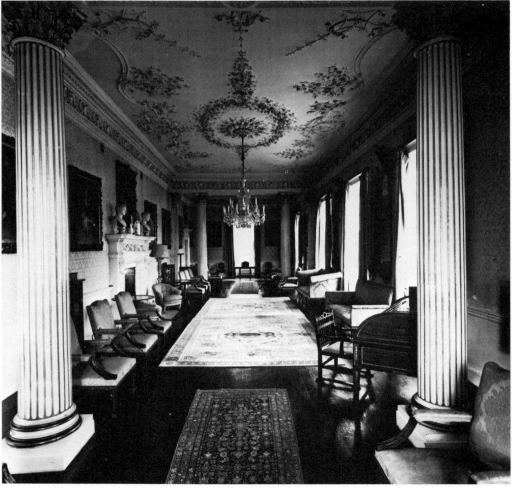

Fig. 15. (top) Hagley Hall, Worcestershire. The ground floor.

120. Hagley Hall, Worcestershire (Sanderson Miller, 1753–9). The gallery.

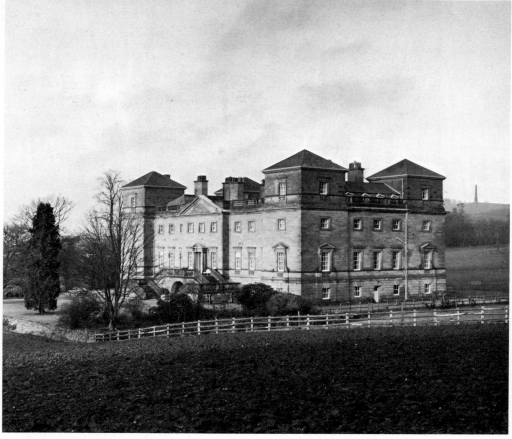

121. Hagley Hall. The exterior.

this position were often very large and decorated with great splendour (Col. Pl. XX); but they were no longer the formal hub of the house.

Saloons, although often used for dancing, were now seldom used for meals. A separate dining room had become an essential element of all houses of any pretensions; the grander ones often had a common parlour, for everyday use by the family as an eating and sitting room, and a dining room (or 'eating room') for entertaining company. The dining room was always one of the best and biggest rooms in the house. Plate on the sideboard or central table and large numbers of footmen waiting in splendid liveries could make a big dinner an impressive sight, but mediaeval ceremony had by now entirely vanished.[24] Each course was carried in by footmen and laid out on the central table; the more lavish the dinner, the greater the variety of dishes. The main meat dish was usually put in front of the host to carve. Footmen attended to the individual wants of guests by taking their plates to the dishes, rather than carrying the dishes round the table. The butler stayed at the sideboard with the wine; the footmen brought glasses to the sideboard to be filled or refilled. If the glasses had been used already the butler rinsed them in a cistern of water under the sideboard (or, as Swift complained, merely filled the dirty glasses).[25] The one element of ceremony was provided by the company not the servants, in the form of toasts. These were either drunk by

203

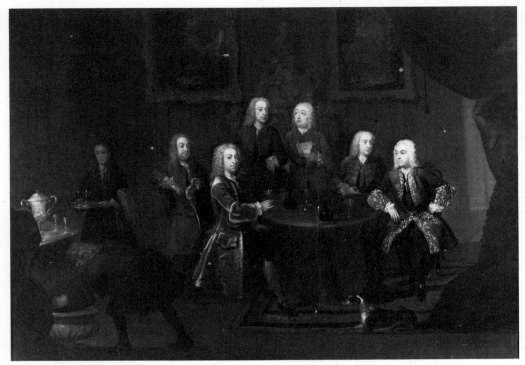

122. The brothers Clarke and others taking wine. By Gawen Hamilton, *c.* 1730.

the whole company, or when one individual asked another to drink with him; in both cases the relevant glasses were taken to the sideboard by footmen to be refilled. On occasions an orchestra in, or more usually next door to, the dining room played music throughout the meal.

The meal normally ended with dessert, after which the ladies removed to the drawing room. At Hagley the drawing room is separated from the dining room by the gallery. In 1752, when the plan was still being worked out, Lyttelton wrote to the architect that 'Lady Lyttelton wishes for a room of separation between the eating room and the drawing room, to hinder the ladies from the noise and talk of the men when left to their bottle, which must sometimes happen, even at Hagley.'[26] By then the English custom of the women leaving the men to drink, smoke and talk in the dining room was well established (Pl. 122). Its origins are somewhat mysterious. It never obtained on the continent, where it was, and still is, regarded as the height of barbarism. There is no trace of it in the many dinners, of all kinds of social grades, described by Pepys in the 1660s. Yet in Congreve's *The Double Dealer* of 1694 the women are described as 'at the end of the gallery, retired to their tea and scandal, according to their ancient custom, after dinner.'[27]

Congreve's reference to tea may provide an explanation. Drinking tea and coffee became fashionable in the 1670s and '80s. Both drinks were normally served after dinner and supper, and brewed by the hostess herself; by about 1680 the Duchess of Lauderdale had an 'Indian furnace for tea garnished with silver' in her closet at Ham.[28] It may be that what was to become one of the institutions of English upper-class life started as a short practical interval in which the ladies

204

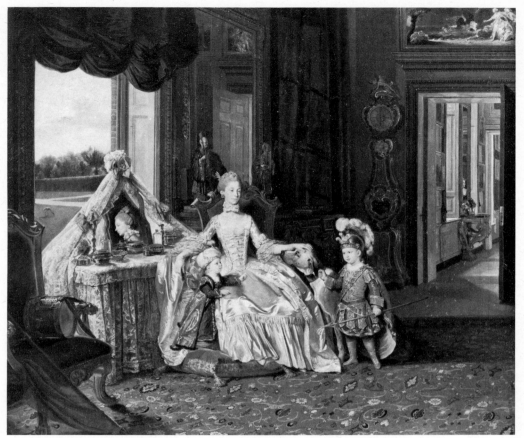

123. Queen Charlotte in her dressing room with her sons. By Johann Zoffany, 1764.

retired to brew tea or coffee, after which the gentlemen joined them to drink it. If so the interval grew longer and longer, until it could last several hours; by 1778 Robert Adam was celebrating it as the period in which the men of the ruling class discussed politics together.[29] They still, however, normally joined the ladies for tea or coffee in the end, unless they were incapable.

The long periods spent by gentlemen and ladies on their own in this way meant that the dining room began to be thought of as a mainly masculine, and the drawing room as a mainly feminine, room. Drawing rooms had now ceased almost entirely to be attached to individual bedrooms and people, or to be rooms used for comparatively short periods of time while dinner was being cleared. They were important rooms. In the seventeenth century they had invariably been smaller than the main eating room; in the eighteenth century they tended to be of more or less the same size.

The fact that so much more space was now being taken up by rooms of general resort by no means implies that the apartment system had been given up altogether. What had happened was that the balance had changed. People in country houses spent more time in the common rooms and less in their own apartments, and the importance and therefore the size of apartments shrank as a result. At the same time the relatively more democratic nature of general society meant that, instead of having a few very grand apartments designed for the entertainment of great people—from the king downwards—and relatively few other bedrooms, the tendency was to have a larger number of smaller apartments. The average apartment consisted of a bedroom and dressing room. Sometimes it also included a closet. A grand apartment for visitors, or the apartments of the owners, could have two dressing rooms, one for the man and one for the woman. Dressing rooms were invariably also used as private sitting rooms; they were often very handsomely furnished, and bigger than the bedroom (Pl. 123). The owner's dressing room was sometimes on the ground floor, even when his bedroom was on the floor above. Such dressing rooms were not so different from studies—except that the owner came down from his bedroom in the morning, and saw people on business while his toilet was being finished off by his valet.[30]

Access for servants to the apartments was now usually by a combination of a single backstairs and corridors; there was a reaction against a plurality of backstairs, probably because of the space they took up. The top floor tended to be given over to a miscellaneous collection of smaller apartments, nurseries and maids' rooms. Bachelor guests were sometimes put in a communal dormitory, known as a 'barracks'; a barracks could also be provided for visiting men-servants.[31] Little effort was made to segregate the sexes. Dorothea Herbert describes how, at Castle Blunden in Ireland in 1780, the girls in the upstairs chamber were serenaded and teased by the 'bold boys' in the barracks; on one occasion they were caught 'en chemise' and 'in our confusion overturned the pot-de-chambre and the two doors being opposite the whole contents meandered across the lobby into their barrack—immediately the house rang with their laughter.'[32] Such an incident would scarcely have been possible in Victorian houses.

The early-eighteenth-century practice of having some family rooms in the rustic continued through the century, especially in houses planned round a single circuit. The arrangements varied greatly from house to house. Sometimes the main entry was into a lower hall in the rustic, and so by an internal staircase up to the main floor. Sometimes the common parlour was in the rustic, or a complete apartment for the owner of the house, or just a billiard room or smoking parlour. A common arrangement was for the owner to have a study or business room in the rustic, with a room or rooms for the land-steward adjacent. In 1786 Lord Pembroke complained that at Wilton 'a steward's office *in the house* would be the very devil. One should never be free an instant from meeting people full of words and wants.' However, after a few month's reflection he became 'convinced of the absolute indispensable necessity of a land-steward, doing nobody's business but mine, living and boarding in the house, and transacting everything in my office.'[33]

Apart from family rooms, and a lower hall if there was one, the rustic normally contained the cellars, the steward's room (in big houses), the servants' hall, and the rooms belonging to the butler and housekeeper. Sometimes it also contained the kitchen and its appendages, but these were often in a separate pavilion, as in earlier houses. Sleeping quarters for servants could be up on the top floor, or in the

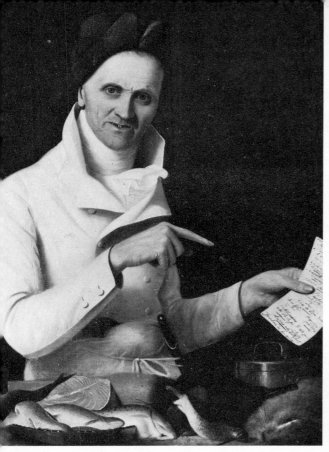

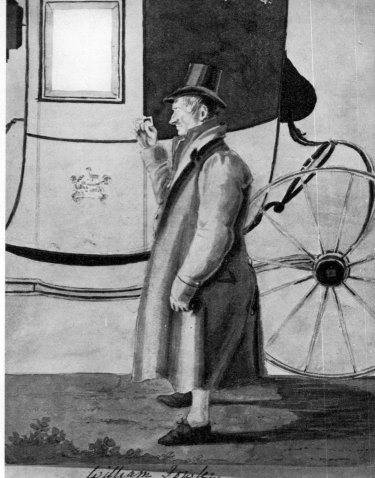

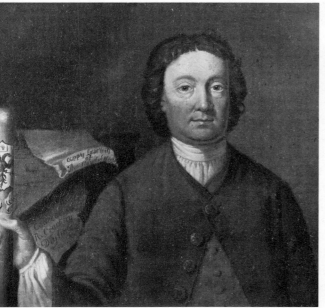

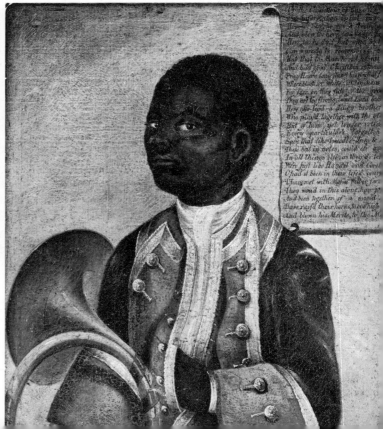

124. (top left) The cook at Drumlanrig, Dumfriesshire, in about 1817.

125. (top right) The coachman at Farnley Hall, Yorkshire, in the early nineteenth century.

126. (lower left) The steward at Hawarden Castle, Flintshire, in the mid eighteenth century.

127. (lower right) A postilion at Erddig Park, Flintshire, in the mid eighteenth century.

kitchen or sometimes, in the case of menservants, over the stables. The tendency for the size of households to decrease continued, as was only to be expected in a society which preferred elegance to grandeur. The household of a peer was likely to vary from twenty-five to fifty people, depending on his wealth and rank (Pls 124 to 127). The proportion of women had increased to a third or even a half. The increase was partly due to a decrease in the showier parts of the male establishment, partly to an increase in the number of house-maids required to clean houses of growing elegance.[34]

The housekeeper accordingly became more important. As few ladies now had gentlewomen to wait on them she was in charge of all the women servants. She was recognized as the female counterpart to the steward (if there was one) or the butler, even if as a woman she was paid little more than half as much as they were. She lived in some comfort in her housekeeper's room, with a store-room and sometimes a still-room next door to it.

Still-rooms first appeared in country houses in the sixteenth century, but only became common in the seventeenth.[35] They were originally so called because they were fitted with stills, to distil the cordial waters used for banquets (in the Elizabethan sense), medicine or scent. At first distilling was one of the skills or hobbies thought proper for the mistress of the house and her gentlewomen, so that the still-room tended to be close to her lodgings. As ladies also concerned themselves with the preparation of delicate dishes for banquets the two functions were often accommodated in the still-room, which was accordingly also fitted with stoves and cupboards for storage.[36] The still-room at Hengrave was used in 1603 for 'preparing and keeping biskett cakes, marchpanes, herbs, spicebreads, fruits, conserves, etc.'[37] In the course of the eighteenth century the housekeeper tended to take over the still-room from her mistress, and the increasing use of doctors and apothecaries made home-brewed medicine less important. Stills gradually disappeared, but preserves and cakes, and the stoves on which to make them, remained in the still-room.[38]

Housekeepers were usually permanently resident in one place. Where families owned more than one house, however, the majority of the household moved round with them, and went up to London for the season. Especially social or political families would be likely to spend more time in London or Bath, and especially sporting or farming families more time in the country. In the country the way of life varied comparatively little. The detailed account that survives of three weeks spent by a party of ten at Welford in Berkshire could have been parallelled in hundreds of other country houses.[39]

The occasion was the marriage, in September 1770, of Jacob Houblon to Susannah Archer, whose parents owned Welford. Apart from the day of the wedding and church-going on Sunday morning, each day passed in much the same way. Breakfast was at nine-thirty, dinner normally at four, supper at ten. Between breakfast and changing for dinner at three-thirty the gentlemen went shooting or fishing or joined the ladies on a walk or an outing or in their dressing rooms, or played billiards in the hall. The ladies spent part of the morning in their

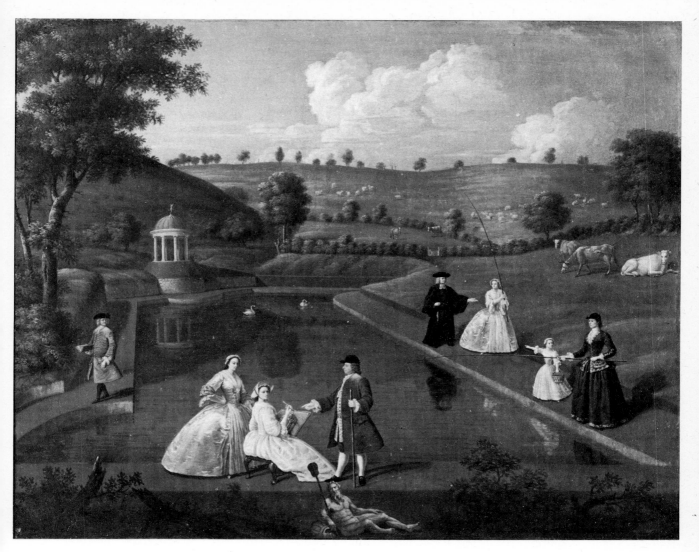

own or Lady Mary Archer's dressing rooms, then walked round the lake and gardens, watched the gentlemen fishing, or went for a drive to a neighbouring town or park. Occasional visitors called, and were received in the drawing room. On one wet day the party spent the whole morning in Lady Mary's dressing room. The Reverend Stotherd Abdy (who was to marry the couple) describes how

> we rummaged all the book-cases, examined the knick knacks upon the toilet, and set a parcel of shells a-dancing in vinegar. Lady Mary and Miss Archer worked; Mr Houblon gazed with admiration upon his future bride; Mrs Abdy and Mr Archer were engaged in stamping crests upon doilys with the new invented composition; and I read to the company a most excellent chapter out of the *Art of Inventing, addressed to the Patronesses of Humble Companions.*

In larger or more sophisticated houses these kinds of wet day activities would probably by now have taken place in the library.

128. The garden of Beachborough House, Kent, in about 1745. Attrib. to Edward Haytley.

After dinner the ladies retired to the drawing room, where the gentlemen joined them around seven for tea and coffee. Cards, 'romping', reading the newspapers, verse-making, fortune-telling or impromptu dancing filled the time before and after supper until everyone went to bed around twelve. On the day of the wedding, the marriage service was held in the church, but the registry was signed in the drawing room; then the party walked round the garden, returned to have cake and wine in the drawing room, and finally dined in state in the great dining parlour. They wore their best clothes and jewels, sixteen servants in rich livery waited on them, the sideboards were loaded with plate, 'the bells were ringing the whole dinner time, and in short everything had the appearance of the true hospitality of a fine old family, joined to the elegance of modern taste.'

Walking round a garden or driving round a park, whether one's own or somebody elses, loomed large in the ample leisure time of people in polite society. Their view of what was elegant extended outside as well as in. The surroundings of their houses were reorganized in much the same way as the interiors, and for rather similar reasons. Axial planning, and straight avenues, canals or walks all converging on the ceremonial spine of the house disappeared in favour of circular planning. A basically circular layout was enlivened by different happenings all the way round the circuit, in the form of temples, obelisks, seats, pagodas, rotundas and so on. The result was like an external version of the circuit at Norfolk House, with its different colour schemes giving a different accent to each room. It was used in much the same way. Guests or visitors, having done the circuit of the rooms, did the circuit of the grounds. Just as, at a big assembly, tea was served in one room and cards laid out in another, the exterior circuit could be varied by stopping at a temple to take tea, or at a rotunda to scan the view through a telescope (Pl. 128), or in general by reading the inscriptions and enjoying the sentiments expressed on the various monuments. Alternatively, special expeditions could be made to individual buildings on the circuits. In summer, people often left the house to take their after-dinner tea or coffee in one of the garden buildings. At some houses outings were made to a fishing pavilion on the lake, equipped with a little kitchen in which to cook the fish and an elegant room in which to eat it.[40] Or a medically-fashionable cold bath might be taken in a bath house somewhere else on the circuit, followed by further refreshments in the bath house or an adjacent temple.

The most famous, elaborate and visited of these garden circuits was at Stowe. By 1760 this had collected well over thirty different garden buildings. The smaller, but almost equally famous circuit at Stourhead was arranged round an artificial lake, and enlivened by a re-erected market cross from Bristol, a Turkish tent, the temple of Flora, a Chinese bridge, a grotto (one portion of which contained a cold bath) a rustic cottage, a pantheon, a temple of the Sun and a Palladian bridge (Pl. 129).

Similar circuits proliferated all over the country. Later on in the century they tended to get larger. New light-weight chaises came in handy for doing the round; the smooth and level turf of the typical late-eighteenth-century park was

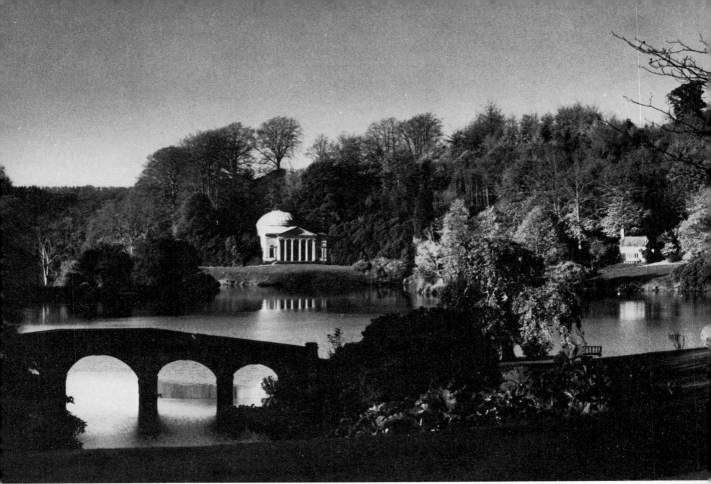

129. Looking across the lake at Stourhead, Wiltshire.

ideally adapted for getting off the gravelled tracks of the circuit and making a diversion or a short cut. It was quite usual to have two circuits, as at Stowe, Stourhead and Blenheim, usually a short circuit through the pleasure grounds, designed for walking, and a long circuit through the park, designed for riding and driving.[41]

The replacement of axial by circular planning, inside houses and out, affected the way people looked at buildings. They no longer thought in terms of rigidly intersecting axial vistas, each neatly ending in a terminal feature. They liked to see buildings in a series and from a variety of constantly changing angles. Their compactly planned houses were visually circumscribable and were made more so by having their extremities hived off instead of being subsidiaries to the main block, as in many formal houses. Stable blocks became separate incidents in the landscape. The sculptural neatness of Harleyford was made possible by putting kitchen and offices in a separate building, connected by a tunnel to the main house, and invisible from most view-points. This arrangement can be found in a number of new eighteenth-century houses. Mrs Lybbe Powys thought it 'a great addition . . . to the look of any place and certainly [it] adds infinitely to the neatness so conspicuous round Harleyford.'[41]

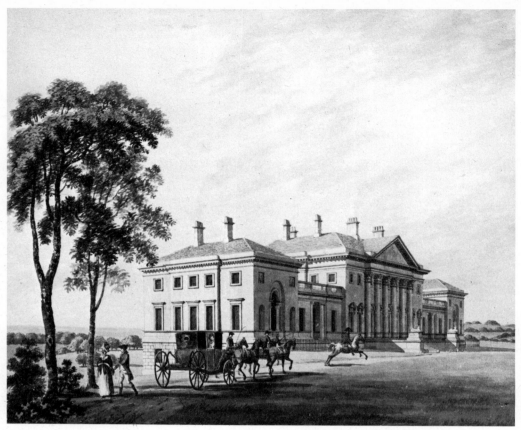

130. Harewood House, Yorkshire, as painted by Thomas Malton in 1788.

The way people looked at houses affected the way they drew them. Up to the early eighteenth century the conventional—and for architects almost the invariable—way to show a house was full-frontal, from a central axis. During the eighteenth century it became increasingly common to draw them from an angle. Harewood, in Yorkshire, as drawn in 1788 by Thomas Malton, is one of innumerable examples (Pl. 130). It was designed by Carr of York in the late 1750s, and superficially it appears to be on the same formal model as houses like Blenheim or Houghton, with a central portico and symmetrical wings ending in pavilions. But the asymmetry of the view corresponds to an asymmetry in the planning. It is a double-circuit house, with big public rooms to the right of the portico, and private apartments arranged in a completely different plan to the left.[42]

Once symmetry of the exterior was no longer the expression of a symmetrical interior, and people were anyway thinking of buildings in terms of views from an angle rather than an axis, there was no very strong reason for even the exterior to remain symmetrical. Nor did it.

131. (right) Sir Brooke Boothby. By Joseph Wright of Derby, 1781.

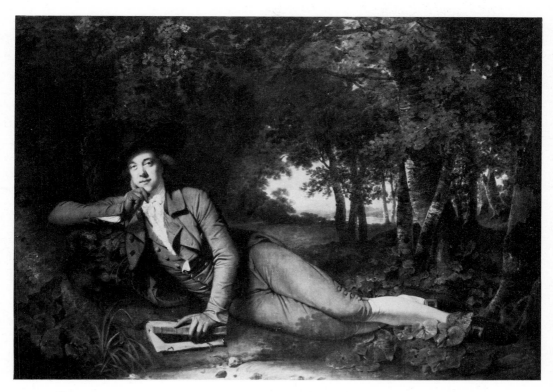

8 The Arrival of Informality: 1770-1830

IN 1776 Mrs Lybbe Powys went for a tour of Wiltshire. She occupied much of her time in going round country houses, as was the normal practice not only for her but for all polite people on holiday,.then as now. Among others, she visited the Earl of Radnor's Longford Castle, near Salisbury and Fonthill House, near Tisbury. William Beckford's amazing Fonthill Abbey was not yet built. She saw its predecessor, the opulent classical mansion built in the 1760s by William's father, Alderman Beckford, on the proceeds of his West Indian plantations.

Mrs Powys was delighted with Longford, but much less impressed by Fonthill. She especially liked Longford because, as she put it, it 'stands in the middle of the garden only one step from the ground, so that you may be instantly out of doors.'[1] She was referring to the main rooms. In Elizabethan times, when the house was built, these had been up on the first floor in the usual way of the time, but in the seventeenth and eighteenth centuries they had been moved down to the parlour floor at ground level. This often happened in Elizabethan and Jacobean houses. Their great chambers were normally up above high-ceilinged parlours or halls, and too inaccessible for later tastes. But their parlours tended to be spacious and lofty, and were easily adapted to become the principal rooms of the house.

At Fonthill, on the other hand, the main rooms were up above the rustic. Although this had been normal practice in the early and mid eighteenth century Mrs Powys now did not like it at all. 'As a contrast to Lord Radnor's,' she wrote, 'which we had that morning admired for being so near the garden, the ground apartments at Fonthill by a most tremendous flight of steps are, I believe, more distant from the terrace on which the house stands than the attic storey of Longford Castle.'[2]

Twenty years previously, when Mrs Powys had been at Holkham as a girl, the elevation of the main rooms, which was almost as tremendous as at Fonthill, had worried her not at all. But towards the end of the eighteenth century people began to feel that the main rooms of a house should be in touch with the outside world—not just by views through the windows, although increasing attention was paid to these, but also by means of having the rooms at ground level, with low-silled windows or actual French windows opening straight into the garden or on to the lawn. The rooms thus flowed out into the garden and correspondingly the garden made inroads into the house, in the form of vases and pots of flowers, or occupied an entire room in the form of a conservatory attached to the house.

The development was a gradual one and was part of a change common to all Europe, but pioneered in England. The upper and upper-middle classes had reached the stage of sophistication at which they could react against their own civilization and endeavour to go back to nature. They found nature both in the countryside, preferably in as wild a state as possible, and in man in the countryside, preferably in the supposedly unconstrained, passionate and pure state as presented in the myth or model of the Noble Savage.

Accordingly, increasing value was put on the spontaneous expression of emotion, on sensibility rather than sense, on love matches rather than arranged marriages, and on life in the country rather than in the town. Young girls sat at

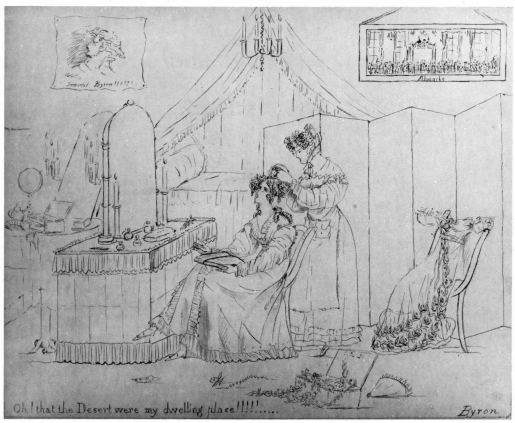

Oh! that the Desert were my dwelling place!!!!......   Byron.

132. A sketch by Olivia de Ros, *c.* 1820.

their dressing tables and had fantasies about Byron, who became the symbol of revolt against convention (Pl. 132). Men and women began to lounge and recline instead of sitting up straight (Pl. 131). The upper classes as a whole became increasingly enthusiastic about the country and country pursuits. During the six months or so which they spent in the country they had always hunted and shot, and even occasionally farmed, but these activities were now upgraded in their hierarchy of values. Instead of just being activities indulged in to pass the time, and ones which were rather looked down on if indulged in excess, they became virtuous and prestigious. A country gentleman on his horse, taking a straight line across country, could feel in direct contact with animals and nature and enjoy the primitive emotions of man the hunter. Such changing attitudes produced a steady increase of sporting pictures, and of portraits of country-house owners shown in sporting dress.

Apart from sporting activities, simple communion with nature in surroundings unsmirched, or apparently unsmirched, by human hands was increasingly valued. Praises of country life were nothing new but earlier examples had been based mainly on moral grounds. The supposed innocence of country life had been used as a stick with which to beat the wickedness of the city. The idea of nature as a positive force, something which one could plug into and get a spiritual charge from, was quite new. But to commune with nature needed a measure of solitude.

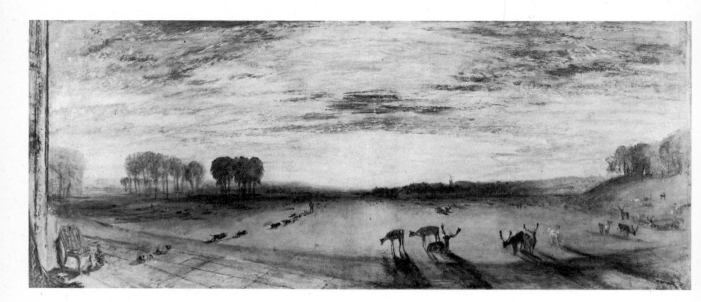

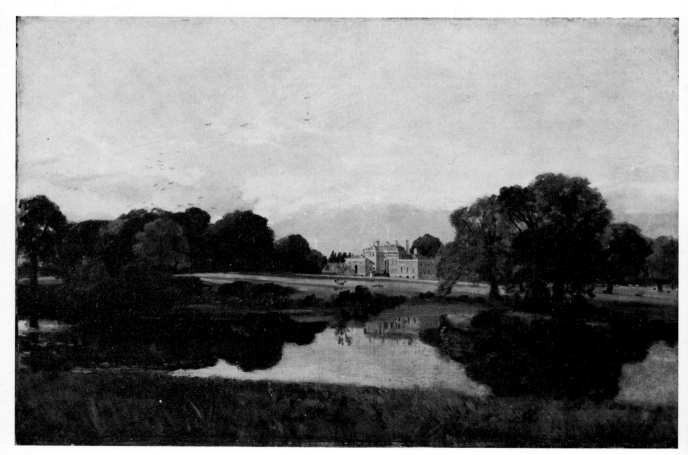

133. (top) Petworth Park from the house. By J. M. W. Turner, *c.* 1828.

134. Malvern Hall, Warwickshire. By John Constable, 1809.

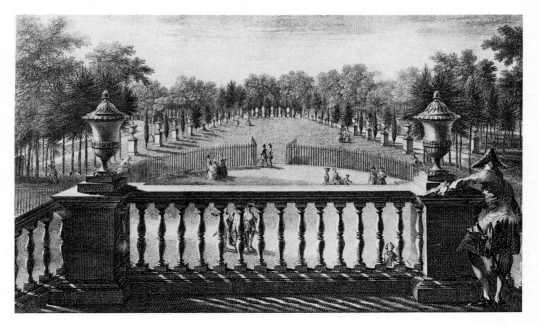

To walk or ride through empty countryside seemed now a highly desirable instead of a rather boring occupation. Pictures of country houses no longer showed them thronged with people, as had been the normal way of representing them up till the mid eighteenth century. Instead they appeared in idyllic solitude, with perhaps just a single figure—a horseman, or a ploughman with his team—or herds of grazing deer or cattle, to add a touch of arcadian life to the scene (Pls 133 to 135).

Two other developments helped boost the prestige of country pursuits. One was a revolution in English agriculture. In the early Middle Ages the landowning classes in England had farmed huge areas of their own land. From the later Middle Ages onwards they had developed into rentiers, drawing rent from their tenants and perhaps keeping one farm by the house in hand, to supply fresh provisions for the household. But during the second half of the eighteenth century the landed classes were caught up by the idea of what was called at the time 'improvement'. They began to plant, drain and enclose, to run farms themselves and to encourage their tenants to improve the farms that were on lease. This new interest, besides greatly advancing farming techniques, and boosting food output, enabled landlords to perhaps double their income. Once it became clear that this was the case, improvement became exceedingly popular.

The first improvers got under way before the mid eighteenth century. At first the idea caught on comparatively slowly. It was still considered a novelty in the 1770s. In 1773, for instance, Lady Grey wrote from Wrest Park in Bedfordshire to her daughter Lady Polwarth, 'we have not yet dealt much in the modern improvements of husbandry.'[3] Within a few years her son-in-law had been bitten by the bugs of farming and fox-hunting, and was spending much more of his time

217

135. The view from Chiswick House. By John Donowell, 1753.

in the country as a result. Fox-hunting and improvement tended to go together. Farming kept landowners in the country for longer periods, and big well-drained fields separated by jumpable hedges, which was the typical land pattern produced by enclosure, resulted in livelier hunting as well as more profitable farming.[4]

There was another encouragement to country life. It was not nearly as remote as it used to be. Many landowners of the early seventeenth century had treated their visits to their country seats like a visit to the dentist. It was something which had to be done, but the quicker it was over the better. They found the remoteness of the country acutely painful after the gay social life in London. In the early eighteenth century Pope wrote his 'Epistle to Mrs Teresa Blount on her leaving the town'.

> She went to plain work, and to purling brooks,
> Old fashioned halls, dark aunts and croaking rooks.

The only visitor was the local squire who

> With his hounds comes hallooing from the stable,
> Makes love with nods, and knees beneath a table
> Whose laughs are hearty, though his jests are coarse
> And loves you best of all things—but his horse.

By the end of the eighteenth century a network of excellent turnpike roads and fast coaches had made country houses much more accessible (Pl. 136), and squires a good deal less provincial. The beginning of this development was discussed in the last chapter. Its first effects tended to be to encourage people to introduce town gaieties to the country. Mid-eighteenth-century country houses, especially the bigger ones, were designed for the kind of sophisticated balls or assemblies which it had previously only been possible to have in London. By the end of the eighteenth century houses were designed less for balls than for house parties. A new situation had produced a new life-style.

The next hundred years were the golden age of the country house. It was possible for people to have their cake and to eat it. They could enjoy the country without feeling imprisoned by it. Nature was refreshing but no longer frightening. Improvement was not only meritorious but extremely lucrative. Solitude was made especially delicious by the knowledge that there was no problem about escaping from it—whether by ordering up one's carriage and driving up to London at what seemed then amazing speed or by filling the house with amusing visitors.

Against this background one can watch country houses gradually sinking into the ground and opening up to the surrounding landscape. Many of them sank literally. As their main rooms moved down closer and closer to ground level, the servants' rooms underneath them were pushed further and further underground. By the end of the eighteenth century they were often sunk so far down that light had to be got to them by digging a pit or dry moat round the house. This was not very enjoyable for the servants. Moreover, it did not even work all that well for the gentry above them. However close their living rooms were to the ground, it

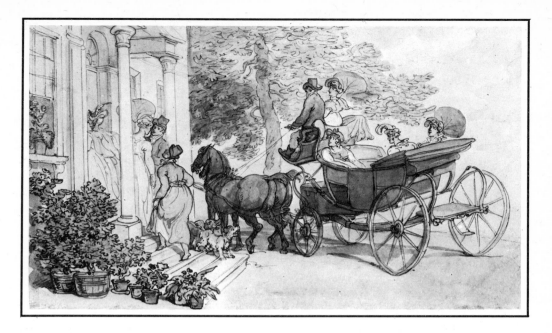

was impossible for them to have French windows opening straight onto gardens or green lawns. There was this pit or moat to be negotiated first.

The solution was, of course, to put the servants into a wing instead of digging a hole for them. In small houses self-contained servants' wings had existed for many years. But in houses of any size, although the kitchens and laundries were often pushed out into a wing, the other day-rooms for servants were normally under the main block, so that the servants could be conveniently on call for upstairs services. The invention of the bell-rope, followed by the bell-pull, changed this situation. Bell systems began to appear in the 1760s and '70s, and were steadily improved until the whole house could be wired and every room put in connection with the servants in their wing.[5] Basements could be got rid of, except to contain cellars. Moreover there was no longer any need to have servants hanging around on hard wooden seats in the hall. Their presence there had been taken for granted in earlier decades, but now grated on people's increasing sense of privacy.

Earlier in the eighteenth century, in houses where the servants or at any rate the kitchens had been put in a wing, the importance attached to symmetry meant that this had to be balanced by another wing. There tended to be an element of artificiality in deciding what to put in the second wing, and moreover it interrupted the contact of the main block of the house with gardens and greenery which was now thought desirable. In addition, the internal balance of the saloon and apartment system, which external symmetry expressed, had by now collapsed. But symmetry was under stress for more than practical reasons. The new feeling for nature meant that it no longer appeared desirable anyway. To make a house lopsided became a positively meritorious gesture, an escape from artificiality.

So the concept developed of the asymmetric country house, with a servants' wing to one side—usually to the north—and with living rooms of different shapes

219

136. Country-house visiting, as depicted by Thomas Rowlandson.

irregularly grouped to enjoy the sun and the view, and opening into conservatories or onto green turf or gardens. It was a radically different model from country houses of the early or even mid eighteenth century. In classical houses the differences were accentuated by a lesser, but very noticeable, change in the organisation of facades. Houses of the early and mid century were based on the convention of a temple standing on a rusticated base. Even if there was no actual portico the division between rustication and smooth exterior expressed this. The main rooms were above the rustic; the rustic contained servants' rooms and sometimes informal family rooms. When the main rooms moved down to ground level the rustic, if the house still had one, had to be increased in height, and the 'temple' upper floors proportionately reduced.

In the houses which remained faithful to porticoes (by now usually attached rather than freestanding), these tended to appear diminutive or skied. Moreover there was something illogical about putting the most expensive ornamental feature in front of the bedrooms. At Bywell in Northumberland (Pl. 137), an early example of a house with its main rooms at ground level, James Paine made some sense of the arrangement by putting a first-floor breakfast room behind the portico, and apartments for the master and mistress to either side of it.[6] But on the whole, upper-floor porticoes tended to disappear, in favour of the typical high-waisted house of the late eighteenth century, with the main rooms in a lofty rusticated ground floor, and the bedrooms above in two lower-ceilinged floors of smoother unadorned ashlar, rendering or brick (Pl. 138).

There was still, however, an element of irrationality in putting the main rooms into a feature which was essentially a base for something more important. The next step was to get rid of the rustic altogether. In this case, if the house had a portico at all, it had to come down to the ground on the Greek model (Col. Pl. XXII). The adaptability of Greek architecture for houses with ground-level living rooms was one reason for its popularity in the early nineteenth century.

Main rooms at ground level, their opening-up to gardens and greenery, asymmetric servants' wings, and houses without rustics appeared gradually from about 1760 to 1800. As early as 1762, at Duddingstone near Edinburgh, Sir William Chambers designed a classical house with no rustic, an entrance portico rising from ground level, and an asymmetric service wing. Horace Walpole's Strawberry Hill, which was of course Gothic rather than classical, started to become mildly asymmetrical in the 1750s and acquired a long irregular wing in the 1760s. Asymmetry was encouraged in its case by the fact that it was gradually enlarged over several decades; but instead of trying to fit the additions into a symmetrical scheme Horace Walpole deliberately kept them irregular out of aesthetic preference.

Both these houses were pioneers. It was not till the 1790s that asymmetric houses began to appear in any numbers. Bonomi's Longford Hall in Shropshire (1794) and Wyatt's Dodington in Gloucestershire (1797) are good and typical examples (Col. Pl. XXII).[7] In the early years of the 1800s the architect John Nash, in association with the landscape gardener Humphry Repton, produced a series of houses in which the potentialities of the irregular house were carried to

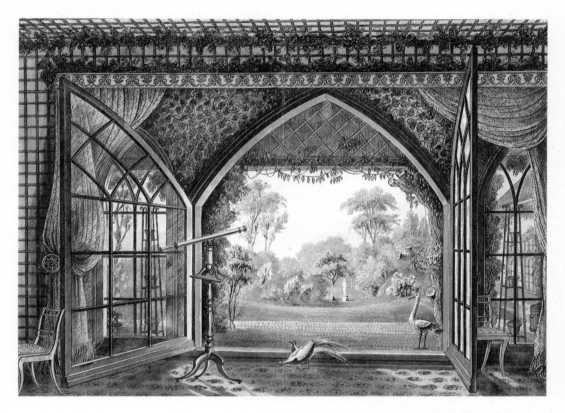

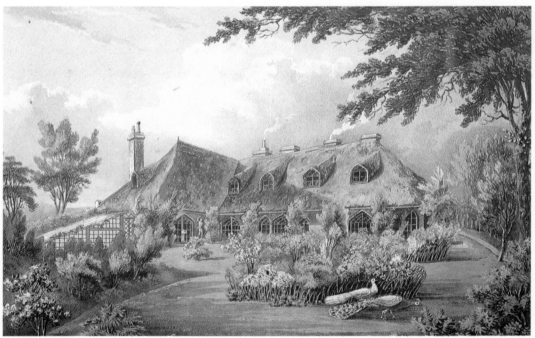

XXI. Knowle Cottage, Sidmouth, Devon, as depicted in 1834.

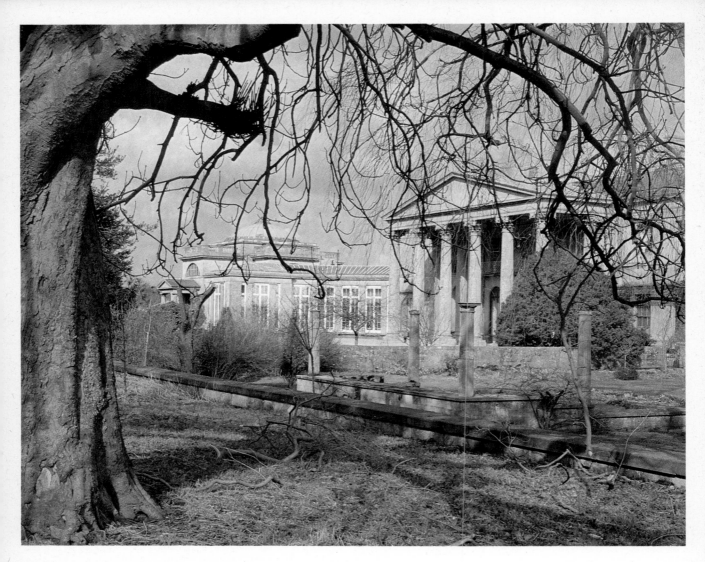

XXII. Dodington Hall, Gloucestershire (1798–1808).
XXIII. (right) Deepdene, Surrey. The circular conservatory in 1823.

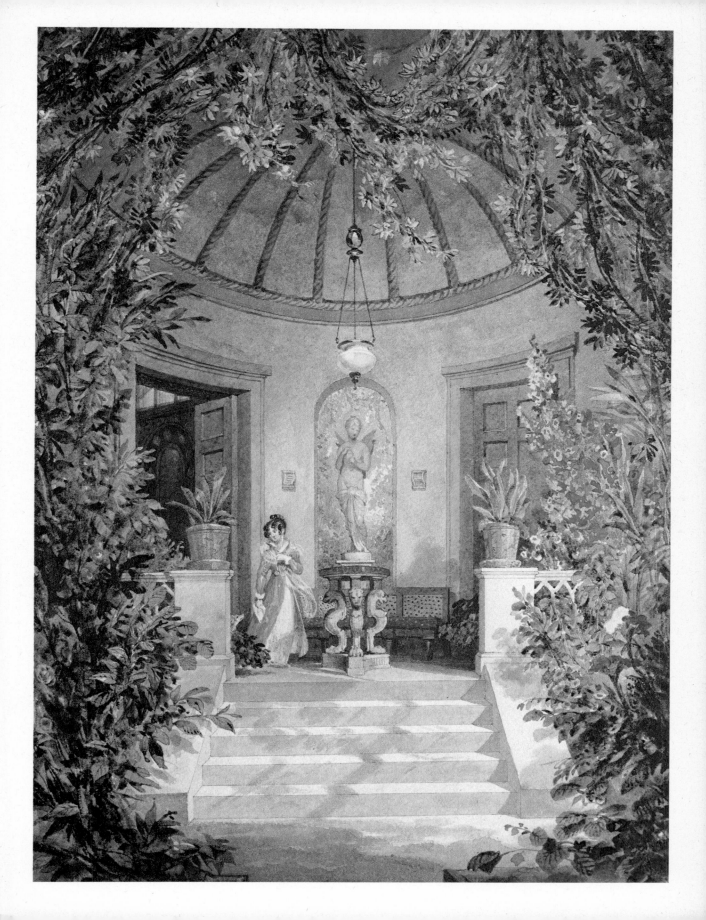

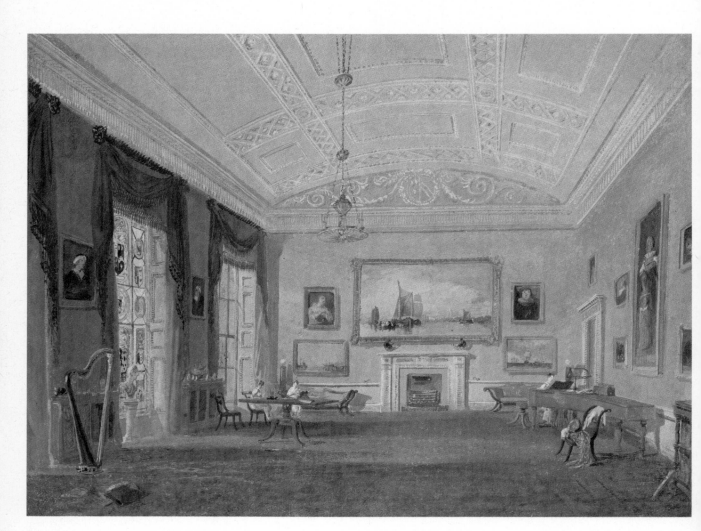

XXIV. Farnley Hall, Yorkshire. The drawing room, as painted by Turner in 1818.

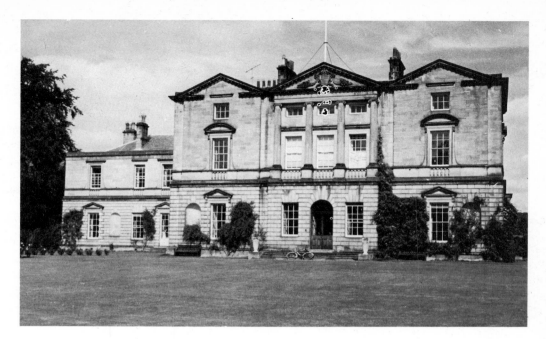

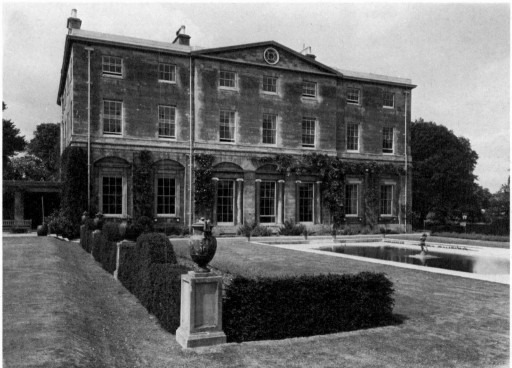

extremes of sophistication. They so exactly matched the new tastes and needs of country-house owners of the period that it is worth looking at two of them in some detail.

Luscombe, in Devon, was designed for Charles Hoare in 1800 (Fig. 16). Two sketches by Humphry Repton show the kind of house which other architects might have designed and the kind of house and setting which he and Nash

137. (top) Bywell Park, Northumberland (James Paine, *c.* 1760).

138. Courteenhall, Northamptonshire (Samuel Saxon, 1791–4).

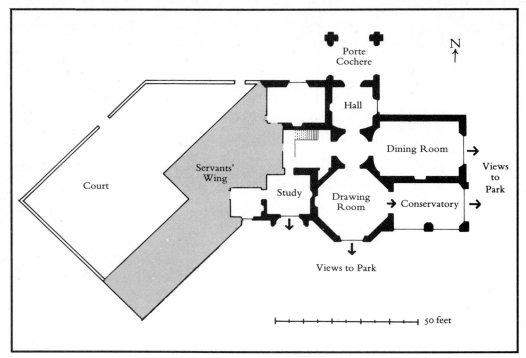

Fig. 16. Luscombe Castle, Devon. The ground floor.

between them were proposing. The first drawing shows a neat free-standing house in an open landscape, on the mid-eighteenth-century model, the second a house of irregular plan and broken outline, designed to settle comfortably into a broken and irregular landscape (Pl. 139). Nash and Repton were, in fact, suggesting a 'natural' house in a 'natural' landscape. And this was exactly what they built. Luscombe was not at all a big house (it has been enlarged since); the servants were tucked away in a wing to one side, the rooms had agreeably varied shapes but very simple decoration, and all the main rooms had windows down to the ground, designed to frame the view in two different directions. From the drawing room one could look either west or south—west across the park, and south through a little conservatory and along the valley (Pl. 140).[8]

The style of the house was gothic. The Gothic Revival was well under way by 1800. It had the great advantage of being without commitment to symmetry or level skylines, so that it could be made as broken and irregular as was desired. But one of Nash's achievements was to show that classicism did not necessarily involve flat roofs and symmetry. He worked out a relaxed and simplified classicism which achieved all that his gothic building did, and had a particular easy-going elegance of its own. A typical example is Sandridge in Devon, designed for Lady Ashburton in about 1805 (Pl. 141). The plan was similar to that of Luscombe.[9] A drawing room and dining room of different shapes both had French windows angled on two different views, up and down the estuary of the Dart. The house originally had two conservatories—a small one, opening into both drawing room and dining room, and a big one opening from the hall and

139. (upper right) Luscombe Castle, Devon (John Nash, 1800–4), as drawn by Humphry Repton.

140. (right) The view through the conservatory from the drawing room at Luscombe Castle.

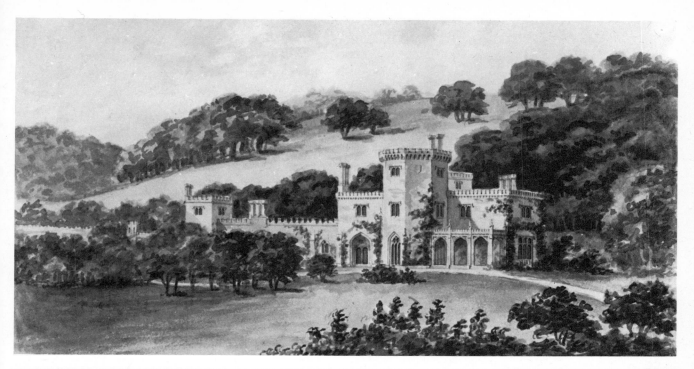

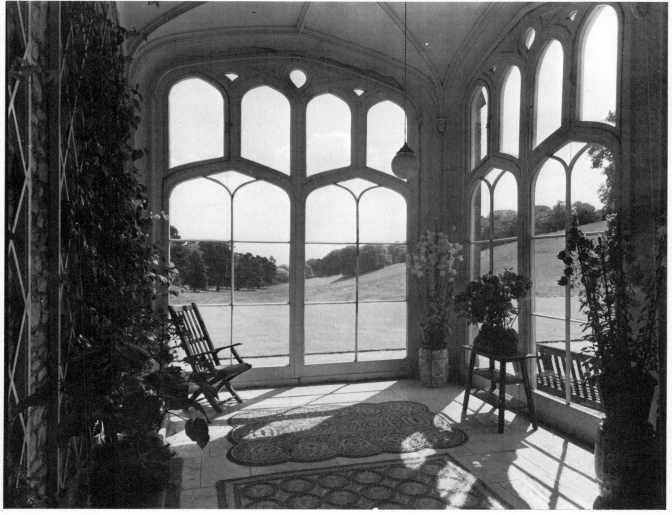

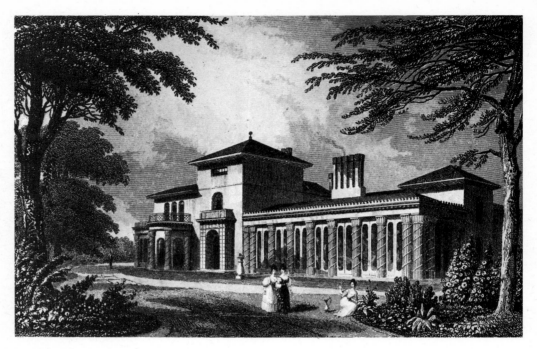

used to mask the servants' wing. This became a common use for conservatories. Over the drawing room the main bedroom was also carefully arranged to enjoy the view and had its own French windows, opening onto a little terrace or balcony on top of the bow-window of the drawing room.

All this was very accomplished, and also very sophisticated. The nature Charles Hoare looked out at through his drawing room windows was 'nature' in quotes— it was an edited and improved version of nature cunningly devised by Humphry Repton. Hoare was able to enjoy it on a solid basis of servants and comfort. It was perhaps significant that neither Luscombe nor Sandridge were designed for straightforward country gentlemen. They were the country properties of a banker in the case of Luscombe, and the sister of a banker in the case of Sandridge. The strong element of artificiality in the whole back-to-nature movement came into the open in one of its most engaging but also ridiculous products, the *cottage ornée*—the simple life, lived in simple luxury in a simple cottage with—quite often—fifteen simple bedrooms, all hung with French wallpapers.

Nash was as good at designing *cottages ornées* as he was at designing picturesque gothic or classical houses. For George IV he designed the biggest and most ridiculously elaborate one of all, the Royal Lodge in Windsor Park.[10] But he by no means had a monopoly of them. They were going up by the dozen in the first decades of the nineteenth century, especially at the new seaside resorts, where the simple life could be enjoyed in conjunction with the natural scenery of sea and cliffs, and in the company of other fashionably simple people. A delightful if totally absurd little book published in 1834 gives, for instance, a contemporary record of Knowle Cottage, a *cottage ornée* at Sidmouth, in Devon (Col. Pl. XXI). It was built originally by Lord Le Despencer, probably about 1820, but at the time the book was published was described as 'the elegant marine villa ornee of Thomas L. Fish Esq.'.

228

141. Sandridge Park, Devon (John Nash, c. 1805).

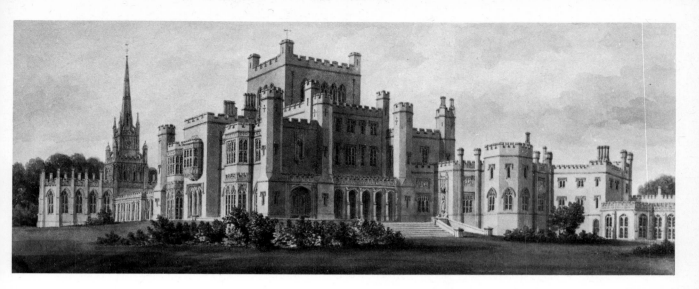

Asymmetric planning and a close relationship between inside and outside were not confined to *cottages ornées* or smaller country houses. They extended right the way up the scale. At Deepdene near Dorking, for instance, Thomas Hope, who was both extremely rich and a gifted amateur architect, remodelled and enlarged a country house for himself. The result was a very large house inextricably mixed up with the landscape by way of conservatories, loggias, pergolas and French windows (Col. Pl. XXIII). It was also exceedingly irregular, even though the detail was all classical.[11] But few houses, small or large, were as adventurous as Deepdene. Few architects were prepared to plan as freely as Nash or Hope, and many clients thought that dignity and propriety still called for a good measure of symmetry.

The result was still very different from symmetrical houses built earlier in the eighteenth century. At Wyatt's Dodington, for instance, although each individual facade is grandly and even pompously symmetrical the total effect is not symmetrical at all; the facades are all different from each other, and the main block is combined in an irregular composition with a large service wing, masked on the entrance front by a conservatory and chapel (Col. Pl. XXII). At the immense Ashridge in Hertfordshire, a gothic house where Jeffrey Wyatville took over as architect from his uncle James Wyatt in 1813, the axial relationship of hall to staircase and of dining room to drawing room is rigidly formal and is expressed on the external facades (Pl. 142). But the total composition sprawls and rambles in the landscape as easily as its splendid owner Lord Bridgwater sprawled on one of his fashionably padded sofas.

Ashridge is a good place at which to stop looking at the houses of this period in more or less general terms, and start examining the rooms they contained in more detail (Fig. 17). On the ground floor almost the whole of its main block was occupied by living rooms. There was a dining room, drawing room and library, all on a scale suitable for a house which was likely to fill its thirty or so guest bedrooms with house-parties. There was a smaller billiard room and breakfast room. A very large conservatory led west from the dining room to the chapel, and concealed the interminable service wing from the garden. The north-west wing

229

142. Ashridge Park, Hertfordshire (James and Jeffrey Wyatt, 1808–17).

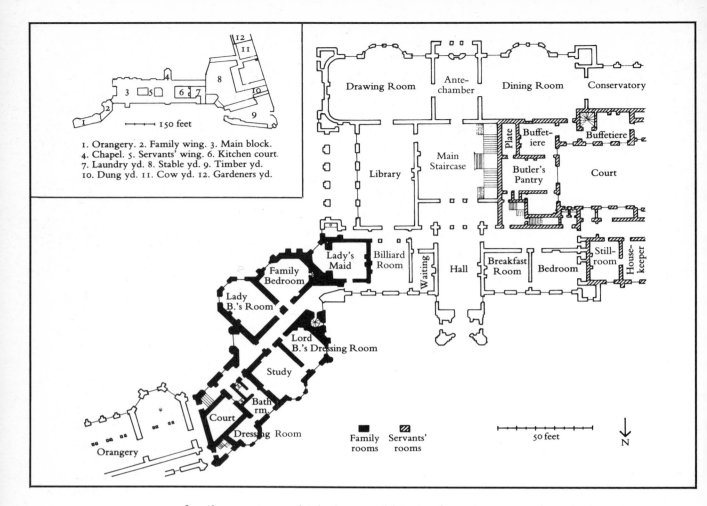

was a family one, into which they could retire for privacy or when the house was empty. Lady Bridgwater's bedroom was next to her sitting room and had a French window on to the terrace. Lord Bridgwater's dressing room was across the corridor from it. The only other bedroom on the ground floor was a small one in one corner of the main block. It was intended, as a contemporary description put it, 'to accommodate any guest, who may find inconvenience in ascending a staircase'.[12] All the other bedrooms were upstairs, including the best one.

A state apartment consisting of bedrooms with attendant dressing rooms or closets continued to be provided on the main floor of some great houses up till about 1770. From then on it was almost invariably upstairs, because there was no room for it down below; and since the concept of state was going out of fashion it was normally called the best apartment rather than the state one. In older houses an existing state bedroom was often moved upstairs as a result of the expansion of the downstairs living rooms. At Wimpole in Cambridgeshire the state bed went upstairs in 1781, and the main floor was gradually absorbed by increasing numbers of bigger and bigger living rooms.[13] A few great houses still had a family apartment on the ground floor, as at Ashridge. But in the majority of houses there were no bedrooms on the ground floor at all. People began to feel that upstairs bedrooms were part of the order of things.

230

Fig. 17. Ashridge Park. The main block and family wing, with insert showing the whole complex.

Bedrooms still normally had dressing rooms attached to them. The apartment system had by no means vanished, although it was still on the decline. Dressing rooms were usually also furnished as sitting rooms, and women guests, at any rate, often spent the morning in them. But they were not normally rooms to which visits were paid by other people. Even christenings, which for centuries had taken place in a bedroom, with the mother in a richly-apparelled bed, began to take place with her lying on a couch in the drawing room, or even standing in church. The only apartment which continued to be used to receive in was the family apartment. But here the reception room was no longer the dressing room. The mistress of the house often had a room off her bedroom or dressing room known variously just as her 'room', or as her sitting room or boudoir, or sometimes as the 'ladies' sitting room or drawing room.[14] The master of the house invited people into his study. This often had a dressing room and sometimes a bathroom next door to it, but the dressing room was now for its owner only. Sometimes both husband's and wife's apartments were grouped together on the ground floor in a separate wing, as at Ashridge. A common arrangement was for the family bedroom and the wife's dressing room and boudoir to be on the first floor, and the husband's study and dressing room on the ground floor.

But it was the social parts of the house rather than the private territories which now dominated it. They dominated it, however, in a comparatively easy-going way, in sympathy with the general reaction against formality. The result was the English house-party, a subject of comment and admiration by visitors to English country houses from all over the world. House-parties often, though by no means invariably, coincided with some local event, such as a race-meeting or a coming-of-age. They were predominantly intended for enjoyment, but they could also have practical purposes. They were useful for planning politics or making matches.

It would be pleasant to be able to trace the English house-party back to Renaissance gatherings as described by Castiglione or Boccaccio, by way of the kind of company collected by the Countess of Pembroke at Wilton under Elizabeth, or Lord Falkland at Great Tew under Charles I. Both of these houses were described by Aubrey as like 'colleges' because of the 'learned and ingeniose persons' that frequented them.[15] But they were learned rather than courtly gatherings, with a strong element of patronage in them. A more valid prototype would be the 'congresses' held by Sir Robert Walpole at Houghton in the 1720s and '30s; the greater part of the government went down to Norfolk during the summer or Christmas recess, and spent a week or more plotting politics in the interval of hunting, feasting and boozing with the local gentry.[16] These congresses were perhaps the first important examples in England of regular country-house gatherings attended, in conditions of relative equality, by large numbers of people not related to the owner. They were considered a phenomenon at the time, but by the end of the century better transport had made the political house-party a common enough event.

The Houghton congresses had been exclusively masculine. Later house-parties, whether or not politically oriented, were attended by both men and women.

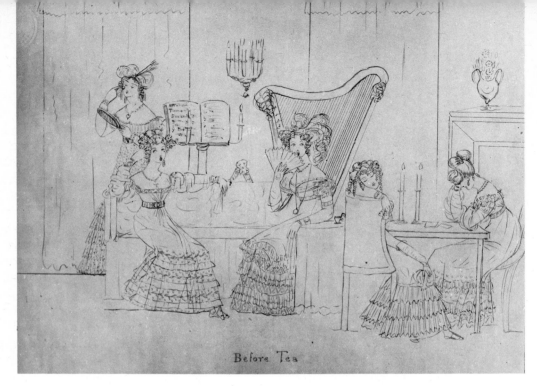

Before Tea

Their match-making function was a side product of this mixture. The arranged marriage largely disappeared in the course of the eighteenth century. Ambitious parents had to engineer marriages rather than arrange them, by seeing that their daughters met the right sort of young man in the right circumstances. London balls, or balls in the local Assembly Room, were a good venue for striking up a first acquaintance; but the relaxed atmosphere of a house-party (Pls 143 and 144) was ideal for the last stages before the proposal.[17]

The basis of house-party life was that between breakfast and dinner guests were left to a considerable extent to do what they liked. Every kind of facility was laid on for their amusement. An early example of what was to become the accepted life style was described at Carton, the Duke of Leinster's house in Ireland, in 1779.

> The house was crowded—a thousand comers and goers. We breakfast between ten and eleven, though it is called half past nine. We have an immense table—chocolate—honey—hot bread—cold bread—brown bread—white bread—green bread—and all coloured breads and cakes. After breakfast Mr Scott, the Duke's chaplain, reads a few short prayers, and we then go as we like—a back room for reading, a billiard room, a print room, a drawing room, and whole suites of rooms, not forgetting the music room ... There are all sorts of amusements; the gentlemen are out hunting and shooting all the morning. We dine at half-past four or five—go to tea, so to cards about nine ... play till supper time—'tis pretty late by the time we go to bed.[18]

By the early nineteenth century dinner was normally at six-thirty or seven rather than four-thirty or five. Country houses had begun to serve a meal called luncheon to fill the growing gap between breakfast and dinner. It was an informal meal, often for women only, since the men were out shooting or hunting.[19] But

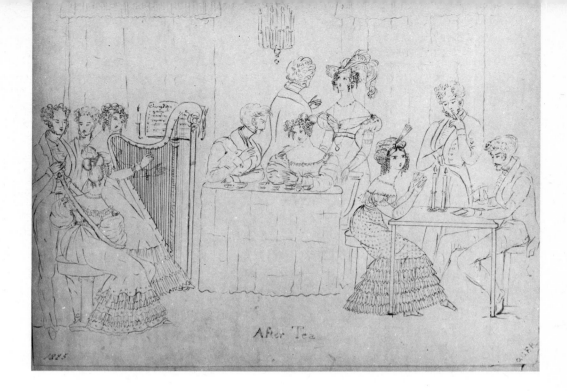

After Tea

dinner remained the one invariable formal ritual at all house parties, and indeed in every country house whenever there were people staying, and even when there were not. It involved assembly in formal dress in the drawing room before dinner, a formal or semi-formal procession of family and guests from the drawing room to the dining room, the serving of the meal in some splendour, with plate on display and numerous footmen waiting, the retirement of the women to the drawing room while the men drank, smoked and talked, and the final return of the men to join the ladies in the drawing room.[20] In a large house drawing room and dining room were now almost invariably separated from each other by one or more rooms, both so that the noise of the men should not disturb the women in the drawing room, and to provide a little state and distance for the procession from drawing room to dining room.

The dining room was now recognized as a masculine and the drawing room as a feminine room. The two reigned as king and queen over the other rooms. The nature of the relationship was quite often underlined by putting a matching drawing room and dining room to either side of a hall or antechamber (sometimes called a saloon), and expressing this externally by a symmetrical facade. It was a way of retaining an element of formality in houses of otherwise irregular disposition and planning. It attracted owners and architects who were unwilling to throw symmetry out of the plan altogether.

There was an arrangement of this kind at Ashridge, and also at Farnley Hall in Yorkshire, where it dated from the 1780s. The drawing room and dining room at Farnley were painted in the early nineteenth century by Turner, who was a friend of its owners, the Fawkes family (Pl. 145 and Col. Pl. XXIV). But although the dining room is shown formally enough in his painting, the drawing room is

233

143, 144. After-dinner tea in 1825. By Olivia de Ros.

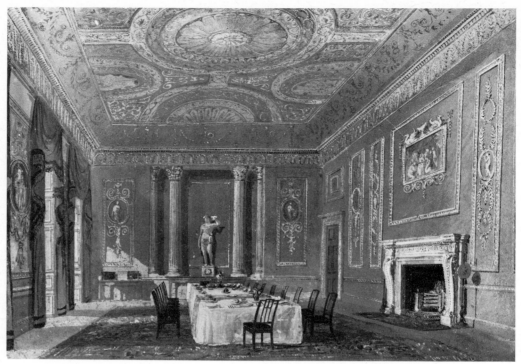

145. Farnley Hall, Yorkshire (1786–90). The dining room, as painted by Turner in 1818.

occupied in a relatively easy-going way, by one lady reading on the sofa, another
working at the table, and a third practising on the piano.

It is, in fact, painted in its informal daytime rather than formal evening aspect.
It was quite common for a drawing room to have these two aspects, but often,
especially in the larger country houses, informal daily life was lived in one or
more other rooms. Many houses had a breakfast room or breakfast parlour, used
not only for breakfast but also as a morning sitting room. Some houses had a
gallery, used for everyday living rather than just as a room for pictures or dancing.
But in big houses the main informal living room was usually the library. In the
late eighteenth and early nineteenth century the country-house library was at its
apogee. Its handsomely designed bookcases were likely to contain an all-round
collection of several thousand books, both new and old, a good many of which
were still being read by the occupants of the house—as was by no means the case
fifty or a hundred years later. But it was also a comfortable, relaxed and
sympathetic living room (Pls 146 and 147).

In 1778 Mrs Lybbe Powys visited Middleton Park in Oxfordshire and found 'a
most excellent library out of the drawing room, seventy feet long—in this room,
besides a good collection of books there is every other kind of amusement, as
billiard and other tables, and a few good pictures. As her ladyship is, according to
the fashion, a botanist, she has a pretty flower garden going out of the library.'[21]
In 1818 Maria Edgeworth described the library at Bowood, in Wiltshire:

the library tho' magnificent is a most comfortable habitable looking room . . .
it was very agreeable in the delightful library after breakfast this day—groups

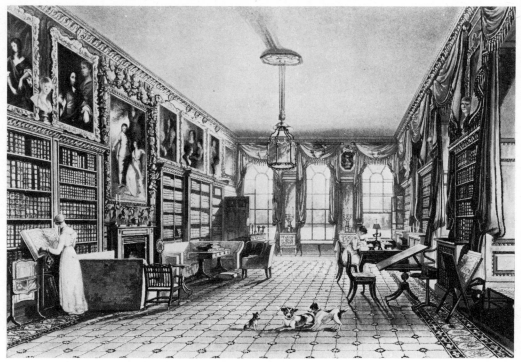

146. Cassiobury, Essex. The library in about 1830.

round various tables—books and prints—Lady Landsdowne found the battle of Roundway for me in different histories, and Lord Landsdowne showed me a letter of Waller's to Lord Hopton on their quarrel after this battle, and Lord Grenville shaking his leg and reading was silent and I suppose, happy.[22]

The description by a clergyman of Lord Spencer's gothic library at Althorp in Northamptonshire is in similar terms, if rather more pompously put. Althorp had one of the biggest private collections of books in the country. The gothic library was designed in 1819, and was the last and most lived-in of a series of libraries filling most of the ground floor of the house. It was a big room, and had a first-floor gallery six feet wide. The latter contained 'ample room for chairs and tables; and the studious may steal away from the animated discussions carried out below, to the more perfect enjoyment of their favourite authors.' Down below, 'sofas, chairs, tables of every comfortable and commodious form are of course liberally scattered throughout the room. The bay-window looks into the pleasure garden where both serpentine and straight walks invite to a ramble among larches elmes and oaks.'[23]

A drawing by Turner of the library at Petworth shows a spinet in it (Pl. 147). Mrs Lybbe Powys describes a billiard table in the library at Middleton. But on the whole the library was reserved for quieter recreations. Music and billiards went on in other rooms, music in the drawing room, or a separate music room, billiards in a billiard room, or in the gallery or hall. Billiard tables had been installed in English houses since the seventeenth century, but in the late eighteenth or early nineteenth they became increasingly fashionable. They were now quite often

235

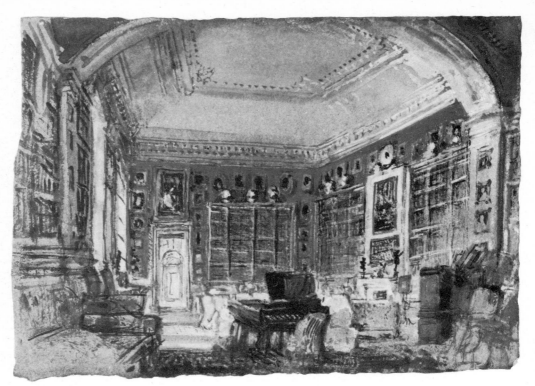

147. Petworth House, Sussex. The library, as painted by Turner in about 1828.

installed in a bay-window or an extension of a bigger room. The sixth Duke of Devonshire thought that 'connected in this manner with an inhabited room, nothing in the world—no nothing can be more enjoyable.'[24]

The duke, who was an incessant giver of house-parties and had the money to give them in the grandest and most capacious of manners, also installed a private theatre at Chatsworth, to provide yet another recreation for his guests. Amateur theatricals, sometimes with a stiffening of professionals to raise the quality, became extremely popular in smart society of the late eighteenth and early nineteenth century. The Chatsworth theatre was fitted up in 1833, and was in fact one of the last in a line of which the earliest was perhaps at Wynnstay in Denbighshire, built in 1771.[25] Lord Barrymore built 'a very elegant playhouse' at his house at Wargrave in Berkshire in 1788, with a ball and supper room attached, for the entertainment of the local gentry and his own house-party.[26] At Blenheim a theatre in the east courtyard was described in 1789 as 'recently fitted up in a style of peculiar elegance'.[27] Apart from the Chatsworth theatre these have all been demolished. More often, however, a temporary stage was fitted up in one of the other rooms, or in an outbuilding. When the Honourable John Yates, disappointed of amateur theatricals at 'Ecclesford, the seat of the Right Hon. Lord Ravenshaw', persuaded his friends to act a play at Mansfield Park, the stage was erected in the billiard room. The possibility of amateur theatricals was yet another reason for providing a string of living rooms on the ground floor.

People were conscious that manners were changing, and convinced that they were changing for the better. Humphry Repton, in his *Fragments on the Theory of*

236

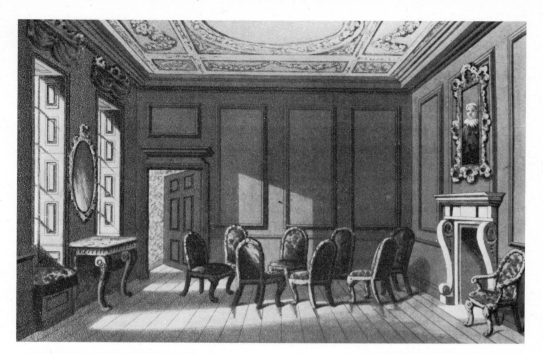

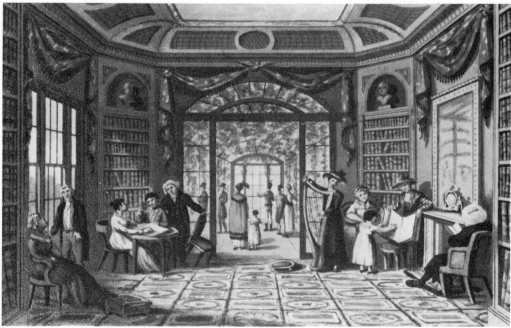

Landscape Gardening published in 1816, illustrated an old fashioned 'Cedar Parlour' and a modern 'Living Room' (Pls 148 and 149). He wrote a poem to go with the pictures:

> No more the cedar parlour's formal gloom
> With dulness chills, 'tis now the living room,
> Where guests to whim, to task or fancy true

148, 149. An old-fashioned cedar parlour and a modern living room, as depicted by Humphry Repton in 1816.

Scatter'd in groups, their different plans pursue.
Here politicians eagerly relate
The last day's news, or the last night's debate.
Here books of poetry and books of prints
Furnish aspiring artists with new hints . . .
Here, midst exotic plants, the curious maid
Of Greek and Latin seems no more afraid.[28]

'Scattered in groups' is the vital phrase in these verses. Everyday social life was no longer a kind of round game, in which everyone joined in together. Different people could now do different things at the same time and even in the same room. They could drift together and separate, form groups and break them up, in an easy informal way. The alternative is drawn by Repton in his cedar parlour. There was no need for him to expand on it in his verses, for everyone knew what he was getting at. It was what society called the 'circle' and is silently but eloquently expressed in his drawing by a circle of empty chairs, just abandoned by their occupants, who have been indulging in general conversation as their ancestors had been doing since at least the seventeenth century.

Sir Ulick O'Shane expostulated against the circle in Maria Edgeworth's novel *Ormond*:

What—no music, no dancing at Castle Hermitage tonight . . . and all the ladies sitting in a formal circle, petrifying into perfect statues . . . of all the figures in nature or art, the formal circle is universally the most obnoxious to conversation . . . all my faculties are spell bound—here am I like a bird in a circle of chalk that dare not move so much as its head or its eyes.[29]

Ormond was published in 1817, but set in about 1780, and Maria Edgeworth, who had a strong social sense, had got the timing exactly right. Around 1780 society was beginning to revolt against the formal circle as the habitual form of social intercourse when people were not actually at a party. One can watch the revolt in action in Fanny Burney's diary. On 8 December 1782, she describes going to visit Miss Monckton and her mother Lady Galway, in Charles Street, off Berkeley Square. 'Everything was in a new style. We got out of the coach into a hall full of servants, not one of which inquired our names or took any notice of us. We proceeded, and went upstairs, and when we arrived at a door, stopped and looked behind us. No servant followed or preceded us.' They finally discovered the drawing room. Fanny Burney describes Miss Monckton's way of receiving guests: 'She kept her seat when they entered, and only turned round her head to nod it and say: "How do do?"', after which they found what accommodation they could for themselves. Finally: 'Some new people coming in, and placing themselves in a regular way, Miss Monckton exclaimed: "My whole care is to prevent a circle", and hastily rising, she pulled about the chairs, and planted the people in groups with as dexterous disorder as you would desire to see.'[30]

The decline of the circle was perhaps not an absolute blessing. It had not been necessarily confined to inane general conversation. In an intellectually high-powered house it could be the vehicle for vigorous intellectual jousting. The relaxed, browsing and chatting life of an early-nineteenth-century house-party could, on the other hand, result in a good deal of superficiality and amiable sloppiness—along with moments of acute boredom, nicely caught in the caricatures of Olivia de Ros (Pls 143 and 144). Moreover, informality could produce its own constraints. By the 1820s house-parties were breeding new conventions. Prince Pückler-Muskau, who toured England in 1826–8, was at first delighted with what he called its 'vie de château'. It was, he wrote, 'without any question the most agreeable side of English life'. But in the end he felt constrained by the lack of privacy which resulted from the supremacy of the common rooms. He found it was virtually impossible for him to have breakfast or write a letter in his own room; it was 'not usual, and therefore surprises and annoys people . . . With all the freedom and absence of useless ceremonies and tedious compliment-ing, there is yet, for a person accustomed to our habits, a considerable degree of constraint.'[31]

The growing importance of the common rooms affected the way rooms were arranged. In the formal house individual rooms were likely to need quick rearranging, depending as to whether they were to be used for meals, cards, conversation or dancing. Chairs were normally kept lined along the walls and were moved into the required positions by servants. Eating-tables were often folding ones, so that they could be put up and taken down with ease. When houses had a string of common rooms, each room tended to be put to a more limited set of uses. Dining rooms became rooms for eating in, and nothing else; the dining-room table stayed permanently in the centre of the room. In the living rooms chairs and sofas remained in frozen positions suitable for conversation or in groups (Pl. 150); lounging life anyway encouraged softer upholstery and therefore heavier and less mobile furniture.

Of course, upper-class life was not entirely confined to informal house-parties. Balls and assemblies continued to take place, in London and out of it. As transport was still improving and polite society growing, the numbers to be entertained grew too. London assemblies could be crammed to bursting with up to a thousand people ('are these really the amusements of civilizations', asked Pückler-Muskau).[32] In the country, balls for four hundred people were being given regularly at Hatfield in the 1780s, with smaller weekly balls in the Christmas season.[33] New forms of entertainment were also appearing. Amateur theatricals have already been referred to. Social 'breakfasts' were nicely in tune with the temper and house-planning of the time, for they enabled large numbers of people to be entertained in both garden and house. They were the ancestors of today's garden parties. Guests ate cold food, walked in the house and garden and listened to music. The earliest breakfast parties were given at breakfast time, but they gradually worked their way into the afternoon. By 1828 a 'Breakfast' given by the Duchess of St Albans at Holly Lodge, on the slopes of Highgate Hill, started at three o'clock. Food was not served till five, by servants got up in fancy dress as gardeners. There was a maypole, archery, and dancing in tents. The party ended at midnight.[34]

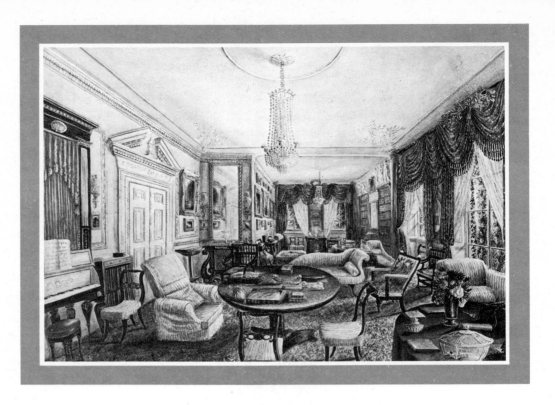

Another quite different kind of social event also came, or rather returned, into fashion. Dinners, dances and other entertainments for tenants, labourers, schoolchildren, local townspeople or yeomanry now often took place on an enormous scale (Pl. 151). Many of these events were based on traditions which had never lapsed, but the evidence suggests a new lavishness, and a new awareness among the upper classes of their importance. At Petworth the annual feasts given by the third Earl of Egremont (d. 1837) for his tenants and workers involved many hundreds of people in all-day festivities.[35] In 1800, when the Marquess of Salisbury invited George III to Hatfield to review the volunteers, 1594 volunteers sat down to an *al fresco* dinner at twenty-four tables, and the royal party and the gentry filled two rooms in the house. The list of what was consumed is reminiscent of the gargantuan mediaeval wallowings at the Neville feast.[36]

But for number and scale of entertaining at this level in the decades around 1800, the marquesses and dukes of Buckingham were probably unequalled. At their three houses, Stowe, Wotton and Avington, they gave separate annual entertainments for the tenantry, the servants, the local corporation or townspeople, and the yeomanry. Events such as comings-of-age or even ordinary birthdays produced more festivities. The news of George III's recovery from madness in 1789 was immediately celebrated by illuminating the front of the house, roasting an ox whole and distributing it to two thousand people, and entertaining the quality of Buckingham to supper in the hall, followed by a dance.[37] In the 1790s Lady Buckingham's birthday was celebrated by a dance and supper for the farmers, followed by supper for three hundred poor people on the next evening; her younger son's birthday a few days later produced a supper for

240

150. Field Place, Sussex. The drawing room in about 1820.

poor children, and a dance for the servants.[38] The family and their guests put in an appearance at all or most of these festivities, and joined in the dancing. In 1804 Lady Buckingham's birthday dance for the tenants was described by a house guest with less than enthusiasm. 'We all danced with the tenants . . . I laughed a great deal to see the different mixture of people. We could hardly breathe it was so hot and the smell was beyond anything.'[39]

In the 1770s and '80s the blue-stocking Elizabeth Montagu had been a pioneer in reviving this kind of entertainment. Apart from her famous annual London dinner for chimney-sweeps, at her country house in Berkshire she gave annual servants' balls, harvest dinners and dances for her farm labourers and dinners for her Sunday school pupils and their teachers. She describes how she made her little son Edward 'sit at the head of the table, and lead up the dance at night, in order to give him more sympathetic feelings for his poor neighbours.'[40] Her descriptions suggest a conscious attempt to create a Rousseauesque atmosphere of natural innocence. The dinners are eaten in a grove 'under the canopy of heaven'; the children 'run about the lawn frisking like lambs'. But such entertainments naturally tended to acquire feudal inflections, and be seen as a revival of the 'ancient English hospitality'.[41] The Stowe dances took place in a large but unpretentious tenants' hall in the rustic, but the tenants' hall built under the new library added to Eaton Hall in the 1820s was vaulted and gothic; it was clearly intended to have a baronial flavour.[42]

At its best, entertaining the lower orders expressed a genuine concern for the

151. A party in the grounds at Ham House, Surrey. By Thomas Rowlandson.

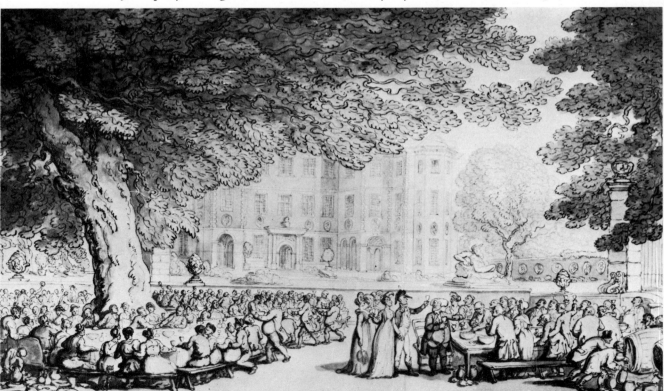

poor and a desire to improve the relations between the classes; at its worst it showed a rather odious condescension. Over the whole revival hovered the spectre of the French Revolution. It is hard to exaggerate the traumatic effect that this had on the English upper classes. They felt that they were sitting on a volcano, a volcano, moreover, which they themselves had helped to stoke, by the reaction against convention and authority, and exaltation of the emotions which some of them had found so delightful when confined to their own house-parties. Moreover, quite apart from what was going on in the towns, the enclosures which had done so much to improve English agriculture and boost the incomes of farmers and landowners had also produced poverty, misery and disaffection among farm labourers and small-holders.

Charity and entertainment for the lower orders were ways of trying to reduce disaffection and show how different English aristocrats were from French ones. But revolutions abroad and discontent at home had uglier effects; they scared many of the upper classes out of their enlightened attitudes. The volunteer yeomanry, however picturesque they may have appeared on parade, could also become an alliance between landowners and farmers to repress anyone in the locality who showed radical or even independent views. The age of the house-party was also the age of the game laws followed by the poor laws, of the autocratic governments of Pitt, Liverpool and Castelreagh, of spies, informers, imprisonment without trial and muzzling of the press. Country houses could project a disconcerting double image—relaxed and delightful to those who had the *entrée*, arrogant and forbidding to those who did not.

A house like Robert Smirke's Eastnor Castle (Pl. 150), designed for Lord Somers in about 1810, can be seen in two lights. The circuit of handsome and comfortable living rooms, grouped round a baronial hall and looking through great plate-glass windows onto garden and parkland, suggests both comfortable house-parties and ancient English hospitality. The towers, battlements and gatehouse are arranged with formidable symmetry to strike a new but not accidental note of authoritarianism; Lord Somers, whose belligerent portrait dominates the dining room, was, after all, to publish *A Defense of the Constitution of Great Britain and Ireland against the Innovating and Levelling Attempts of the Friends of Annual Parliaments and Universal Suffrage.*[43]

The revival of the castle style in the early nineteenth century was not only an expression of romanticism—or rather, it expressed a particular kind of romanticism, looking back with nostalgia to an age when the lower classes had known their places. Similarly a classical portico could be more than a symbol of its owner's education and culture. It could also symbolize his authority. This may be one reason why porticoes, having gone out of vogue in the second half of the eighteenth century, had a revival in the early nineteenth. Certainly the architect Gilbert Scott, who was brought up in the 1820s under the shadow of Stowe and the dukes of Buckingham, saw authoritarianism in great classical houses. 'Their cold and proud Palladianism', he wrote, 'seems to forbid approach—the only rural thoughts they suggest are of game keepers and park rangers.'[44]

242

152. (right) A corner of Eastnor Castle, Herefordshire (Robert Smirke, 1811–20).

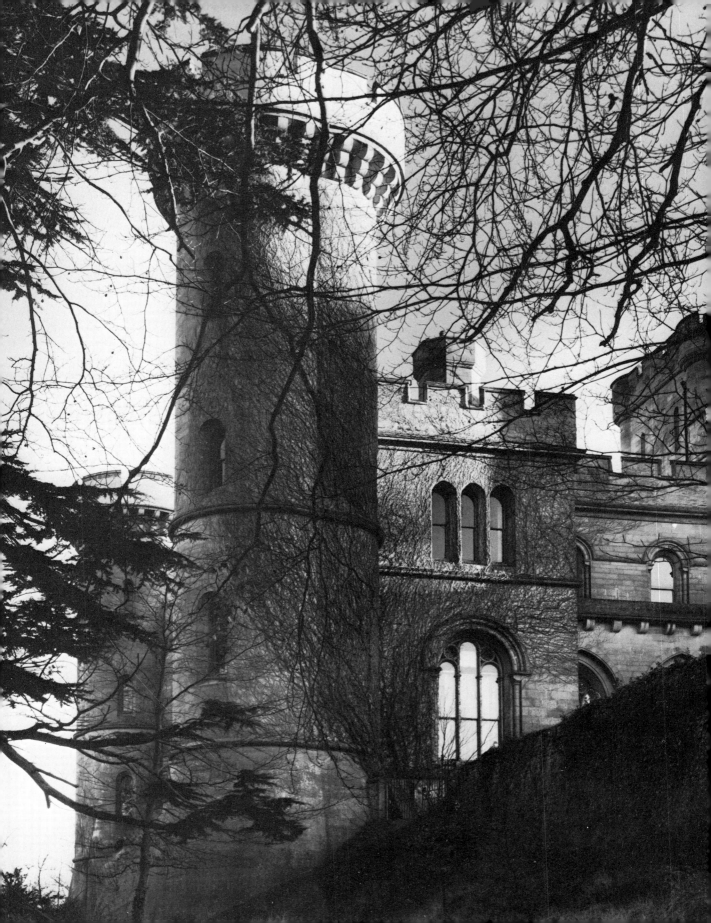

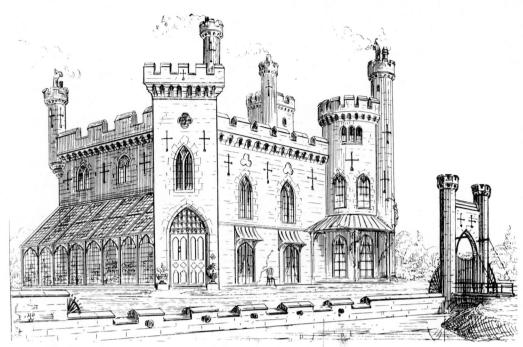

153. A. W. Pugin's parody of a 'modern castellated mansion'.

Pugin's satirical drawing of a 'modern castellated mansion' (Pl. 153) had a point to it, though not perhaps exactly the point he was trying to make in the accompanying text:

> What absurdities, what anomalies, what utter contradictions do not the builders of modern castles perpetrate! How many portcullises which will not lower down, and drawbridges which will not draw up! . . . On one side of the house machicolated parapets, embrasures, bastions and all the show of strong defence, and round the corner of the building a conservatory leading to the principal rooms through which a whole company of horsemen might penetrate at one smash into the very heart of the mansion! For who would hammer against nailed portals when he could kick his way through the greenhouse?[45]

To use the language of castle architecture for symbolic reasons is not necessarily absurd. But there *was* a conflict between the authoritarian and the recreational aspects of early-nineteenth-century houses—between the company gathered round the billiard table and the man-traps waiting in the woods. It was a conflict which the Victorians recognised and tried to get rid of.

244

154. (right) Bill-head showing an early-nineteenth-century water-closet. Thomas Thirkill was employed at Tythegstone Court, Glamorgan, in 1815.

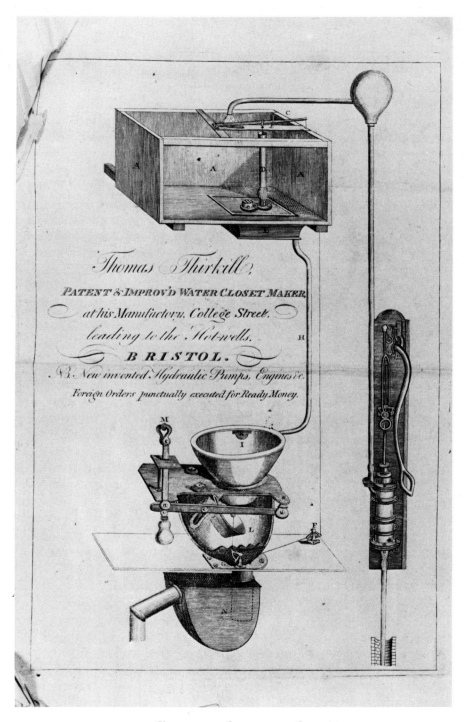

9 Second Interlude:
Early Country-House Technology

COUNTRY houses have always had to be warmed, lit, and supplied with water. Food has always had to be cooked in them, and sewage disposed of. But until the eighteenth century the technology which this involved moved slowly. So did technology of all kinds; but country houses tended to be a stage behind industry and the cities. The numbers involved were smaller and the profit motive largely absent.

Wall fireplaces, for instance, first appeared in England in the late eleventh century. Although at first they were luxuries, by the end of the Middle Ages they had become standard fittings for all the inhabited rooms in a country house. Coal began to supplement wood or turf in the fourteenth century, and came into general use in the sixteenth, along with grates and firedogs. But in spite of minor improvements, the grossly uneconomic combination of wide-arched opening and big chimney-flue remained the standard arrangement from the early Middle Ages to the late eighteenth century. During the same period techniques of cooking and lighting were equally static. Little advance was made on the apparatus already available in the Middle Ages; brick-lined ovens for baking, open fires for every other kind of cooking, and lighting by means of inefficient lamps fuelled with vegetable oil, or by wax and tallow candles in need of constant snuffing.

More progress was made in the provision and use of water. Even so it was a long time before country houses could match mediaeval monasteries. These were always carefully sited so as to have a running water supply. It was usually brought from a stream or spring on higher ground reasonably near the monastic buildings. The water was channelled into a conduit of stone, lead or wood and connected at least to the kitchen and the lavatorium, the long trough in the cloisters where the monks washed their hands before and after meals. Equal care was taken to provide a drainage system and to link it to a necessarium, or rere-dorter. This was usually built immediately above the main drain, and contained one or more rows of pierced seats, usually subdivided by partitions.

Royal palaces could be as well supplied with water as monasteries, and were considerably more luxurious. As early as 1169 the hall of the Palace of Westminster was being supplied with water by lead conduits. In the mid thirteenth century the supply was extended from the hall to the king's chamber, and to bathrooms for the king and queen. In 1351–2 the king's bath was fitted with 'two large bronze taps . . . to bring hot and cold water in to the bath.'[1] The royal accounts contain many payments for supplying running water and bathrooms to other royal houses. But on hill-top sites running water was often out of the question. Windsor Castle, for instance, had to rely on wells, and on what rainwater was collected in a lead cistern on the roof of the great tower.[2]

A few great noblemen could also afford to bring running water into their houses but the majority of mediaeval manor houses and castles had no such supply, and had to rely on rainwater or water carried in containers from springs or wells. This was probably the case even in houses surrounded by moats, since these were invariably used as receptacles for sewage. All mediaeval houses of any size were amply supplied with privies, connected by vertical shafts either to water or

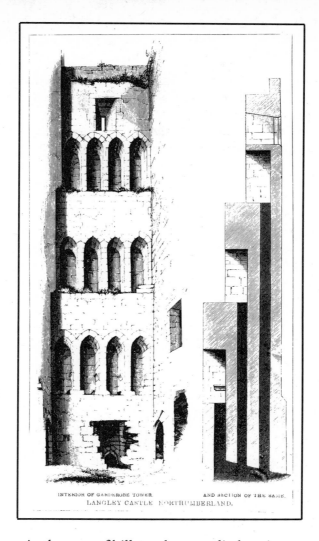

INTERIOR OF GARDEROBE TOWER.   AND SECTION OF THE SAME.
LANGLEY CASTLE NORTHUMBERLAND.

to sewage pits—or in the case of hill-top houses, discharging onto the hillside. In early examples the privies were sometimes grouped together in a single tower. A formidable example of this arrangement at Langley Castle in Northumberland dates from the late fourteenth century (Pl. 155). Three layers of parallel vertical shafts are connected to three floors of privies. There are four privies in each tier; each privy is in an arched recess built over its respective shaft.[3] By the fifteenth century, however, the usual arrangement was to have the privies dispersed, with one privy to each of the more important chambers. In a range of two-storey lodgings the series of projections built to contain the privies and their shafts could be an impressive feature.

Mediaeval techniques of water supply continued through the sixteenth century with only minor modifications. The dissolution of the monasteries provided many secular landowners with a ready-made system. When the Byron family acquired Newstead Abbey in Nottinghamshire and converted its cloister into corridors, they continued to use the monastic water supply, including the lead cistern which the monks had installed as a *lavatorium* in the south cloister walk.[4] At Longleat the many privies installed in the mid sixteenth century by Sir John

247

155. View and section of the fourteenth-century privy tower at Langley Castle, Northumberland.

Thynne were connected to a subterranean water channel, probably installed in the time of the Austin Friars, whose buildings Thynne took over and remodelled.

Beckley Park near Oxford is another house where an Elizabethan builder probably took over a mediaeval system, but a royal rather than a monastic one. Beckley had been the hunting lodge of Henry III's brother, the Duke of Cornwall. Its water system, which includes two concentric moats, now much silted up, probably dates from his time. But the present house was built in about 1560 as a hunting lodge for Sir John Williams of Rycote (Col. Pl. XXV). Its east front is dominated by three slender gabled towers. Two of these were built as privy towers and contained privies on the top floor, connected by shafts to a water channel threaded beneath them.[5]

A good many sixteenth-century houses acquired new water supplies, rather than taking over old ones. The most ambitious system was that which finally brought running water to Windsor Castle from Blackmore Park, five miles from the castle. It took at least four years to construct, between about 1551 and 1555. The water was piped in a lead conduit and the head of water brought it up the castle hill to a great lead cistern in the upper court. From here more conduits distributed it to other points in the castle.[6]

Little if any of the Windsor system survives. But charming little conduit houses of about 1545–50 still cover the springs from which conduits supplied water to Lacock Abbey in Wiltshire (Pl. 157) and Sudeley Castle in Gloucestershire. The two buildings are similar in design, not surprisingly since Sir John Sharington of Lacock was a close associate of Lord Seymour of Sudeley. The main purpose of such buildings was to protect the springs from being dirtied by cattle. A number of them survive, and there are records of many others.[7] At Sir Nicholas Bacon's Gorhambury the conduit supply, which probably dated from the 1560s, was especially elaborate and served all parts of the house. At Holdenby the supply ran from a conduit house over a spring about a mile from the house to a second building on the edge of the garden; this contained a still room at ground level, and a big storage cistern above it. In 1585 plumbers were installing lead pipes for the 'water works' at the Earl of Shrewsbury's Worksop in Nottinghamshire.[8]

But as in the Middle Ages the majority of country houses had no such supply. To install one was expensive, and the fondness of many Elizabethans for building on high ground often made it difficult or impossible. In the 1580s, when Sir Francis Willoughby pulled down his family home at Wollaton and rebuilt it on a neighbouring hill top, he had to rely for water on an underground spring a considerable way down the hillside from the house. Although a spacious brick-vaulted tunnel ingeniously connects this to the basement, fetching and carrying water cannot have been a convenient operation. A number of country houses economized on human labour by using donkey-wheels to draw up buckets from their wells. The energy was provided by a donkey installed inside the wheel, in order to turn it on the treadmill system. Late-sixteenth-century examples still survive at Carisbrooke Castle and Grey's Court in Oxfordshire. Donkey-wheels continued to be installed and used in country houses into the nineteenth century.[9]

Hand pumps seem to have appeared at about the same time as donkey-wheels. At Hardwick, on another hill-top site, water was pumped from a source which has not yet been identified into a cistern raised on a handsome stone-arched structure by the Old Hall. The pumping was almost certainly done by hand. From there a lead conduit fed it by gravity into a cistern in the scullery of the New Hall.[10]

There were privy-shafts in the Old Hall at Hardwick, but none in the new one. It and many other Elizabethan and Jacobean houses relied entirely on close-stools. These were pierced wooden seats, with removable containers in a box underneath them. The close-stools of the great were handsomely fitted up; Bess of Hardwick's one at Hardwick was 'covered with blue cloth stitched with white, with red and black silk fringe'.[11]

As long as plenty of labour was available, to abandon privy-shafts for close-stools was not as retrogressive as it might seem. The contents of the close-stool could be disposed of tidily in a pit at a convenient distance from the house, whereas privy-shafts in the house needed constant maintenance if they were not to become offensive. Even if the drainage system at or below ground level was efficient, the walls of the shafts needed regular flushing, which they did not always receive. Efforts were made to use rainwater for this purpose. Fourteenth-century examples are known at Caernarvon, Denbigh and Warkworth Castles.[12] A similar system at Longford Castle in Wiltshire probably dated from the building of the house in the 1580s, and was described in 1678:

> Nay, art here hath so well traced Nature in the most ignoble conveyances (which are no less needful than the most visible conveniences) as to furnish every storey with private conduits for the suillage of the house, which are washed by every shower that falls from the gutters, and so hath vent from the very foundations to the top for the discharge of noisome vapours, by a contrivance not enough followed elsewhere in England, tho' recommended by Architects.[13]

Rainwater was also put to other uses. In the alterations made by Lord Lumley to Lumley Castle around 1570, the roof drains were connected to cisterns which fed two lavatory basins in alcoves to either side of the hall porch.[14] At Hardwick Old Hall a stone down-pipe ran from the flat roof of the Hill Great Chamber (built in 1588) and fed a stone trough in the kitchen.[15] Rainwater was such an obvious source of supply that it would be surprising if more examples of its use at this and earlier periods did not come to light: it was usually the only, if highly variable, means by which water could be brought without inconvenience to upper floors. Houses supplied by conduit seldom had a head of water sufficient to carry the supply above the ground floor. A hand pump, such as seems to have been installed at Hardwick, could only raise water about fifteen feet, and in very limited amounts. It could supply the kitchen, but little else.

More ambitious and efficient methods of pumping water were in fact available, but it was a long time before they were used for country houses. Pumps powered by water-wheel were in operation to drain mines in Saxony in the early sixteenth century, and could raise water to heights of up to a hundred feet. They seem to have made their first appearance in England in the late sixteenth century. Water-wheels were pumping Thames water to parts of the City from 1581, and up ninety-three feet to other parts of London from the 1650s; the latter supply was the work of an ingenious gentleman virtuoso, Sir Edward Ford.[16]

But it was only in the second half of the seventeenth century that water and water-power, fostered by the Royal Society and the virtuosos, really came into their own. Water was the ruling power of the next hundred and fifty years, just as steam was the ruling power of the hundred years that followed them. More and more country houses acquired a running water supply, whether supplied by pumping or by gravity. The excitement of being able to move and control great masses of water, and to harness water to raise itself or to turn machinery, produced its own aesthetic—the aesthetic of formal water gardens, of cascades, ponds and fountains.

On 30 July 1681, the London Gazette reported a remarkable achievement of pumping at Windsor Castle. 'Sir Samuel Morland, with the strength of eight men, forced the water (mingled with a vessel of red wine to make it visible) in a continuous stream, at the rate of above sixty barrels an hour, from the engine below at the park pale, up to the top of the castle, and from thence into the air above sixty foot high.' The water came from the Thames, and the total height involved was about 250 feet; the 'engine' was almost immediately adapted so as to be worked by a water-wheel rather than man-power.[17] Morland was the great maestro of water supply in the reign of Charles II. He improved the efficiency of pumps, and experimented with powering them by steam, water and gunpowder. Charles II appointed him his 'magister mechanicorum', and Louis XIV consulted him about the waterworks at Versailles. His services were engaged to pump water out of mines, to install machinery for mills and, in at least one case, to supply water to a country house. When Evelyn visited Euston Hall in Suffolk in 1671 and 1676, he described the 'pretty engine . . . the invention of Sir Samuel Morland' which was turned by a cascade supplied from the formal canal in front of the house. This 'turns a corn-mill, that provides the family and raises water for the fountains and offices'.[18]

Euston was perhaps the first example of a country house with more than a hand-pumped water supply, but it was soon followed by others. In about 1689 water was pumped, probably by water-wheel, up a formidable hill of about three hundred feet to supply Lord Tankerville's new house at Uppark in Sussex.[19] At Broadlands, in about 1695, Celia Fiennes noted 'a water house that by a wheel casts up the water out of the river just by and fills the pipes to serve all the house and to fill the basin designed in the middle of the garden with a spout in the middle.'[20] In the early decades of the eighteenth century such water pumps (usually described as 'engines') became much commoner in country houses. They were powered by water, horse or donkey-wheel, and occasionally by steam. They were country relations of the great engines which were installed at the same

250

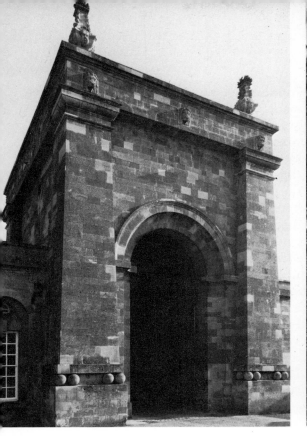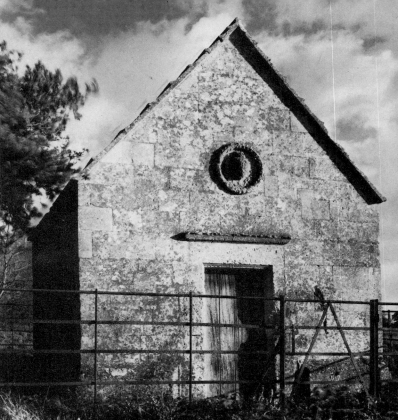

time in the towns. Not surprisingly one of the most up-to-date country water supplies was at Blenheim. It was installed in 1706–9 by 'Mr Aldersey'. An 'engine' (of an unspecified nature) pumped water to a great wooden cistern at the top of a neighbouring hill. From there water was fed to a massive lead cistern over the entrance gateway through which the approach from the Oxford road passed into the kitchen court. The cistern tower (as it became known) was perhaps the first English water-tower (Pl. 156). It supplied water to the gardens, kitchen, offices and 'other places in the east end of the house'. Another cistern in the stable court supplied water to the stables and the western half of house and gardens.[21]

At the very end of the seventeenth century the use of steam for power, first adumbrated in the 1650s by the Marquess of Worcester, was made effective by Thomas Savery. Savery supplied what he called 'fire-engines' (soon to be radically improved by Newcomen) to a number of houses in the early eighteenth century. In 1712 a pump worked by a Savery engine was installed at Campden House in Kensington.[22] It could raise 3000 gallons an hour up fifty-eight feet to a cistern at the top of the house. Savery was also employed at the Duke of Chandos's house at Sion Hill, Isleworth. Here 'the engine was placed under a delightful Banquetting-House, and the water being forced up into a cistern on the top thereof used to play a fountain contiguous thereto in a very delightful manner.'[23]

In about 1730 Houghton was furnished with a running water supply from a well a hundred feet deep and about half a mile from the house. A wheel was turned

156. (above left) The cistern tower at Blenheim Palace, Oxfordshire.

157. (above right) A conduit house at Bowden Hill, Wiltshire. Water was supplied from it to Lacock Abbey.

by a horse-worked pump, and sent water up through a lead conduit into a great cistern in a nearby water-house in the park. This was an extremely elegant Palladian building designed by the Earl of Pembroke; above the tank was a belvedere portico and two inspection rooms with hatches into the tank. From there water was fed to the house by gravity. The water-house, the well, a brick-lined inspection shaft giving access to it, the pump, the wheel and the original design for the wheel all survive, although the pump may be a replacement and the wheel is in decay. The system was in operation until the 1920s.[24]

Water systems, new or old, and pumped or fed by gravity were also being used to supply the formal gardens which were now being laid out all over England. But the owner who proudly contemplated his spouting fountains and tumbling cascades was likely to be able to look with equal pride at water flowing in basins, baths, buffets and water-closets inside his house. These enviable novelties were not taken for granted, or kept out of view, as internal plumbing tends to be today. They were trimmed out with marble and put on show—water-closets included.

Indoor fountains, baths and possibly even water-closets had been installed in country houses in the late sixteenth and early seventeenth century, but they were rare. The great chamber at Theobalds had a fountain which spouted water into a circular basin supported by figures of two savages. When Sir John Harington pioneered the water-closet in the 1590s he may have installed an example in his own house at Kelston in Somerset; if so, it did not work well enough to find imitators. According to John Aubrey there were two 'bathing rooms' in the lodge built by Francis Bacon at Verulam, near St Albans, in the early seventeenth century. Water was piped to basins in two alcoves in the grotto installed as part of the remodelled range of Woburn Abbey in the 1630s.[25]

In 1664 Pepys was impressed by the bathroom in Thomas Povey's house in Lincoln's Inn Fields.[26] Around 1670 Sir Samuel Morland was involved in improving, and possibly installing, a bathing room for Charles II in Whitehall Palace. In 1673 he provided Sir Robert Howard, Auditor of the Receipt, with a luxuriously decorated bathing house in the garden of his official Westminster lodgings. Water was pumped up from the Thames to a stone cistern and heated in a copper, before being run into an oval bathing cistern surrounded by a white marble pavement.[27] By 1681 Lord Craven was planning to introduce these London luxuries to Combe Abbey in Warwickshire. The new north-east pavilion designed by William Winde was to contain bathing and sweating rooms, but was never built.[28]

By the time Celia Fiennes was touring England in the late seventeenth and early eighteenth century, water was on the move everywhere, but was sufficiently novel for her to describe it. Apart from actual water-pumping devices and ornamental water in the gardens, she was intrigued by water-closets, bathrooms and buffets. The latter, in the new and fashionable form that they assumed in the late seventeenth century, were usually made of marble and could contain a running water supply, shelves for the display of glasses, plate or china, and a basin or cistern in which to wash hands, faces or glasses.

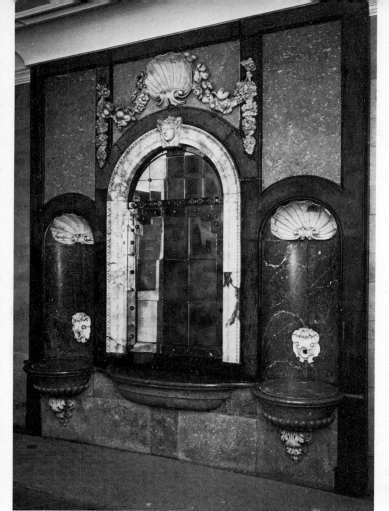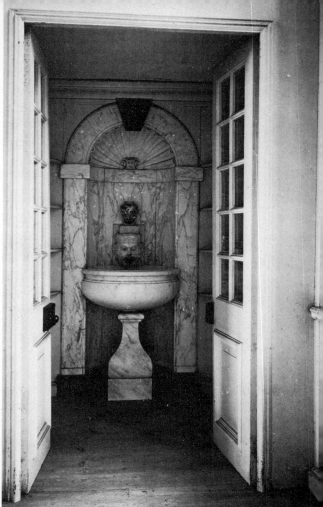

Early in the eighteenth century she visited Windsor and admired the water-closets in 'the little box the Queen has bought of Lord Godolphin's . . . for a little retreat out of the palace.' A closet in Prince George of Denmark's apartment led 'to a little place with a seat of easement of marble with sluices of water to wash all down'. There was a matching arrangement in the queen's apartment, above the duke's.[29] At Mr Rooth's house at Epsom, in about 1705, she found a canal and a great fountain in the garden, and a bathing room and 'a neat booffet' in the house. The buffet was in a little parlour, and was 'furnished with glasses and china for the table, a cistern below into which the water turned from a cock, and a hole at bottom to let it out at pleasure.'[30]

At Chatsworth (where an ample water supply from the moors above the house made pumping unnecessary) the elaborate waterworks in the gardens were paralleled by almost equally elaborate fittings inside the house. Celia Fiennes described the grotto and bathroom in 1697:

There is a fine grotto all stone pavement, roof and sides, this is designed to supply all the house with water besides several fancies to make diversion; within this is a bathing room, the walls all with blue and white marble, the

158. (above left) A buffet of 1704 originally at Chatsworth but now at Thornbridge Hall, Derbyshire.
159. (above right) The buffet of 1703 at Swangrove, Gloucestershire.

pavement mix'd one stone white, another black, another of the red rance marble; the bath is one entire marble all white finely veined with blue and is made smooth, but had it been as finely polished as some, it would have been the finest marble that could be seen; it was as deep as one's middle on the outside, and you went down steps into the bath big enough for two people; at the upper end are two cocks to let in, one hot the other cold, water to attemper it as persons please; the windows are all private glass.[31]

At the same period Chatsworth also acquired a considerable number of water-closets and an exceptionally fine marble buffet. At least ten water-closets were installed in and around 1691–4; their woodwork was mostly of cedar, their fittings of brass, and their bowls of local alabaster, except those for the duke and duchess which were of marble. The buffet was installed in 1705 in what seems to have been a private family dining parlour on the ground floor of the newly-remodelled west range. The bathroom and water-closets have long ago disappeared; the grotto is still there and contains a handsome fountain decorated with a marble relief of Diana bathing; the buffet (Pl. 158) has been removed to Thornbridge Hall, a few miles away.[32] There is a much smaller, but enchantingly pretty buffet in the main room of Swangrove, a lodge or banqueting house built by the Duke of Beaufort on the edge of Badminton park in 1703 (Pl. 159). The basin in the buffet was connected to a cistern immediately above it; water was pumped to the cistern from a spring a hundred yards or so from the house.[33]

The best surviving example of domestic water-architecture of this period is the water-tower at Carshalton House in Surrey (Pl. 160). It was erected in 1719–20 for Sir John Fellowes, one of the directors of the South Sea Company. The architect may have been Henry Joynes; the engineer was Richard Cole. A vaulted engine-room under the tower contained a water-wheel, powered by a mill-stream running under the building. An artificial lake, between the house and the tower, acted as a mill-pond. The water-wheel turned a pump which pumped water up to a lead cistern in the tower. This supplied water to the house, and to a bathroom at the base of the tower (Col. Pl. XXVI). The bathroom was one of a series of rooms grouped round the engine-room. They included an orangery or greenhouse, a room probably used as a dining and banqueting room, and a little room which may originally have contained a boiler. The bathing room is still lined with Dutch tiles, and preserves its black and white marble floor and coved ceiling; the bath is a sunk 'cistern' about 8 ft by 11 ft, and has three tiled alcoves in the wall at one end. The actual bath has been covered in, but was probably fitted with cocks for hot and cold water, and steps to descend by.[34]

The water-system at Blenheim included a 'bagnio', with hot and cold water laid on. It was in the basement under the duchess's bedroom, and connected to it by a backstair.[35] The Duke of Chandos's country houses, Cannons in particular, were especially well provided with water.[36] Shaw Hall in Berkshire had running water on all floors, and Cannons on at least two. This was scarcely surprising for the duke's chaplain, Dr Desaguliers, was also an eminent virtuoso, and engineer

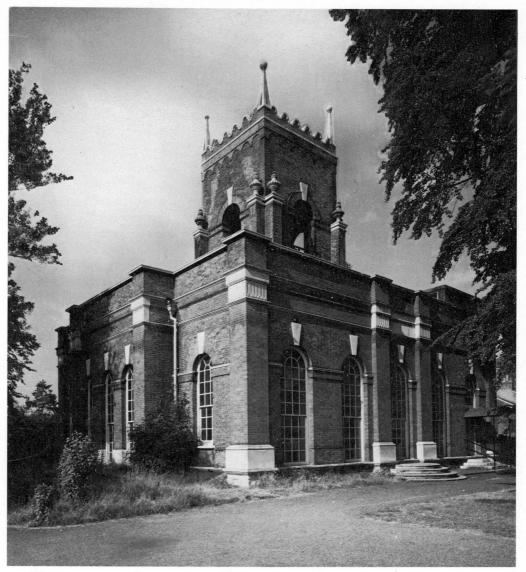

160. The water tower of 1719–20 at Carshalton House, Surrey.

to the York Water Company, which pumped water by means of a Newcomen steam engine from the Thames up to the new Cavendish-Harley estate in North London. Cannons had elaborate water gardens, a bathing room, four water-closets and two buffets in the house, all richly tricked out with marble. The duke's own water-closet, off his dressing room, contained a marble pavement, walls, and bowl, a japanned seat, an ornamental and gilded plaster ceiling and an Italian painting by 'Mr Scarptena'. Another marble water-closet complete with 'plug cock and handles' was exposed for all to see in the corridor outside his library. There were buffets in the eating parlour and in a separate marble-floored room known as the 'beaufett' next to the great dining room. In spite of Pope's denials, his couplets:

But hark! the chiming clocks to dinner call,
A hundred footsteps scrape the marble hall;
The rich buffet well coloured serpents grace,
And gaping Tritons spew to wash your face,

were generally taken to refer to Cannons, along with the rest of his description of Timon's villa.[37]

By 1730, when the description was written, any country house could in theory have running water on all floors, and as many baths and water-closets as its owner wanted or could afford. But comparatively little use was made of this technology in the next fifty years. Some handsome or elegant baths (invariably plunge-baths) were installed, but they remained the exception rather than the rule, and were almost invariably in the basement or on the ground floor. Running water above ground-floor level remained a rarity. Water-closets became, if anything, less common. Instead, a fashion started for outdoor earth closets. In 1751 the requirements for the 'little house' in one of the less prominent parts of the garden at Felbrigg in Norfolk were described in detail by its owner William Windham. 'Should not the inside be stucoed, or how do you do it? How many holes? There must be one for a child; and I would have it as light as possible. There must be a good broad place to set a candle on, and a place to keep paper . . . though the better the plainer, it should be neat.'[38]

The lack of progress in sanitation was due to a combination of cheap labour, lack of demand and technical disadvantages. Personal cleanliness did not rank high enough on the eighteenth-century list of priorities to offset the expense of installing an elaborate water system, especially since water in small quantities could very easily be carried by servants. Moreover, since no adequate valve had yet been invented, water-closets were still malodorous and inefficient.

But although water-closets went out of fashion, cold baths came into it. They were recommended, for reasons of health not cleanliness, by Dr Oliver in his influential treatise *A Practical Dissertation on the Bath Waters* (1707). Public cold baths were opened at Clerkenwell in 1697 and at Widcombe, near Bath, in 1707. Although their water had no medicinal content they were extremely successful. In 1715 Dudley Ryder, a young London attorney, described how 'Mr Porter, who is an apothecary, was talking of the cold bath and the service it had done him by making him of a more strong, firm constitution than before. He says it is extremely good against the headache, strengthens and enlivens the body, is good against the vapours and impotence, and that the pain is little. I have almost determined to go in them myself.'[39]

Many country-house owners did determine to take them, and cold baths were built all over England. As they were used on a weekly or even monthly rather than daily basis there was no special need for them to be in the house. They were often constructed in the park or garden, where they could be made the object of an afternoon's outing. The bath was sometimes in the open air, sometimes in a garden building or grotto, as at Stourhead. There was usually accommodation

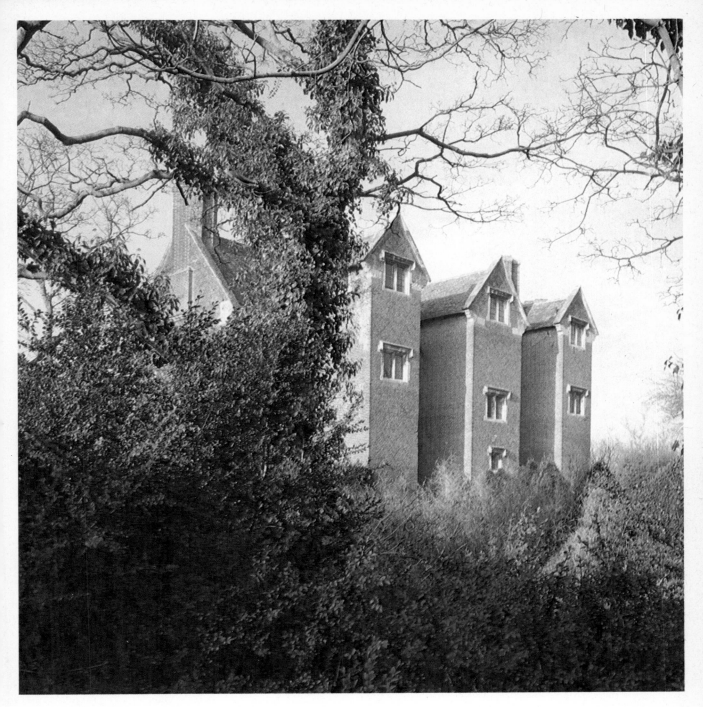

XXV. Beckley Park, Oxfordshire (*c.* 1560). The privy towers.

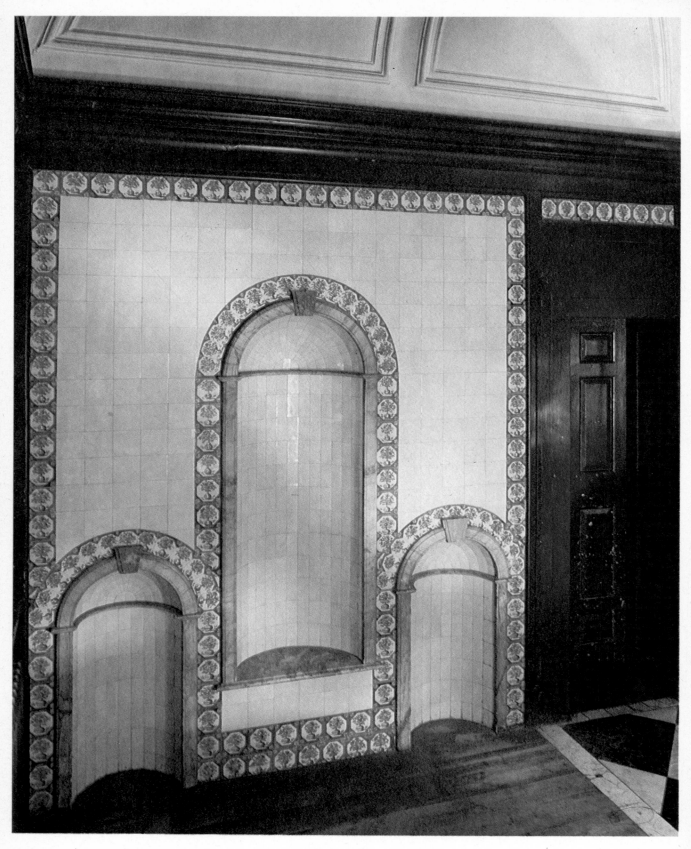

XXVI. Carshalton House, Surrey. The bathroom in the water tower (1719–20).
XXVII. (right) The Princesses Louise, Victoria and Maude visiting Cragside, Northumberland in 1884.

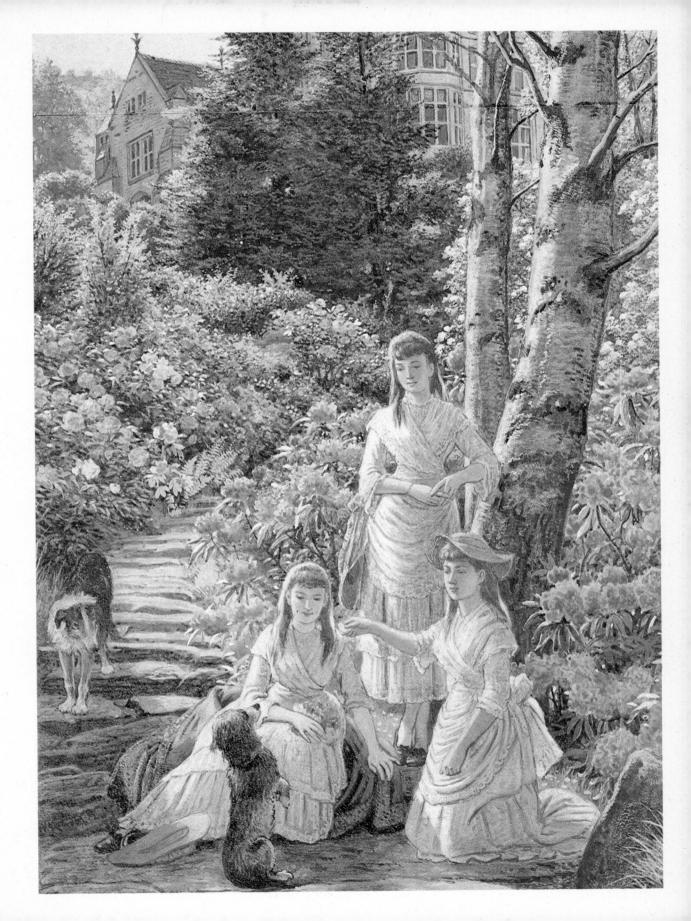

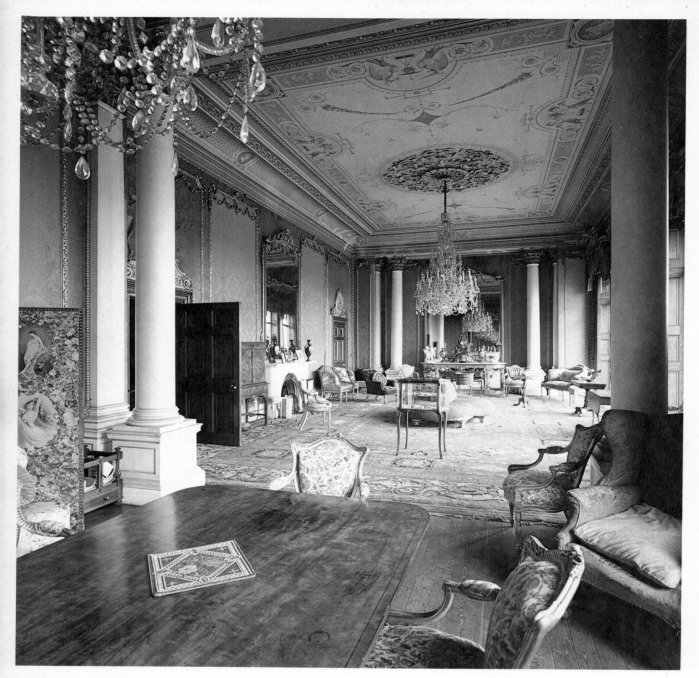

XXVIII. Brodsworth Hall, Yorkshire (1861–70). The drawing room.

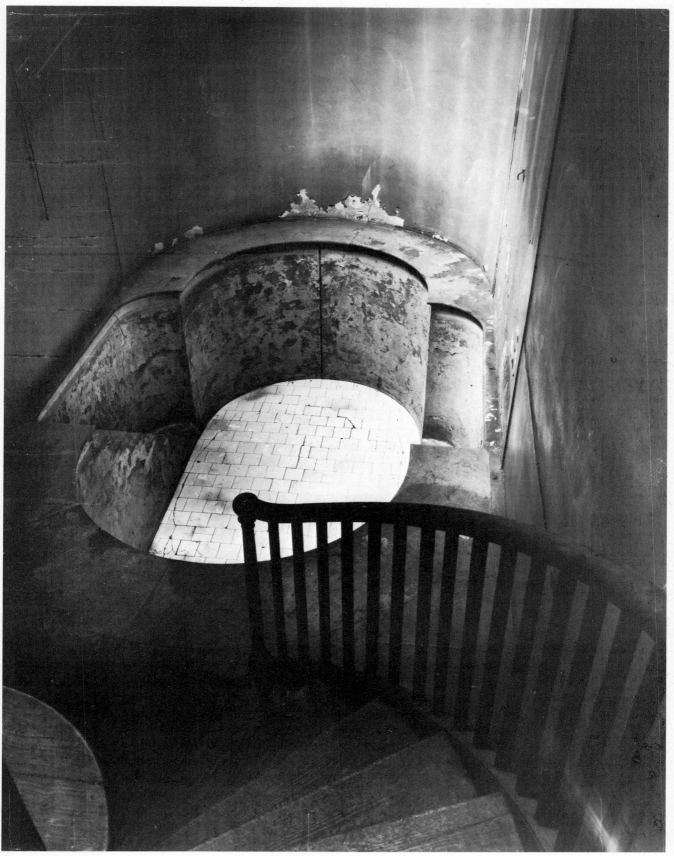

161. A plunge bath of about 1790–1800 at Wimpole Hall, Cambridgeshire.

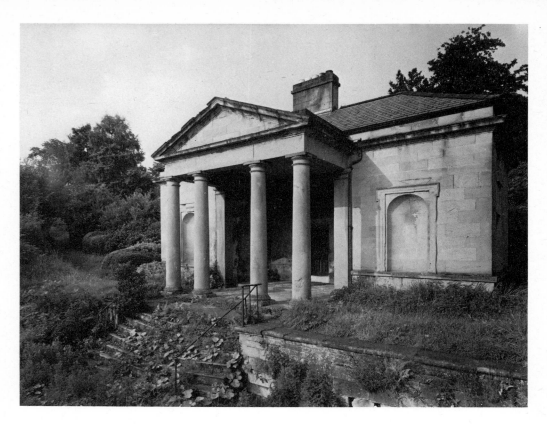

above or near the bath, for dressing and undressing, and for taking some self-congratulatory refreshment after the plunge. The baths varied a good deal in size. The cold bath at Rousham in Oxfordshire, constructed in the 1730s, is only a few feet across; the cold bath at Wynnstay in Denbighshire, which dates from about 1780, consists of a large stone-lined pool, the size of a big swimming-bath (Pl. 162). A broad flight of steps leads down into the water from the porticoed changing room which adjoins it.[40]

By the 1780s most big houses probably had an ice-house as well as a cold bath. The first reference to such an amenity in England is perhaps in 1666–7, when a 'snow-well' was installed at St James's Palace for the Duke of York. It was sunk in the ground and thatched with straw.[41] In the eighteenth century ice-houses were usually vaulted in brick or stone and built conveniently near a lake or pond, so that winter ice could be packed into them, insulated between layers of straw for use in the summer.[42]

If, cold baths and ice-houses apart, plumbing made little advance in mid-eighteenth-century country houses, neither, for that matter, did technology of any kind. 'Nothing can be more preposterous and inappropriate than the prevailing construction and management of a gentleman's kitchen,' wrote Charles Sylvester in 1819. 'As for the boasted comfort of an Englishman's fireside, we see it accompanied with evils which loudly call for remedy.'[43] But Sylvester, while attacking the general situation, was also celebrating the beginnings of what he called domestic economy—by which he meant science applied to home life. By the end of the eighteenth century, domestic technology, following in the wake of the Industrial Revolution, was starting to move again. The pioneers were mainly

262

162. The bath house and remains of the cold bath at Wynnstay, Denbighshire (c. 1780).

radicals, utilitarian factory-owners and reformers rather than virtuoso gentlemen; on the whole, hospitals, prisons and lunatic asylums were centrally heated and lit by gas long before country houses. But Regency country gentlemen, however suspicious of radicals, were by no means averse to comfort; by the early 1800s new scientific gadgets were being installed at country houses in considerable numbers.

Designs for fireplaces were being produced throughout the eighteenth century, but made little impression until the American Count Rumford introduced his so called 'Rumford stove' in 1796. This was in fact no more than an efficient fireplace, which could easily be introduced into existing openings. By narrowing the throat of the chimney, reducing the size of the fireplace opening, and placing it between inclined surrounds of brick to absorb and reflect the heat, Rumford was able to make open fires dramatically more effective. He also experimented with completely closed cooking-stoves.[44] Although such stoves were ultimately to reduce kitchen smells to manageable dimensions, and make it possible to place even a big kitchen close to the dining room, most English country houses continued to spit-roast before open fires (Pl. 163). A feature of some country-house kitchens which seems first to have appeared in the late eighteenth or early nineteenth century was what were called stewing stoves—a row of individual cooking plates, each heated by charcoal placed in a flueless archway underneath them. Examples can still be seen in the kitchens at Hardwick and Tullynally.[45]

As early as 1754 William Day of Lambeth was advertising a device 'which rarifies cold air until it is hot, and conveys it into Gentleman's libraries and grand rooms.'[46] In 1760 the kitchen garden at Thoresby in Nottinghamshire acquired what was known as a 'hot wall'—a brick wall incorporating horizontal flues warmed from a central stove, the whole designed to bring about early ripening.[47] Hot walls in kitchen gardens became common enough, but central heating inside the house was seldom found until the early nineteenth century. In the 1790s William Strutt, the mill-owner, was experimenting with heating by hot air and by 1819 had installed complete systems in his own house at Derby and in Derby County Infirmary. His stove, which he called a 'cockle', was adapted and improved by Charles Sylvester and marketed with some success 'particularly to warm halls, staircases and passages'.[48] Hot air heating was installed in the hall of Pakenham Hall (now known as Tullynally Castle) in Ireland in about 1807 and at Coleshill in Berkshire in 1811. The Earl of Shelburne (who had numerous utilitarian friends) introduced steam-heating into the library at Bowood in the 1790s; Walter Scott followed suit at Abbotsford in 1823.[49] At much the same time Prince Pückler-Muskau was revelling in the luxury of the gallery round the courtyard at Woburn: 'this affords a walk as instructive as it is agreeable in winter or bad weather, and is rendered perfectly comfortable by the "conduits de chaleur" which heat the whole house.'[50] This heating system was almost certainly worked by hot-air; hot-water heating came a little later. Several hundred feet of hot-water piping were installed at Stratfield Saye for the Duke of Wellington in 1833. The system included rudimentary radiators, of which two ponderous examples still survive.[51]

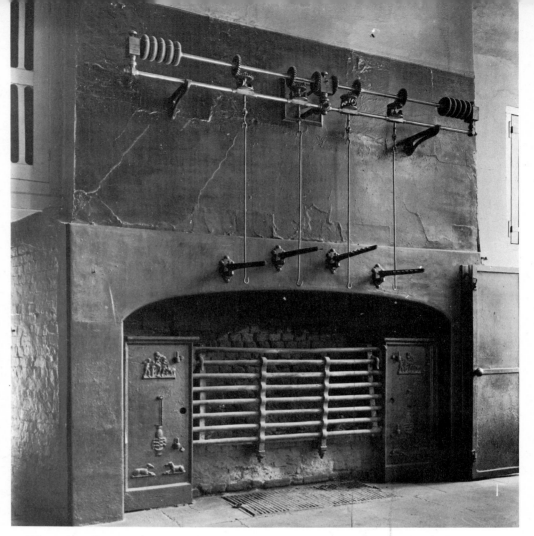

The comfort and convenience of English houses at this date was much commented on by European visitors. Prince Pückler-Muskau was quick to notice fittings and habits which were not to be found in Germany. At Penrhyn in 1828 he commented on another novelty, the bells outside the servants' hall: 'They are suspended in a row on the wall, numbered so that it is immediately seen in what room any-one has rung: a sort of pendulum is attached to each which continues to vibrate for ten minutes after the sound has ceased, to remind the sluggish of their duty.'[52]

To Englishmen such rows of bells were already familiar. They survive today in many country houses, although invariably long since disconnected. They marked a considerable advance in sophistication from the bell which Pepys had hung outside his bedchamber door in 1663 'to call the maids'.[53] The next stage was to have a bell or bells connected to a rope in another room. Zoffany's portrait of Sir Lawrence Dundas and his grandson, painted in 1769, shows a bell rope hanging between the pictures. In 1774 bells and bell-ropes were installed in the main rooms at Harewood.[54] In the next few decades the technique was improved by the introduction of wires and cranks, until it became possible to wire up the whole

264

163. A late-eighteenth-century kitchen fireplace.

house and connect all the main rooms and bedrooms to the bell-board outside the servants' hall.

Around 1800 candles in country houses were increasingly supplemented by oil, and to a lesser extent by gas. Lord Dundonald installed gas in the hall of Dundarane Abbey in Scotland in 1787; the chandeliers in the music and banqueting rooms at Brighton Pavilion were fitted for gas in 1818; and Walter Scott introduced gas to Abbotsford in 1823.[55] But before the improvements of the mid nineteenth century gas-light was too expensive, hot and malodorous to be practical for private houses. The introduction of colza-oil in 1834 provided a new and more efficient lighting-fuel which became very popular. In the 1830s Belvoir Castle was largely lit by oil. The rooms in the basement where the lamps were prepared were described as 'the most complete in their arrangement in the kingdom'. They were vaulted and fireproof: 'the lamps are filled over cisterns, which receive the unavoidable waste of oil in the operation . . . In the season of his Grace's residence, about sixteen or seventeen weeks, four hundred burners are required, and about six hundred gallons of oil consumed.'[56]

Improvements in heating and lighting were accompanied by improvements in sanitation. The shower-bath was invented, bath-tubs replaced the elegant but much more expensive plunge-baths of the eighteenth century, and most important of all, really efficient water-closets, fitted with valves that worked, at last became available (Pl. 154). The breakthrough came with Joseph Bramah's water-closet, patented in 1778. By 1797 Bramah claimed to have made 6000 closets.[57] In the early decades of the nineteenth century water-closets (often still supplemented by outside earth-closets for the servants) became a common though far from universal phenomenon in country houses. Water was piped and often pumped to the upper floors to service them, in addition, perhaps, to a sink in the housemaid's closet and one or occasionally two bathrooms. But in some houses the water-closets were run, not very effectively, off rainwater. At Pakenham Hall in Ireland, where there was no running water supply until 1875, a four-storey tower for water-closets was added to the rear of the house in about 1800. It was surmounted by a rainwater cistern, into which the main roof drained, and contained three two-seater and one single-seater water-closets.[58]

As early as 1813 the Earl of Moira's Donington Park in Leicestershire had two bathrooms and at least six water-closets, on two floors. His wife had a water-closet and bathroom off her dressing room; the bathroom was furnished with a gilded wash-hand stand, a dressing stand with gilded basin and ewers, a rosewood book stand, a thermometer and a copper tea kettle. Immediately below, her husband had a water-closet and bathroom off his study and powdering room.[59] By the late 1830s and early 1840s the dukes of Buckingham were equipping Stowe with plumbing almost as lavishly as their predecessors had equipped it with temples. By 1844 it had at least nine water-closets, a shower-bath and four bathrooms.[60] The shower-bath, which was in the duke's apartment and had piped hot and cold water, was not an altogether new phenomenon; the Duc de Levis had described it as a 'machine . . . now very much in use' by the English in

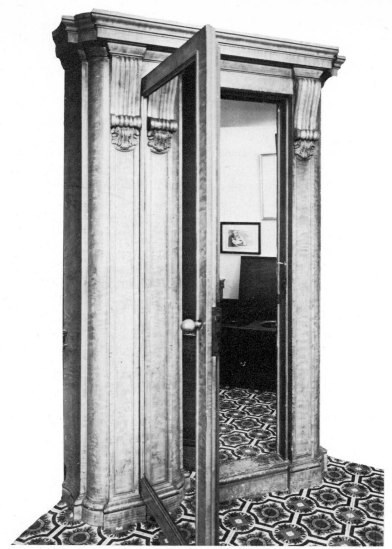

164. One of the cupboard water-closets installed by the first Duke of Wellington at Stratfield Saye, Hampshire.

1815.[61] Designs survive for the most ingenious of the Stowe water-closets, which was neatly hidden in a cupboard surmounted by a ducal coronet. Similar cupboard-lavatories (without the coronet) were installed at about the same time by the Duke of Wellington at Stratfield Saye, and can still be seen there (Pl. 164).

An English nobleman of the 1820s or '30s, purged and refreshed after a visit to his water-closet and bathroom, reclining in his dressing room on a richly upholstered sofa, reading the latest novel by the light of a colza-oil lamp and able, whenever he felt like it, to tug a bell handle and summon a servant to bring him an iced drink, had reached a pinnacle of luxury which was the admiration of all his European contemporaries. In the next fifty years, advances in the available technology were not matched by equivalent advances in comfort. Luxury, to the Victorians, tended to be a suspect word.

266

165. (right) 'Home, Sweet Home', Lord and Lady Folkestone and their son, Jacob. By Edward Clifford, c. 1879.

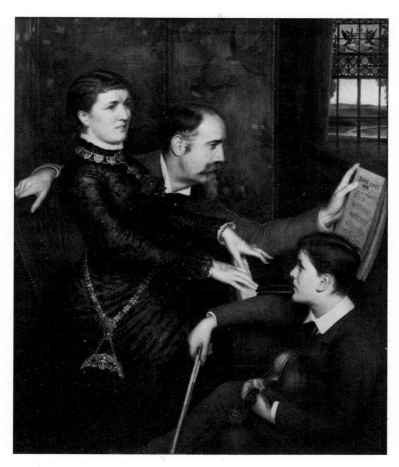

10 *The Moral House: 1830-1900*

'You will, I think,' wrote the Dowager Lady Buxton in 1858, 'be astonished when you see poor dear Shadwell again.' She was referring to Shadwell in Norfolk, the family home of the Buxton family. It had already been given a considerable face-lift in the time of the dowager, in the 1840s; it was now being done over again by her son. The results were sensational, some might say alarming (Pls 166 to 168).[1] But such transformations were a commonplace in Victorian days. At Highclere in Hampshire, in the 1840s, the Earl of Carnarvon turned a house condemned at the time as exemplifying the 'flatness and insipidity of bare classicism' into a house which, however it might be described, was certainly not flat. At Kelham in Nottinghamshire, in the late 1850s, J. H. Manners Sutton inherited a house not unlike Highclere and turned it into a version of the St Pancras Hotel in London—both buildings being by the same architect, Sir George Gilbert Scott. A few years later John Walter took the modest classical house built by his father at Bear Wood in Berkshire, and with the wave of a wand and the expenditure of about £120,000 transformed it into the enormous house that is there today.[2]

So impressive an attack of elephantiasis within two generations was the result of the soaring circulation of *The Times*, of which the Walter family were the printers and principal proprietors. Remodellings of country houses had, of course, been going on since the Middle Ages. They were bigger and more frequent in Victorian days not so much because tastes and needs were changing faster as because money was coming in faster. The soaring circulation of *The Times* reflected the soaring size of the middle classes. Behind the middle classes lay all that the Industrial Revolution was producing in the way of mines, factories, railways, ships, warehouses, banks and cities to contain and support them. As a result the number of newly rich people who were able to invest in landed property, to buy or build a house, and to set up as landed gentry was greater than it had ever been. Moreover, the older landed families often found their own incomes agreeably and sometimes sensationally increased, as coal was found under their fields or towns spread over their property.

So much new money in both new and old families tended to make the country-house world competitive. The old families built to keep up with the new ones. But on the whole the new arrivals did none of the things that *nouveaux riches* are supposed to do. They were neither aggressive, inept nor ostentatious. They subscribed to local charities, sent their sons to the right schools and hunted, shot and fished with enthusiasm, if not always with skill. They were eager to be accepted. After relatively few years, and as long as they kept the rules, they generally were accepted. But what were the rules? The elaborate code of behaviour devised by the Victorian upper classes was partly a defensive sieve or initiatory rite, designed to keep out the wrong sort of people. What to wear when, how to address whom, the ritual of making morning calls and leaving cards—here were plenty of traps for the uninitiated, especially when most of the rules were unwritten. However, books of etiquette soon appeared, to help new families in their troubles. They revealed the code with reasonable accuracy, and

268

166–8. (right) Shadwell Park, Norfolk, as it was in the eighteenth century, as enlarged in 1840–3, and as further enlarged in 1856–60.

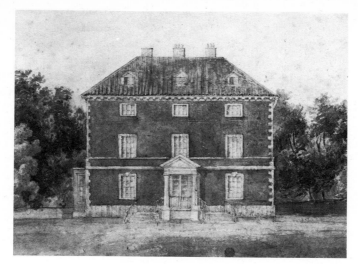

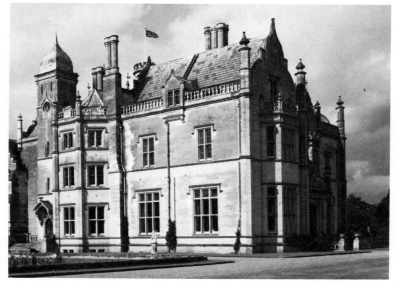

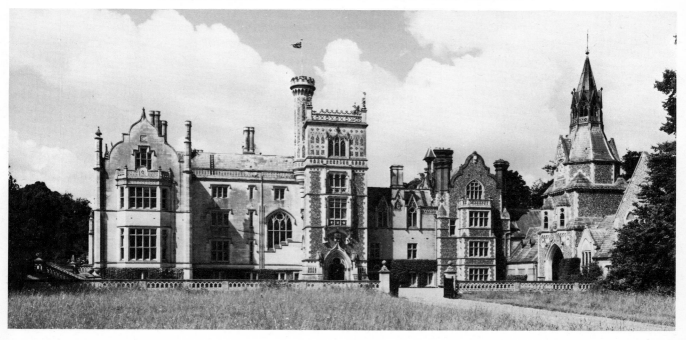

their rules were obeyed by new families with even more enthusiasm than by old ones.[3]

New families were eager to join the landed upper classes because of the power and prestige which still remained to them. But while this prestige was, if anything, increasing the power was gradually dwindling. The Industrial Revolution had altered the balance. The middle classes in the new towns—or the rapidly growing old ones—had demanded and obtained a share in running the country. During the course of the nineteenth century their power gradually increased at the expense of the upper classes, as a result, to quote a few examples, of new towns being given representation in parliament, of the corn laws being repealed, of more people getting the vote, and of the civil service being gradually enlarged and opened to competitive examination. Upper-class patronage largely disappeared and so did upper-class sinecures.

In the 1820s and '30s the middle classes had been violently critical of the arrogance, immorality and inefficiency of the upper classes who, they considered, ran the country badly and for their own benefit. Such criticism continued all through the century, but it grew noticeably milder, for a number of reasons. The upper classes gradually surrendered more and more of what the middle classes wanted. During the 1840s working-class agitation at home and a series of revolutions abroad convinced upper and middle classes that they must stick together. As the middle classes sent their sons to public schools and universities, and the new rich moved on to the second and third generation, the social gap between upper and middle classes narrowed—even among those members of the middle classes who lacked the money or the inclination to transfer themselves to the gentry. Finally, the upper classes adjusted their image to make it acceptable to middle-class morality. They became—some quite genuinely, others at least superficially—more serious, more religious, more domestic, and more responsible. They behaved, in fact, with considerable sense and circumspection. The result was the mutually admiring partnership of middle and upper classes which ran Victorian England. The upper classes had given up a good deal of power, but they remained the senior partners. As a rich industrialist told Hippolyte Taine in the 1860s: 'It is not our aim to overthrow the aristocracy; we are ready to leave the government and high offices in their hands . . . Let them govern, but let them be fit to govern.'[4]

In the 1870s Lord and Lady Folkestone chose to be painted singing 'Home, Sweet Home' with their eldest son (Pl. 165). A portrait of Lord Armstrong, the millionaire arms dealer, shows him reading the newspaper in his dining room inglenook at Cragside, over the fireplace of which is inscribed 'East or West, Home is Best'. An essential part of the new image cultivated by both new and old families was their domesticity (Col. Pl. XXVII); they were anxious to show that their houses, however grand, were also homes and sheltered a happy family life.[5]

This life often contained a strong element of religion. Accounts of going to church, visiting the poor, or reading religious books filled the diaries of upper-class girls, as well as, and sometimes instead of, descriptions of parties and clothes.[6]

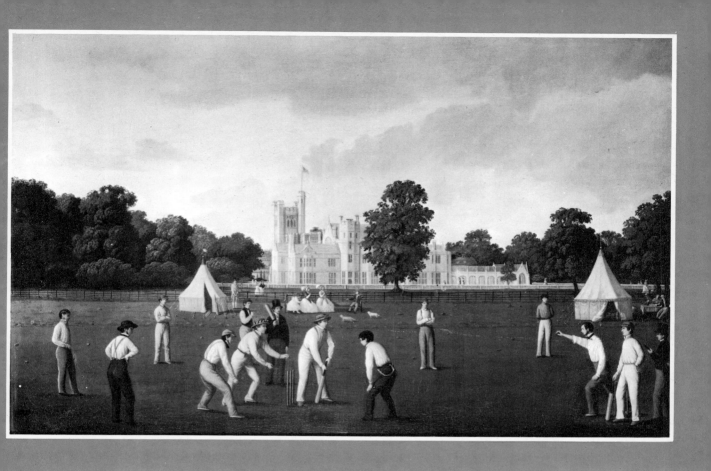

169. A cricket match at Canford Manor, Dorset (Sir Charles Barry, 1848–52).

In Jane Austen's *Mansfield Park,* when Fanny visits the family chapel at Sotherton, she finds to her regret that daily prayers are no longer said there. But family prayers came back in force under the Victorians; family chapels began to be built again in considerable numbers, and in houses where there was no chapel the whole household assembled for prayers every morning in the hall or dining room. On Sundays the household walked through the garden or across the park to the church—often newly built or restored at the pious expense of the owner of the house. The family walked too, so that grooms and coachmen could be free to observe their Sunday duties.

The numerous potted biographies of county worthies, which began to be printed in local newspapers or reprinted in book form in the later nineteenth century, spotlight the other qualities which the public considered necessary for 'the beau-ideal of an English country gentleman'. He must be courteous, hospitable, a good sportsman, a model landlord, interested in agriculture and preferably chairman of one or more local societies. Intellectual and artistic interests were acceptable but not essential. The emphasis was on what were considered country virtues. Perhaps the entries, and the photographs that go with

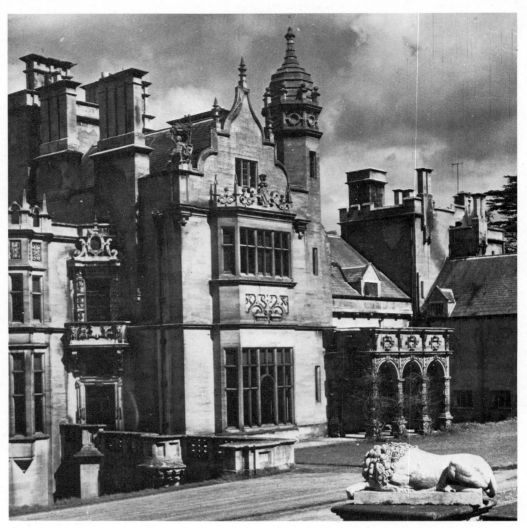

them, suggest that partnership between the classes was leading towards a new
type, the gentlemanly figurehead who left the brainwork to professionals.[7]

Many country-house owners did in fact possess most or all of the requisite
virtues. Others kept up a facade, and only let it down in London or abroad. Their
houses were designed to go with their image. The desired effect could be
produced in a number of ways. One of these was negative, the avoidance of the
wrong symbols. The porticoes or sham fortifications of the early nineteenth
century had acquired unwelcome connotations of arrogance, authoritarianism
and ostentation. Moreover porticoes were un-English and fortifications not at all
domestic. Both types went right out of fashion. If classical houses were built, they
were usually in what was called the 'rural-Italian style'—basically the informal
classical style pioneered by John Nash and developed by Charles Barry from the
starting-off-point of 'the charming character of the irregular villas of Italy'. But in
spite of a modest spate of Italianate villas and an occasional flirtation with French
chateaux, much the most popular source of inspiration was now the gothic,
Tudor or Elizabethan manor house (Pls 169 to 171). To the Victorians such
houses conjured up images of an old-style English gentleman, dispensing

272

170. A corner of Harlaxton Manor, Lincolnshire (Anthony Salvin, 1831–8).

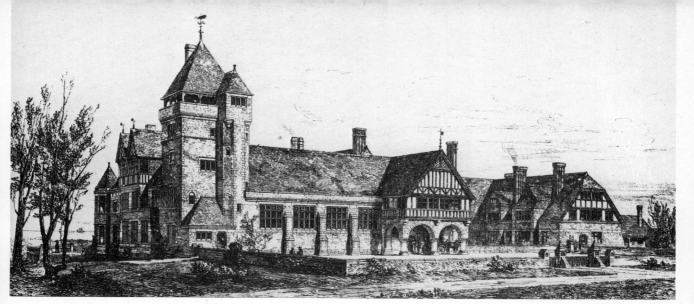

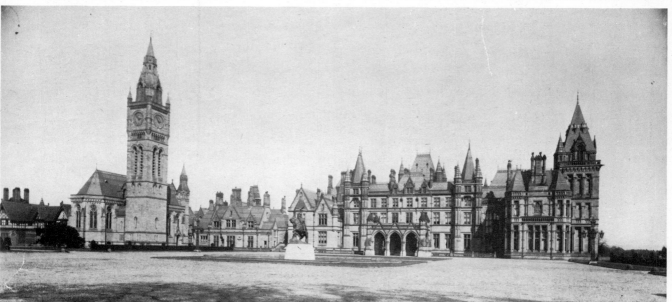

hospitality in a great hall, with fires blazing in the great arched fireplaces, smoke rising from innumerable chimney-stacks, comfortable groups gossipping in ingles and oriels, and generous sheltering roofs over all.

Houses in the gothic style had the extra advantage that, as a result of the writings of Pugin, Ruskin and others, gothic was increasingly associated both with Christianity and with truthfulness. A gothic house stood for good principles as well as good cheer. Especially pious families could give their gothic houses an extra flavour of religion by an admixture of tracery and stained glass—or by building a chapel and tower grand enough to dominate the whole building, as was the case at Eaton Hall in Cheshire, as it was remodelled by the Duke of Westminster in the 1870s (Pl. 172). Others contented themselves with having pious inscriptions carved or painted in appropriate places; 'Except the Lord buildeth the house they labour in vain that build it' was a special favourite.

171. (top) Rousdon, Devon (Ernest George, 1874).

172. Eaton Hall, Cheshire (Alfred Waterhouse, 1870–82).

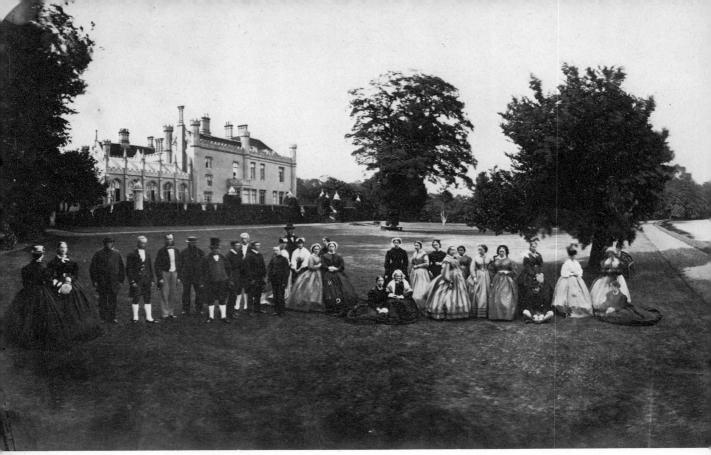

173. The household of Sir John Boileau at Ketteringham Hall, Norfolk, *c.* 1850. The Gothic hall is on the left.

But a Victorian landowner, however pious, hospitable and concerned for the welfare of his tenantry, seldom forgot that, as the architect Gilbert Scott put it, 'he has been placed by providence in a position of authority and dignity; and no false modesty should deter him from expressing this, quietly and gravely, in the character of his house.'[8] Porticoes and fortifications suggested authority too crudely; but the old English manor house supplied the answer in the form of the tower—sufficiently dignified, sufficiently prestigious, but not at all aggressive. One or two towers—seldom more, for that would have been ostentatious—were almost always part of the equipment of Victorian country houses of any pretensions. Towers, moreover, could combine dignity with usefulness and contain a water tank to service the plumbing.

The Victorian upper classes were reasonably keen to seem up-to-date, but their modernity tended to be put under pressure by other values. In the 1850s and '60s, huge sheets of undivided plate glass were proudly installed in country houses both new and old, and gave a contemporary flavour to their various period dresses. Later on in the century tradition began to seem more important than progress, and small panes and leaded lights came back in force. Many, though by no means all, country houses had central heating and gas or oil lamps in their main rooms and corridors, but candles and coal fires everywhere else. Electric light began to

174–6. (right) The Marquess of Lansdowne's footmen in everyday, semi-state and state liveries in about 1899.

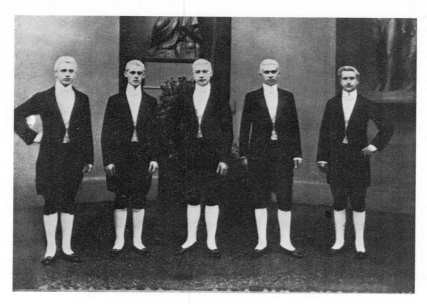

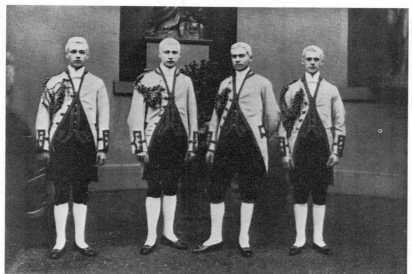

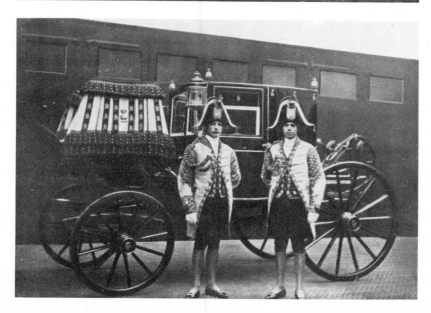

be installed in a few houses after 1880. All new houses had running water on every floor and an ample supply of water-closets; but hip-baths or toilet jugs and basins, supplied from brass cans of hot water brought by the housemaids, remained the usual means of washing. Few houses had more than one or two bathrooms until the end of the century. Those that did tended to be condemned as 'luxurious'.[9]

The area of a country house in which technology and organisation were especially on show was the servants' wing. This had begun to grow bigger in early-nineteenth-century houses. At Ashridge it seems to sprawl for ever; at Penrhyn in 1828 Pückler-Muskau was so impressed by the elaborate servants' accommodation that he described it in detail.[10] Under the Victorians the growth became universal. It was not produced by an increase in the number of servants. Although the Victorians tended to employ more gardeners, keepers, foresters and estate workers than in previous generations, these did not eat in the servants' hall. The size of the main household remained much what it had been in the late eighteenth and early nineteenth century. It ranged from about fifty in very large country houses to less than ten in very small ones—including stable and laundry staff in both cases (Pl. 173). Grand households were still run by a steward, and usually included one or more grooms of the chambers, an under-butler, and at least three footmen (Pls 174 to 176). Households with stewards seldom had a butler as well, and good sense combined with political awareness to make liveries less gaudy (except on special occasions) and to get rid of postillions. No new type of servant appeared until the end of the century, when new technology produced the chauffeur and the resident electrician.

The peculiar character of Victorian servants' wings was the result of early-nineteenth-century arrangements being revised to make them more moral and more efficient. Efficiency involved analyzing the different functions performed by different servants, giving each function its own area and often its own room, and grouping the related functions into territories accessible to the gentry part of the house which they serviced. Morality meant—in addition to compulsory attendance at daily prayers and Sunday church—separation of the sexes except when they were under supervision. The organisation of related jobs into territories achieved this fairly efficiently in the daytime. At night, infinite care was taken to see that men and women slept in different parts of the house, without access one to the other. Within the male and female sleeping quarters it was normal for the servants to sleep one, or at most two, to a room. Servants' dormitories had survived into the early Victorian period, but were regarded with suspicion and soon got rid of.

The results of organisation and morality in terms of the plan can be seen in its most elaborate and carefully worked out form in houses designed by William Burn in the 1840s and '50s. Burn (who worked, incidentally, more for old families than for the new rich) was regarded at the time as providing houses that were the last word in organisation and efficiency. The servants' wing at Lynford in Norfolk, designed by him in 1856 for Mr Lyne Stephens, was a typical example of his work (Fig. 18). It was divided into four zones—the butler's, the cook's, the

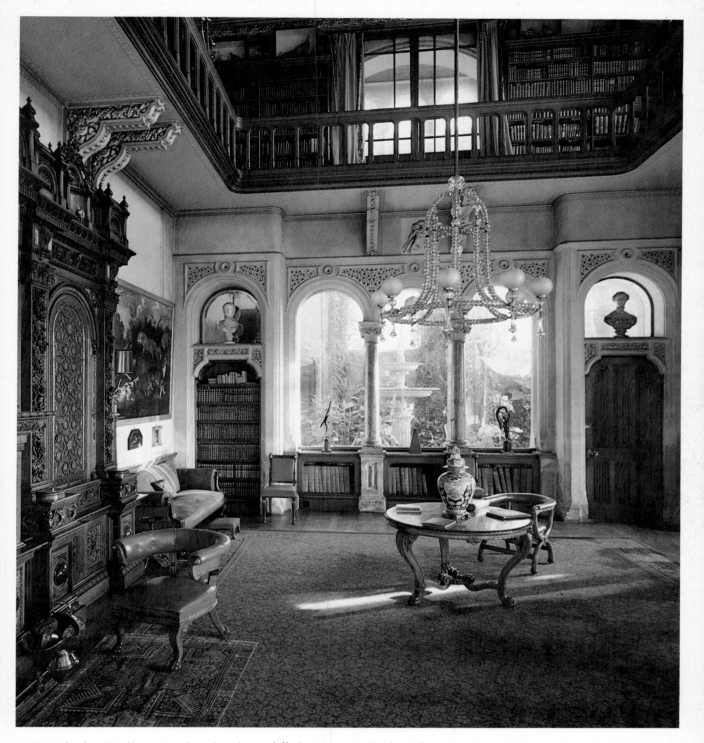

XXIX. Flintham Hall, Nottinghamshire (remodelled *c.* 1851–4). Looking from the saloon into the conservatory.

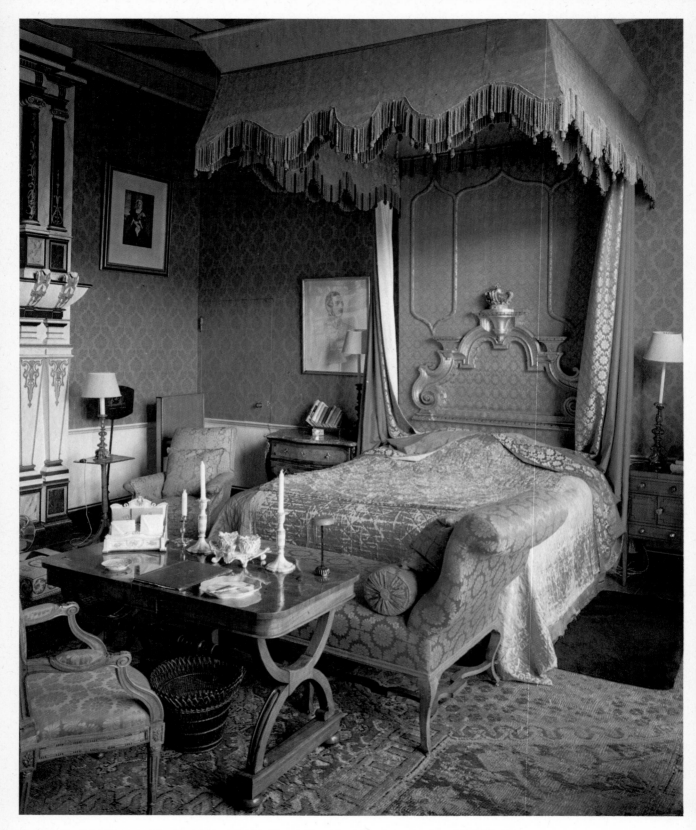

XXX. Hatfield House, Hertfordshire. The bedroom furnished for Queen Victoria's visit in 1846.

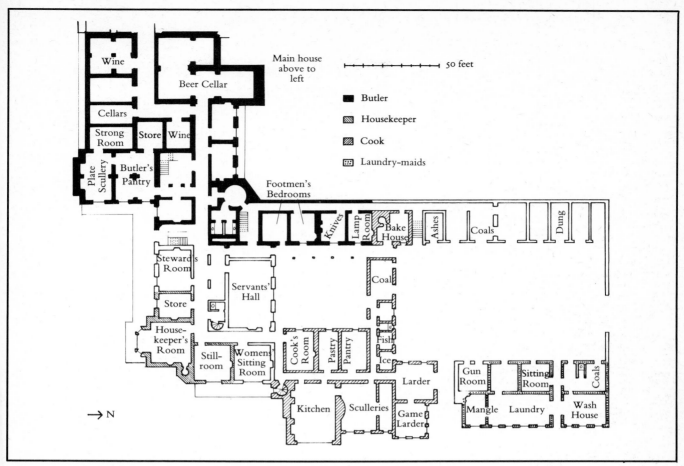

Fig. 18. The servants' floor at Lynford Hall, Norfolk (William Burn, 1856–61).

housekeeper's and the laundry-maid's. The butler's zone was entirely male, the other three entirely female, except, possibly, for a male chef at the head of the cook's department. Male and female zones were kept separate, each with its own staircase to its own bedrooms. The servants' hall and steward's room occupied the neutral ground between them.[11]

In grand houses the steward, housekeeper and head cook ate in the steward's room, along with the head gardener, the senior lady's maids and valets, the coachman, and visiting servants of the same rank. A footman or steward's-room boy waited on them. The other servants ate in the servants' hall, usually looked after by the odd man. In less grand houses the upper servants had breakfast and tea in the housekeeper's room, ate the main courses of dinner and supper in the servants' hall, and retired to the housekeeper's room to eat their pudding—just as their betters had retired to the drawing room to eat their dessert in the seventeenth and eighteenth centuries.

The housekeeper was in command of the housemaids and one or more still-room maids. She was responsible for cleaning the house, looking after the linen, and providing, storing, and where necessary preparing tea, coffee, sugar, groceries, preserves, cakes and biscuits. The institution of afternoon tea in the 1840s added to her responsibilities. Her central territory consisted of her own housekeeper's room, the still-room and sometimes a separate store-room and closet. Her own room was usually lined with china-cupboards and linen-presses but was also furnished as a comfortable parlour; it had the agreeable atmosphere of a room used for both business and gossip.

There was a similar atmosphere in the butler's pantry (Pl. 177), with its cupboards for storage, sinks and table for cleaning, and comfortable chair by the fire. The butler ruled over the footmen and any other indoor men-servants, except for the valets. He was in charge of the plate, drink and table linen, and his many responsibilities included (by way of footmen or groom of the chambers) furnishing all writing-tables and, in some houses, polishing the mirrors. In a big house like Lynford his pantry was the centre of a little kingdom of satellite rooms, including a safe or storage room for plate, a scullery to clean it in, cellars for wine and beer, and separate little cells in which the footmen or odd man brushed the clothes, cleaned the shoes, cleaned the knives, and trimmed, cleaned and filled the oil lamps. In some houses a footman, or even the butler himself, had a bedroom next to the safe, for security. Some pantries had a view of the front of the house from their windows, so that visitors could be seen in advance, and the front door open magically as their carriages drew up at the front steps.

The butler's pantry was often close to the dining room, as at Lynford; the kitchen almost never was. The Victorians, like earlier generations, thought it more important to keep kitchen smells out of the gentry end of the house. Although the closed range had been pioneered at the beginning of the century, in most houses roasting was still conducted at open fires; the bigger the house the greater the smell. In houses the size of Lynford the kitchen was usually a considerable distance from the dining room and had its own louvered roof, for ventilation. One or more kinks in the connecting corridor helped to keep smells from travelling, and a hot plate in the serving-room warmed the food up again (Pl. 178).

The grandeur of a house could be measured by the number of chefs in the kitchen. Less grand houses had a single chef presiding over female under-cooks, kitchen-maids and scullery-maids; in many houses all the kitchen staff were women. A big country-house kitchen, bustling with chefs and kitchen-maids and lined with all that the latest Victorian technology had to offer, was an impressive sight (Pl. 179); Robert Kerr in his invaluable contemporary book *The Gentleman's House* described it as 'having the character of a complicated laboratory'.[12] The Victorians were proud of their kitchens, and of their complex equipment of roasting-ranges, stewing-stoves, boiling-stoves, turnspits, hotplates and hot closets. The kitchen was usually the only servants' room which owners or architects bothered to have photographed. By present-day standards its technology was, of course, cumbersome and limited. There were no washing-machines, no extractors, no refrigeration, except what was provided by a marble

177. (upper right) The butler's pantry at Ashburnham, Sussex.

178. (right) Looking from the serving room to the dining room at Lanhydrock, Cornwall.

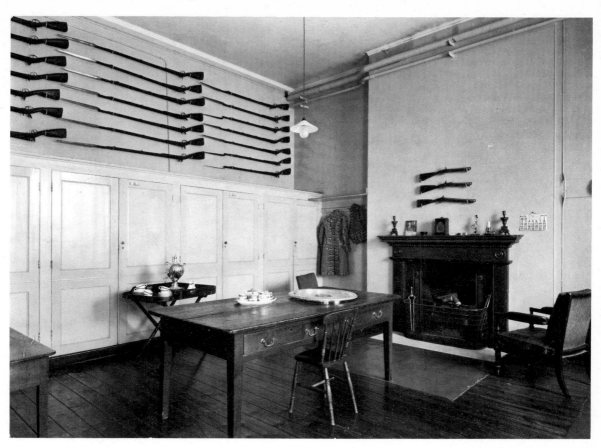

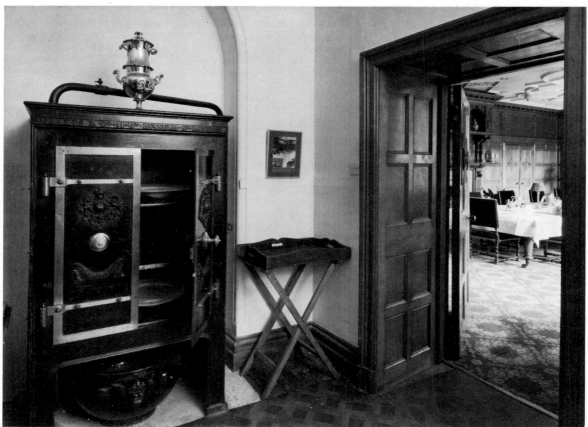

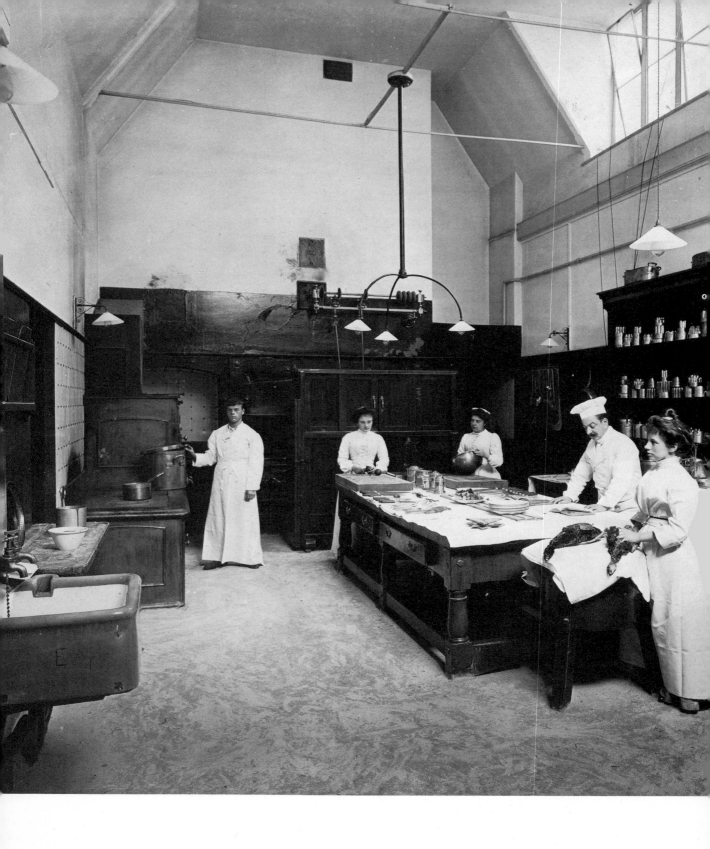

179. The kitchen at Minley Manor in the 1890s.

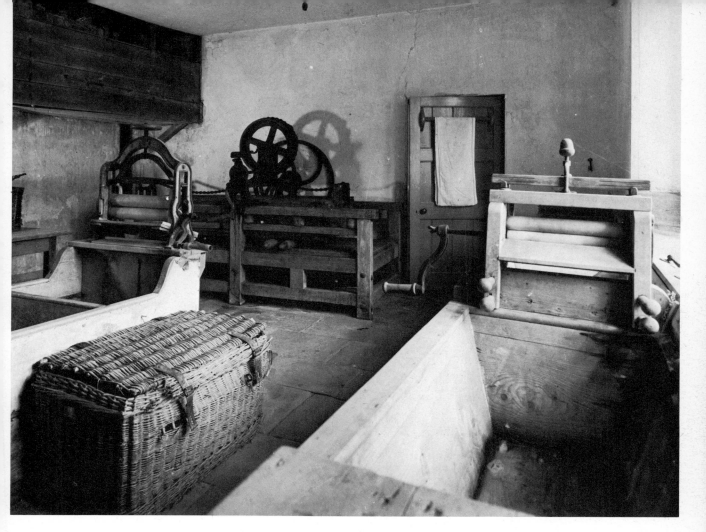

slab or a box cooled with ice brought up from the ice house. Larders were kept cool by natural ventilation. Most big country houses had a game larder, planned for ventilation as a free-standing and often rather decorative building in the kitchen courtyard. Larder accommodation could be further subdivided into a pantry or dry larder, for cooked materials, and separate meat and fish larders for uncooked ones—in addition to the inevitable scullery, and occasional rooms for baking, salting, and smoking.

The laundry department was in a unique position, the result both of history and of the process of laundering. Laundry-maids had been working in country houses for many centuries before housekeepers and housemaids; they formed an independent group and were not always under the control of the housekeeper. Before the invention of washing-machines and tumble-driers laundering produced a great deal of steam and smell, and had to be accessible to a drying-ground; so laundering was usually on the periphery of the servants' quarters. The independence of the job tended to bring pretty girls into it, and the position of the laundry to make it easily accessible to outside workers—especially to the grooms in the stable. As far as sexual segregation was concerned, the laundry was the Achilles' heel of the Victorian country house.[13]

283

180. The laundry at Pakenham Hall (now Tullynally Castle), County Westmeath, Ireland.

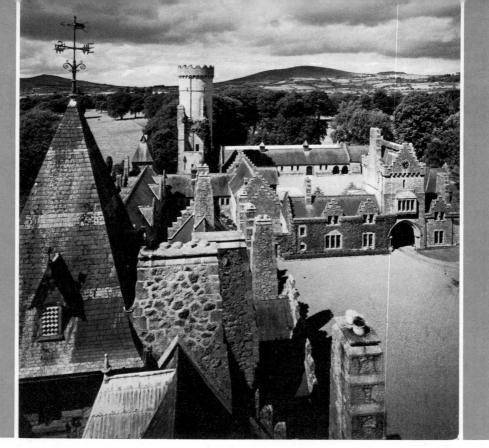

At Pakenham Hall in Ireland the laundries (Pl. 180) were linked to a drying-ground by a sunken passage. It ran along the front of the stables, through a tunnel under the approach to the stable-gateway, and round to a flight of steps leading up to the drying-yard. This route, which was installed in the 1840s, enabled the laundry maids to pass to and fro without meeting the grooms. In about 1860 drying-yards and this kind of subterfuge were made redundant at Pakenham Hall and elsewhere by the introduction of efficient drying-rooms. These contained a series of heavy wooden racks, which could be trundled out on rails, loaded up with washing, and pushed back into a chamber heated by hot water pipes. With its processes efficiently organized into washing-room, drying-room and ironing-room, the laundry then became the technological counterpart of the kitchen.[14]

Steward's room and servants' hall, the spreading domains of butler, housekeeper and cook, and the outer extremities where the laundry-maids shared quarters with wood stores, coal stores, an engine-room for pumping water and even (though this was growing rare) a brew-house, could encompass between them at least two courtyards and a little townscape of roofs and chimneys. A skilful architect could deploy gateways, covered walks, clock-towers, game larders, and the louvered or lanterned roofs of kitchens and laundry so as to suggest the lively and complex life that was going on beneath them (Pl. 181). But indoors it was almost impossible to avoid long dark passages and labour-consuming journeys to the main house. The solution of putting all the offices in a basement was not popular in Victorian times. Compunction made owners

284

181. Looking along the servants' wing and stables at Humewood, County Wicklow, Ireland (William White, 1866–70).

unwilling to sink their servants in a hole, love of privacy made them equally unwilling to give them a view from a semi-basement out onto the garden. A solution adopted in a number of houses, including Lynford, was to build on a slope, so that a sunk basement for the servants (or more often the cellars) on the garden side became the ground floor in other parts of the house.

Segregation from the garden was one of the prices which Victorian servants had to pay for their owner's domesticity. An Englishman's castle, however large, was now his home, and an essential quality of a home was privacy. As Robert Kerr put it: 'It becomes the foremost of all maxims, therefore, that the Servants' Department shall be separated from the main house, so that what passes on either side of the boundary shall be both invisible and inaudible to the other . . .'[15] As far as possible the servants were kept invisible even when they came into the main house. An intricate system of backstairs and back corridors ensured that housemaids could get up to the bedrooms, dinner to the dining room and the butler or footman to the front door with the least possible chance of meeting the family on the way.

To quote Kerr again: 'The idea which underlies all is simply this. The family constitute one community: the servants another. Whatever may be to their mutual regard and confidence as dwellers under the same roof, each class is entitled to shut its door upon the other, and be alone . . . On both sides this privacy is highly valued.'[16] The Victorians saw the concept of two communities—so evocatively symbolized by Victorian house plans—as an advance on the single integrated 'family' of earlier centuries. But Kerr's language is rather too reminiscent of the language of apartheid. Separation in Victorian country houses could be carried to uncomfortable limits.

At Welbeck the Duke of Portland (admittedly eccentric if not mad) sacked any housemaid who had the misfortune to meet him in the corridors. Housemaids in a country house in Suffolk had to flatten themselves face to the wall when they saw family or guests coming. In Wiltshire an anonymous Lord M., as reported by his footman and valet, 'never spoke to an indoor servant except to give an order and all the ten years I was with him he never, except on Christmas and New Years' Days, gave me any kind of greeting.'[17] There were friendlier houses where employers took a kindly interest in their servants, and where the children and young men of the family looked in for tea or a chat in the housekeeper's room or butler's pantry, captained an estate cricket eleven, or came down in the evenings for an impromptu dance in the servants' hall.[18] There were innumerable houses in between the two. Ample food, security, companionship and the hopes of travel and outside contacts helped to compensate the younger servants for long hours, low pay, and strict discipline. For the upper servants life was less hard and more interesting, and relationships with their employers often much closer; after retirement there was the prospect of pensioned old age in an estate cottage, or savings invested in a pub, a small business or even a hotel. In general, service in great houses had enough attractions to make it comparatively easy to get servants all through the nineteenth century. But it can still be a disconcerting experience to

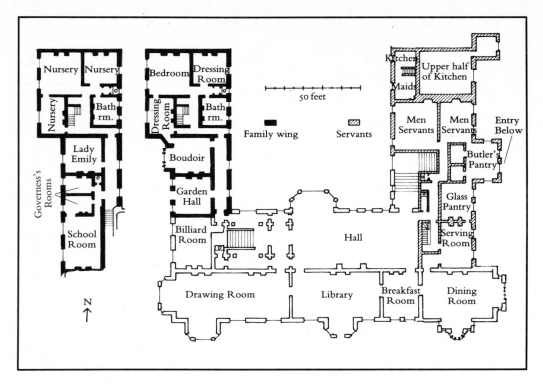

Family wing ■   Servants ▨

50 feet

push through the baize doors, studded with brass nails, that divided the servants from the family, and pass from carpets, big rooms, light, comfort and air to dark corridors, linoleum, poky rooms, and the ghostly smell of stale cabbage.

In observing life on the gentry side of the baize door one can once again watch the early-nineteenth-century model being modified by Victorian concern for morality, domesticity, organization and hospitality. In typical mid-Victorian houses the children of the family slept and worked above, or next door to their parents. Visiting bachelors were put along one corridor and visiting young ladies along another. A capacious porch, with 'Welcome' inscribed on the threshold or doormat, led (by way of a vestibule to keep out the draught) to a great hall in which to entertain tenants, servants or the county.

The pedigree of Victorian family quarters can be traced back by way of early-nineteenth-century houses like Ashridge to the family apartments and lodgings of earlier centuries. What gave them their peculiar Victorian character was that they were designed for husband, wife and children, not just for husband and wife. Before the nineteenth century the need to accommodate children had had little if any influence on country-house planning. The children's rooms were normally up on the top floor, but there was nothing to differentiate them from other rooms; they were fitted in wherever it happened to be convenient. But in most Victorian country-house plans great care was taken to see that the children were properly accommodated (Pl. 182), and within easy reach of their parents. Many houses had a self-contained family wing, on two or three floors, with the nurseries up above the parents' boudoir, study, bedroom and dressing room, and a little private stair to enable a fond mother to run up from her boudoir and see how the children were (Pl. 183 and Fig. 19). At Eaton Hall, where the family wing was in

Fig. 19. Thoresby Hall, Nottinghamshire. The ground floor, and the first floor of the family wing (Anthony Salvin, 1864–75).

182. (right) Minley Manor, Hampshire. The nursery in 1899.

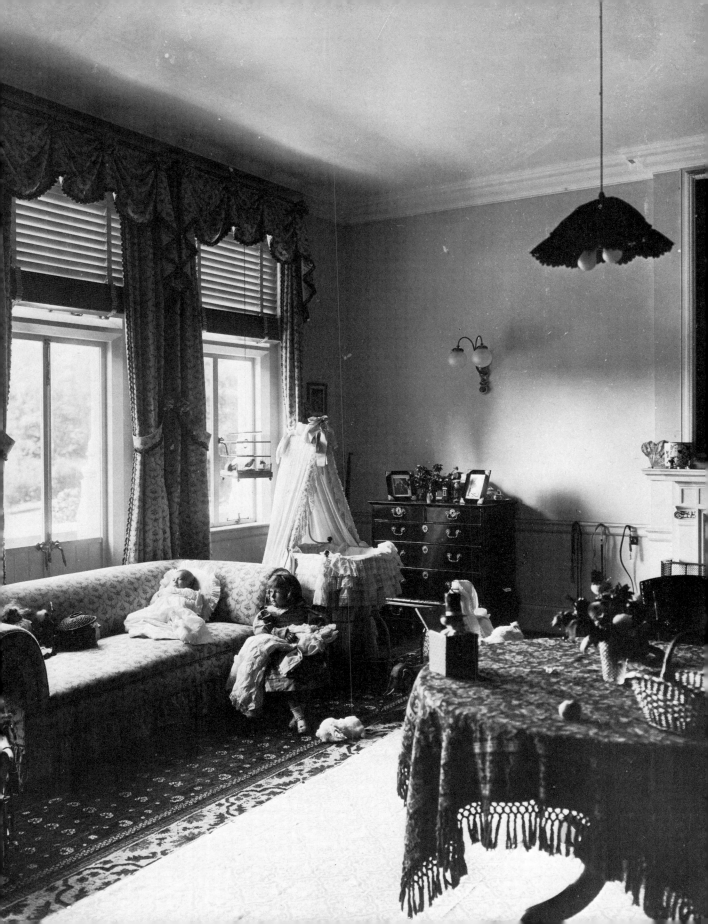

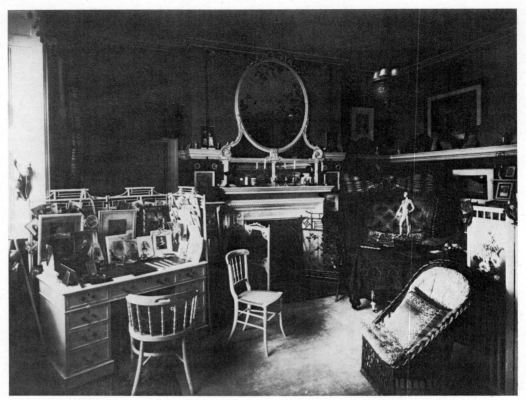

183. White Lodge, Richmond Park, Surrey. The Duchess of Teck's boudoir in 1892.

effect a self-contained house with its own dining room, the schoolroom was between the duke's study and the duchess's boudoir on the ground floor. Here the family could live in self-contained domesticity when there were no house-parties to fill the great rooms in the main block of the house.

The family wing or quarters was the one vestige of the traditional apartment system to survive in country houses. Guests were now expected to spend the day downstairs in the communal rooms, except when they were changing for meals. The one exception was that in some houses women guests could pass part of the morning in their bedrooms writing letters. The more comfortable bedrooms were furnished with a writing-table and one or two upholstered chairs, but they were definitely not bed-sitting rooms (Col. Pl. XXX). Dressing rooms lost their eighteenth-century character and became no more than rooms for a husband to dress, or if needs be to sleep in. Bachelor rooms were usually considerably less comfortable than rooms for married couples or single women. They were often on a corridor of their own, even if the segregation was not always as pointed as at Stokesay, where the gentlemen's bedrooms were in a wing to the east, securely separated by the whole main block of the house from the ladies' bedrooms in a wing to the south.[19]

The planning of the main living rooms remained much the same as in the early nineteenth century. The main changes were the arrival of the smoking room, and the revival of the great hall. Pioneer great (or 'baronial') halls had already appeared earlier in the century.[20] In the 1830s and '40s they began to be built in

288

184. (right) Canford Manor, Dorset. The hall.

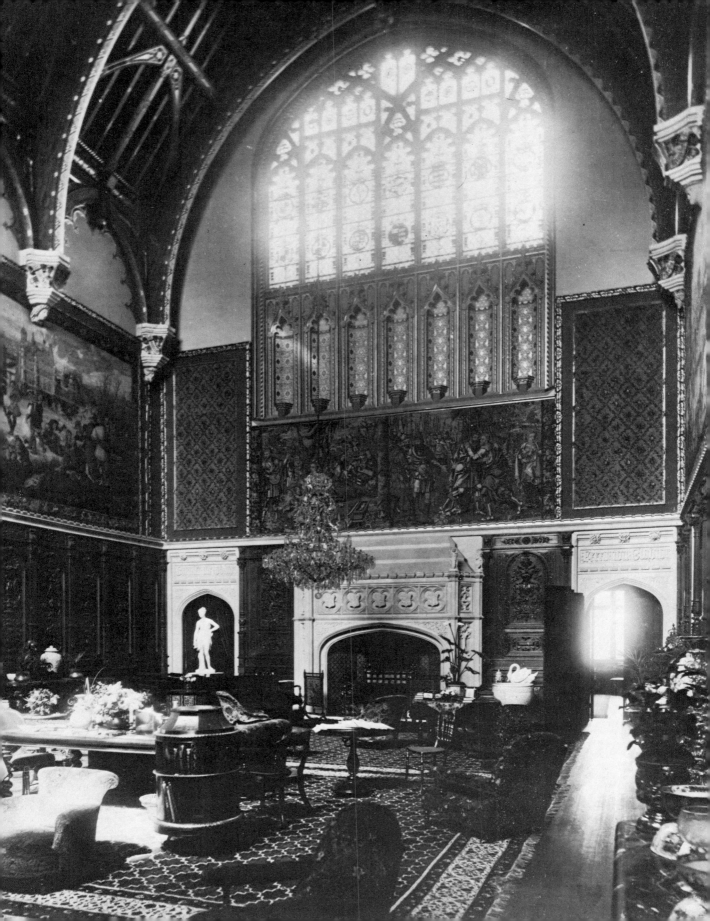

large numbers (Pl. 184), as part of the general revival of 'old English hospitality'. Amongst their strongest advocates was the architect Augustus Welby Pugin. He designed numerous ones himself, some for imaginary and some for real clients, and wrote with enthusiasm about their mediaeval builders: 'They did not confine their guests to a few fashionables, who condescended to pass away a few days occasionally in a country house; but under the oak rafters of their capacious halls the lords of the manor used to assemble all their friends and tenants at those successive periods when the church bids all her children rejoice.'[21]

It is worth looking at what went on in the Gothic Hall which Sir John Boileau built at Ketteringham in Norfolk in 1840 (Pl. 173). It was described at the time (with some exaggeration) as 'fit for the hospitalities of the chivalrous ages, and occasionally the scene of hospitalities rivalling those of the times of which it recalls the remembrance.'[22] The hospitalities included dances for the gentry, dinner for the tenantry and an annual servants' dance, attended by family, servants, gardeners, the estate carpenter and the village schoolmistress. As in most country houses of the time, the high point of entertaining was the coming-of-age of the eldest Boileau son in 1848. Festivities included a tenants' dinner and dance, a servants' ball, a ball for the county, a dinner for the local school children and a dinner for two hundred cottagers and labourers. All these festivities took place in the Gothic Hall, except for the labourers' dinner, which was held out of doors. The tenants' dinner was attended by the men of the Boileau family; the women looked on from the gallery. The children's dinner was preceded by 'old English' games, such as sack races, blindfold races and climbing a soapy mast for a shoulder of mutton.[23]

There was nothing specifically Victorian about any of these ceremonies; what was new was that both gentry and non-gentry entertainments were being held in the same room. The Ketteringham hall was an addition, tacked onto one side of the house, but in new houses the great hall was usually in a central position. Sometimes it was entered directly from the front door, as in the Middle Ages, but often it was preceded by a vestibule, for greater warmth and convenience.

Great halls continued to be built all through the nineteenth century and on into the twentieth. Such halls were not necessarily modelled on mediaeval or Elizabethan ones; a common type was a top-lit central room, like a roofed-in courtyard. But halls of all types experienced a noticeable change in character; although they continued to be used on occasions for balls and dinners, they also began to be used all the year round as living rooms.

As so often with Victorian practice, one can see the seeds of this development in the early nineteenth century. Once an efficient bell system had removed waiting servants from the hall, it began to be put to miscellaneous uses by the gentry. By 1820 there were writing-tables in the hall at Harewood.[24] A number of early-nineteenth-century halls had billiard tables in them. By the 1850s and '60s halls were often being supplied with organs, and with armchairs and sofas on which the house-party could listen to them. They rapidly developed into comfortable informal living rooms, which could also be used for games, charades and amateur

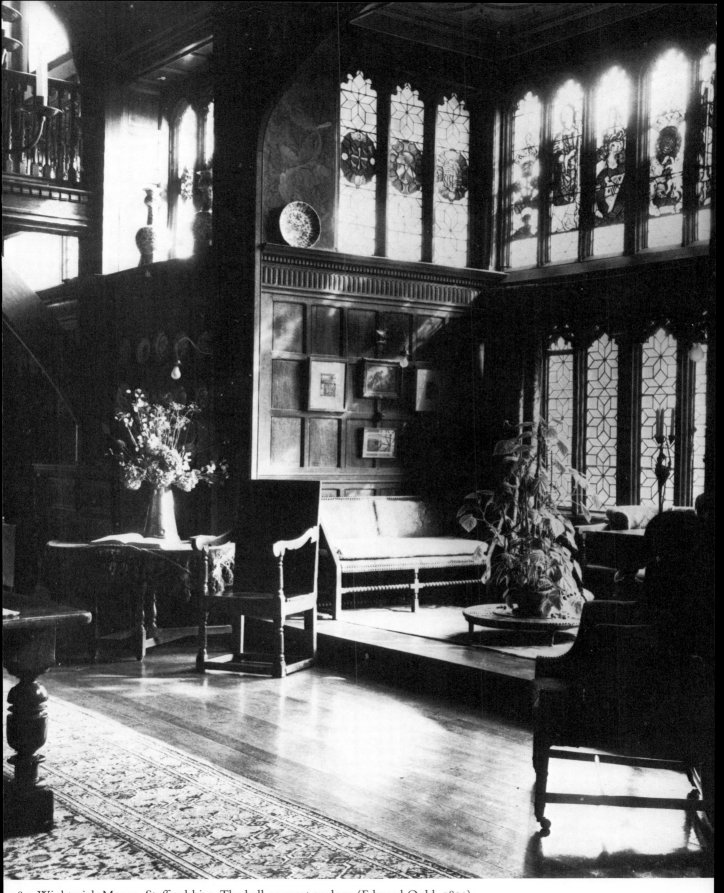

185. Wightwick Manor, Staffordshire. The hall or great parlour (Edward Ould, 1893).

theatricals (Pl. 185). They came especially into their own with big house-parties. Once the rest of the house was stratified into areas for men and women, they made a useful common meeting-place. In some houses the family and guests assembled in the hall before dinner rather than in the drawing room. Halls with staircases down into them became especially popular in the late nineteenth and early twentieth century, perhaps because they were nicely adapted for these evening gatherings. The descent of the ladies in their evening splendour could be watched by the party assembled below.

Dining room, drawing room and library remained in much the same relationship to each other as in earlier houses. The drawing room was still considered an essentially feminine and the dining room a somewhat masculine room. Their characteristics were defined by Robert Kerr as being 'masculine importance' and feminine delicacy,[25] which in effect usually meant massive oak or mahogany and Turkey carpets in the dining room and spindly gilt or rosewood, and silk or chintz in the drawing room (Col. Pl. XXVIII). A dignified dinner route between them was still of the greatest importance. The drawing room or dining room still frequently opened into a conservatory (Col. Pl. XXIX); Victorian advances in glass and iron technology often made it a building of great size and richness. The library was still often a pleasant living room, although perhaps rather less so than in the late eighteenth or early twentieth century; it now seemed less important for an English gentleman to be cultivated, and the library tended to suffer as a result. Kerr could even describe it as 'rather a kind of morning room for gentlemen than anything else'.[26]

A number of new developments brought new usages to drawing room and dining room without at first much altering their size or arrangement. In the mid nineteenth century it became usual to serve both luncheon and dinner what was called *à la Russe*. Instead of the dishes of each course being placed on the central table, each dish was carried round in succession to all the guests, in the manner which has remained standard up to the present day. Prince Pückler-Muskau remarked that this method (which he called 'the more convenient German fashion') was already being adopted by 'some of the more travelled gentlemen' in 1828.[27] An intermediate stage was for all the dishes to be served *à la Russe* except joints or birds, which as in the eighteenth century were still placed on the main table in front of the master of the house (Pl. 186). This practice had disappeared from big houses by about 1880, but survived in middle-class households for much longer.[28]

The old system had made it convenient to have a servant for every guest, whereas meals *à la Russe* could be served by one servant to every three or even four guests. In theory this should have made it possible to have smaller dining rooms, to accommodate smaller tables and fewer servants. In fact there was little change. The tradition of having a dining room of the same size as the drawing room died hard, and at important dinners it was still considered prestigious to have a servant for each guest, even if there was not enough for them to do. But fewer servants in simpler liveries made ordinary dinners considerably less

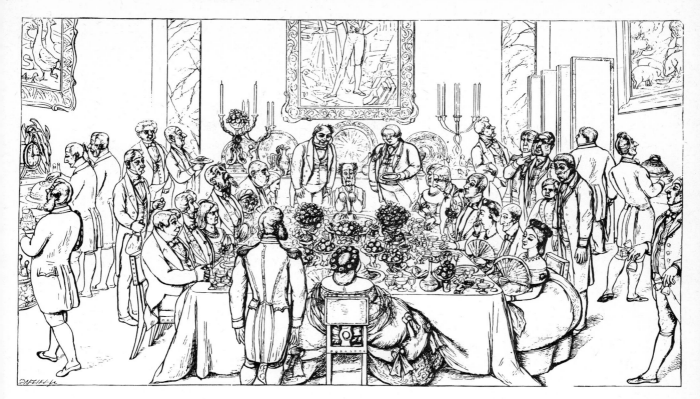

pretentious than they had been at the beginning of the century. In some fashionable late-nineteenth-century houses, breakfast, luncheon and even dinner were served to a large house party at numerous little tables, as in a restaurant.[29]

The drawing room acquired two new functions in the Victorian period, as a result of the inane ceremony of morning calls and the more genial celebration of afternoon tea. Morning calls (which by the late nineteenth century took place in the afternoon) were the ritualization of an earlier practice. They involved carriage visits from one local hostess to another, and a quarter of an hour's polite conversation in the drawing room.[30] Afternoon (or 'five o'clock') tea was the result of the inexorable movement of the dinner hour. By the 1840s, when this had advanced to seven-thirty or eight o'clock, the gap between it and luncheon at one or one-thirty became uncomfortable. Ladies began to take a meal of tea and cakes in the afternoon, at first surreptitiously in their boudoirs or bedrooms, and then openly in the drawing room. The Duchess of Rutland was dispensing tea in her boudoir at Belvoir by 1842, and by 1850 drawing room tea had become customary in all fashionable houses.[31] By the end of the century an elaborate five o'clock tea, attended by both sexes and served in the drawing room in cold or bad weather, and on the lawn by the house when it was fine, had become one of the major institutions of country-house life.

Consecrated as it now was to morning calls, afternoon tea, assembly before and after dinner, and the occasional ball, the drawing room became more than ever a formal room. Informal life, safe from the menace of the morning caller, tended to go on in the morning room and the library. Morning rooms, which first appeared in the early nineteenth century, had a somewhat similar function to the breakfast

293

186. 'A state party', portrayed by Richard Doyle in about 1850.

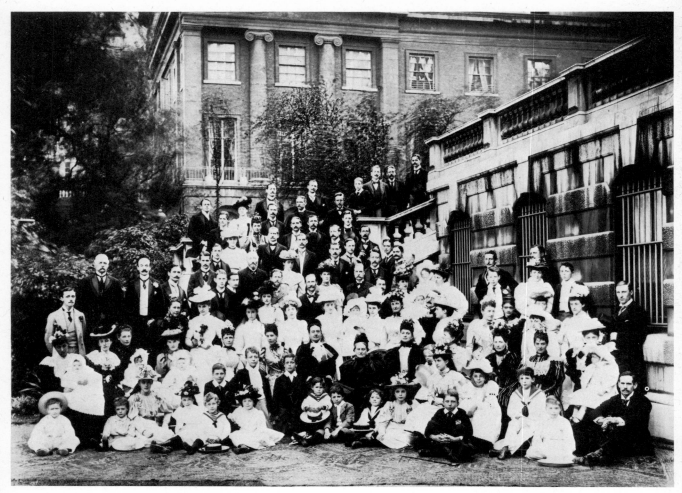

parlours, except that they were normally sitting rooms only, and for women rather than for men; men, if Kerr is to be believed, congregated more in the library. But Kerr was writing before the great days of the smoking room. Tobacco had a stronger influence on Victorian planning than tea.

The smoking habits of the upper classes came and went in a slightly mysterious manner. There were smoking parlours or smoking rooms at, for instance, Charborough in about 1690, Cannons in 1727, and Kedleston in 1767.[32] In 1735 Peter Wentworth smoked an after-dinner pipe in the handsome dining parlour of his cousin, the squire of Lillingstone Lovell in Buckinghamshire.[33] But by the end of the century tobacco had been banished from polite society. It returned as a result of royal patronage. In 1827 Prince Pückler-Muskau attended a dinner at which the guest of honour was George IV's brother, the Duke of Sussex. The duke had spent much time in Germany and picked up the German habit of smoking cigars. In compliment to him cigars were handed round the dinner table after the ladies had left it—'which I never before saw in England' according to the prince.[34] But a somewhat disreputable royal duke was not important enough to make cigars fashionable; that was left to Prince Albert and even more to Edward VII when Prince of Wales. Both were inveterate cigar smokers.

294

187. Louisa, Duchess of Abercorn, with 103 of her descendants in the garden of Montagu House, London, in 1894.

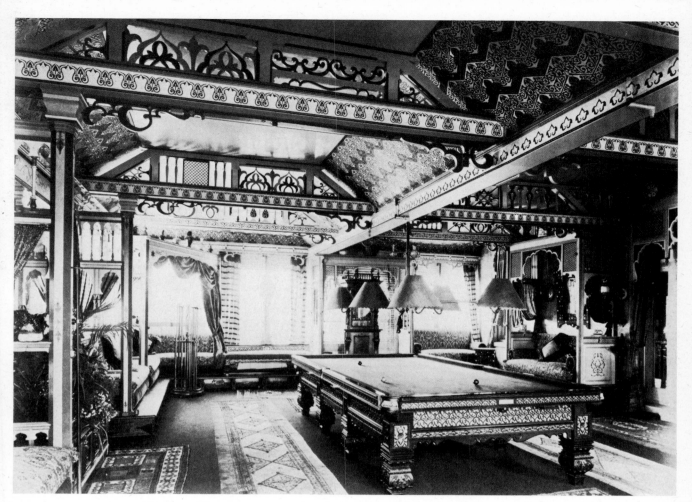

Even so, for many years smoking was still regarded as an undesirable and even unforgivable habit by many country-house owners. The Duke of Wellington made his guests smoke in the servants' hall; in the 1850s Sir John Boileau of Ketteringham never invited a guest again if he found him smoking; in 1855 the Bishop of Rochester admitted that he would have refused to accept a candidate for ordination if he had known that when staying in the Bishop's Palace he had smoked in his bedroom; as late as the 1890s W. O. Hammond of St Alban's Court in Kent made guests smoke in the kitchen, after the servants had left it.[35] In increasing numbers of houses, however, smoking was accepted as long as it took place in a smoking room. Smoking rooms first started to appear in a small way around 1850. They rapidly became one of the most important features of Victorian houses. They acted as a safety-valve. The male half of the house party could retire to them and talk about all the subjects concerning which Victorian women were expected to be ignorant.

Smoking rooms were especially supported by Victorian bachelors. One of the results of domesticity without contraception was very large families (Pl. 187), and therefore numerous younger sons. Younger sons, as had been the case in previous centuries, were usually left to fend for themselves on a few hundred pounds a

295

188. Newnham Park, Hertfordshire. The billiard room in 1897.

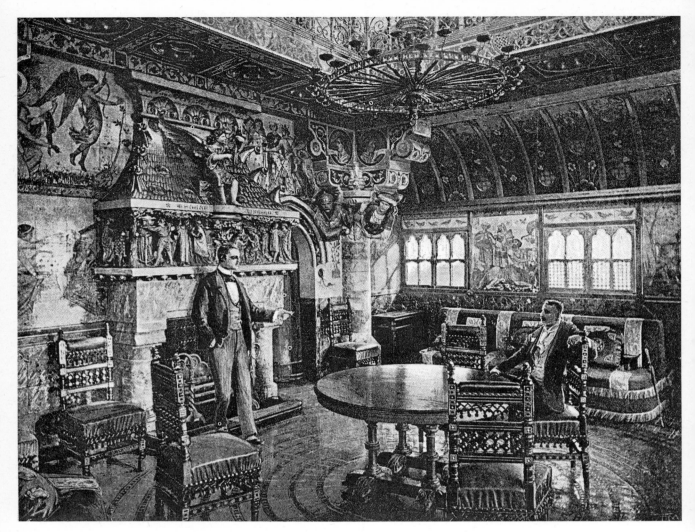

year, which they supplemented by the modest salary of a commission in the armed forces, a position in the diplomatic service, or one of the other comparatively few jobs considered suitable for a gentleman. Their incomes often remained too small to support a wife to the standard required by a lady; to marry someone who was not a lady was socially unthinkable, but Victorian morality made setting up a mistress less common than it had been. The country house and the London club provided two havens for their bachelor existence; and the growing network of the railways made it easy to get from one to the other. Suitably equipped for the season with rods, guns, hunting boots or tennis rackets, they passed their week-ends and ample holidays in moving round the houses of their numerous relations, connections or friends.

It became the accepted ritual for the men in a house-party, after the women had gone to bed, to don elaborate smoking jackets and retire to the smoking room, where a tray of spirits was laid out for them, in addition to a supply of cigars. Refusal to join the smoking party was considered bad form, and those who failed to do so were liable to find themselves hauled out of bed.[36] Smoking was often

296

189. Cardiff Castle. The summer smoking room (William Burges, 1868).

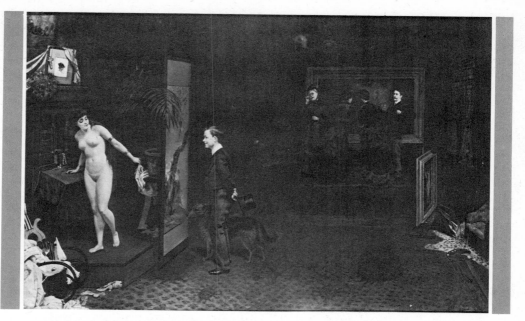

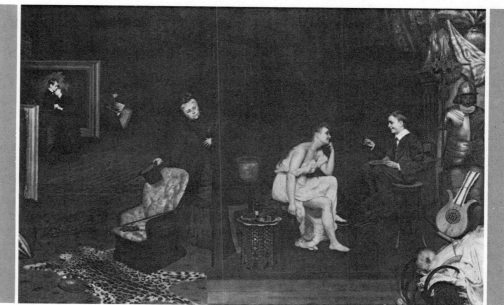

combined with a game of billiards, and as a result the billiard room and smoking room tended to be placed side by side. Many smaller houses just had one smoking-cum-billiard room. Billiards, as a result, became more and more of a man's game. The extent to which this happened can be exaggerated, however. Women continued to play billiards in some houses; the sixth Duke of Buccleuch and his wife played billiards together daily until the end of their married life.[37]

Both billiard and smoking rooms could be as elaborately decorated as the smoking jackets of their occupants. The Moorish style was an especial favourite (Pl. 188). At Cardiff Castle in 1868 the young and as yet unmarried Marquess of

297

190, 191. 'A visit to the studio'. Two paintings by Frank Hyde, now at Callaly Castle, Northumberland.

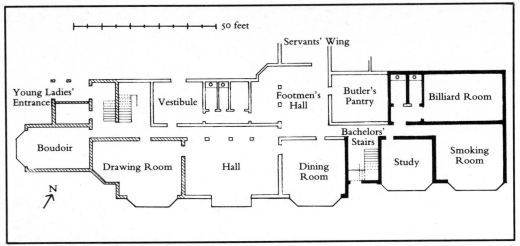

Fig. 20. Abbeystead Hall, Lancashire (John Douglas, 1886–8). Sketch plan showing male and female zones.

Bute built himself bachelor quarters in a tower 150 feet high. It contained his own bedroom and bathroom, and both a winter and summer smoking room (Pl. 189), the latter decorated with unparallelled magnificence by his architect, William Burges.[38] In many houses the smoking room became the nexus of a whole male territory, sometimes balanced by a female territory at the other end of the house. At the Earl of Sefton's Abbeystead in Lancashire—a very large shooting lodge designed in 1886—the male territory included billiard room and smoking room, with attendant lavatories, the owner's study or business room, and a bachelor staircase leading to a clutch of bachelor bedrooms (Fig. 20). There was a corresponding female territory of boudoir and morning room on the other side of a large living hall. In some houses the male territory included a gun room, furnished as a sitting room as well as with cupboards for guns. These male rooms could contain books and pictures of a mildly naughty nature (Pls 190 and 191), to go with the smoking-room stories.

A late-Victorian household with its troop of bachelors retiring to talk ritual smut in the male preserves, its animated house-party seated at separate tables in the dining room, and a certain amount of discreet adultery along the bedroom corridors, had moved a long way from the domesticity, earnestness and godliness of a typical mid-Victorian house. By the end of the nineteenth century inevitable reaction had begun to set in. Mid-Victorian earnestness was beginning to seem a little ridiculous and even the treasured finesses of Victorian planning considerably overdone—why on earth separate rooms for cleaning shoes and knives for instance? The country house was moving into the rather more relaxed atmosphere of the twentieth century when, in spite of slowly decreasing wealth and quickly decreasing power, country houses retained enough money, enough prestige and enough finesse in the art of living to enjoy an exceedingly agreeable Indian summer.

298

192. Miss Penelope Chetwode and her horse taking tea with Lord Berners at Faringdon House, Berkshire, in the 1930s.

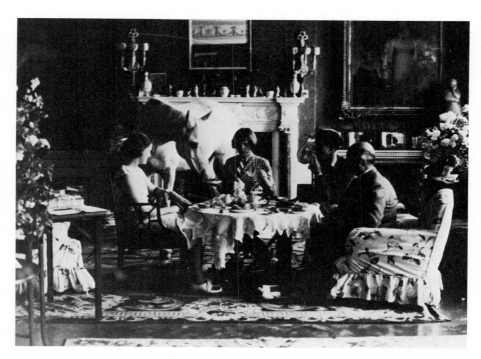

11 The Indian Summer: 1900-40

ONE of the rocks on which the upper classes rested was the belief that land was safe. Money invested in anything else was likely to do the dirty on one, but it was impossible for land to burn down, or be stolen, or blow up, or sink at sea. It was irremoveably there, and one could rely on it. This belief was one of the main reasons why people invested in land, often to the exclusion of everything else, and why it was the most prestigious form of investment. Anyone who owned land had a permanent stake in the country. The belief survived through most of the nineteenth century, even when the power conferred by the ownership of land was diminishing, and temptingly larger returns could be obtained by investing in something else.[1]

And then it turned out that land wasn't safe at all. In the years around 1880 the influx of cheap corn from America—which the landed interest was no longer strong enough to keep out—led to twenty years of deep depression in the British farming industry. Upper-class families who were entirely dependent on the income from their land found themselves in difficulties. A good many had to sell up altogether—perhaps especially those who had rebuilt their houses in more optimistic days and had borrowed money to do so. Numerous country houses were standing empty, or were let or up for sale. Of houses which have featured in this book, Houghton was up for sale but did not find a buyer, Apethorpe was sold to one of the Brasseys, the great Victorian contractors, Hengrave to a cotton-spinner from Lancashire, Gilling to a colliery owner, Shadwell to a northern businessman. Although the depression was over by 1900 and rents gradually began to recover, their recovery was a short one; after a brief burst of prosperity in the early 1920s they began to sink again, and continued to sink until the end of the 1930s.

The mystique of land had been exploded, but the mystique of the country house remained as strong as ever. On green lawns or under spreading cedar trees countless tea-tables were still being spread with white table cloths, and hostesses pouring out tea from silver tea pots. Nothing, it might seem, had changed. But in fact a great deal had changed.

The families that survived the agricultural slump in the best order were those which had eggs in other baskets. If rents were coming in from a comfortable slice of London property, or money from a family business, or a handy portfolio of shares, it was possible to watch the dwindling income from one's farms with relative equanimity. The lesson was taken to heart. The landowning classes entered into an increasingly close merger with the business world.

The merger could take various forms. Many peers supplemented their sinking incomes by sitting on company boards, often as comatose directors brought in as icing to help make prospectuses attractive to shareholders. In the worst days of the slump there was an undignified rush of indigent peers scrambling for directorships. Shady financiers had no difficulty in finding gullible ones to lend an air of respectibility to their operations. The most famous case was that of the Marquess of Dufferin and Ava, ex-Viceroy of India, who sat in all innocence as chairman of the companies set up by Whitaker Wright—until their sensational collapse in the early 1900s, and Wright's subsequent suicide in the dock, a few minutes after he had been given a stiff sentence for fraud.

But many landowners were shrewder. They sold the outlying farms on their property and invested the money in shares. They sent their younger and sometimes even their elder sons into the City. They married the daughters of rich bankers, brewers or industrialists, who brought them enough, and often more than enough, money to do up the house, re-gravel the drive, renew the gates, install central heating and generally plug the holes eroded by agricultural decline.[2]

Much of this was, of course, by no means new. Landowners had been marrying the daughters of new men from the city since at least the sixteenth century. But the shift in the economy meant that the new men now had a much stronger hand. Up till the middle of the nineteenth century anyone who wanted to be accepted as a full member of the upper classes had to cut all his links with business. He had not only to cease working in his office or warehouse but to give up any financial stake in it. He had to sell out and reinvest the money in land. The only exception made was for bankers, who were so essential to the upper classes that they had acquired a special position. But even bankers were not quite given full membership. They had no hope, for instance, of getting a peerage until the 1830s, and even then there were a good many raised eyebrows when the first two banking peers were created.[3]

By 1900 the situation had changed completely. The new rich were setting up in country houses, being given titles and continuing to take the train up to their offices in order to deal in newspapers, ships, tobacco, coal, gold or linoleum. To be a captain of industry and the owner of a country house had become an entirely acceptable combination. The supply of British tycoons was supplemented by American and South African ones, either buying or building houses themselves or supplying well-endowed daughters to bring more much-needed money into the country-house world.

The merger between business and land was not a complete one. There were still families too dim, proud or set in their ways to do anything but continue to live off the rents of their farms, as they always had done; and as agriculture remained unprofitable and prices, taxes and wages continued to rise, many of them lived in increasing shabbiness. There were other upper-class families who owned so much anyway, whether in land or other forms of property, that they could afford to be independent. These two groups, from their separate positions of strength and weakness, might make derogatory comments about new families, but this was only an expression of superficial and sometimes rather enjoyable friction within the system. Basically, the country-house world had been saved by the merger. Provided with new sources of money, and therefore of power, country houses sailed into the calm waters of their Indian summer.

The merger, of course, had to work both ways. New families had to be eager to join, as well as old families prepared to accept them. Yet the old arguments for buying a country property were wearing very thin. To invest in thousands of acres of land was now politically and socially unnecessary and financially—or so it seemed at the time—unwise. It was possible, as Asquith discovered, to get on very comfortably with a house in the country rather than a country house, that is to say with a house with no parkland or farms attached to it. Politically it became possible to get to the top with no country house or even country-house connections at all—as was conclusively demonstrated in 1922, when Curzon, in spite of his blue blood and string of country houses, was beaten to the job of Prime Minister by Bonar Law, who had neither.

Although there were still elements of social or political climbing in the motives of some of the new people who bought or built country houses—and for some of them perhaps these still predominated—increasing numbers did so for other reasons. A hard-working politician or businessman found that a country house provided a pleasant retreat from the cares of his office and the round of London. But many people were impelled less by convenience than by romanticism. They wanted to own a country house not because it was a step on the way to Parliament but because they were in love with the idea of a country house—because it represented to them peace, tradition, beauty and dignity. They wanted to be country gentlemen not because it would help them to get a title but because they were in love with the idea of being country gentlemen, strolling with gun under arm round their own acres—like John Buchan's Richard Hannay, the South African engineer, who dreamt all through the 1914–18 war of putting down roots in the English countryside, and finally bought Fosse Manor in the Cotswolds. He describes it at the opening of *The Three Hostages*: 'As I came out of the Home Wood onto the lower lawns and saw the old stone gables that the monks had built, I felt that I was anchored in the pleasantest of harbours . . .' Even its smell made him feel romantic. 'There is an odour about a country house that I love better than any scent in the world. Mary used to say it was a mixture of lamp and dog and woodsmoke, but at Fosse, where there was electric light and no dog indoors, I fancy it was wood smoke, tobacco, the old walls, and wafts of the country coming in at the windows.'[4]

This kind of country-house romanticism is everywhere in Buchan's books, just as it was everywhere in Buchan's own life, the life of a self-made son of the manse who ended up in his own modest but mellow country house in Oxfordshire. It is equally present in the books of Buchan's contemporaries, sometimes with the tug-in-the-throat quality one finds in Buchan, sometimes treated with rather more gaiety. The world of Wodehouse is very much a send-up of the world of Buchan, but one carried out with the greatest affection. Moreover, accurate knowledge of what was going on in real country houses lies behind his characters: the Earl of Emsworth, whose resources are clearly widely enough based for no threat of financial difficulty to cloud the lawns of Blandings Castle; Lord Biskerton and his father Lord Hoddesdon, desperately trying to let Edgeling Court to T. Paterson Frisby, the American president of Horned Toad Copper Mine Inc.; Sir Watkyn Bassett, whose relative has died and 'left him a vast fortune' so that he can buy Totleigh Towers 'from a Lord Somebody, who needs the cash, as so many do these days'; and Aunt Agatha's husband Spencer Gregson, who is on the Stock Exchange and by 'cleaning up to an amazing extent in Sumatra Rubber' has enabled Aunt Agatha to 'lash out on an impressive scale' in selecting a country seat.

The country houses portrayed by Buchan, Wodehouse and others are mellow, dignified, creeper-clad, lawn encompassed, and bathed in perpetual sunshine. They are, in fact, exactly like the houses that were to be seen week after week and page after page in *Country Life*. *Country Life* was started in the late 1890s by a romantic and country-loving businessman called Edward Hudson, whose family owned a printing works. It was extensively bought by equally romantic businessmen, in Britain, America and the dominions. They read it with yearning, and resolved that when they had made their pile they, too, would acquire a country house. Many of them did make their pile, and built or restored country houses on the strength of it—and the results were duly recorded in *Country Life*.

But *Country Life*, as its name makes clear, was not entirely devoted to articles on country houses, although they were its principal feature. It was started because the country and all that it stood for was being threatened by industrialization and the growth of the towns. It aimed to cover every aspect of country life. Behind it lay two assumptions: that life in the country was inherently better than life in the town, and that the life of an English country gentleman was the best life of all. A large part of the urban middle classes agreed with the assumptions and (ignoring the fact that their own activities were helping to cause it) deplored the threat. They did their best to escape to the country and, if they had the means, to set up as country gentlemen—if only at week-ends.

Of course *Country Life* was not only bought by country-loving businessmen. It quickly made its appearance on the drawing-room tables of old country-house families as well. Nobody minds being admired. Just as the complaining, censorious, reforming attitude of the early-Victorian middle classes had helped to make the upper classes more moral and more religious, the idealistic, romantic country-loving enthusiasm of a large section of the early-twentieth-century middle classes helped to make them very much more conscious of what they possessed, and careful and conservative in the way they looked after it.

Romanticism about the country does not, however, necessarily imply romanticism about the country house. There were many comfortably-off business or professional people who came to the country in order to walk through it rather than hunt and shoot through it, and wanted to get to know country characters rather than county society. Their romanticism worked at the level of farm houses and cottages rather than country houses. They believed in simple living and homespun virtues, and their politics were more likely to be socialist than conservative. In spite of their admiration of country virtues they were often consciously 'progressive'; they thought that society needed changing. If they wanted to build a house they went to architects like Voysey and Baillie Scott, who supplied them with progressive plans designed to catch the sun, whitewashed simplicity on the exterior and apple-green paint or scrubbed oak combined with uncomfortably original furniture in the interior. *Country Life* gave such houses a certain amount of coverage, but its sympathies, and probably most of its readership, remained with the owners or would-be owners of traditional country houses.

It was usually would-be owners rather than existing owners who ended up by building. Since the most admired kind of country house was now an old one, old families were under no pressure to rebuild in order to keep up to date. Taxation, declining income and fears for the future made it unlikely that they would have the means, confidence or desire to enlarge. Unless their house was burnt down, or they were forced to sell it and build a smaller one on what remained of their property, they tended to confine themselves to minor alterations. The initiative in country-house building passed more than ever to new families.

But many new people were more anxious to buy an old house than build a new one. Thanks to the agricultural depression there was no shortage of country houses on the market. Many of them were relatively small ones, sold by small gentry who lacked resources and had failed to weather the depression. They were often not large enough for the house-parties envisaged by their owners. They needed to be enlarged. If one had been looking for the typical country house of the first thirty years of this century—perhaps of its nature an impossible task—the most likely candidate would have been neither an altogether new nor an altogether old house, but an old house rescued from decay, lovingly restored, carefully enlarged, and surrounded by new gardens (Pl. 193). The Victorians tended to be insensitive in the way in which they tacked service wings, bachelor wings, vestibules, *portes-cochères* and conservatories onto older houses; the Edwardians and Georgians were infinitely tactful.

Two examples, both in Kent, give some idea of their methods: Hever Castle, which was bought by the American millionaire, William Waldorf Astor, in the early 1900s, and Lympne Castle, bought in 1905 by F. J. Tennant, son of a Scottish chemical millionaire and one of a family which much enlivened society in the years around 1900. At Lympne the old house was restored and the additions designed by the Scottish architect Robert Lorimer, who had a reputation for the tactful handling of old houses. He more than doubled its size; but by keeping the new work low and set back to one side, and by matching its flint walls with the original flintwork, he carefully blended it in with the mediaeval house. At Hever the moated castle was not nearly large enough for the lavish scale of Astor hospitality. Guests were accordingly put up in new accommodation designed to look like a mediaeval village (Pl. 194). A series of what appeared to be cottages were all in fact connected, and were finally joined onto the castle by a covered bridge across the moat.[5]

The demand for country houses was so great, however, that there were not enough suitable old ones for sale in suitable places. Moreover there were always people who were irresistibly attracted to the idea of building something new. New country houses were in fact put up in considerable numbers. But their appearance was heavily conditioned by what was now admired in old ones.

304

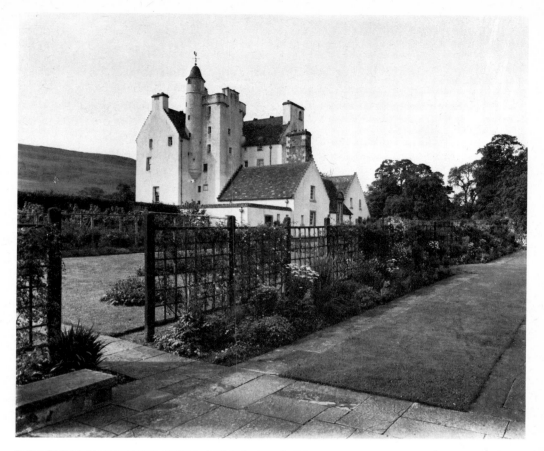

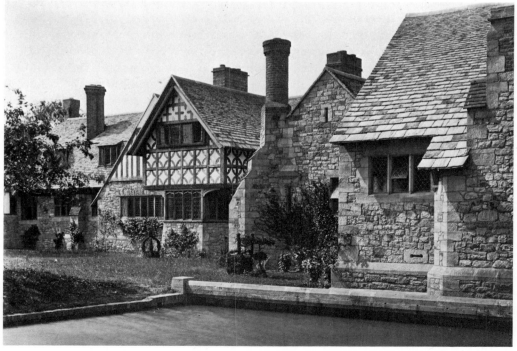

193. (top) Balmanno Castle, Perthshire. An old castle added to by Sir Robert Lorimer in 1915.

194. The guest wing at Hever Castle, Kent (F. L. Pearson, 1903–7).

Country houses were no longer expected to express authority—not even 'quietly and gravely' as recommended by Gilbert Scott. The authority of country-house owners was being eroded all the time, and it seemed impolitic to draw too much attention to what remained of it. Not only did porticoes remain out of fashion; even towers all but disappeared. Living halls continued to be built, but baronial halls became a thing of the past because there was no role for them. New families were now unwilling to lumber themselves with too much land, and normally only bought enough to provide adequate shooting and fishing, and a home farm with a pedigree herd; they had no tenants to entertain. Even old families had usually reduced the number of their tenants by sales of land; and after the shake-up of the agricultural depression, those that remained were often new people who confined their relationship to a cash one.[6]

The emphasis was now on the country house as a country product rather than a seat of authority. The country houses which were most admired were ones which seemed, as Vita Sackville-West put it, 'essentially part of the country, not only *in* the country but part of it, a natural growth.' Houses in the grand manner were 'false to the real tradition'. They had not been allowed 'to grow with the oaks and elms and beeches'.[7]

This kind of organic approach to country houses had first begun to appear in the mid nineteenth century. Houses that had grown bit by bit over the centuries, that rambled round several courtyards and had matured in greenery like port in the cellar had been not only admired but imitated by architects like George Devey in the 1870s and '80s.[8] They were still being admired and imitated in the 1930s. But alongside admiration of rambling irregular houses began to appear a new appreciation of symmetry and order—and therefore of the eighteenth century.

This appreciation perhaps owed something to imperialism, as expressed architectually for instance by the Admiralty Arch, the Mall, and the new front of Buckingham Palace. There are a few country houses, mostly built about 1900, that might be described as proconsular because of the grandeur of their architecture and the politics of their owners.[9] But the general development of the country house was so much away from grandeur that there are very few of them. The order that now came into fashion was more a domestic orderliness, of the kind that seemed to Vita Sackville-West 'as quiet as the country squires and the country existence where they belonged.'[10] It was an orderliness that went with hipped roofs, pleached avenues and clipped hedges. It came as a relief after an excess of rambling; to people who supported the existing order and feared that it was threatened, there was something reassuring about it.

Anyone who wanted to build himself a country house that would be new but not too new, orderly but not overbearing, gratifyingly inventive and yet reassuringly traditional could, and very often did, go to Lutyens—or if he were building in Scotland to Lorimer, sometimes described as the 'Scottish Lutyens'. Both tend to be thought of as aristocrats' architects but in fact, although they had a number of aristocratic clients, their practice was mainly supported by new families and romantic businessmen. Both—but Lutyens to a considerably higher

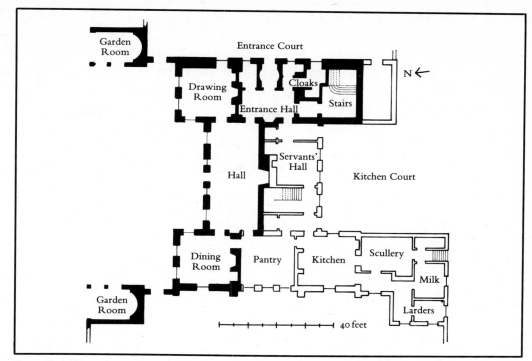

degree—had the gift of all good architects, of sensing what their clients wanted and giving it to them in heightened and transmuted form.

Houses designed by Lutyens invariably had what Vita Sackville-West called 'the peculiar genius of the English country-house . . . its knack of fitting in.'[11] He used second-hand bricks, or carefully scaled and delicately coloured new ones. His oak, where it was exposed, was grey and gentle, not black and shiny. He had an extraordinary feeling for texture, and for settling his houses into their surroundings. The lines of his houses and gardens were softened from the earliest possible moment by creepers and planting (Pl. 195).

Architecturally, all his houses were securely linked to the country-house tradition—in his early days to irregular and sometimes half-timbered mediaeval or Tudor manor houses, in his later days increasingly to symmetrical houses of the seventeenth and eighteenth centuries. But his symmetry, like his detail, had its own special quality. The courts, outbuildings and terraces which he deployed with such skill were used to fuse the main house into its setting rather than to suggest social hierarchy. He loved generous roofs and bold chimney stacks, but only once supplied a country house with a full-scale portico and used even pediments very sparingly. Even if his facades suggest formal houses of the late seventeenth or early eighteenth century, his plans never do. The formal relationship of hall to saloon or saloon to apartments is virtually never found in them. His houses are more often entered from the side than from the front, and wherever the entrance the route from the front door to the main reception room is circuitous and full of pretty incident, rather than along a formal axis (Figs 21 and 22).[12]

The grandest of Lutyens's symmetrical houses is Gledstone Hall in Yorkshire. Its cotton-manufacturing owner, Sir Amos Nelson, as he bowled up to it in his

307

Fig. 21. Ednaston Manor, Derbyshire (Sir Edwin Lutyens, 1913).

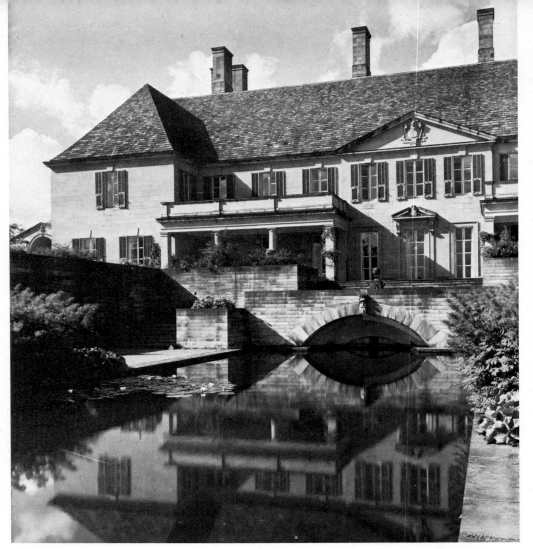

Rolls Royce or Daimler, could feel himself linked to the great Palladian houses of the neighbourhood. But he could also contemplate the fact that there was ample garaging discreetly concealed in a wing, that the house was equipped with central heating, electric light and eight bathrooms, that its south-facing loggias were designed for afternoon tea, that its balconies could be used as open-air bedrooms, and that a portion of its formal canal was kept clear for swimming (Pl. 195). [13] New country houses had to be fitted for life as lived at the time, and keep reasonable pace with new technology. Their owners, however romantic about the past, usually wanted to be comfortable.

Changes in country life were conditioned by two developments, rather fewer servants and rather less formality. Fewer servants were the result of less money and more technology. Families hit by the agricultural depression were forced to reduce their households. Death duties were first imposed in 1894, and the rate was increased in 1909 and 1919. Income tax rose steadily, and so did servants' wages. On the other hand, families whose income was supplemented or derived from sources other than land could get by with only minor economies. The Astors still had thirty indoor servants at Cliveden in the 1930s, exclusive of three dailies. [14]

308

195. Gledstone Hall, Yorkshire (Sir Edwin Lutyens, 1925–7).

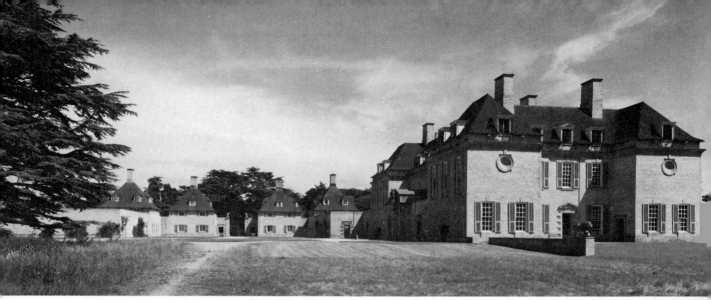

But labour-saving devices were making some household departments luxuries rather than necessities, and reducing the numbers needed in others. There was a laundry and a still-room at Cliveden until the second World War, but after 1920 many sizeable new houses had neither. Commercial laundries, groceries and confectioners, complete with vans to collect and deliver, made them unnecessary; such cakes and preserves as were still made in the house became the responsibility of the cook. Cars needed fewer people to run them than carriages. Vacuum cleaners saved time for the housemaids. Central heating meant fewer fires to be laid or grates to be cleaned. More baths and wash-basins meant fewer cans of water to be carried to the bedrooms. Electric light meant no dirt from gas or oil lamps, and no staff needed to fill and clean the lamps. More efficient kitchen ranges meant fewer kitchen smells and shorter distances from kitchen to dining room.[15]

Many of these improvements had been available since the nineteenth century. The pressure to install them became greater as servants became harder to get. The 1914–18 war broke the old secure supply of domestic staff. The upper and middle classes had long ago deserted service in big households because there were better opportunities for them elsewhere; now the lower classes were beginning to follow the same pattern. Jobs in offices or factories offered better hours, better pay and more independence. Servants had to be tempted by houses that were easier to clean and run, and rooms that were better furnished and had a better outlook. The emphasis was now on comfort and convenience rather than morality; separate flats or houses for married couples began to be provided. Relations between staff and employees grew little if any closer; the two communities still lived independent lives but the life of the servant community was considerably more comfortable.

The height of improvement and luxury was reached with Middleton Park in Oxfordshire, designed by Lutyens (with the collaboration of his son) in 1935 for the Earl of Jersey (Pl. 196 and Fig. 22). It had fourteen bathrooms, electric light generated in the house, an engine-driven service lift, and a refrigerated cold store. There was no laundry, still-room or steward's room and the kitchen was linked direct to the dining room through a serving lobby. Free standing pavilions

309

196. Middleton Park, Oxfordshire (Sir Edwin and Robert Lutyens, 1938).

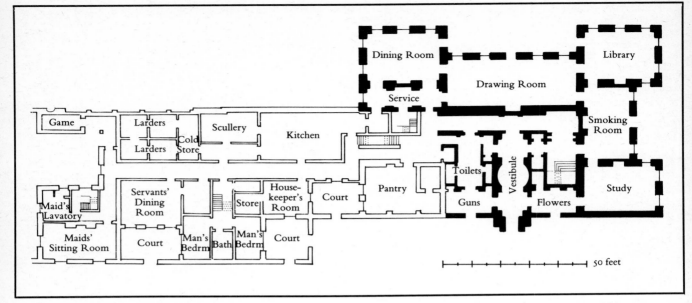

provided a house for the butler and rooms for visiting servants. There was garaging for fifteen cars.[16]

The shrinkage of servants' quarters from sprawling tails to relatively modest appendages helped to make country houses less ponderous. In the main body of the house less ceremony and more mixing between the sexes had a similar effect. Fewer servants, the influence of America and the reaction of the post war generation against their parents all played their part. Some houses were consciously unconventional but for the most part the changes were only minor ones. Guests no longer changed for tea but still changed for dinner and for tennis. They always helped themselves at breakfast, sometimes at luncheon but never at dinner. Men ceased to arm women into dinner in the country, but continued to do so at big dinner parties in London. Smoking was allowed in the drawing room, but a smoking room, with or without a billiard table, tended to survive as a sitting room for men only.

Even so, both male and female territories were in decay. Bachelors' wings ceased to be built after 1920. Few new houses had both a billiards and a smoking room; billiard tables tended to sink to the degradation of billiards fives. Billiards was gradually replaced by bridge, which brought the sexes together in the drawing room. Morning rooms disappeared, at least as separate women's rooms. Many houses made do with a relatively small dining room; it was the room which could be contracted with least inconvenience, especially as there were likely to be fewer people waiting at table.

Living halls remained popular, but suffered from a reaction. Edwardian ones were often huge (Pl. 197 and Col. Pl. XXXI). H. F. Goodhart-Rendel, who had experienced them, commented ruefully on 'the strange Edwardian fashion . . . of sitting not in one's sitting rooms but in the hall outside them. A central hall in Edwardian times, with a stream of housemaids issuing with slop-pails from the bedrooms after breakfast in full view from below, left much to be desired as a sitting room, however invitingly it might be furnished with sofas, screens, palm trees and perhaps a grand piano.'[17] In the 1920s living halls tended to become

310

Fig. 22. Middleton Park. The ground floor.

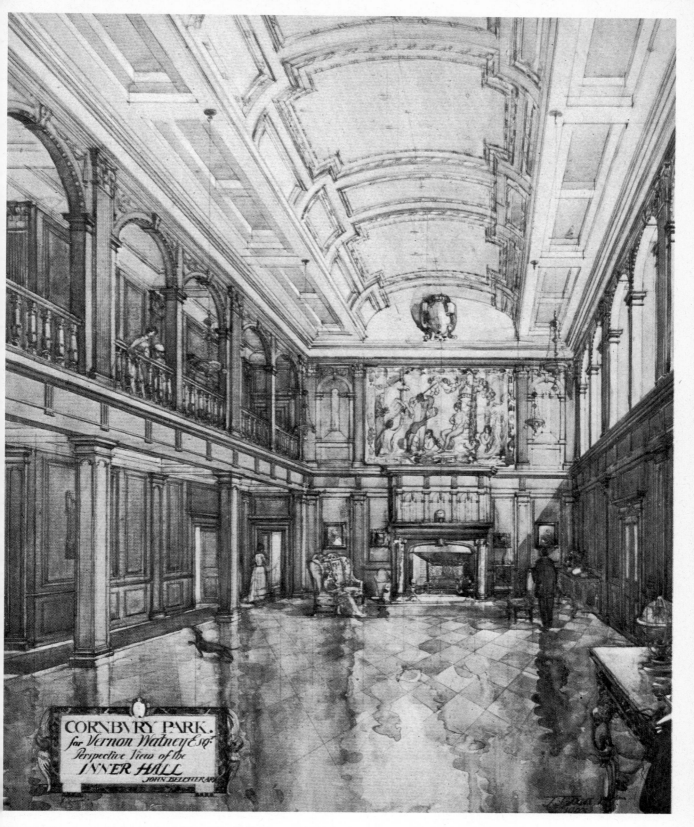

Within the drawing:

CORNBVRY PARK.
for *Vernon Watney* Esqᵉ
Perspective View of the
INNER HALL
JOHN BELCHER ARᵗ

XXXI. Cornbury Park, Oxfordshire. The hall, from a drawing by the architect, John Belcher, *c.* 1901.

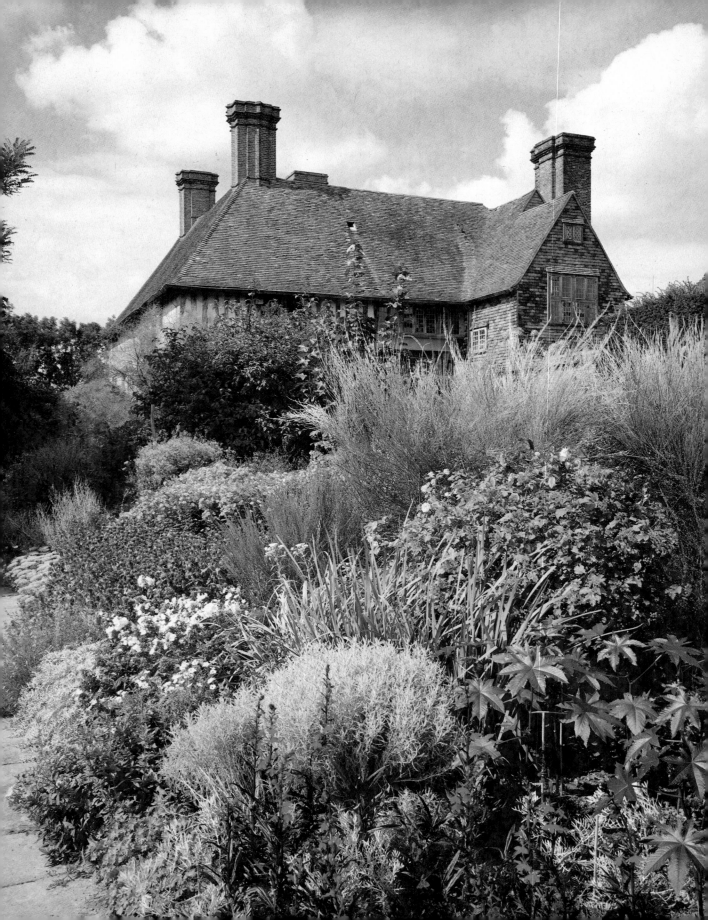

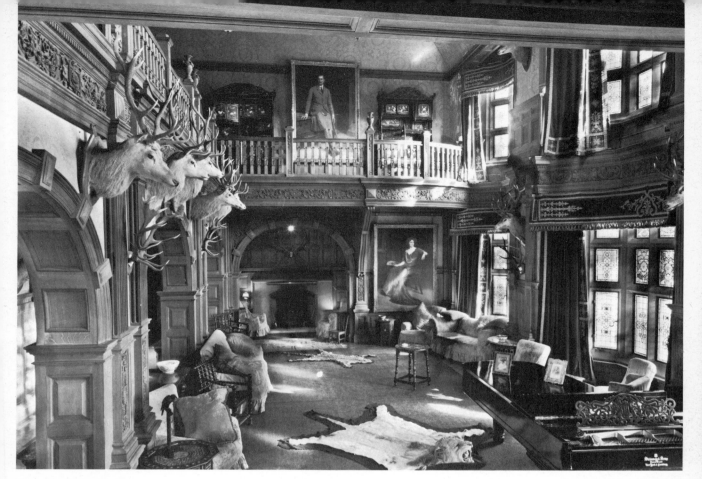

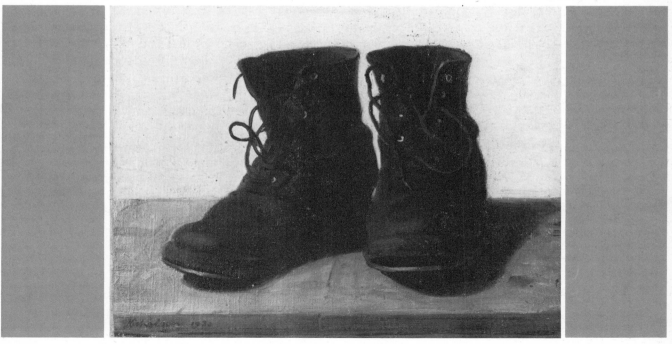

XXXII. (left) Great Dixter, Sussex. A mediaeval house embellished by Lutyens and Jekyll in about 1910.

197. (top) Kinloch Castle, Isle of Rhum. The hall (Leeming and Leeming, c. 1899–1903).

198. Gertrude Jekyll's boots. The gardening boots of the queen of Edwardian gardeners, painted by William Nicholson in 1920.

smaller and less exposed; some of those designed by Lutyens were scarcely distinguishable from ordinary rooms.

An attached conservatory began to grow rare after 1900, and is almost never found in houses built after 1920. Its disappearance is the result, not of less interest in gardens and plants, but of a different kind of interest. The garden had become the supreme symbol of the good life lived in the country. But it had to be a country garden, full of outdoor plants growing naturally. Conservatories were too artificial and placed too much of a barrier between indoors and outdoors. Belief in the virtues of country air led to a passion for open windows, and for living, working, eating and sleeping in or above the garden, in loggias, outdoor rooms, sleeping porches or on bedroom balconies (Pl. 199). When P. G. Wodehouse's Freddy Widgeon threw a cat out of his bedroom window, it was not altogether surprising that it hit his host, who was sleeping in a hammock on the lawn.[18]

For early-Victorian gentry to work in the garden had been something of a rarity. In the 1880s gardening ladies began to supplement the labour of their staff as well as to direct them. From then on there were more and more upper-class gardeners—not only gardening wives but gardening husbands and any gardening guests who wished to ingratiate themselves with their host and hostess. Over the whole country-house scene floated the image of Gertrude Jekyll's boots as painted by William Nicholson—the symbol of the greatest of Edwardian country-house gardeners as painted by the best of Edwardian country-house painters (Pl. 198).

For those who wanted to get away from the garden, motor cars were at hand to take them on the other favourite occupation of house-parties—sight-seeing expeditions along roads which, if dusty and narrow, were still blessedly empty. But when the motor cars were not on the road somewhere had to be found to put them. They were one of the novelties which country houses had to incorporate but had no language to deal with. The whole ethos of country romanticism made owners unwilling to flaunt their garages, as their predecessors had flaunted their plate glass windows. At Marsh Court (Pl. 200) Lutyens put the cars into a garage disguised as a barn (with the power-house in another barn next door to it), but in most country houses they were concealed altogether in an invisible back yard.[19]

In general, technology was accepted but disguised. Radiators were modestly veiled behind screens of lattice work. Electric bulbs were hidden in eighteenth-century-style lanterns or disguised as candles. In the bedrooms at Lutyens's Folly Farm, cupboards of massive joinery opened to reveal wash-basins of the latest design. The only rooms in which technology was let relatively loose were kitchens and bathrooms. Kitchens were out of view and bathrooms were secret places set apart. In bathrooms, especially, country-house architects tended to let themselves go, and indulge in untraditional and often expensive fantasies in glass, marble, metal or mosaic (Pl. 203).[20]

Outside the house there was seldom a problem about incorporating tennis courts, since up till 1939 they were usually grass courts; while nothing could be more English and rural than a cricket field and a cricket pavilion. Swimming

199. (right) A bedroom balcony at Monkton House, Sussex (Sir Edwin Lutyens, 1903).

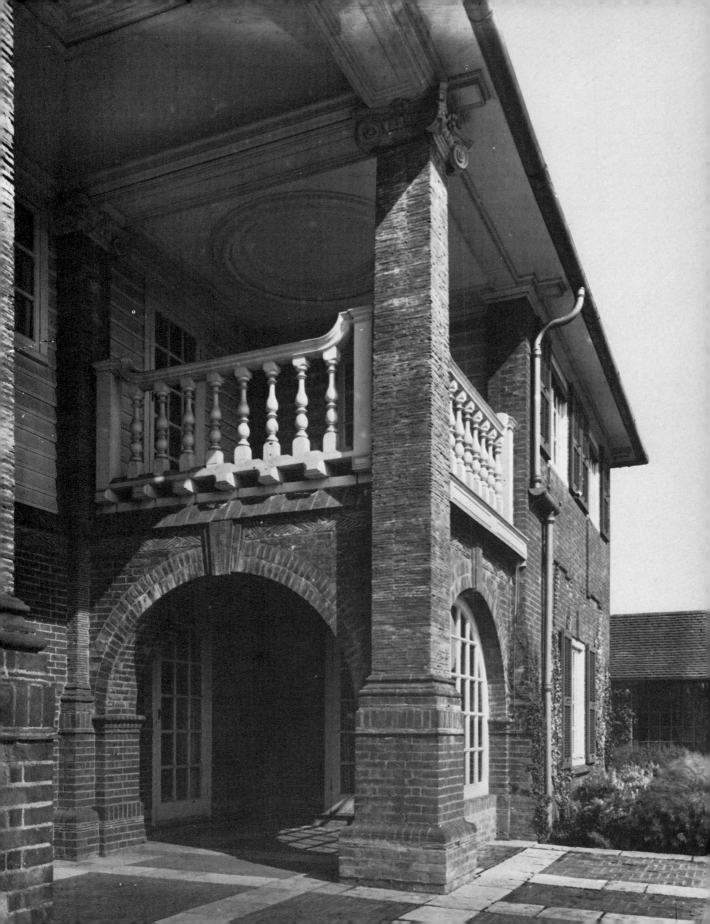

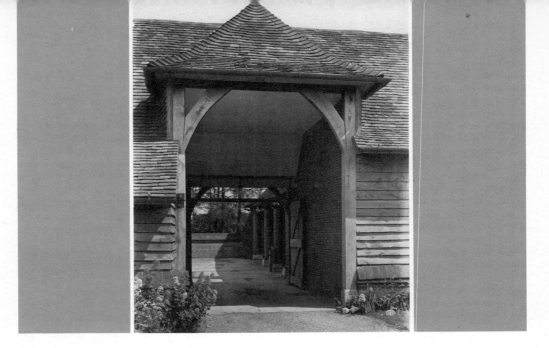

pools were more of a problem; unlike bathrooms they were public places and were normally treated with much more circumspection. Before the last war swimming pools were still a comparative rarity in English country houses (and heated or indoor swimming pools even rarer). But those that there were tended to be disguised as something else or carefully incorporated into the garden layout, with the scaffolding of diving boards conspicuously absent (Pl. 202).[21]

Occasional owners chafed against the standards of quiet good taste expected of a country gentleman. At Port Lympne in Kent the extravagant bathrooms, Moorish patio and Roman swimming pool (Pl. 201) combined with more conventional features to suggest that its exotic and intriguing owner, Sir Philip Sassoon, was torn between the standards of *Country Life* and Metro-Goldwyn-Mayer. But on the whole gentlemanly good taste prevailed, sometimes in unexpected quarters. No-one was more of a squire, more tweedy, garden-loving or gentlemanly than Ramsay Macdonald, resting for the week-end at Chequers (Pl. 204).

Chequers had been given to the nation by Lord Lee of Fareham as a country house for prime ministers, who by now were less likely to have one of their own. It had previously been his own home; he himself describes how, after many years of nostalgically turning the pages of *Country Life*, he finally made his pile (or, to be exact, married his pile) and bought his country house.[22] Its possible use as a means of taming radicals may have occurred to him. Certainly, Chequers and Lady Londonderry between them tamed Ramsay Macdonald more than the Labour Party could stomach.

But it was Ramsay Macdonald who went under, while the party survived. The power structure continued to change. Today the coherence of the country-house world, which survived, even if under stress, up till the second World War, has largely vanished. Many country houses have been destroyed, many more are no longer privately owned. Of those that are, some belong to foreigners, some are week-end retreats for businessmen. Some have little or no land attached to them,

316

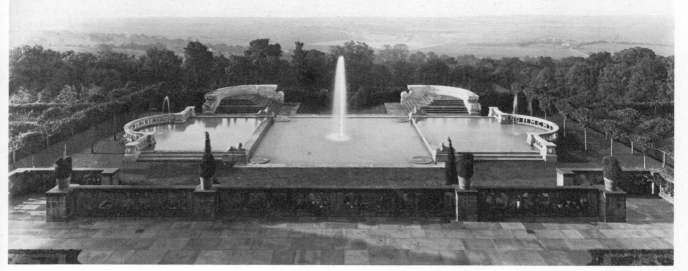

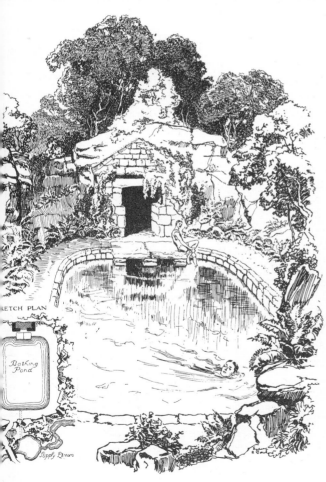

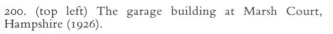

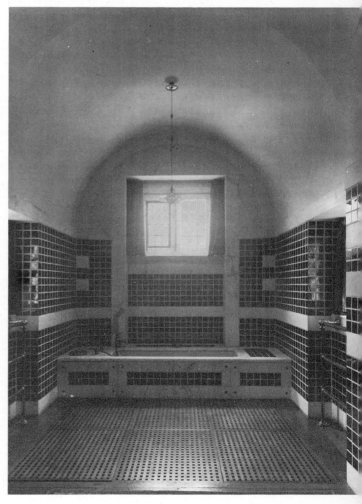

200. (top left) The garage building at Marsh Court, Hampshire (1926).

201. (top right) The swimming pools àt Port Lympne, Kent (Philip Tilden, c. 1925).

202. (lower left) Design for an Edwardian bathing pond.

203. (lower right) A bathroom at Marsh Court (1926).

some are the headquarters of property empires or large areas of farmland. Even if a considerable number belong to families who have owned them for many generations, such families could no longer conceivably be described as a ruling class. A few owners of country houses are still engaged in running the country or the county, but the old automatic correlation between the ownership of an estate and the right to execute power has vanished. The most that country houses now bring their owners is an accepted constitutional position, as patrons of local and national good causes.

Financially, country houses are not as badly off as is sometimes suggested. The surge in property and agricultural values since the war has produced a bonus which could never have been foreseen in the dark days of the 1880s and '90s. The beauty and associations of the houses themselves, and the romance of what Evelyn Waugh described as their 'secret landscapes', bring them sympathy, visitors and grants; in a curious reversal of history, instead of the houses existing as means to support the ends of their owners, their owners now tend to be seen as means to support the survival of their houses. On the other hand, most of them are engaged in a constant, often gallant, but all too often losing battle against taxation and rising costs.

The situation, though by no means hopeless, is not calculated to continue an architectural tradition. Country-house owners are mainly concerned with adapting, redecorating, maintaining and often reducing old houses, rather than building new ones. When they do build, they seldom produce anything creatively new, or even convincingly traditional. They have lost the coherence of an integrated and powerful class, which knew the kind of buildings it wanted and had the confidence and money to produce them.

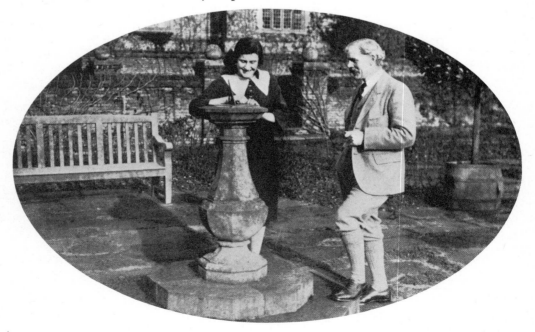

204. Ramsay Macdonald with his daughter in the garden at Chequers in the 1920s.

NOTES TO THE TEXT

ABBREVIATIONS

B.M.	British Museum	P.R.O.	Public Record Office
E.E.T.S.	Early English Text Society	R.C.H.M.	Royal Commission on Historical
H.M.C.	Historic Manuscripts Commission		Monuments
Huntington	Huntington Library, San Marino, California	R.I.B.A.	Royal Institute of British Architects

HOUSEHOLD REGULATIONS

The list that follows is of the household regulations, from the Middle Ages till the early eighteenth century, made use of for the earlier chapters of the book. If referred to in the footnotes I have used the abbreviations listed in the margin. A number of later eighteenth and nineteenth-century household regulations also survive (e.g. the Hatfield regulations printed as end-papers) but on the whole these are much less informative than the earlier ones, and I have made comparatively little use of them.

I. ROYAL HOUSEHOLD REGULATIONS

Tout T. F. T. F. Tout, *Chapters in the Administrative History of Mediaeval England* (Manchester, 1920) II, pp. 158–63. Brief regulations of 1279.

Edward II H.R. T. F. Tout, *The Place of the Reign of Edward II in English History* (Manchester, 1936) pp. 241–84. Household Regulations of Edward II, 1318 and 1323.

Edward IV H.R. A. R. Myers, *The Household of Edward IV* (Manchester, 1959) pp. 63–230. Various household regulations, including the immensely detailed *Black Book* of *c.* 1471.

Royal H.R. Society of Antiquaries, *A Collection of Ordinances and Regulations for the Government of the Royal Household* (London, 1790). Contains ordinances from time of Edward III to William and Mary.

Charles II H.R. Nottingham University Library, Portland MSS. PWV 92 and 93. Regulations of 1661 and 1673 for Charles II's Privy Lodgings.

II. OTHER HOUSEHOLD REGULATIONS

Fleta H.R. *Fleta* (Selden Society, LXXII, Pt II) pp. 241–60. A short section on duties of various household officials, in this fourteenth-century compendium of general information.

Grosseteste H.R. *Statuta Familiae*, written by Bishop Grosseteste for the Countess of Lincoln in the late thirteenth century. MS. versions include B. M. Sloane MS. 1986, f. 193. The Sloane version published by F. J. Furnivall, *The Babees Book* (see *Nurture H.R.*, below) pp. 328–31.

Fairfax H.R. Bodleian Library, Fairfax MS. 24 (3904). Fragment of a mid-fourteenth-century treatise on the organisation of a seignorial household, written in French.

Baron-bishop H.R. 'The service to the Baron-bishop of Yorke'. Printed by Thomas Hearne, *Lelandi Collectanea*, VI (1774) p. 7. Hearne assumes this is contemporary with the Neville Feast (1465), but the ceremony suggests a considerably earlier date.

Chambers H.R. B.M. Add. MS. 37969. Published as *A Fifteenth-Century Courtesy Book*, ed. R. W. Chambers (E.E.T.S., XLVIII, 1914).

Nurture H.R. John Russell, *The Booke of Nurture* (*c.* 1450), ed. F. J. Furnivall (E.E.T.S., XXXII, 1868) pp. 115–239. Furnivall's text was modernized as *The Babees Book*; *Mediaeval Manners for the Young etc.* (1908) ed. Edith Rickert. References are to the Rickert edition, unless stated.

Courtesy H.R.	*The Booke of Courtesy* (*c.* 1420?), ed. Furnivall as above, pp. 297–327, and Rickert, pp. 79–121.
Harleian H.R.	B.M. Harleian MS. 6815. 'Orders of service belonging to the degrees of a duke, a marquess and an erle used in there owne howses'. Elizabethan copy of what appears to be late-fifteenth-century original. Only the service for an earl is in fact covered. Extremely long and detailed. Unpublished.
Northumberland H.R.	*The Northumberland Household Book*, ed. Thomas Percy (London, 1770). Immensely detailed regulations for all aspects of the household of Henry Algernon Percy, fifth Earl of Northumberland, at Wressel and Leconfield in Yorkshire, *c.* 1520. Much supplementary material printed in the notes.
Derby H.R.	*Stanley Papers*, II (Chetham Society, XXXI, 1853) pp. 8–10, 20–2. Short regulations of 1568 and 1572 for the household of the Earl of Derby.
Willoughby H.R.	*Manuscripts of Lord Middleton* (H.M.C., 1911) pp. 538–41. Regulations for household of Sir Francis Willoughby of Wollaton, *c.* 1572.
Montagu H.R.	W. H. St J. Hope, *Cowdray and Easebourne Priory* (London, 1919) pp. 119–134. Long and detailed regulations for household of the second Viscount Montagu, of Cowdray, Sussex, 1595.
Berkeley H.R.	John Smyth, *Lives of the Berkeleys* (1618), ed. Sir J. Maclean, (Gloucester, 1883) II, pp. 365–7, 418–20. Regulations of *c.* 1590 and 1601 for household of Henry, seventh Baron Berkeley.
Donegall H.R.	*Archaeologia*, XIII (1800) pp. 315–89. 'A Breviate touching the Order and Government of a Nobleman's House', 1605. From a MS. bought by Sir Joseph Banks from the library of the first Marquess of Donegall.
Ellesmere H.R.	Huntington Library, California, Ellesmere MSS. EL 1179 and 1180. Regulations of *c.* 1603 for household of Sir Thomas Egerton, created Lord Ellesmere, 1603, and Viscount Brackley, 1616.
'R.B.' H.R.	*Some Rules and Orders for the Government of the House of an Earle*, printed for R. Triphook (London, 1821). 'Set downe by R.B. at the instant request of his loving frende, M.L.', and wrongly attributed to Richard Brathwait. Dating from *c.* 1605. Long and detailed.
Huntingdon H.R.	J. Nichols, *History and Antiquities of the County of Leicester: West Goscote Hundred* (1804) pp. 594–8. Regulations of 1609 for household of the Earl of Huntingdon, at Ashby-de-la-Zouch Castle and Donington Park, Leicestershire.
Fairfax H.R.	Northumberland Household Book (see *Northumberland* above) p. 421. Short regulations of *c.* 1620 for household of Lord Fairfax (probably Thomas, first Baron Fairfax (1560–1640) of Denton and Nunappleton, Yorks.).
Bridgwater H.R.	H. J. Todd, *History of the College of Bonhommes, Ashridge* (London, 1823) pp. 47–55. Household regulations of John, first Earl of Bridgwater, of Ashridge, Hertfordshire, 1652, with additions 1670 and 1673.
Chandos H.R.	Huntington Library, California, Stowe MS. ST 44. Household regulations of James Brydges, first Duke of Chandos, of Cannons, Middlesex, 1721.

NOTES TO CHAPTER 1

1. Christopher Hussey, *English Country Houses: Early Georgian* (London, 1955) p. 197, quoting Lyttelton's own estimate. In fact he was promoted almost immediately to Chancellor of the Exchequer.

2. See *Lord Hervey's Memoirs*, ed. Romney Sedgwick (London, 1952) pp. 46–7, and R. W. Ketton-Cremer, *An English Country Neighbourhood* (London, 1951) pp. 97–8.

3. Hussey, *Country Houses: Early Georgian*, pp. 244–52.

4. For literary praises of country life see especially G. R. Hibbard, 'The Country House Poem of the Seventeenth Century', *Journal of the Warburg and Courtauld Institutes*, 109 (1956) pp. 159–74; Richard Gill, *Happy Rural Seat: the English Country House and the Literary Imagination* (New Haven and London,

1972), especially pp. 227–52; H. Erskine-Hill, *The Social Milieu of Alexander Pope* (New Haven and London, 1975), especially pp. 279–317.

5. Lawrence Stone, *The Crisis of the Aristocracy, 1558–1641* (Oxford, 1965) pp. 391–2.

6. Analysis of account books at Chatsworth, 1659–73, excluding plague and fire of London years.

7. The schedule can be worked out in some detail from e.g. Earl of Bessborough, *Georgiana Duchess of Devonshire* (London, 1955), and *Hary-o: The Letters of Lady Harriet Cavendish, 1796–1809*, ed. G. Leveson-Gower (London, 1940).

8. M. Girouard, *Robert Smythson and the Architecture of the Elizabethan Era* (London, 1966) pp. 184–7.

9. H.M.C., *Manuscripts of the Earl of Carlisle*, 15th Report, Pt VI (London, 1897) p. 143.

10. *British Sporting Painting, 1650–1850* (Arts Council Catalogue, London, 1974) p. 63 and illustration.

11. The word derives from the Latin *Familia*, meaning 'household' or 'clan' but never 'family' in the modern sense.

12. David Durant, *Bess of Hardwick: Portrait of an Elizabethan Dynast* (London, 1977) pp. 190–2.

13. John Smyth, *Lives of the Berkeleys* (1618) ed. Sir J. Maclean (Gloucester, 1883) II, p. 363.

14. Pückler-Muskau, *Tour in England, Ireland and France in the Year 1828 and 1829* (London, 1832) IV, p. 333.

15. *Ibid.* III, pp. 95–6.

16. Consuelo Vanderbilt Balsan, *The Glitter and the Gold* (London, 1953) p. 68.

NOTES TO CHAPTER 2

1. This account of a household on the move is mainly based on *Northumberland H.R.*, especially pp. 386–91.

2. C. D. Ross, 'Household Accounts of Elizabeth Berkeley, Countess of Warwick', *Trans. Bristol & Gloucester Archaeological Society*, LXX (1951) pp. 81–105; John Gage, 'Extracts from the Household Book of Edward Stafford, Duke of Buckingham', *Archaeologia*, XXV (1834) pp. 318–41; E. M. Richardson, *The Lion and the Rose* (London, 1923) I, pp. 69–82; *Northumberland H.R.*, pp. 43–5, 253–5. The estimate for the Warwick household is obtained by adding the earl's riding household when returning from France to the countess's household in England.

3. Smyth, *Lives of the Berkeleys*, I, p. 305; George Cavendish, *The Life and Death of Thomas Wolsey*, ed. F. S. Ellis (London, 1908) pp. 22–6.

4. The organisation is listed in detail in *Northumberland H.R.*, and much information is also provided by Smyth, *Lives of the Berkeleys*; *Nurture H.R.*; Ross,

'Household Accounts of Elizabeth Berkeley'; *Harleian H.R.* See also C. D. Ross, 'Estates and Finances of Richard Beauchamp, Earl of Warwick', *Dugdale Society, Occasional Papers, 12* (Oxford, 1956).

5. *The New Inn*, I. i. 148–59.

6. *The Babees Book*, ed. F. J. Furnivall, with several similar treatises and long forewords, as *Manners and Meals in Olden Time* (E.E.T.S., XXXII, 1868).

7. *Ibid.* p. VI.

8. *Ibid.*

9. Cavendish, *Thomas Wolsey*, pp. 25, 38.

10. *Northumberland H.R.*, p. 254.

11. Smyth, *Lives of the Berkeleys*, I. p. 305.

12. *Northumberland H.R.*, p. 34.

13. For retaining see especially K. B. McFarlane, 'Bastard Feudalism', *Bulletin of the Institute of Historical Research*, XX (1965); McFarlane, *The Nobility of Later Mediaeval England* (Oxford, 1963); W. H. Dunham, *Lord Hastings' Indentured Retainers* (Newhaven, 1955).

14. J. M. W. Bean, *The Estates of the Percy Family, 1416–1537* (Oxford, 1958).

15. *The Paston Letters*, ed. J. Gardner (London, 1904) III, p. 125.

16. Bacon, *Historye of the Raigne of King Henrye the Seventh* (London, 1622) p. 216.

17. The main source for mediaeval ceremony are the household regulations listed on pp. 319–20.

18. Ross, 'Household Accounts of Elizabeth Berkeley'. The original MS. is at Longleat.

19. Smyth, *Lives of the Berkeleys*, I, p. 305; Gage, 'Household Book of Edward Stafford', pp. 321, 325; Richardson, *The Lion and the Rose*, I, pp. 79–80, based on the household book of the Duke of Norfolk formerly in the library of Pembroke College, Cambridge, but now lost or stolen.

20. *Northumberland H.R.*, pp. 340, 343–6. For the Lord of Misrule see also the introduction to *Monumenta Antiqua Anglicana* (London, 1816).

21. *Stonor Letters and Papers*, ed. C. L. Kingsford (Camden Miscellany, XIII, 1924) II, p. 40.

22. Thomas Hearne, *Lelandi Collectanea*, VI (1774) pp. 2–6.

23. *Ibid.* pp. 16–34.

24. M. E. James, *The Life of Sir Rhys ap Thomas* (Tenby, n.d.).

25. *Northumberland H.R.*, pp. 4–29.

26. *Northumberland H.R.*, pp. 23, 24, 253; Ross, 'Household Accounts of Elizabeth Berkeley', pp. 81–105.

27. *Northumberland H.R.*, pp. 53–4. For part-time servants in a great Elizabethan household see *Stanley Papers*, II, pp. 8, 22, 23–4.

28. *The Chronicles of Froissart*, tr. Lord Berners, ed. W. P. Ker (London, 1903) IV, p. 331.

NOTES TO CHAPTER 3

1. *Grosseteste H.R.*, pp. 329, 331.
2. Langland, *Piers Plowman*, Text B, Passus X. 97–101.
3. *Sir Gawain and the Green Knight*, modernized by J. R. Tolkien (London, 1975) p. 26.
4. *Ibid.* pp. 27–8.
5. *Ibid.* ed. Tolkien and Gordon (Oxford, 1925) ll. 807–10.
6. *Ibid.* ll. 1664–7.
7. For the King's Champion see Samuel Lodge, *Scrivelsby: The House of the Champions* (London, 1893) pp. 20–9.
8. Hearne, *Lelandi Collectanea*, VI, pp. 2–6. The Earl Marshal, Lord High Steward and Lord High Constable escorted the first course in on horseback at Coronation banquets up to that of George IV.
9. *The History of the King's Works*, ed. H. Colvin, II (London, 1963) p. 611.
10. For a full list of the sizes of mediaeval halls see Margaret Wood, *English Mediaeval House* (London, 1965) pp. 62–6.
11. *Harleian H.R.*, ff. 25, 33.
12. *Royal H.R.*, p. 148.
13. Langland, *Piers Plowman*, 97–101.
14. E.g. in the house of Canon Thomas Morton of York in 1448, and at Caister Castle in 1459. *Testamenta Eboracensia*, III (Surtees Society, XLV, 1864) pp. 106–115; Caister inventory, *Archaeologia*, XXI (1827) pp. 232–80.
15. *E.E.T.S.*, XXV (1875) p. 87.
16. *Chronicles of Froissart*, VI, pp. 129–34.
17. *Sir Gawain*, p. 46.
18. *Grosseteste H.R.*, p. 331.
19. *E.E.T.S.*, XXV (1975) p. 5.
20. *King's Works*, II, pp. 494–500.
21. *Edward II. H.R.*, e.g. pp. 257, 259, 266.
22. *Edward IV H.R.*, pp. 106, 115, 143.
23. *Nurture H.R.*, p. 71.
24. *Courtesy H.R.*, p. 79.
25. *Harleian H.R.*, f. 26 and *passim*, f. 38v.
26. *Harleian H.R.*, ff. 26–30, 33v–34v.
27. *Edward IV H.R.*, p. 91, *Harleian H.R.*, f. 28v.
28. *Nurture H.R.*, pp. 71–2.
29. See list on pp. 319–20.
30. E.g. *Baron-bishop H.R.* and descriptions in *Chronicles of Froissart*.
31. *Chronicles of Froissart*, IV, p. 331.
32. Quoted Mrs Henry Cust, *Gentlemen Errant* (London, 1909) pp. 38–9.
33. William Harrison, *Elizabethan England*, ed. L. Withington and F. J. Furnivall (1921) p. 95.
34. L. F. Salzmann, *Building in England down to 1540* (Oxford, 1952) pp. 465–6.
35. *Chronicles of Froissart*, I, p. 194.
36. *Courtesy H.R.*, pp. 101–2; *Harleian H.R.*, f. 24.
37. *King's Works*, I, p. 506.
38. Hearne, *Lelandi Collectanea*, V, pp. 363–4.
39. Inventory in Northants Record Office, Stopford-Sackville MS. 2308, published in *Northamptonshire Past and Present*, II (1962) I, p. 17. Sir Henry Vere, the owner, occupied the parlour chamber.
40. Dudley inventory, *Archaeologia*, LXXI (1921) pp. 39–42. Dudley occupied the great chamber and kept his papers and money in the closet within it.
41. *Northumberland H.R.*, p. 99.
42. P.R.O. inventories, Prob. 2/199 (1508). The inventory needs to be treated with caution as its membranes appear to have been restitched in the wrong order.
43. *E.E.T.S.*, XXV (1875) p. 4.
44. *Courtesy H.R.*, p. 100.
45. *Royal H.R.*, p. 148.
46. *King's Works*, II, p. 926.
47. *Archaeologia*, LXXI (1921) pp. 39–42.
48. *Harleian H.R.*, f. 23.
49. There are or were other mediaeval chapel galleries at e.g. Ashby-de-la-Zouch, Bolton Castle, Chibburn (Northumberland), East Hendred (Berkshire), and Blackmoor (Somerset).
50. Inventory (*Archaeologia*, LXVI (1915) pp. 320–48) apparently for a house within the precinct of Colne Priory, Essex, of which the earl was patron.
51. For a further account of privies see Ch. 9, pp. 246–7.
52. *The Paston Letters*, II, pp. 281–2.
53. As far as I know, this explanation of the origins of the terms has not been advanced before.
54. *King's Works*, II, pp. 935–6.
55. *Troilus and Criseyde*, II. i. 78–154.
56. E.g. Horton, c. 1425 (*Stonor Papers*, I, p. 43); Caister Castle, 1459 (*Archaeologia*, XXI (1827) pp. 232–80); Mautby, Norfolk, 1482 (*Paston Letters*, VI, pp. 46–53); Addington, 1493 (*Northamptonshire Past and Present*, II (1962) I, p. 17).
57. *Montacute House* (National Trust Guide, 1977) p. 27.
58. For such spaces off the hall see Wood, *English Mediaeval House*, pp. 99–121.
59. D. J. C. King and J. C. Perks, 'Carew Castle, Pembrokeshire', *Archaelogical Journal*, CXIX (1962) pp. 270–307.

60. M. Binney, 'The Bishop's Palace, Wells', *Country Life*, CLVIII, pp. 1666, 1738.

61. For the inventory see n. 14. The position of both halls can be traced in the surviving ruins.

62. Information J. T. Smith, from forthcoming R.C.H.M. volume on mediaeval houses of Hertfordshire.

63. *Harleian H.R.*, f. 38; *Derby H.R.*, p. 9, forbids 'slaves or boys' to eat in the hall. Hinds' halls are shown by Thorpe at Slaugham, Sussex, and on two designs possibly for Burley-on-the-Hill, Rutland (*The Book of Architecture of John Thorpe*, ed. John Summerson (Walpole Society, XL, London, 1966) Pls 39, 48, 109). There was a 'carters' hall' at Ingatestone in 1601 (Inventory, Essex Record Office Publications, No. 22).

64. *King's Works*, I, pp. 506–7.

65. Hearne, *Lelandi Collectanea*, VI, pp. 2–6.

66. For part-time officials see *Northumberland H.R.*, pp. 53–4. For multi-hall castles see P. A. Faulkner, 'Castle Planning in the Fourteenth Century', *Archaeological Journal*, CXX (1963) pp. 215–35.

67. *Harleian H.R.*, ff. 32v, 33, 37v, 38v.

68. For Ely see Wood, *English Mediaeval House*, p. 26 and Fig. 9.

69. Plan reproduced *King's Works*, II, p. 913 (from Borenius and Charlton, 'Clarendon Palace: an Interim Report', *Antiquaries Journal*, XVI (1936)).

70. Binney, 'Bishop's Palace, Wells', pp. 1666, 1738.

71. Thomas Tropenell of Great Chalfield worked for the Hungerford family as steward or in some other senior capacity, but is also said to have 'had the livery' of Henry VI and Edward IV. *The Tropenell Cartulary*, ed. J. S. Davies (Devizes, 1908) pp. X–XIV.

72. The twelfth-century Sherborne castle in Dorset, a rectangular building with small internal courtyard, seems to have had little influence.

73. Fantosme's *Chronicle* of the rebellion of 1173–4 (Surtees Society, II, 1839) p. 15, l. 267.

74. For a list of great towers see Wood, *English Mediaeval House*, pp. 175–6.

75. W. D. Simpson, 'Bastard Feudalism and the Later Castles', *Antiquaries Journal*, XXVI (1946) pp. 145–71.

76. J. C. Hodgson, *History of Northumberland*, V (Newcastle, 1899) pp. 57, 61.

77. Inventory in Huntington, Huntingdon MS. L5/B1.

78. See W. D. Simpson, 'Buckden Palace', *Journal British Archaeological Association*, 3rd series, II (1937) pp. 121–32.

79. The 'unit system', providing self-contained accommodation apparently for two members of the same family in one complex is discussed (mainly in a sixteenth- and seventeenth-century context) by R. Machin in 'The Unit System: Some Historical Explanations', *Archaeological Journal*, CXXXII (1975) pp. 187–94.

80. *Stanley Papers*, II, pp. 63, 89.

81. *The Itinerary of John Leland*, ed. L. Toulmin Smith (London, 1907) I, p. 46.

82. E. P. Shirley, *Some Account of English Deer Parks* (London, 1807) pp. 21–2.

83. *The Travels of Cosmo III through England*, ed. L. Magalotti (London, 1821) p. 331.

84. E. Hasted, *History of Kent* (Canterbury, 1778) I, p. 19; G. Puttenham, *Arte of English Poesie*, ed. Willcock and Walker (Cambridge, 1936) p. 268.

85. W. Weber, *Metrical Romances* (1810) II, p. 285.

86. H. S. Bennett, *Life on the English Manor* (Cambridge, 1937) pp. 262–4.

87. *Nurture H.R.*, ed. Furnivall, p. 195.

88. *Canterbury Tales*, Prologue, ll. 99–100.

NOTES TO CHAPTER 4

1. The Derby household books and regulations were edited, with valuable biographical footnotes, by F. R. Raines for the Chetham Society as *Stanley Papers*, II (Chetham Society, XXXI, 1853).

2. See 'An Account of how the Earl of Worcester lived in Raglan Castle before the Civil Wars', *Northumberland H.R.*, p. 419.

3. For Burghley's household see R. C. Barnett, *Place, Profit and Power: A Study of the Servants of William Cecil, Elizabethan Statesman* (Chapel Hill, 1969).

4. See list on p. 320.

5. References on p. 41 of R.B.'s treatise suggest he was in the household of the third Earl of Huntingdon in the 1580s. A possible suggestion is Robert Bainbridge, for whom see J. Nichols, *History and Antiquities of the County of Leicester: West Goscote Hundred* (London, 1804) p. 632.

6. See Barnett, *Place, Profit and Power*, pp. 50–55; M. Girouard, 'Trevalyn' and 'Plas Teg', *Country Life*, CXXXII, pp. 78–81, CXXXIV, pp. 134–7.

7. For the two duchesses and their marriages, see D.N.B. The attribution of the well-known portrait by Hans Eworth (Coll. Wynne-Finch) as being of the duchess and Adrian Stokes is almost certainly incorrect.

8. *The Autobiography of Thomas Whythorne*, ed. J. M. Osborn (Oxford, 1961 and (modern spelling) 1962).

9. *Romeo and Juliet*, I. v. 9–11.

10. E. Carleton Williams, *Bess of Hardwick* (London, 1959) p. 258; Stone, *Crisis of the Aristocracy*, p. 209.

11. Quoted *Babees Book*, p. IX.

12. Francis Peck, *Desiderata Curiosa*, II (1779) p. 255; David Durant, *Bess of Hardwick: Portrait of an Elizabethan Dynast* (London, 1977) p. 150.

13. Bodleian, Ashmole MS. 836, p. 235.

14. Stone, *Crisis of the Aristocracy*, pp. 201–11, from which the examples in this paragraph are drawn.

15. In *Huntingdon H.R.* (1609), 'retainer' is used in the sense of servants (such as foresters and bailiffs) on the payroll but not resident in the household, i.e. in something approaching its modern use.

16. Smyth, *Lives of the Berkeleys*, pp. 364–5.

17. Stone, *Crisis of the Aristocracy*, pp. 484, 516, 528, 778.

18. Durant, *Bess of Hardwick*, p. 169, and information kindly supplied by the author.

19. '*R.B.*' *H.R.*, p. 11.

20. For a discussion of devices, especially in relation to Elizabethan architecture see Girouard, *Robert Smythson and the Architecture of the Elizabethan Era*, pp. 35–42.

21. For an analysis of such Elizabethan attitudes and beliefs see E. M. W. Tillyard, *The Elizabethan World Picture* (London, 1943).

22. 'Raby Castle', *Country Life*, CXLVI, p. 153.

23. The importance of family prayers is stressed in many sixteenth and early-seventeenth-century household regulations. See also Lawrence Stone, *The Family, Sex and Marriage in England, 1500–1800* (London, 1977) pp. 154–5.

24. *Donegall H.R.*, p. 322.

25. According to Elizabethan and Jacobean practice, cloths of estate (of varying type, according to degree) were only allowed to those of the rank of earl and above (e.g. *A Booke of Precedence*, ed. Furnivall (E.E.T.S., E.S. VIII, 1869); Huntington, Ellesmere MS. EL 1118) or viscount and above (B.M. Add. MS. 6032).

26. J. G. Gage, *History and Antiquities of Hengrave* (London, 1822) p. 22. The original now in Gage MSS., University Library, Cambridge.

27. J. Nichols, *Progresses of James I* (London, 1828) II, pp. 145–52.

28. Huntington, Ellesmere MSS.

29. Roger North, *Of Building*, B.M. Add. MS. 32540, f. 51v.

30. '*R.B.*' *H.R.*, p. 44.

31. The Toddington carving is now in the Victoria and Albert Museum, London.

32. *Montagu H.R.*, p. 128.

33. *Berkeley H.R.*, p. 419.

34. Huntington, Ellesmere MS. EL 1118.

35. B.M. Add. MS. 38141, ff. 8–9. Amongst other numerous surviving MS. regulations for sixteenth and seventeenth-century funerals are the Ellesmere MS. (n. 34) of 1587; College of Arms MS. Vincent's Precedents 151 (1610); Bodleian, Ashmole MS. 836 (funerals of various dates). See also Stone, *Crisis of the Aristocracy*, pp. 572–9.

36. Smyth, *Lives of the Berkeleys*, II, p. 408.

37. Burghley to Hatton, 10 Aug. 1579, quoted in E. S. Hartshorne, *History of Holdenby* (1868).

38. This seems to have happened at Slaugham Hall in Sussex. See *Book of Architecture of John Thorpe*, p. 104 and Pls 109–11.

39. George Whetstone. *An Heptameron of Civil Discourses* (London, 1582) H. 11.

40. Inventory, P.R.O., Prob. 2/122.

41. *Montagu H.R.*, p. 129 (20).

42. Whetstone, *Civil Discourses*, C.1 (verso).

43. *Diary of Lady Anne Clifford*, ed. V. Sackville-West (London, 1923) pp. 62, 63.

44. E.g. in designs by Robert Smythson for an unidentified house, *c.* 1600 (R.I.B.A., Smythson 11/2) and John Smythson for Bolsover Castle, *c.* 1630 (R.I.B.A., Smythson 111/1(4)).

45. Galleries appear to have originated in France. In 1440 Bernardinus of Toulouse referred to 'ambulacrum quos nos galeriam vocamus'. See N. Pevsner, *A History of Building Types* (London, 1976) p. 112, and accompanying footnote.

46. Hearne, *Lelandi Collectanea*, VI, pp. 2–6.

47. Dudley inventory, *Archaeologia*, LXXI (1921) pp. 39–42.

48. *Archaeologia*, XXV (1834) p. 312 (Thornbury); *Archaeologia*, LXXI (1921) pp. 39–42 (Exeter House); J. Nichols, *Progresses of Queen Elizabeth*, 2nd edn (London, 1821–3) p. 413 (Richmond).

49. While exercising on the leads of his house Sir Thomas was accosted by a lunatic who threatened to throw him over the parapet.

50. B.M. Harleian MS. 1419.

51. Hatfield House MS. Family Papers 3370.

52. Edmund Lodge, *Illustrations of British History* (London, 1791) III, p. 336.

53. Inventory, Essex Record Office Publications, No. 22.

54. Nichols, *Progresses of James I*, II, pp. 128–31.

55. *Faerie Queene*, II. ix. 33–4.

56. *The Taming of the Shrew*, v. ii. 102; *Countess of Pembroke's Arcadia*, ed. A. Feuillerat (Cambridge, 1912) p. 29.

57. Shovelboards were shaped and used like very large-scale shove-halfpenny boards. An example, made in 1702, survives at Boughton in Northamptonshire (ill. *Country Life*, CXLVIII, p. 568).

58. B.M. Lansdowne MS. 118, ff. 37–40.

59. G. C. Williamson, *Lady Anne Clifford* (1922) p. 477.

60. *Bridgwater H.R.*, p. 55.

61. '*R.B.*' *H.R.*, p. 11.

62. Inventory in Huntington, Huntingdon MS. L5/B1.

63. For a useful account of voids, desserts and banquets (but without references) see G. B. Hughes, 'The Old English Banquet', *Country Life*, CXVII, p. 474.

64. Markham, *The English Housewife* (1615). There are numerous recipes for banquets in Sir Hugh Plat, *Delightes for Ladies* (1602) ed. G. E. and K. R. Fussell (London, 1948).

65. Smyth, *Lives of the Berkeleys*, II, p. 362.

66. Richard Carew of Anthony, *The Survey of Cornwall, etc.*, ed. F. E. Halliday (London, 1953) pp. 175–6. Bourne Mill, Colchester (ill. Pevsner, *Buildings of England: Essex*, Fig. 53) is a converted banqueting-cum-fishing lodge of 1591.

67. A plan and elevation of the Holdenby banqueting house are in *The Book of Architecture of John Thorpe*, Pl. 84. It is shown on a Holdenby survey of 1585 but not on one of 1580 (Northants Record Office).

68. Thomas Fuller, *The Worthies of England*, 1st edn (1662) p. 280.

69. Hunting lodges are a building type in much need of further research.

70. *Countess of Pembroke's Arcadia*, p. 91.

71. *Much Ado about Nothing*, II. i. 224.

72. *Stanley Papers*, II, p. 89.

73. See especially *Royal H.R.*, pp. 109–29. (Henry VII, 1494) and pp. 137–239 (Henry VIII, 1526).

74. Thomas Platter, *Travels in England*, ed. Clare Williams (1937) pp. 193–5.

75. The incorporation of a royal coat of arms into a chimney-piece is therefore no evidence that it derives from a royal palace. The 'Holbein' fireplace at Reigate Privy, for instance, is more likely to have always been at Reigate than to have been removed from Nonsuch or some other royal residence, as has frequently been suggested from the time of Evelyn onwards.

76. Nichols, *Progresses of Elizabeth*, III, pp. 101–2.

77. *Ibid.* II, pp. 400–4.

78. For Theobalds see John Summerson, 'The Building of Theobalds', *Archaeologia*, XCVII (1959).

79. Hartshorne, *History of Holdenby*.

80. Lawrence Stone, *Family and Fortune: Studies in Aristocratic Finance in the Sixteenth and Seventeenth Centuries* (Oxford, 1973) pp. 3–160.

81. The existence of this arrangement is suggested by an analysis of Thorpe's plan. (*Architecture of John Thorpe*, Pl. 85) and by the fact that under royal ownership the house was similarly divided into king's and queen's lodgings (Parliamentary Survey, 1650, quoted in Hartshorne, *History of Holdenby*).

82. This is my own analysis of Audley End. Unfortunately no seventeenth-century plan of its first floor survives. The two porches are suggestive of later king's and queen's entrances planned, for instance, for Greenwich, Hampton Court and Winchester.

83. E.g. at Holdenby, Castle Ashby and Audley End.

84. Inventory of 1611, Hatfield papers.

85. There are or were best lodgings and great chambers on the second floor at Charlton House (Kent), Chatsworth, Theobalds (before its final enlargement) and, almost certainly, Holdenby.

86. See Fuller, *Worthies of England*, p. 280.

87. Durant, *Bess of Hardwick*, p. 205.

NOTES TO CHAPTER 5

1. *Architecture of John Thorpe*, p. 29. The surviving house is Somerhill, Kent (*c.* 1610–13).

2. E.g. Plas Teg, Flintshire (*c.* 1610); Charlton, Kent (1607).

3. O. Hill and J. Cornforth, *English Country Houses: Caroline* (London, 1966) pp. 75–89.

4. John Harris, 'Inigo Jones and the Prince's Lodging at Newmarket', *Architectural History*, II (1959) pp. 26–40; M. Whinney, 'John Webb's drawings for Whitehall Palace', *Walpole Society*, XXXI (1943) p. 45.

5. North, *Of Building*, f. 40v (see Ch. 4, n. 29).

6. A set of plans and drawings in the R.I.B.A. show all three floors of Raynham as arranged for a visit of Charles II and the Duke of York in 1671.

7. *The Architecture of Sir Roger Pratt*, ed. R. T. Gunther (Oxford, 1928) p. 64.

8. Kingston Lacy, Dorset, 1663–5; Horseheath, Cambs., 1663–5 (wings added *c.* 1700); Clarendon House, Piccadilly, 1664–7.

9. Charles II dined in the great room at the Mauritshuis on the eve of his return to England in 1660. The dinner is depicted in an engraving in Sir William Lower, *A Relation of the Voyage and Residence which Charles the II hath made in Holland (1660)*.

10. For a valuable account of French (and other) palace planning at this period, see H. M. Baillie, 'State Apartments in Baroque Palaces', *Archaeologia*, CI (1967) p. 169.

11. *Charles II H.R.*, Add. order 5.

12. Webb's designs for the king's bedchamber recess at Greenwich are in the R.I.B.A. Drawings Collection.

13. By the mid seventeenth century 'cabinet council' had become an accepted term for any inner group, and it is possible that the term was applied to Charles II's inner ring of ministers in this general sense rather than because they met in his cabinet.

14. *The Diary of Samuel Pepys*, ed. R. Lathum and W. Matthews (London, 1970 etc.) V, pp. 188–9.

15. He built one wing of a new palace at Greenwich and the shell of a palace at Winchester.

16. The house as built was rather simpler than the design reproduced as Pl. 75.

17. Isaac Ware, *Complete Body of Architecture* (London, 1756) p. 335.

18. Description by Henry Pelate, ed. H. C. Brentnall, 'A Longford Manuscript', *Wiltshire Archaeology and Natural History Magazine*, LII (1947) p. 39.

19. Huntington, Stowe MS. ST24, I/282.

20. See p. 123. John Webb's unexecuted plans for Belvoir, *c.* 1654, show separate servants' and steward's dining rooms leading off the main entrance hall (R.I.B.A.).

21. North, *Of Building*, f. 48v.

22. *Architecture of Roger Pratt*, p. 62.

23. See North, *Of Building*, f. 40v. The treatise is full of shrewd comment and interesting examples, and deserves publication.

24. *Ibid.* f. 59v.

25. *Architecture of Roger Pratt*, p. 64.

26. The original arrangement at Kinross is shown in a plan of *c.* 1684 reproduced by J. G. Dunbar, 'Kinross House', *The Country Seat*, ed. H. Colvin and J. Harris (1970) p. 64.

27. *Stanley Papers*, II, pp. 123–7; Williamson, *Lady Anne Clifford*, p. 477.

28. Huntington, Stowe MS. ST 44/37–8.

29. *Chandos H.R.*, orders for usher of the hall.

30. C. H. and M. I. Collins Baker, *The Life and Circumstances of James Brydges, First Duke of Chandos* (Oxford, 1949) pp. 174–5.

31. Table seating and wages at Cannons are given in Huntington, Stowe MS. ST 44/27–30.

32. E.g. *Courtesy H.R.*, p. 320; Cavendish, *Thomas Wolsey*, Ch. V; Gage, *History of Hengrave*, p. 190.

33. At Raglan Castle in the 1630s footmen were waiting at the second table in the great chamber and the steward's table in the hall (*Northumberland H.R.*, p. 419). In the 1660s control of the Earl of Bedford's footmen was being disputed between the house steward and the gentleman of the horse (G. Scott-Thomson, *Life in a Noble Household* (London, 1937) p. 118).

34. Huntington, Stowe MS. ST 24, *passim*.

35. The household at Badminton is described in Roger North, *Lives of the Norths*, ed. A. Jessopp (1905) I, p. 172.

36. *The Journeys of Celia Fiennes*, ed. C. Morris (London, 1947) p. 334.

37. For contemporary theory, see *Patriarcha and other Political Works of Sir Robert Filmer*, ed. P. Laslett (Oxford, 1949) pp. 174–5.

38. Stratford Hall, Virginia (*Country Life*, CXLV, pp. 118–21) is a perfect example of a small formal house of *c.* 1730.

39. Obadiah Walker, mostly on the basis of an Italian book of etiquette *Il Maestro di Camera*, describes these and similar niceties in *Of Education*, 6th edn, pp. 224–6. *The Travels of Cosmo III through England*, are full of actual examples in an English context.

40. J. Dallaway, *West Sussex* (1832) II, p. 329 (quoting *Annals of Reign of Q. Anne* (1704) II, App. 3).

41. Nottingham University, Portland MS. PWB/79. B.M. Add. MS. 22226, f. 79.

42. A lively satirical poem describing the Duke of Argyll's levée in the early eighteenth century is in Nottingham University, Portland MS. PWV/718.

43. See 'The Political Function of Charles II's Chiffinch', *Huntington Library Quarterly*, XXXIX (1976) pp. 277–90.

44. For Dr Johnson's supposed indignation at being kept waiting by Lord Chesterfield while Colley Cibber was introduced by the backstairs, see Boswell's *Life*, Everyman edn (London, 1906) I, p. 153.

45. Goldsmith, *Double Transformation* (1765) quoted in O.E.D.

46. Evelyn, *Diary*, 4 October 1683.

47. See Ch. 3 p. 54 and n. 41.

48. North, *Of Building*, f. 61.

49. E.g. at Easton Neston, *c.* 1685.

50. North, *Of Building*, ff. 26v–27.

51. The bed was originally on a raised dais, probably behind a balustrade. A reconstruction in model form is on show at Ham House.

52. In contemporary records it is described as the ante-room, painted room or upper saloon. F. Thompson, *A History of Chatsworth* (London, 1949).

53. North, *Of Building*, f. 57v.

54. The much reproduced plan of Blenheim in *Vitruvius Britannicus* can be usefully supplemented by that in Kip and Knyff, *Nouveau Théâtre de la Grande Bretague* (1714–16), I, which gives the arrangement of the basement.

55. Macky, *Journey through England* (London, 1724) II, p. 106.

56. For villas see John Summerson, 'The Idea of the

Villa', *Journal of the Royal Society of Arts*, CXVII (1959) pp. 570–86.

57. Macky, *Journey through England*, I, pp. 20–1.

58. Joyce Godber, 'Marchioness Grey of Wrest Park', *Bedfordshire Historical Society*, XLVII (1968) p. 142, quoting diary of Philip Yorke.

59. *Lord Hervey and his Friends, 1726–38*, ed. Earl of Ilchester (1950) p. 71.

60. *Ibid.*

61. H.M.C., *Earl of Carlisle*, p. 85.

NOTES TO CHAPTER 6

1. Quoted in Stone, *Crisis of the Aristocracy*, p. 674.

2. See K. B. McFarlane, *The Nobility of Later Mediaeval England* (Oxford, 1973) Ch. 6.

3. *Northumberland H.R.*, pp. 99, 101, 378, 452.

4. Quoted *ibid.* pp. 452–3.

5. *Testamenta Eboracensia*, I (Surtees Society, IV, 1836) pp. 398–402.

6. Thomas Elyot, *The Booke named the Governour*, Everyman edn (1907) pp. 34–41.

7. Stone, *Crisis of the Aristocracy*, p. 676.

8. S. Jayne, *Library Catalogues of the English Renaissance* (Berkeley and Los Angeles, 1956) pp. 93–172.

9. *Ibid.* In 1545 Vincent Mundy had 15 books at Markeaton Hall, of which 6 were kept in the chapel and 9 in his closet or study.

10. *Ibid.* p. 136; J. Evans, 'Extracts from the private account book of Sir William More', *Archaeologia*, XXXVI (1885) pp. 290–2.

11. R.I.B.A., Smythson drawings 11/13.

12. *Diary of Lady Anne Clifford*, p. 66.

13. See John Harris, 'A rare and precious room: the Kederminster Library, Langley, Buckinghamshire', *Country Life*, 1 Dec. 1977, pp. 1576–9.

14. North, *Lives of the Norths*, I, p. 231.

15. Inventories of 1679 and 1683 (typescript copies in Victoria and Albert Museum, Dept. of Furniture).

16. B.M. Harleian MS. 1419.

17. For virtuosos see Walter E. Houghton, 'The English Virtuoso in the Seventeenth Century', *Journal of the History of Ideas*, III (1942) on which I have drawn heavily for this portion of the chapter.

18. *Ibid.* p. 56.

19. Henry Peacham *The Compleat Gentleman*, reprint of 1634 edn, ed. Gordon (1906) pp. 160–1.

20. Houghton, 'English Virtuoso', p. 65.

21. Inventory of 1679 (n. 15).

22. Evelyn, *Diaries*, 29 Sept. 1645.

23. *Tatler*, No. 216, 26 Aug. 1710.

24. Houghton, 'English Virtuoso', p. 212.

25. *Ibid.* p. 193.

26. Shaftesbury, *Characteristics*, 1723 edn, I, p. 338.

27. An eminent result of this attitude of mind was the Society of Dilettanti, for which see L. Cust, *History of the Society of Dilettanti* (London, 1898).

28. Horace Walpole, *A Description of Strawberry Hill* (Strawberry Hill, 1784) pp. 55–71.

29. *The Diary of Sylas Neville*, ed. Basil Cozens-Hardy (Oxford, 1950) pp. 329, 331.

30. Godber, 'Marchioness Grey of Wrest Park', p. 30.

31. *Correspondence of Emily, Duchess of Leinster* (Irish MSS. Commission, 1949 etc.) I, p. 18.

NOTES TO CHAPTER 7

1. For the Duke of Somerset, see relevant entries in the D.N.B. and *Complete Peerage*.

2. But the Duke of Norfolk was still dining under a canopy at Norfolk House in the 1750s (Diaries of Countess of Pomfret).

3. Goldsmith, *The Life of Richard Nash of Bath, Esq.* (London, 1772) p. 36.

4. There is an admirable contemporary analysis of the connection between property and interest in a letter written by Lord Strafford to his wife in 1729, B.M. Add. MS. 22226, ff. 427–9.

5. *Diaries of a Duchess*, ed. J. Greig (1926) p. 35.

6. *Chandos H.R.*, orders for usher of the hall.

7. B.M. Add. MS. 33137, f. 472.

8. E.g. Henry Pulteney to Elizabeth Montagu, 1764, Huntington, Montagu MS. MO 4204.

9. For contemporary theories of government, see especially P. Laslett's edn of J. Locke, *Two Treatises of Government* (Cambridge, 1960).

10. *Passages from the Diaries of Mrs. Lybbe Powys*, ed. E. J. Climenson (London, 1899) pp. 24–5, 50.

11. *Evelina*, Letter LXIII.

12. E.g. *Autobiography and Correspondence of Mrs. Delany* (London, 1861–2) 1st series, I, p. 224.

13. Quoted in O.E.D. under 'Assembly'.

14. B.M. Add. MS. 22227, f. 209.

15. Ware, *Complete Body of Architecture*, p. 434.

16. For a good description of an assembly of this type (given in Dublin in 1731) see *Delany*, I, 1, p. 305.

17. See *The Survey of London*, ed. F. H. W. Sheppard, XXIX (1960) pp. 287–302; Desmond Fitz-Gerald, *The Norfolk House Music Room* (Victoria and Albert Museum, London, 1973).

18. From R. O. Cambridge's *Elegy written in an empty Assembly Room*, quoted in Fitz-Gerald, *Norfolk House Music Room*, p. 49.

19. Fitz-Gerald, *Norfolk House Music Room*, pp. 48–9.

20. In the anonymous *Critical Observations on the Buildings and Improvements of London* (1771).

21. See Marcus Binney, 'The Villas of Sir Robert Taylor', *Country Life*, CXLII, pp. 17–21, 78–82.

22. *Diaries of Lybbe Powys*, p. 247.

23. For Hagley see Hussey, *Country Houses: Early Georgian*, pp. 195–9.

24. Eighteenth-century household regulations are uninformative about the serving of meals. My account is mainly based on contemporary descriptions, pictures, and diagrams of the table lay out for courses, and Swift's satirical *Directions to Servants* (1745) new edn (Oxford, 1959).

25. *Ibid.* (1959) p. 17.

26. Hussey, *Country Houses: Early Georgian*, p. 196.

27. *The Double Dealer* (1694) I. 1.

28. An extra entry (described as 'added since') in the 1679 inventory (Ch. 6, n. 15).

29. *Works in Architecture of R. and J. Adam*, I (London, 1778) pp. 8–9.

30. E.g. Herbert Pugh's caricature of Lord Granard in his dressing room (*c.* 1771) reproduced in J. Cornforth and J. Fowler, *English Decoration in the Eighteenth Century* (London, 1974) Fig. 200.

31. E.g. John Macdonald, *Memoirs of an Eighteenth-Century Footman*, ed. J. Beresford (London, 1927) p. 46; William Adam, *Remarks on the Blair Adam Estate* (1834) p. 111.

32. *Retrospections of Dorothea Herbert*, ed. G. F. Mandeville (London, 1929–30) I, p. 68.

33. *Pembroke Papers*, ed. Earl of Pembroke (London, 1950) pp. 299, 304.

34. Lord Petre's household at Thorndon in 1742 contained 19 men and 14 women. Lord Salisbury's household at Hatfield in 1797 contained 18 men and 18 women (Essex Record Office, D/DP Z14/10; Hatfield MS. Family Papers XI, p. 177). Both totals inclusive of indoor and stable servants only.

35. At Holdenby there was a 'still-house' under the water cistern in the conduit house in the garden, probably dating from the 1570s (Parliamentary Survey, 1650 quoted in Hartshorne, *History of Holdenby*).

36. For the skill of Queen Elizabeth's gentlewomen in 'devising delicate dishes' and 'distillation of waters' see Harrison, *Elizabethan England*, p. 219.

37. Gage, *History of Hengrave*, pp. 36–7.

38. Distilled waters still figure prominently in Samuel and Sarah Adams, *The Complete Servant* (London, 1825) pp. 176–90.

39. Alice Archer-Houblon, *The Houblon Family* (1907) II, pp. 118–52.

40. See Martin Drury, 'The Architecture of Fishing', *Country Life*, CLII, pp. 202–4.

41. *Diaries of Lybbe Powys*, p. 119.

42. Plan in *Vitruvius Britannicus*, V, reproduced in Christopher Hussey, *English Country Houses: Mid Georgian* (London, 1956), p. 63, and M. Mauchline, *Harewood House* (Newton Abbot, 1974) Fig. 3.

NOTES TO CHAPTER 8

1. *Diaries of Lybbe Powys*, p. 165.

2. *Ibid.* pp. 166–7.

3. Godber, 'Marchioness Grey of Wrest Park', pp. 93–5.

4. For hunting see Raymond Carr, *English Foxhunting: A History* (London, 1976).

5. See Ch. 9, pp. 264–5.

6. The plan is given in Paine, *Plans, Elevations and Sections of Noblemen's and Gentlemen's Houses*, Vol. I.

7. For Longford see G. Richardson, *New Vitruvius Britannicus*, I (1802–8).

8. For Luscombe see Christopher Hussey, *English Country Houses: Late Georgian* (London, 1958) pp. 55–65.

9. For Sandridge see Terence Davis, *The Architecture of John Nash* (London, 1960) p. 27 and plan.

10. A superb surviving *cottage ornée* which may be by Nash is the Swiss Cottage Cahir (*Country Life*, CXL, pp. 688–91).

11. David Watkin, *Thomas Hope 1769–1831, and the Neo-classical Idea* (London, 1968) pp. 158–92.

12. H. J. Todd, *A History of the College of Bonhommes at Ashridge* (London, 1823) p. 74.

13. C. Hussey, 'Wimpole Hall, Cambridgeshire, III', *Country Life*, CXLII, pp. 1594–7.

14. For examples, see the plans of Putney Park, Surrey, *c.* 1794 (Richardson, *New Vitruvius Britannicus*, I, 1802–8); Donington Park, Leics., 1790–1800; Lislee, Cork, *c.* 1803; Loudoun Castle, Ayrshire; Osterton Hall, Notts., *c.* 1806 (all *New Vitruvius Britannicus*, II, 1808–10).

15. John Aubrey, *Brief Lives and other Selected Writings*, ed. A. Powell (London, 1949) pp. 33, 356.

16. See Ch. 5, pp. 161–2.

17. For the decline of the arranged marriage in English upper-class society see Stone, *The Family, Sex and Marriage*, especially Ch. 7.

18. Brian Fitzgerald, *Emily, Duchess of Leinster* (1949) p. 166.

19. Pückler-Muskau, *Tour in England*, III, pp. 313–14, describing luncheon at Cobham Hall, Kent, in 1827.

20. For a blow-by-blow description of a country-house dinner see *ibid.* pp. 83–7.

21. *Diaries of Lybbe Powys*, pp. 197–8.

22. M. Edgeworth, *Letters from England, 1813–44*, ed. C. Colvin (Oxford, 1971) pp. 84, 91.

23. T. F. Dibdin, *Aedes Althorpianae* (London, 1822) I, pp. 27, 31.

24. *Handbook to Chatsworth and Hardwick* (1845).

25. Derek Linstrum, *Sir Jeffry Wyatville* (Oxford, 1972) p. 158; P. Howell and T. W. Pritchard, 'Wynnstay, Denbighshire, III', *Country Life*, CLI, pp. 851–2.

26. *Diaries of Lybbe Powys*, pp. 238–40, 244–5.

27. W. Mavor, *New Description of Blenheim*, new edn (1789) pp. 41–2.

28. Repton, *Fragments*, p. 58.

29. Edgeworth, *Ormond*, opening of Ch. I.

30. *The Diary of Fanny Burney*, ed. L. Gibbs (London, 1940) pp. 79–85. And see p. 22 (January 1779) for another example of circle-breaking.

31. Pückler-Muskau, *Tour in England*, IV, p. 333.

32. *Ibid.* p. 261.

33. Newspaper cuttings at Hatfield, filed in Hatfield Family Papers XI, p. 150 and Supp. 4, p. 173.

34. Pückler-Muskau, *Tour in England*, IV, pp. 339–40. Breakfasts of this sort seem indistinguishable from the 'fêtes champêtres' and 'déjeuners champêtres' also given at the period.

35. The scene is vividly evoked in a painting of 1835, by W. F. Witherington, at Petworth.

36. *A Narrative of the Preparations at Hatfield House*, printed for J. J. Stockdale (London, 1818).

37. H.M.C., *Manuscripts of J. B. Fortescue*, 13th Report, App. 3 (1892) I, pp. 433–4.

38. *The Wynne Diaries*, ed. A. Freemantle (1940) III, *passim*.

39. *Ibid.* p. 147.

40. Huntington, Montagu MS. MO 3647.

41. *Ibid.* and Montagu MSS. MO 3896 and 3644.

42. J. Seacane, *The Eaton Tourist* (1825); J. and J. C. Buckler, *Views of Eaton Hall in Cheshire* (1826).

43. Alistair Rowan, 'Eastnor Castle, Herefordshire, I', *Country Life*, CXLIII, p. 527 and Fig. 2.

44. G. G. Scott, *Secular and Domestic Architecture* (London, 1857) p. 147.

45. A. W. Pugin, *True Principles of Pointed or Christian Architecture* (London, 1841) pp. 48–9.

NOTES TO CHAPTER 9

1. *King's Works*, I, pp. 549–50.

2. W. H. St J. Hope, *Windsor Castle, An Architectural History* (1913) p. 61.

3. Parker, *Some Account of Domestic Mediaeval Architecture in England*, II (1853).

4. For a drawing of the cloister cistern see B.M. Add. MS. 15544, ff. 94–7.

5. Beckley, complete with privies, was the model for Crome in *Crome Yellow*, by Aldous Huxley.

6. Hope, *Windsor Castle*, pp. 156–8.

7. For a contemporary description of the conduit house erected at Shrewsbury in 1578–9 see 'Dr. Taylor's MS.', *Trans. Shropshire Archaeological Society*, III (communicated by Derek Sherborne).

8. Surveys of Holdenby 1580 and 1585 (Northants Record Office); Parliamentary Survey, 1650 (Hartshorne, *History of Holdenby*); Girouard, *Robert Smythson and the Architecture of the Elizabethan Era*, pp. 99–100.

9. For donkey and horse powered wheels see the article and list by H. Brunner and J. K. Major, *Industrial Archaeology*, IX (1972) pp. 117–51.

10. Stallybrass, 'Bess of Hardwick's Buildings and Building Accounts', *Archaeologia*, LXIV (1913) pp. 368–9.

11. 'The Hardwick Hall Inventories of 1601', ed. L. Boynton, *J. of the Furniture History Society*, VII (1971) p. 32.

12. Wood, *English Mediaeval House*, p. 387.

13. Pelate, 'A Longford Manuscript', p. 33.

14. *Country Life*, XXVII, p. 896.

15. Hardwick building accounts (information from D. Durant).

16. D.N.B., Ford.

17. D.N.B.; Hope, *Windsor Castle*, p. 322; Evelyn, *Diaries*, 16 June 1683.

18. Evelyn, *Diaries*, 16 Oct. 1671; 10 Sept. 1677.

19. Hussey, *Country Houses: Mid Georgian*, p. 29.

20. *Journeys of Celia Fiennes*, pp. 55–7.

21. *Complete Works of Sir John Vanbrugh* (London, 1928) IV (the *Letters*, ed. G. F. Webb) pp. 32–3; Kerry Downes, *Hawksmoor* (London, 1959) p. 236.

22. Stephen Switzer, *An Introduction to a General System of Hydrostatics and Hydraulics* (London, 1729) pp. 326–8, with illustration.

23. *Ibid.* p. 334.

24. The design is at Houghton. Surviving brass cocks piped to the wall and originally feeding into cisterns from the shells of the marble tables in the dining room appear to be part of the eighteenth-century system.

25. Summerson, 'The Building of Theobalds'; D.N.B., John Harington; Aubrey, *Brief Lives*, p. 194.

26. *Diary*, 19 May.

27. *King's Works*, V, pp. 176, 412–13.

28. Drawings in Bodleian Library, MS. Gough Drawings a. 2, f. 72.

29. *Journeys of Celia Fiennes*, pp. 358–9.

30. *Ibid.* pp. 345–7.

31. *Ibid.* p. 100.

32. Francis Thompson, *History of Chatsworth* (London, 1949) p. 73 etc.

33. *Country Life*, LXXXVI, p. 626.

34. Colvin, *Dictionary of British Architects*, under Joynes; *Country Life*, CV, pp. 480–3; Field and Bunney, *English Domestic Architecture of the Seventeenth and Eighteenth Centuries* (London, 1905) Pls LXV–LXIX.

35. Plan in Kip and Knyff, *Nouveau Théâtre*, I.

36. Inventory of Cannons, 1721, in Huntington, Stowe MS. ST 83 (photostat copy in Victoria and Albert Museum, Dept. of Furniture).

37. *Moral Essays*, Epistle IV (to Lord Burlington), 'On the Use of Riches'.

38. R. W. Ketton-Cremer, *Felbrigg: the History of a house* (London, 1962) p. 135.

39. *Diary of Dudley Ryder*, ed. W. Matthews (London, 1939) p. 58; Walter Ison, *Georgian Buildings of Bath* (London, 1948) pp. 116–17.

40. Howell and Pritchard, 'Wynnstay', pp. 852–3.

41. *King's Works*, V, p. 235.

42. Comparatively little work has been done on English ice-houses. But see *Industrial Archaeology*, VI (1969) p. 42; IX (1972) pp. 152–71.

43. Charles Sylvester, *Philosophy of Domestic Economy* (1891) pp. 1–11.

44. J. A. Thompson, *Count Rumford of Massachussets* (New York, 1935) pp. 109–10.

45. For stewing stoves see J. C. Loudon, *Encyclopaedia of Cottage Farm and Villa Architecture* (London, 1859) pp. 715–16.

46. S. J. Wearing, *Georgian Norwich: Its Builders* (Norwich, 1926) p. 60.

47. R.I.B.A. Drawings Collection K4/30/8, K4/33/6–10.

48. Sylvester, *Domestic Economy*; Edgeworth, *Letters from England*, p. 26.

49. For Tullynally see Elizabeth Inglis-Jones, *The Great Maria* (London, 1959) p. 92; for Coleshill, plans by J. C. Loudon in Berkshire County Record Office, Reading; for Bowood, Bernan, *Warming and Ventilating Rooms and Buildings* (London, 1845) Essay XIV; for Abbotsford, Lockhart, *Life of Scott*, 1896 edn, pp. 500–1.

50. Pückler-Muskau, *Tour in England*, III, p. 209.

51. C. J. Richardson, *Popular Treatise on the Warming and Ventilating of Buildings* (London, 1837) pp. 48–9.

52. Pückler-Muskau, *Tour in England*, I, p. 44.

53. Pepys, *Diary*, 3 and 6 Oct. 1663; 16 Nov. 1664.

54. Mauchline, *Harewood House*, p. 93.

55. *Encyclopaedia Britannica*, 11th edn (London, 1910) p. 483; Clifford Musgrave, *Royal Pavilion* (London, 1959) p. 68; Lockhart, *Life of Scott*, pp. 500–1.

56. Eller, *Belvoir Castle* (1841) p. 334.

57. D.N.B.; for an example in 1785, see J. D. Williams, *Audley End: The Restoration of 1762–97* (Chelmsford, 1966) p. 32.

58. M. Girouard, 'Modernizing an Irish Country House', *Country Life*, CL, p. 1780.

59. Richardson, *New Vitruvius Britannicus*, II; Huntington, Huntingdon MS. L5/B2.

60. Huntington, Stowe MS. L8/F5-7.

61. Quoted O.E.D.

NOTES TO CHAPTER 10

1. M. Girouard, *The Victorian Country House* (Oxford, 1971) pp. 95–8.

2. *Ibid.* pp. 68–70, 108–11, 121–4.

3. A typical example, which ran into many editions, is *Manners and Tone of Good Society* by 'a member of the aristocracy' (London, *c.* 1880).

4. Hippolyte Taine, *Notes on England* (1860–70) tr. Edward Hyams (London, 1957) p. 155.

5. For Cragside see Girouard, *Victorian Country House*, pp. 141–6.

6. *Diary of Lady Frederick Cavendish* (London, 1927), I, gives an excellent picture of a serious-minded upper-class girl in the 1850s.

7. E.g. C.A.M. Press, *Norfolk Notabilities* (Norwich, 1893).

8. Scott, *Secular and Domestic Architecture*, p. 142.

9. E.g. Augustus Hare, as quoted in Girouard, *Victorian Country House*, p. 19.

10. Pückler-Muskau, *Tour in England*, I, p. 44.

11. The planning of servants' quarters is dealt with in great detail in Robert Kerr, *The Gentleman's House* (London, 1864) pp. 220–309.

12. *Ibid.* p. 227.

13. See *The Recollections of a Northumbrian Lady*, ed. L. E. O. Charlton (London, 1949) pp. 195–6; Dorothy Henley, *Rosalind Howard, Countess of Carlisle*, (London, 1958) p. 89.

14. For the Victorian services at Tullynally, see Girouard, 'Irish Country House', pp. 1834–7.

15. Kerr, *Gentleman's House*, pp. 74–5.

16. *Ibid.* p. 76.

17. Ronald Blythe, *Akenfield: Portrait of an English Village* (London, 1969) pp. 103–4; typescript

recollections of Gerald Horne, originally steward's-room boy at Blenheim, kindly communicated by David Green (see also *Country Life*, 23 Feb. 1945, pp. 326–8.

18. E.g. recollections of other households by Gerald Horne.

19. Plan communicated by Jill Franklin.

20. E.g. at Corsham Court, Wiltshire, *c*. 1797; Arundel Castle, Norfolk, 1806; Eastnor Castle, Herefordshire, *c*. 1810.

21. Pugin, *True Principles*, p. 51.

22. Joseph Hunter, *The History and Topography of Ketteringham* (Norwich, 1851) p. 54.

23. Owen Chadwick, *Victorian Miniature* (London, 1960) pp. 44, 103 etc.

24. Mauchline, *Harewood House*, p. 121.

25. Kerr, *Gentleman's House*, pp. 105, 119.

26. *Ibid*. p. 129.

27. Pückler-Muskau, *Tour in England*, III, p. 83.

28. There is no mention of it in *Manners and Tone of Good Society*.

29. Examples quoted and illustrated in Girouard, *Victorian Country House*, p. 50 and Pl. 48.

30. *Manners and Tone of Good Society*, pp. 21–39.

31. *Two Generations*, ed. Osbert Sitwell (1940) pp. 129–30.

32. *Journeys of Celia Fiennes*, p. 15; Huntington, Stowe MSS. ST 24/2/113; *Vitruvius Britannicus*, IV.

33. B.M. Add. MS. 22227, f. 170v.

34. Pückler-Muskau, *Tour in England*, IV, pp. 49–50.

35. John Hames, *Memoirs of a House Steward* (London, 1949) p. 93; Chadwick, *Victorian Miniature*, p. 148; Girouard, *Victorian Country House*, p. 106; E. Wingfield-Stratford, *This Was a Man* (London, 1949) p. 143.

36. Lord Ernest Hamilton, *Old Days and New* (London, 1924) p. 69.

37. Information Mary, Duchess of Buccleuch.

38. Girouard, *Victorian Country House*, pp. 126–8.

NOTES TO CHAPTER 11

1. For an example of a successful Victorian lawyer investing in land for reasons of prestige, in spite of financial misgiving, see M. Girouard, 'Blackmoor House, I', *Country Life*, CLV, pp. 554–7.

2. For country house finances in this period see F. M. L. Thompson, *English Landed Society in the Nineteenth Century* (London, 1963) pp. 292–345.

3. *Ibid*. pp. 59–60.

4. John Buchan, *The Four Adventures of Richard Hannay* (London, 1930) pp. 852, 863.

5. *Country Life*, XXVIII, p. 682 (Lympne); XXII, pp. 522, 558 (Hever).

6. Thompson, *English Landed Society*, pp. 269–91.

7. V. Sackville-West, *English Country Houses* (London, 1941) pp. 7, 9.

8. Girouard, *Victorian Country House*, pp. 53–4.

9. E.g. Norman Shaw's Bryanston, Dorset (for Viscount Portman, 1890).

10. Sackville-West, *English Country Houses*, p. 40.

11. *Ibid*. p. 8.

12. Lutyens's house planning can be studied in A. S. G. Butler, *Architecture of Sir Edwin Lutyens* (London, 1950) I.

13. For Gledstone see *Country Life*, LXXVII, pp. 374, 400.

14. Rosina Harrison, *My Life in Service*, paperback edn (London, 1977) pp. 46–7.

15. Vacuum cleaners were invented by an Englishman, H. Cecil Booth, in 1901.

16. *Country Life*, C, pp. 28, 74, 354, 378.

17. *Victorian Architecture*, ed. Peter Ferriday (London, 1963) p. 65.

18. P. G. Wodehouse, *Young Men in Spats* (London, 1922) Ch. 5.

19. *Country Life*, LXX, pp. 316, 354, 378.

20. See the chapter on bathrooms in *The House and its Equipment*, ed. Laurence Weaver (London, 1912), and examples at Port Lympne and Middleton.

21. There are (or were) good 'architectural' swimming pools by Lutyens at Middleton Park (n. 16) and Tyringham, Bucks. (*Country Life*, LXVI, pp. 740, 780).

22. *Country Life*, 18 May 1935, p. 507.

LIST OF ILLUSTRATIONS

LIST OF ILLUSTRATIONS

BLACK AND WHITE PLATES

LIST OF ILLUSTRATIONS

LIST OF ILLUSTRATIONS

TEXT FIGURES

ENDPAPERS

INDEX

338